The struggle between orthodox Anglicans and the deists, freethinkers, and "atheists" who opposed their exclusive claims to religious power and political authority reveals cultural practices and ideological assumptions central to an understanding of eighteenth-century thought. In this collection of essays, leading scholars look beyond the clash of philosophical propositions to examine the role of deists and freethinkers as the producers and the subjects of literary, philosophical, and religious controversy. They explore the curious symbiosis between the defense of orthodoxy and the elaboration of new forms of heterodox argument; they examine the practical implications of the debate in specific areas such as the libel laws and the growing influence of Lockean philosophy; and they show how the assault on orthodoxy influenced the development of historiography, public policy, and even the rise of the novel.

THE MARGINS OF ORTHODOXY

THE MARGINS OF ORTHODOXY

Heterodox Writing and Cultural Response, 1660–1750

EDITED BY

ROGER D. LUND

Le Moyne College, Syracuse

CAMBRIDGE
UNIVERSITY PRESS

Published by the Press Syndicate of the University of Cambridge
The Pitt Building, Trumpington Street, Cambridge CB2 1RP
40 West 20th Street, New York, NY 10011-4211, USA
10 Stamford Road, Oakleigh, Victoria 3166, Australia

© Cambridge University Press 1995

First published 1995

Printed in Great Britain at the University Press, Cambridge

A catalogue record for this book is available from the British Library

Library of Congress cataloguing in publication data
The margins of orthodoxy: heterodox writing and
cultural response, 1660–1750 / edited by Roger D. Lund.
p. cm.
"Eight of the essays in this collection were
first presented at the Le Moyne Forum on
Religion and Literature, September 26–28, 1991" – Acknowledgment.
Includes bibliographical references and index.
ISBN 0 521 47177 X (hardback)
1. Free thought – England – History – 17th century – Congresses.
2. Free thought – England – History – 18th century – Congresses.
3. Dissenters, Religious – England – History – 17th century – Congresses.
4. Dissenters, Religious – England – History – 18th century – Congresses.
5. England – Intellectual life – 17th century – Congresses.
6. England – Church history – 17th century – Congresses.
7. England – Intellectual life – 18th century – Congresses.
8. England – Church history – 18th century – Congresses.
I. Lund, Roger D., 1949–
BL2765.G7M37   1995   273'.7'0942 – dc20   94-44773   CIP

ISBN 0 521 47177 X hardback

For Walter O. Lund

Contents

Contributors

RICHARD ASHCRAFT is Professor of Political Science at the University of California at Los Angeles. He is the author of *Revolutionary Politics and Locke's Two Treatises of Government* (1986), *Locke's Two Treatises of Government* (1987), and numerous articles on political theory.

SHELLEY BURTT is Associate Professor of Political Science at Yale University and author of *Virtue Transformed: Political Argument in England 1688–1740* (1992).

JEFFREY S. CHAMBERLAIN is Assistant Professor of History and Chair of the Department of History and Political Science at the College of St. Francis, Joliet, Illinois. He has published articles on eighteenth-century theology and churchmanship and is at work on a book concerning the accommodation of high churchmen in Sussex to the Whig administration of the early eighteenth century.

CHRISTOPHER HILL has been a Fellow and Tutor of Balliol College, Oxford, where he was Master from 1965 to 1978 and where he is now an Honorary Fellow. Professor Hill is the author of numerous articles and books on the seventeenth century, including *The World Turned Upside Down* (1972), *A Turbulent, Seditious and Factious People: John Bunyan and His Church* (1988), and most recently *The English Bible and the 17th-century Revolution* (1993).

JOSEPH M. LEVINE is Distinguished Professor of History at Syracuse University. He is the author of *Dr. Woodward's Shield: History, Science and Satire in Augustan England; Humanism and History: Origins of Modern English Historiography* and *The Battle of the Books: History and Literature in Augustan England* (winner of the Gershoy Prize of the American Historical Association and the Gottschalk Prize of the American Society for Eigheenth-Century Studies). He is presently

xi

completing a new work entitled *Avenues to Antiquity: Ideas of History in Eighteenth Century England.*

ROGER D. LUND is Professor of English at Le Moyne College, Syracuse, New York. He has written essays on Pope, Swift, and the English deists and is currently at work on a study of wit and ideology in the long eighteenth century.

RONALD PAULSON is the Mayer Professor of the Humanities at the Johns Hopkins University. The world's leading expert on the works of William Hogarth, his most recent book is entitled *The Beautiful, the Novel, and the Strange: Aesthetics and Heterodoxy* (1994).

J. G. A. POCOCK is Professor Emeritus of History at the Johns Hopkins University. He recently edited *The Varieties of British Political Thought, 1500–1800* (1994) and is working on a study of Edward Gibbon.

G. A. J. ROGERS is Professor of Philosophy at the University of Keele and the editor of the *British Journal for the History of Philosophy*. He is currently editing Locke's philosophical manuscripts and is the author of many books and papers.

GORDON SCHOCHET is Professor of Political Science at Rutgers University and a founding member of the Steering Committee of the Center for the History of British Political Thought of the Folger Shakespeare Library. The author of *Patriarchalism in Political Thought*, Professor Schochet is currently completing a book entitled *John Locke and the Politics of Religious Toleration*, and editing Locke's unpublished writings on toleration.

Acknowledgments

Eight of the chapters in this collection were first presented at the Le Moyne Forum on Religion and Literature, September 26–28, 1991. Ronald Paulson's discussion of Henry Fielding and my own chapter on Thomas Woolston were prepared specifically for this volume.

A number of people have provided invaluable encouragement and advice over the past four years. During the early stages of conference planning Paula Backscheider and J. C. D. Clark offered generous assistance; I thank them both. When telephoned for advice about possible speakers and seminar topics, Ralph Cohen and James Winn were kind enough to consult their rolodexes on my behalf. One perquisite of organizing a national conference is that one has the chance to invite friends to participate. It is a pleasure to acknowledge the contributions of Frank Shuffleton, Frank Palmeri, A. G. Roeber, John O'Neill, Anna Battigelli, and the late Laura Ann Curtis, whose participation helped to make the conference a success. I must also acknowledge an old debt to Martin C. Battestin, whose graduate seminar some twenty years ago, "Augustan Form and Mock Form," first introduced me to the guilty pleasures of heterodox writing in the eighteenth century.

I am indebted to Michael McGiffert for his wise counsel and support, to the Institute of Early American History and Culture who cosponsored the Le Moyne Forum, and to the Lynde and Harry Bradley Foundation for a generous grant which supported the conference. Additional grants from the Le Moyne Committee on Faculty Development and Research, the National Endowment for the Humanities Travel to Collections Program, and the William Andrews Clark Memorial Library have also provided support for the preparation of this volume. I am also grateful to the staffs of the British Library, the Bodleian Library, and most particularly to the librarians of Le Moyne College.

It is impossible to overestimate the value of sane and congenial colleagues, and it is a pleasure to express my gratitude to Frans De Bruyn and Patrick J. Keane who read portions of the manuscript and whose sage and humane advice has grown more valuable with every passing year. My department chairman, David Lloyd, has smoothed the path in many ways; W. Richard Merriman, Jr. was instrumental in obtaining outside funding; and Sharyn Knight, who prepared the manuscript, has proven herself almost sibylline in unriddling the mysteries of Word Perfect 5.1. Special thanks are due to my editor, Josie Dixon, who has patiently and expertly nursed the manuscript through to publication.

I owe much to my wife, Sheila Murphy-Lund, and to my children, Sarah Min and David, whose good humor and forbearance are completely unmerited but deeply appreciated, nonetheless. I am also deeply in the debt of my father, an honorable antinomian who first taught me the joys of religious argument, to whose memory this book is dedicated.

Introduction

Roger D. Lund

In *Tom Jones* Henry Fielding treats his readers to a debate between Parson Thwackum, representative of "narrow and rigid" Anglican orthodoxy, and the philosopher, Square, deist and defender of the *"unalterable Rule of Right* and the *eternal Fitness of Things."*[1] They are wrangling over the nature of honor, whether it may be said to exist independent of religious belief. "If by Honour you mean the true natural Beauty of Virtue," argues Square, "I will maintain it may exist independent of any Religion whatever. Nay (added he) you yourself will allow it may exist independent of all but one; so will a *Mahometan,* a *Jew,* and all the Maintainers of all the different Sects in the World." Thwackum, for whom honor is a "Mode of divine Grace," accuses Square of "arguing with the usual Malice of all the Enemies of the true Church." He doubts not but that "all the Infidels and Hereticks in the World would, if they could, confine Honour to their own absurd Errors, and damnable Deceptions." For honor, according to Thwackum, "is not therefore manifold, because there are many absurd Opinions about it; nor is Religion manifold, because there are various Sects and Heresies in the World."[2]

Here Fielding provides an epitome of the struggle between Anglican orthodoxy and the heterodox promulgators of "new modish systems" in religion and government:[3] a representative deist attacks the hegemony of the established church, implying that Christianity, Mohammedanism, and Judaism make equal (and equally dubious) claims to moral authority, while his Anglican counterpart responds with charges of heresy, infidelity, and malice aforethought. Denying the suggestion that Christian truth could ever be reduced to "absurd Opinion," or the church transmogrified to a mere "Sect," Parson Thwackum offers a definition of religion that would come to mark the most stiff-necked and restrictive defenses of Christian orthodoxy: "When I mention Religion," the parson thunders, "I mean the

I

Christian Religion; and not only the Christian Religion, but the Protestant Religion; and not only the Protestant Religion but the Church of *England*."[4]

The conflicts adumbrated here – between revealed truth and the claims of reason, private conscience and the authority of the church, the desire to expand the range of acceptable belief and the insistence upon narrowing definitions of orthodox behavior – provide the substance for much of the debate concerning the role of the Church of England, which as J. C. D. Clark has reminded us, stood center stage in the drama that was the long eighteenth century.[5] This struggle, somehow to define and defend the margins of orthodoxy, provides the focus for the chapters of this volume. Taken together, they explore a series of related questions regarding the status of authority (Scriptural, clerical, political), the relationship between private conscience and public action (the presumptive linkage between freethinking and free acting), and the role of the civil magistrate in protecting the church as by law established. From a variety of disciplinary perspectives these chapters examine the prospect of Anglicanism threatened from without by an onslaught of skepticism and infidelity – variously ascribed to deists, freethinkers, and atheists – and from within by factional rancor as well as the fear that the roots of modern infidelity might actually find a nurturing soil in the very beliefs and habits of the orthodox themselves. As the chapters in this volume suggest, much of the struggle between defenders of the faith and their deist critics occurs at the margins where orthodox assertions and heterodox responses almost seem to merge.[6]

I

Despite the apparent confidence of Thwackum's *ukase*, there were contemporary observers, many within the Church of England, who questioned whether orthodoxy could be defined at all. To quote Bishop Watson,

What is the thing called Orthodoxy, which mars the fortunes of honest men, misleads the judgment of princes, and occasionally endangers the stability of thrones? In the true meaning of the term, it is a sacred thing to which every denomination of Christians lays an arrogant and exclusive claim, but to which no man, no assembly of men, since the apostolic age, can prove a title.[7]

In purely formal terms Anglican orthodoxy was defined in the *Book of*

Common Prayer and the Thirty-Nine Articles.[8] Yet just as heterodoxy could not easily be reduced to a set of philosophical assertions, so Anglican Christianity could not be "simply entertained as a collection of propositional beliefs." As J. A. I. Champion has argued, "Religious belief was a complex fabric of doctrine, devotion and institution. It was not enough to subscribe to the Thirty-nine Articles, worship by the Book of Common Prayer or believe in the Trinity. Christian belief also included and absorbed ideas about the legitimacy of government by bishops, the sanctity of Churches, and the truth and authority of the Scriptures."[9] In other words, to speak of orthodoxy in the eighteenth century is often to say less of theological positions than of cultural practices and ideological assumptions. As a result the effort to more clearly define the precise characteristics of orthodoxy would continue unabated throughout the eighteenth century.

It was, however, the more aggressive assertion of orthodox claims which riveted the attention of the church's critics, and which led them to charge the Church of England with various forms of tyranny. This was certainly the response of Francis Hare, whose controversial pamphlet, *The Difficulties and Discouragements which attend the Study of Scriptures in the Way of Private Judgment* (1714), provides witness to the difficulties that contemporary observers encountered when attempting to trace the precise outlines of Anglican orthodoxy. Noting the disjunctions between Scriptural teaching and the doctrines of the church, Hare concludes that the very notion of orthodoxy could not be derived solely from the Scriptures, but was itself an artificial imposition. Orthodoxy was in effect a tautology, Hare concludes; the church was orthodox because it had declared itself to be so. "The *established Church*, you will allow, is *Orthodox* in all necessary Points," Hare argues. "If therefore you know the Sense of the *established Church*, you have in Epitome the *Church Catholick;* and therefore you need only study *her* Opinions to make you *Orthodox*. And this, the most illiterate Man may find in the *Liturgy and Articles*."[10] This seems on the face of it to endorse received wisdom; yet as Hare's readers soon discovered, his argument was ironic to the core. For in terms that cast a jaundiced eye on orthodox claims, Hare's pamphlet (published anonymously) outlines the putative dangers which attend the private interpretation of Scripture. And much in the manner of Jonathan Swift's *Argument Against Abolishing Christianity* (to which he owes obvious debts), Hare provides a thoroughly ironic defense of Samuel Clarke's *Doctrine of the Scripture Trinity* (1712), a work particularly offensive to orthodox sensibilities because it denied any Scriptural basis for the Trinity, at least of the Athanasian variety. Although Hare claimed to be defending a fundamental tenet of Anglican belief - the right of individual Protestants to interpret Scripture for themselves – his pamphlet, like Clarke's, seemingly threatened other notions dear to the hearts of the Anglican clergy. The Lower House of Convocation condemned Hare's pamphlet for casting "injurious Reflexions on the Fathers and Councils of the Antient Church," for insinuating that "the Doctrines and Articles of the Established Church, are not grounded on Scripture," and for exposing the "Discipline of the Church under the Notion of Persecution." As if this were not enough, Convocation also lumped Hare's pamphlet with the works of deists and freethinkers for treating "Things Sacred, in a Ludicrous and Prophane manner."[11] The irony here is that all this recrimination was reserved not for a Toland or a Tindal, but for a Christian "infidel" who would later become the bishop of Chichester.

True enough, Hare's suggestion that the Thirty-Nine Articles, like the Athanasian Creed, were clerical impositions bears a strong resemblance to similar arguments by deists and freethinkers. And it struck a particularly tender nerve because it came from within the orthodox fold. As Hare suggests, even the Thirty-Nine Articles, which presumably served as the benchmark of Anglican orthodoxy, could be interpreted in radically different ways by equally devout believers, a fact which provided the basis for conflict throughout the eighteenth century. *"We do not suffer any man to reject the 39 Articles of the Church of England at his pleasure,"* writes Edward Fowler, Bishop of Gloucester, *"yet neither do we look upon them as essentials of Saving Faith, or Legacies of Christ and his Apostles; but in a mean, as pious opinions fitted for the preservation of unity; neither do we oblige any man to* believe *them, but onely not* contradict *them."*[12] Fowler's emphasis on the political value of public adherence to the Thirty-Nine Articles casts in bold relief both the ideological dimension of Anglican orthodoxy and the recognition by members of the church that there was a necessary distinction between private faith and the public practice of religion. As several contributors here point out, the redefinition of Anglican doctrine as "opinions fitted for the preservation of unity," left them open to debate not only by members of the church, but by deists and freethinkers anxious to reduce Christian belief to a mere matter of speculative opinion.

As Hare recognized, ambiguity in the significations of "orthodoxy" led in turn to uncertainty as to what it meant to be an enemy of the church. Thus, asking even the simplest questions regarding clerical authority qualified the most sincere pilgrim of the spirit for the same forms of abuse reserved for deists and infidels. Even if you did not actually disturb the peace of the church, Hare argues,

tis all one, you will be *intepreted* to do it; and That will bring on you more Evils, than I would wish to my greatest Enemy. In a Word, you will be thought a *Heretick*; a Term, which there is a strange *Magick* in, though it has *no determinate Meaning* in the Mouth of the People, nor any *ill Meaning* in it self. 'Tis supposed to include in it every thing that is bad . . . And from the time a Man is deem'd a *Heretick*, 'tis Charity to act against all Rules of Charity; and the more they violate the Laws of God in dealing with him, 'tis, in their Opinion, doing God the greater Service.[13]

Indeed, Hare argues, once you have been condemned for heterodox opinions there is nothing you can do to regain your reputation.

If you are guilty of no open Vices, secret ones will be imputed to you; Your Enquiries will be called *Vain, Curious* and *Forbidden* Studies. Pride and Ambition will be said to be the secret Springs of them. A *Search after Truth,* will be called a *Love of Novelty*. The doubting of a single Text, will be *Scepticism;* the denial of an Argument, a *renouncing of the Faith*. To say what the Scriptures have said, and in the very same Words too, if not explained in the common Way, will be *Blasphemy*; and the most sincere Concern for the Honours of Almighty God, you cannot be sure will not be interpreted *down-right Atheism*.[14]

In short, to be termed a heretic, a skeptic, or an atheist was to trigger an interpretive process by which orthodox exegetes then combed your writings for evidence that you deserved the labels they had already applied to you.

As Hare suggests, the problem of defining infidelity, deism, or atheism in the early-eighteenth century could be traced directly to the absence of "determinate meanings" where such labels were involved. Indeed critics of the deists and freethinkers complained that so nuanced and so contradictory were their arguments that one could only assume they practiced deliberate deception, and as a result even the freethinkers could not be certain what freethinking actually meant. In the words of an anonymous critic of Collins's *Discourse of Free-Thinking*,

the Author has a Design to impose upon his Readers Things which he does not believe himself. In order to the doing which he has made use of a Term, to signifie the Subject of his Discourse, which is a wandring and indefinite

Term; a Term capable of various Significations, and which like the *Camelion* varies its Colour, as often as it changes its Subject."[15]

Michael Hunter observes that from the time of its introduction into English in the middle years of the sixteenth century, "the word 'atheist' was frequently used to mean 'godless' in a rather broad and loose sense," and by a "process of elision" various attitudes and forms of behavior came to be condemned as atheistic.[16] Indeed this conflation of error becomes a standard tactic of orthodox writers seeking to imply the necessary connection between a variety of arguments and ideas that to the untutored eye might otherwise seem quite distinct, and even innocent.[17] Thus the author of the assault on Collins's *Discourse* quoted above links him with a rag-tag assemblage of heretics and sectarians, "by what names it seems soever they are dignified or distinguished, whether *Atheists, Deists, Arians, Socinians, Quakers, Mugletonians, the Sweet-Singers, and the Family of Love.*"[18] There is no effort here to discover nice distinctions between the outright atheist who denied the existence of God, the Socinian who acknowledged his existence but denied the Trinity, and the Quaker who believed in God, had doubts about the Trinity but felt quite certain that some form of divine presence had taken up residence in his own individual soul. For the rough purposes of Anglican polemic it was sufficient to suggest that because of similarities in their response to established verities in church and state they naturally belonged together. Here, as with so many of the assaults on presumptive heterodoxy, there is no attempt to test the propositional validity of what these individuals have actually said, because in effect such terms as "atheist" and "deist" are used not to distinguish philosophical or theological propositions at all, but rather to designate a shifting repertoire of attitudes and public behavior that the orthodox, for whatever reasons, found threatening. Take for example Swift's memorable characterization of the Earl of Wharton as a "Presbyterian in Politics, and an Atheist in Religion who chuseth at present to whore with a Papist."[19] Whatever one might say about Swift's intentions here, the desire for philosophical precision does not seem to have been a primary motivation.

This practice of eliding or conflating error was necessary in part because the task of separating the heterodox from the faithful had become so difficult. In the words of one observer, "if after all, the Atheists must be admitted abroad into Company; 'tis a Thousand pities they are not all bound to wear Red Hats, as the *Jews* do in *Italy*, to distinguish them from the Christians."[20] Some such expedient was necessary, because as William Nicholls complained, atheists and deists were otherwise indistinguishable from the regular righteous. "Now because such Infidels lie herded among divers Sects of Christians, as they are not so easily discerned, so they are not so vigorously opposed; and by this means they have of late gained such strength, so that now they begin to look formidable."[21] Nothing would change. In the mid-eighteenth century Philip Skelton gives voice to continuing orthodox frustration, arguing that because the deists stand in awe of fines, afraid to speak out their principles, "lest they should shock or alarm," they are therefore "forced to borrow the name and cloak of Christianity, in order to attack it; and dare seldom or never rejoin to their answerers, lest they should lose the benefit of their present concealment, from which the greater part of their success is hoped for." As if this weren't bad enough, "our modern Apologists for Christianity often defend it on Deistical principles; and, besides, are too apt to give a new model to their own *credenda;* hoping, thereby, to gain some advantage to their cause; or, at least, to acquire the reputation of having contrived a better sort of Christianity."[22]

In the face of such uncertainty, then, the best the orthodox could hope for in their refutations of putative deists, atheists, and freethinkers was not a standard of definitive proof but only a relative scale of inference, a rough "profile" of the Augustan "atheist" of the sort modern criminologists might use to identify a serial killer. Not that every individual fitting such a profile has actually killed anyone, any more than the "atheist" had actually denied the existence of God, but only that he revealed "tendencies" which might eventually produce that result.[23] Such a specimen presumably denied the authority of the Scriptures, the immortality of the soul, and eternal rewards and punishments, preferring natural to supernatural explanations, and rejecting the established religion as the imposition of clever priests. As a result the modern "atheist" could be expected to favor some form of radical Whiggery or republicanism (Swift remarks that "in every hundred of professed *Atheists, Deists,* and *Socinians* in the Kingdom . . . ninety-nine at least, are staunch thorow-paced *Whigs*"[24]). The modern "atheist" could also be expected to express, or at least imply these attitudes in a rhetoric marked by its wit and its willingness to scoff at the sacred. Admittedly such an inventory of heterodox tendencies makes it difficult to speak of eighteenth-century atheism in any clear-cut fashion. As Michael Hunter and David Wootton point out, "the multifaceted character of unbelief in the early modern period . . . means that there is probably no single 'history of atheism' to be written, any more than there is one cause of early modern unbelief, or any particular form of modern irreligion towards which it should be seen as developing."[25]

Such ambiguity and breadth of definition create special problems for those seeking to separate real atheistical arguments from the rhetorical draperies in which they were so often disguised. And we must acclimate ourselves to a process of defining intellectual positions that owes less to the rational analysis of clear propositional statements (although these are sometimes present) than to interpretations of behavior and readings of rhetorical gesture. As David Wootton points out, it was generally conceded that "those who lived evil lives must lack religious faith, just as those who lacked faith would be bound to live evil lives. The term 'atheist' was thus to be applied to people who were in fact believers, because their conduct was held to imply unbelief." Wootton acknowledges that for moderns who "do not share this view of the relationship between thought and action, we cannot follow this aspect of early modern usage, for we would end up with a history of unbelief that concerned itself with the aberrant behaviour, not of atheists, but of believers."[26]

As several of these chapters suggest, however, that is precisely the kind of history that must be written, and they deal in various ways with the ambiguous consequences resulting from the struggle to defend Anglican orthodoxy against the protean variety of heterodox behavior; to defeat enemies who refused to announce themselves unequivocally as atheists or deists, and who often seemed to emerge from within the camp of the orthodox themselves.[27] It is worth remembering that Tindal, Woolston, and Locke all identified themselves as Christians. It fell to their critics to demonstrate, based upon an examination of their behavior and the implications of their rhetoric, that such infidels couldn't possibly mean what they had actually said. No one was exempt from such scrutiny; even an archbishop like Tillotson could be widely vilified as a Socinian because of the heterodox tendencies of his theological writings. For High Church polemicists, a Latitudinarian bishop like Gilbert Burnet was little better than an atheist. In lines dripping irony Swift denies the common rumor that Burnet, like his Whig compatriots, "had a real formed Design of establishing *Atheism* among us." Rather, Swift is willing to concede that the atheism of the Whigs is not a matter of religion but only of policy. "The Reason why Whigs have taken the *Atheists* or *Free-thinkers* into their Body, is because they wholly agree in their political Schemes and differ very little in Church Power and Discipline."[28] In the hands of a trained dialectician like Dean Swift, the conclusion seems self-evident: since by definition Whigs are atheists, and since Burnet is a Whig, we can only conclude that Burnet is an atheist as well. Swift's bland confidence that he has discovered a connection between Burnet's writings, atheism, and the political agenda of the modern Whigs is characteristic of the conspiratorial predisposition of orthodox readers of heterodox texts. This determination to find ultimate connections between all manifestations of religious and political dissent helps to explain why so many seventeenth- and eighteenth-century polemicists bent their efforts not only to interpret the encoded discourse of heterodox books and pamphlets, but also to expose the threat from covert "atheism" disguised in orthodox works as well.

While this interpretive penchant provided inspiration for countless pamphlets outlining the true intentions of heterodox writers, both within and outside the church, it has often frustrated the modern scholar's desire to see these deists and freethinkers clearly as part of a developmental continuum of heterodox propositions, or to assign them unambiguous roles in the history of British atheism.[29] Although scholars have recently begun to address questions of the cultural centrality of freethinking, deism, and atheism in the Augustan Age, it is fair to say that many of those heterodox writers felt to be of enormous significance by their contemporaries have yet to receive the kind of attention which this volume aspires in some measure to provide.[30] It is worthy of note that with all the recent emphasis on expanding the canon, on a "more inclusive view" of the eighteenth century "than those which are limited to the dominant culture alone," we still lack extended treatments of Blount (at least in English), Gildon, Gordon, Trenchard, Asgill, Chubb, Morgan, Wollaston, and Tindal – writers relegated to the margins of historical and literary discourse, not by virtue of their race, gender, or class (categories favored by the New Historicists), but as a result of their heterodox ideas and their anomalous relationship to the literary canon.[31]

Of course if Edmund Burke is to be credited, the deists and

freethinkers have received all the attention they deserved. "Who, born within the last forty years, has read one word of Collins, and Toland, and Tindal, and Chubb, and Morgan, and that whole race who called themselves Freethinkers?" he asks. "Who now reads Bolingbroke? Who ever read him through? Ask the booksellers of London what is become of all these lights of the world."[32] Burke may wonder who had read one word of Collins, Toland, or Tindal, but if we take seriously the literature, theological debate, and political pamphleteering of the early eighteenth century we are led to conclude that almost everyone had. It is one of the ironies of eighteenth-century attitudes toward reputed deists, libertines, and atheists that while they were dismissed as marginal writers (Burke's conclusion), they could also be feared as credible threats to the very foundations of church and state.

For evidence of this concern one might consult obscure country parsons who describe modern atheism as "a vaunting *Goliath* [bidding] defiance . . . to God and Heaven, to Reason and Religion, and the whole Armies of Israel."[33] Or, one might look to the counsellors of kings, who complain that

Such is the degeneracy of the Age we live in that the very Fundamentals of Religion are struck at; and though Modesty was never any Quality of the Devil . . . and though Practical Atheism hath been the Strategem he hath made use of all along, yet his grand Endeavour now, and of late Years is to lead Men into Speculative: And we see it hath so far prevail'd with abundance of Men, that they are grown very Indifferent, whether they believe anything at all concerning God or Religion.[34]

One would expect churchmen to complain. But the fear of heterodoxy also permeates the literary culture of the day. Swift contends that *A Tale of a Tub* (itself condemned as heterodox) was written to defend orthodox Anglicanism against "those heavy, illiterate Scriblers, prostitute in their Reputations, vicious in their Lives, and ruin'd in their Fortunes, who . . . are greedily read, meerly upon the Strength of bold, false, impious Assertions, mixt with unmannerly Reflections upon the Priesthood, and openly intended against all Religion."[35] Nor was poetry immune from attack. John Edwards insists that "This Poetic Age hath prov'd the most Atheistical and Immoral" and that "Those who are excessively addicted to [poetry], have generally their Minds and Manners distorted."[36] While Alexander Pope would doubtless have disagreed with Edwards's blanket indictment, he complained nevertheless that the "Press groan'd with Licenc'd Blasphemies" and that Dulness flourished "In Toland's, Tindal's and in Woolston's days."[37] Not surprisingly in "this lubrick and adulterate age" (the phrase is Dryden's), heterodoxy was also implicated in the corruptions of the theater. And it is useful to point out that the assault on the evils of the stage spearheaded by Jeremy Collier was inspired as much by theatrical dismissals of Christian doctrine and ridicule of the clergy as it was by the sexual libertinism of the Horners and Dorimants of Restoration comedy.

Even the stock exchange, so dear to Addison, is implicated in this riot of impiety! *Fog's Weekly Journal* boldly links atheism, rebellion, Whiggery, and stock manipulation, insisting that "Your Tolands, Tindals, Collins, &c. have made loud Professions of Revolution Principles, nor is there any Antitrinitarian, Deist, Socinian, Atheist, Stockjobber, Projector ... but what (if you'll take their own Words) is a staunch Whig."[38] Fog was not alone in his suspicions. In the estimation of William Nicholls, "*Atheism* and *Theism* are now got from the Court to the *Exchange*, they begin to talk them in Shops and Stalls, and *Spinosa* and *Hobbs* are grown common, even to the very Rabble."[39] Conduct manuals like *The Apprentice's Vade Mecum* (1734), with its thirty pages of "Cautions Against Scepticism and Infidelity," offer strong evidence of widespread fear that having poxed the gentry, the infection of heterodoxy was now spreading to the lower orders.[40]

Although it is impossible for us to tell how many deists or atheists might actually have inhabited the British Isles in the later seventeenth and early eighteenth centuries, clerical observers like the Lower House of Convocation would lead one to believe that their numbers were legion, that they had opened the sluice-gates to "that Deluge of Impiety and Licentiousness, which hath broke in upon us, and overspread the Face of this Church and Kingdom; eminent, in former times, for Purity of Faith, and Sobriety of Manners."[41] Despite the insistence of orthodox polemicists that modern infidels – variously described as hordes, tides, shoals, herds, etc. – threatened to overwhelm the nation, one is struck by their numerical insignificance in comparison with a *perceived threat* assuming near-mythical proportions. In short, heterodoxy, however loosely defined, becomes a universal bogey for those baffled by the intellectual ferment of the eighteenth century and frightened by the implications of a new secularism visible in areas as diverse as Latitudinarian theology, Restoration comedy, mercantile capitalism, and republican political theory.[42] Burke may argue that the deists and freethinkers vanished without a trace, but if we are to believe the writers noted above, there was no area of British life left unmolested or unchanged by the threat of atheism, deism, and libertinism, no form of expression, no political institution, no economic fact of life immune to the corrosive effects of heterodox ideas.

This book seeks in some measure to reassess the importance of heterodox writers, not merely as systematic philosophers (which they so often were not), but as active participants in the rough and tumble of eighteenth-century life. It addresses the role of heterodox writers and their readers as innovators and *agents provocateurs*, as both the producers and the subjects of literary, philosophical, and religious controversy in the first half of the eighteenth century. The contributors also examine the variety of orthodox responses which the deists and freethinkers inspired. And they pay particular attention to the curious symbiosis between the defense of Anglican orthodoxy and the elaboration of new forms of heterodox argument, the kinds of esoteric encoding, or "theological lying" that have frustrated previous attempts to find clear statements of heterodox intent in such writers as Hobbes, Locke, and their disciples.[43] Drawing upon a variety of disciplinary perspectives, contributors explore the manner in which works by such writers as Tindal, Toland, Woolston, Shaftesbury, Blount, and Locke – roughly the same crew consigned by Burke to premature oblivion – undermined comfortable orthodoxies of the age, influenced the development of law, historiography, public policy, philosophy, and literature, as well as contributing to the redefinition of orthodoxy itself. For the purposes of organization, the chapters have been divided into discussions of the origins of eighteenth-century infidelity and definitions of orthodoxy, considerations of Locke's ambiguous role as a model for opponents of orthodox Anglicanism, chapters exploring attempts to police the margins of orthodoxy, and finally three discussions of the unforeseen (and frequently ironic) consequences of the effort to define and defend orthodox belief.

II

In *Examiner* 21, Swift complains of the "Pedantry of Republican Politicks" to which might be traced "those noble Schemes of treating Christianity as a System of *Speculative Opinions,* which no Man should be bound to believe."⁴⁴ Swift's attempt to defend Christian truth against the inroads of opinion echoes a leitmotif of eighteenth-century Anglican polemic. For as J. G. A. Pocock points out in "Within the Margins: The Definitions of Orthodoxy," reducing any fundamental belief to a matter of speculative opinion was the first step on the path to skepticism. And as he observes, every defense of religious freedom as the "freedom to form opinions" carried with it the "reduction of faith to opinion and communion to association." This was roughly the conclusion reached by Charles Leslie, who saw in Tindal's redefinition of the church as a purely voluntary association the diminution of Christianity to a mere "Sect . . . to which there goes no more than to be of this or that Opinion" which may be changed "Ten times a day, or as a Man may change his Lawyer, or Physician, without any Hazard or Penalty." ⁴⁵ But as Pocock observes, the defense of Christ as one with whom the church held communion, not as one about whom they had opinions, led the orthodox to conclude that all discourses of religious toleration were in some measure a polemic "against the orthodox theology of Christ's divinity."

Pocock reveals just how closely linked were questions of orthodox belief and issues concerning the legitimacy of political authority. He focuses on the inevitable tensions produced by two basic propositions which characterized Anglican orthodoxy: (1) that the Church of England was the church as by law established; and (2) that the Church of England was Christ's presence, in some sense his body in the world. These beliefs opened the church to a number of challenges from without and left it to steer a course between Popery, Hobbism and enthusiasm, elements of which were in some sense implicit within orthodox Anglicanism itself.⁴⁶ Pocock explores the contradictions implicit in the Anglican dedication to Scripture and reason (the kind of ambiguity noted by Francis Hare) and he points to the anomaly of a church determined to maintain its spiritual authority as a communion of believers even as it endorsed varieties of opinion and systems of analysis (empiricism, for example) capable of undermining the essentials of orthodox belief. In contradistinction to that notion of orthodoxy which sees it as largely static, always in danger of subversion by a more active heterodoxy, Pocock argues for an understanding of the dynamic of orthodoxy that "has its own history, is in history, and has history in it." He also observes a curious fact that will be central to many of the chapters in this book, that in the later seventeenth and early-eighteenth centuries, "orthodoxy generates its

own skepticism, and skepticism has its own relations with orthodoxy."
Pocock points out that we will never comprehend the long
eighteenth century if we "do not understand that it lived with the
memory of the civil wars as a nightmare from which it was struggling
to awake." Certainly, where religious heterodoxy was concerned,
eighteenth-century observers were quick to trace the deism, atheism,
and libertinism of their age to the upheavals of the mid-seventeenth
century. According to the Lower House of Convocation, this "Deluge
of Impiety" emerged directly from

that long unnatural Rebellion, which loosen'd all the Bands of Discipline
and Order, and overturn'd the goodly Frame of our Ecclesiastical and Civil
Constitution. The Hypocrisy, Enthusiasm, and variety of wild and monstrous
Errors, which abounded, during those Confusions, begat in the Minds of
Men (too easily carried into Extremes) a disregard for the very Appearance
of Religion, and ended in a Spirit of downright Libertinism and Profaneness,
which hath ever since too much prevail'd among Us.[47]

Like the cauldron of Dulness in Pope's *Dunciad*, the Interregnum was
presumably the "chaos dark and deep" from which all embryonic
errors would later emerge in their full maturity.

In "Freethinking and Libertinism: the Legacy of the English
Revolution," Christopher Hill traces the beginnings of eighteenth-
century heterodoxy in a variety of works written during the two
decades preceding the Restoration. In so doing he examines one
genetic explanation of eighteenth-century heterodoxy which located
its origins in the intellectual and political upheaval of the Interregnum.[48]
This account certainly had staying power. Nearly a century after the
Restoration Philip Skelton still maintains that "Libertinism had no
considerable footing in *England* before *Cromwell's* time, when it was
covered, down to the very cloven hoof of contradictory absurdities, in
the long cloak of cant, hypocrisy, and Enthusiasm."[49] As Hill makes
clear, such complaints were not unfounded; for the seventeenth
century articulated much that the forces of orthodoxy would reject in
the eighteenth. Drawing on a variety of seventeenth-century sources,
Hill briefly traces the route by which the appeal to private interpretation
of Scripture by the people themselves, and the introduction of
patterns of interpretation which reduced the Bible to the status of
other books, led by degrees to a general skepticism regarding the
validity of Scripture and the very existence of God.[50]
Hill points out that even the Restoration could not restore the

political authority which had previously been vested in the Bible; for once individual believers had been given the opportunity to interpret the Scriptures freely for themselves, it was difficult to persuade them that the church's interpretation was the only one available. So, for example, even an Anglican cleric like Francis Hare was forced to admit that those undertaking to interpret the Scriptures by themselves must necessarily arrive at heterodox conclusions.

> Nor can it well be otherwise. For what Security has a Man that sets out in this Way; that attempts to *study the Scriptures* in a free and impartial manner, laying aside all Prepossessions and previous Notions, himself, and to believe nothing that he is not upon his own Search convinced is clearly contained in them; What Security has such a Man, that he shall not fall into some *Opinions* that have been *already condemned* as erroneous and heretical, or which may interfere with those that are commonly received.[51]

The growth of antinomianism, with its emphasis on the supremacy of the individual conscience, and the popularity of the notion that religion itself had been invented by cunning priests to keep the lower orders in place encouraged habits of heterodox dissent that the Restoration church found impossible to eliminate. Hill also points out that while Tory pamphleteers and High Church polemicists were eager to trace eighteenth-century heterodoxy to the Interregnum, the radicals of the 1690s were far less willing to acknowledge their debts to the writers of the 1640s and fifties; they were, as Hill argues, "too prudent to stress the origin of their ideas in the regicide republic."

As Hill suggests, anticlericalism – a series of attitudes and rhetorical gestures linking the works of seventeenth-century sectarians with the deists and freethinkers who were said to have imitated them – is one visible legacy of the Interregnum. In the opinion of Francis Atterbury, they shared the impious conviction "that all religion was, like theirs, a convenient trick and pretence only; invented by cunning men to keep silly people in awe, to make princes reign safely, and the priesthood live easily."[52] As J. A. I. Champion has recently argued, anticlericalism was a centrally important strategy of heterodox writers and radicals who instead of denying God directly, "were concerned to debunk the false authority of the Church." From this anticlerical perspective, "The conflict was not just about the competing epistemological hierarchy of revelation and reason but about who or what institution held the authoritative interpretation of truth."[53]

In "Anticlericalism and Authority in Lockean Political Thought,"

Richard Ashcraft considers Locke's lifelong critique of clerical authority, and his rejection of any group, be they philosophers or clerics, who would arrogate to themselves "the authority to instruct mankind in religious matters." In terms that would find an echo in works by deists and freethinkers, Locke argues that the people had been "hoodwinked" by the clergy, and Ashcraft locates Locke's anticlericalism within the context of contemporary discussions of natural right, popular sovereignty, consent, and a defense of democratic practices. In contrast to the Church of England, Locke offers a decentralized claim for authority based upon private judgment and the duty of the individual to assert his or her own conscience against the teaching of the established church. But unlike the church, which had sought through the imposition of civil constraints to impose uniformity of religious practice, Locke accepted diversity and conflict of opinion as the context within which the individual could exercise rational judgment.

Ashcraft traces Locke's anticlericalism to the example of the Levellers, who argued that even the poorest individuals presumably had the capacity to understand and perform their moral duties set forth in Scripture and in natural law. And, Ashcraft argues, this presumption led "directly to a defense of religious toleration, since reliance upon individual judgment necessarily defined a church as a voluntary society based upon the consent of its members, thus placing all churches upon an equal plane of authority." By linking the Levellers with Locke and Tindal, Ashcraft notes significant continuities between seventeenth- and eighteenth-century anticlericalism and suggests that redefinitions of authority, including calls for greater freedom of speech and press, were rooted in the anticlericalism of the seventeenth century.

As I have argued above, charges that the heterodox purposely masked their true intentions resonated in orthodox polemic throughout the later seventeenth and early eighteenth centuries. But as Ashcraft points out, the unmasking of ideological assumptions worked for critics of orthodoxy as well. He draws attention to Mannheim's definition of ideology as "the tearing off of disguises – the unmasking of those unconscious motives which bind the group existence to its cultural aspirations and its theoretical arguments." In their assault on the clerical monopoly on truth, the Levellers, Locke, and Tindal all engaged in this process of unmasking, arguing that there simply was no special authority attaching to the clergy in society, that their arguments, therefore, must be "assessed in terms of this existential fact."

In a recent essay on the histories of atheism, David Wootton notes that we need "a better understanding of the role of John Locke's philosophy in the development of an enlightened skepticism towards religion. Locke himself was probably a Socinian: which is to say that he believed in the Gospel narrative and in the Resurrection, but not in original sin or the Trinity. But whatever his private beliefs, his uncompromising subordination of revelation to reason had revolutionary implications."[54] In "John Locke: Conservative Radical," G. A. J. Rogers discusses some of these revolutionary implications, concluding that the ambiguity of Locke's assertions regarding doctrines like the Trinity can be traced, not to a radical agenda, but to an epistemology that limited theological certainty. For Locke, Rogers argues, theological assertions needed to meet "the standards set by his philosophy of knowledge or probable opinion. The notion of what might be acceptable on grounds of faith was itself circumscribed by these other standards and could not override them."

The result, Rogers suggests, is that Locke, who was otherwise a committed Christian, endorsed a philosophical system which was implicitly subversive of the faith he practiced, a system that necessarily reduced many forms of private belief (like trinitarianism) to mere species of opinion. Paradoxically, while Locke may not have been aggressively heterodox, his uncertain conjectures on theology and his refusal to publicly assert any belief of which there could be no certain knowledge provided a basis for the more radical assertions of his followers. John Edwards, one of his most dogged pursuers, had argued that the Socinians, like Locke, propounded falsehood "not in a simple and naked Way, lest it should easily be found out," but "craftily polish'd and cover'd [it] over with a specious Pretence; that so by this external Gloss it may seem to the Simple to be more plausible than Truth it self."[55] What for Edwards seemed the product of conscious artifice, however, is for Rogers a natural result of Locke's prudence and his endorsement of a distinction between esoteric and exoteric forms of knowledge.

Since esoteric heterodoxy was so difficult to demonstrate, it was always much easier, at least for the state, to deal with overt actions rather than covert beliefs. After the Restoration orthodoxy, with its linkage to notions of "true" belief, would be redefined in terms of what had been established by law. By requiring that all acts of public worship be conducted in keeping with the *Book of Common Prayer*, the

Act of Uniformity (1662) effectively redefined orthodoxy by legal fiat. And in the process, it was hoped, it also provided instrumental means to eliminate the religio-political confusion, which, as Christopher Hill points out, was the legacy of the Interregnum. Put simply, heterodoxy could now be defined not only as a spiritual threat to the individual soul, but as a positive danger to the body politic. In the words of Samuel Parker, "the Principles of Irreligion unjoynt the Sinews and blow up the very Foundations of Government: This turns all sense of Loyalty into Folly; this sets men at Liberty from all the effectual Obligations to Obedience."[56]

Given such a threat, civil penalties for religious nonconformity made a certain kind of sense. Not all were convinced of course. Tindal argues that the calls for the persecution of religious belief were most "hotly maintain'd by self-interested and designing Men."[57] In "Samuel Parker, Religious Diversity, and the Ideology of Persecution," Gordon Schochet discusses the career of an orthodox defender who must be numbered among the most self-interested and designing foes of toleration. And he outlines the logic of religious coercion and persecution that Parker so forcefully advocated. Schochet discusses the various strategies from comprehension to outright persecution, which were designed to deal with the variety of nonconformists, and he offers a guide to the vocabulary of "toleration," "comprehension," "indulgence," and "religious liberty" that emerged after the Restoration but whose distinctions have become muddled with the passage of time.

As Schochet points out, the extremity of Parker's position was a natural by-product of the sectarian confusion that characterized English Protestantism after the Restoration. The only defense against such chaos, Parker argued, was a strict adherence to the religion as by law established. Otherwise one could expect the church to consist entirely of dissenters, "a Reformed Church of Protestant Atheists, that is, a Church without Religion." In this respect Parker concurs with numerous other defenders of the faith, all of whom had experienced to one degree or another, this paradoxical vision of a church without religion, of pews filled with atheists. Such a threat was not to be answered by mere theological refutation. And, as Schochet observes, Parker was far less concerned with theological correctness than with the political stability which would only emerge from religious uniformity. With Parker, as with many of the figures discussed in these chapters, religious heterodoxy had less to do with philosophical propositions than with public practice. Hence for

Parker persecution seemed a logical extension of the conviction that religion was an important public concern, not merely a matter of private conscience, a notion about which he had the gravest misgivings. In his theory of the legitimate role of the civil magistrate in the enforcement of religious conformity, Parker incorporated into Anglican doctrine an almost Hobbesian conception of the absolute power of the sovereign. And, as Schochet points out, such assertions of the role of government in policing the margins of orthodoxy played no small role in retarding the emergence of true religious liberty in England.

The desire for religious conformity assumed numerous forms in the later seventeenth and early eighteenth centuries, from the passage of the Clarendon Code to the formation of the Societies for the Reformation of Manners. Although such efforts were directed at different manifestations of modern heterodoxy, they were all born of a sense that for whatever reasons the moral climate was growing less hospitable. To quote Convocation: "tho' it may with Truth be affirm'd, that the Good Christians among Us were never better than now; yet can it not withal be deny'd that the Bad were never worse; and that the Instances of a Profane and dissolute Behaviour, have of late Years, been very Numerous, and very Scandalous."[58] Complaining of the efflorescence of swearing and Sabbath breaking, Convocation seems to share a familiar bafflement as to which came first, speculative or practical atheism, whether human beings followed vicious courses because they had been influenced by heterodox ideas or whether they had adopted deism and freethinking as the only philosophies providing a justification for their sensual appetites. Although critics of "modern atheism" acknowledged the varieties of heterodoxy which often appeared under that heading, the orthodox presumed "a kind of circular connection . . . between theoretical irreligion and bad behaviour."[59] To quote one worried cleric: "Wickedness of Life . . . naturally proceeds from or is necessarily accompanied with a disbelief of the Nature and Attributes of God." Conversely, "the more open Vice and Wickedness, barefac'd Debauchery and avowed Profaneness get ground in the World, so much the greater proportion of Atheism and Infidelity must there necessarily be."[60]

One immediate corollary of this circular argument was the expressed hope that the punishment of wicked behavior might somehow lead to the correction of heterodox opinion. In "The Societies for the Reformation of Manners: between John Locke and the Devil in Augustan England," Shelley Burtt discusses the attempts of these societies to actually reduce the levels of practical atheism by insisting on the prosecution of offenses like drunkenness, bear baiting, prostitution, and swearing and by sending out squadrons of well-intentioned citizens to issue summonses to the scofflaws in question. The Societies for the Reformation of Manners (SRMs) were ripe for ridicule and critics were only too happy to oblige; for the most part, history has tended to side with the critics. But, as Burtt points out, the SRMs played a more important and more ambiguous role in the attempted defense of Christian orthodoxy than has generally been allowed. Just as blasphemy and heresy had been reinterpreted as types of nonconformity punishable by law, so transgressions from swearing to Sabbath breaking came to be redefined as violations of the public order. Burtt points out the gradual transformation of Anglican ideology from within which this effort inspired, as the defense of moral behavior lost its purely religious justification, assuming instead a political rationale. But just as persecution failed to achieve religious uniformity, so too the intervention of the civil magistrate in questions of religious practice and moral reform was, as Burtt observes, a *de facto* confession that the church's efforts to preserve order through persuasion were no longer effective.

Calls for the intervention of the civil magistrate were not restricted to cases of practical atheism, however; defenders of the Church of England were also insistent that because heterodox arguments so frequently defied open refutation, the state had an active interest in suppressing various forms of esoteric and encoded discourse, irony and ridicule in particular.[61] It has often been the modern habit to treat heterodox writers from Hobbes to Hume as if they were straight-forward expositors of philosophical systems. But as numerous critics pointed out deists and freethinkers were actually masters of disguise whose assault on the church and its teachings more frequently came masked in rhetorical indirection. Hobbes, after all, genuflected politely in the direction of conventional belief – "Miracles are Marvellous workes" – even as he implied just how foolish he found those beliefs to be – "but that which is marvellous to one, may not be so to another."[62]

Such clever insinuations so frustrated clerics like Bishop Parker that they came to demand suppression of heterodox wit as a danger to church and state. "There is no man that laughs at the Folly of Religion," Parker writes, "who is not angry at the Superstition of Government. And therefore I leave it to Authority to consider, how much it concerns them to restrain the Insolence of this wanton

Humour; and to punish those, who make it their Business to propagate Irreligious Principles, as the worst and most dangerous Enemies to the State."[63] In "Irony as Subversion: Thomas Woolston and the Crime of Wit," I examine attempts on the part of parliament and the courts to redefine the esoteric and often witty discourse of heterodox writers as a form of libel punishable by civil statute. The chapter focuses on the ideological presuppositions that allowed the church to demand that all forms of wit directed at established religion be prosecuted by the civil magistrate, a conflation of church and state so complete that Woolston's ridicule of the Scriptures would be condemned as an assault on the constitution itself.

One might argue that the treatment reserved for Woolston merely recapitulated in secular and legal terms interpretative procedures that had first been developed to deal with other forms of deviation from the straight and narrow path. Because esoteric heterodoxy could appear in such a variety of encoded or disguised forms, defenders of orthodoxy were determined to unmask dangerous tendencies of those, like Locke, who remained within the Anglican fold. Therefore there may well be a connection between the efflorescence of encoded heterodoxy in the early eighteenth century and the growing conviction that the church was about to be betrayed from within, that it was "too *Strong* to be *Shaken*, but thro' the *Treachery* or *Supine Negligence* of its own *Members*, or those at least that *pretend* to be such and as such palm themselves frequently upon their *Country* and *Church*, to the irreparable Damage of Both."[64] Just as it would later become an item of faith that wit was a token of heterodoxy, so it had first been a truism of High Church polemic that "false brethren" could be recognized by their "latitude," that in effect the Latitudinarians were a kind of fifth column inveigling deist and Socinian principles into the church itself. So, for example, in Sacheverell's anatomy of the Low Churchman one finds the conflation of categories which, as I have suggested, marks the orthodox response to heterodox dissent in all its forms. In order to "Cloak" their impiety, Sacheverell argues, these new men of Latitude "Stile themselves in *Indefinite* Terms, *Protestants at Large*, that is, of all Religions, besides the *Popish*, which they will not allow to be such; and so by an *Universal Latitude, Comprehension*, and *Indifference* to every Sect and Party, but that of the *True Establish'd Church*, they run into the common Herd, and are *Deists, Socinians, Quakers, Anabaptists, or Independents*; *Turks* or *Jews* upon occasion, [and] take all to be equally Orthodox, as it suits best with their Interest."[65]

Jeffrey S. Chamberlain's "The Limits of Moderation in a Latitudinarian Apologist: or, High Church Zeal in a Low Churchman
Discover'd" provides a corrective to such High Church propaganda
while exploring one of the most contentious issues of the later
seventeenth and early eighteenth centuries: how to define the true
Church of England Man. Chamberlain offers a detailed profile of
Thomas Curteis, a Latitudinarian sympathetic to dissent but
unalterably opposed to deism and freethinking, a Low Churchman
whose treatment of religious heterodoxy revealed all the righteous
fervor (and intolerance) of the doughtiest defenders of the faith.
While Curteis was the most tolerant of clerics where Dissenters were
concerned, he was so horrified by the arguments and the behavior of
heterodox writers that he denied them the toleration he freely
recommended for other forms of religious dissent. With a battery of
books and pamphlets, Curteis carried on the struggle to disprove the
assertions and unmask the deceptions of deists and freethinkers. One
of the great virtues of Chamberlain's chapter is that it introduces
modern readers to a significant body of orthodox polemic that has
largely and unfairly been overlooked by intellectual historians of the
period.[66]

The effort to tar the Latitudinarians with the brush of heterodoxy
was a fairly obvious tactic in the struggle to buttress the claims of
Anglican orthodoxy, a struggle that would also take place in such
unlikely venues as the quarrel of the ancients and moderns and the
rise of the eighteenth-century novel. As J. A. I. Champion has
recently remarked, deists and freethinkers attempted to undermine
the exclusive claims of Christianity "not by denying God but [by]
rewriting the history of religion. . . . radicals like Charles Blount and
John Toland sidestepped propositional debates about the existence of
God, and proposed alternative histories of the Christian past."[67] In
"Deists and Anglicans; the Ancient Wisdom and the Idea of
Progress" Joseph M. Levine explores the paradoxes that emerged
when the defenders of the faith themselves invoked this new historical
criticism in the study (and thus presumably the defense) of Biblical
history, a history that provided an anchor for orthodox belief in the
modernity of the Christian dispensation *and* evidence for those
defending a Christianity as old as the creation. Levine shows how
even the quarrel between the ancients and moderns figured in
discussions of the authority of the Scriptures, the chronology of the
Old Testament, and the status of the Church Fathers: all cruxes in the
argument between heterodox writers and the defenders of orthodox

Anglicanism. And ironically, as Levine points out, modern philological investigations of the authenticity of ancient texts also provided the methodology by which the universalist claims of orthodox Christianity would be undermined. Levine provides yet one more example of a defense of orthodox belief that planted the seeds of its own undoing, and his analysis of the religious implications of the ancients/moderns controversy reminds us that no area of British intellectual life remained untouched by the struggle to somehow define and defend the margins of orthodoxy.

Ronald Paulson's "Henry Fielding and the Problem of Deism" provides a fitting conclusion to this volume. For Paulson explores in detail the tensions between deism and orthodoxy as manifest in the career of Henry Fielding, a writer whose reputation for orthodoxy has alternately waxed and waned over the past two centuries. Here the ambiguous relationship between orthodox aspiration and heterodox temptation so typical of the age is seen to be incarnated in one man's career: Fielding the artist, whose choice and elaboration of literary form incorporates assumptions most characteristic of ethical deism, versus Fielding the man, who eventually embraced Anglican orthodoxy, effectively renouncing attitudes and positions adumbrated if not openly proclaimed in his earlier works.

Paulson addresses the question of Fielding's anticlericalism, most evident in his portrayals of the clergy in *Joseph Andrews*, including his portrait of Parson Adams, the ideal of Christian goodness which was itself condemned by contemporary clerics as an example of heterodox anticlericalism.[68] And he traces analogies between Fielding's Lucianic skepticism, particularly in the farces of the 1730s, and the Woolstonian iconoclasm of Hogarth. Paulson is primarily concerned, however, to discover links between the critical attitudes connected with ethical deism and the rise of historical consciousness essential to the development of the novel. In this regard he draws our attention to the influence of the Third Earl of Shaftesbury, "not only his subtle pragmatism but his equation of beauty and virtue, the principle of internal balance and harmony, shared by the work of art and the virtuous individual." Like Shaftesbury, Fielding "utilizes the deist strategy of shifting attention from the question of revealed religion to the observable facts of human virtue and happiness in a social situation." In particular, Paulson traces Shaftesbury's influence on Fielding's secularization of providence as an aesthetic principle, contrasting the ordered world of the philosopher/artist with the flawed cosmos defined by orthodox Christianity. Reevaluating Fielding's concept of "design", Paulson concludes that, for Fielding, providential order was to be found only in art, not in the sublunary creation.

The point to be made, then, is not so much that Fielding is "necessarily himself a deist as that he accepts the consequences of deism," consequences that Paulson carefully uncovers in Fielding's work. In the process, he draws attention once again to the difficulty of defining eighteenth-century orthodoxy. Because for all the apparent clarity of the debate between Parson Thwackum and Philosopher Square with which this introduction began, the problem of defining orthodoxy was for Fielding as difficult and ambiguous as it was for other orthodox defenders of Anglicanism.[69] Here, we reencounter one of the threads woven throughout this volume. For whether – in answer to Burke – Toland, Tindal or Woolston continued to be read is not the issue. What matters is the recognition that their ideas and their critique, like Shaftesbury's treatment of beauty and virtue, continued to survive even in the works of those, like Fielding, who finally claimed to have rejected the deists completely.

NOTES

1 Henry Fielding, *The History of Tom Jones A Foundling*, introduction and commentary by Martin C. Battestin, ed. Fredson Bowers, 2 vols. (Middletown, CT, 1975). See Battestin's notes, pp. 123–27.

2 *Tom Jones*, book III, chapter 3. All subsequent references to *Tom Jones* will use this form of citation.

3 This useful phrase is coined by Jonathan Swift in his *Ode to the Athenian Society* (1692) when he complains of:

> The Wits, I mean the Atheists of the Age,
> Who fain would rule the Pulpit, as they do the Stage,
> Wondrous *Refiners* of Philosophy,
> Of Morals and Divinity,
> By the new *Modish System* of reducing all to Sense. (ll. 103–97).

See *The Poems of Jonathan Swift*, ed. Harold Williams, 2nd edn, 3 vols. (Oxford, 1958).

4 *Tom Jones*, III.3

5 J. C. D. Clark, *English Society 1688–1832: Ideology, Social Structure and Political Practice During the Ancien Regime* (Cambridge, 1985).

6 Although various eighteenth-century historians have attempted to provide a history of atheism and infidelity in the period, there has been no real effort to account for the various ways in which this debate suffused the culture.

7 Richard Watson, *Anecdotes of the Life of Richard Watson, Bishop of Llandaff; Written by Himself* (London, 1817), p. 451.

8 Donald Greene's discussion of the "Augustinianism" in the eighteenth century is perhaps the most notable recent attempt to define orthodoxy. See *The Age of Exuberance* (New York, 1970), p. 95. Greene's view has enjoyed enormous currency, particularly in North America. For the full development of Greene's argument and the following debate, see also "Augustinianism and Empiricism: A Note on Eighteenth-Century English Intellectual History, *Eighteenth-Century Studies*, 1 (1967), 33–68; "The *Via Media* in an Age of Revolution: Anglicanism in the Eighteenth Century," in *The Varied Pattern: Studies in the Eighteenth Century*, ed. Peter Hughes and David Williams (Toronto, 1971); "How 'degraded' was Eighteenth-Century Anglicanism?" *Eighteenth-Century Studies*, 24:1 (Fall 1990), 93–108. For notable responses, see Frans De Bruyn, "Latitudinarianism and its Importance as a Precursor of Sensibility," *Journal of English and Germanic Philology*, 80 (July 1981), 349–68; Gregory F. Scholtz, "Anglicanism in the Age of Johnson: The Doctine of Conditional Salvation," *Eighteenth-Century Studies*, 22:2 (Winter 1988/89), 182–207.

9 J. A. I. Champion, *The Pillars of Priestcraft Shaken: The Church of England and its Enemies, 1660–1730* (Cambridge, 1992), p. 9.

10 [Francis Hare], *The Difficulties and Discouragements which attend the Study of Scriptures in the Way of Private Judgment* 2nd edn (London, 1716), p. 9.

11 Ibid., p. 39.

12 Edward Fowler, *The Principles and Practices of Certain Moderate Divines of the Church of England (Greatly mis-understood) Truly Represented and Defended* (London, 1670), pp. 191–92.

13 [Hare], *Difficulties and Discouragements*, p. 15.

14 Ibid., pp. 15, 17.

15 [Anon.] *Free Thoughts Upon the Discourse of Free-Thinking* (London, 1713), p. 6.

16 Michael Hunter, "The Problem of 'Atheism' in Early Modern England," *Transactions of the Royal Historical Society*, (1985), 135–57.

17 See Roger D. Lund, "Strange Complicities: Atheism and Conspiracy in *A Tale of a Tub*," *Eighteenth-Century Life*, 13 (November 1989), 34–58.

18 *Free Thoughts on Free-Thinking*, p. 6.

19 Jonathan Swift, *A Short Character of Thomas Earl of Wharton* (1710), reprinted in *The Prose Works of Jonathan Swift*, ed. Herbert Davis, 16 vols. (Oxford, 1939–75), III, p. 179. For Michael Hunter, it is precisely the imprecision of such heightened rhetorical descriptions of atheism in the literature before the Interregnum that he finds most significant.

Some might argue that this juxtaposition displays – and will encourage – muddled thought. But, on the contrary, I think that it is precisely from such a combination that we stand to learn most. Not only are we likely to discover how contemporaries experienced and responded to the threat of irreligion in the society of their day. In addition, by re-examining the relationship between the real and exaggerated in their perceptions of such heterodoxy, we may be able to draw broader conclusions about early modern thought. ("The Problem of 'Atheism'," 135.)

20 [Anon], *Moral Essays and Discourses Upon Several Subjects Chiefly Relating to the Present Times* (1690), p. 141.

21 William Nicholls, *A Conference With a Theist* (1696), preface.

22 Philip Skelton, *Ophiomaches: or Deism Revealed* ed. David Berman, 2 vols. 1749; (rptd. Bristol, 1990), I, pp. xvi–xvii. Daniel Waterland observes that the deists and freethinkers "understood the Policy of introducing *new* Doctrines gradually, and imperceptibly, under the Cover of the *old* Names: So they retained the *Terms*, but shifted the *Ideas* as they pleased. They retain'd the *Name*, but labour'd to destroy the *Thing* under affected and foreign Names, viz. *Credulity, Superstition, Priestcraft*, and the like." (*Christianity Vindicated Against Infidelity: A Second Charge Deliver'd to the Clergy of the Archdeaconry of Middlesex* [1732], p. 64.)

23 This belief in atheistic tendencies provides one of the interpretive norms for all readings of heterodox texts. Thus expositors are less concerned with what writers actually say than with what they presumably mean. So for example, when William Wotton approaches Toland's *Letters to Serena* (1704), he assumes that since they embody a variety of insinuated messages, it is his job to demonstrate the "natural tendency of these Discourses. What Mr. Toland meant he best knows." (*Letter to Eusebia* [London, 1704], p. 72.)

24 Jonathan Swift, *Mr. C–n's Discourse of Free-Thinking. Put into Plain English . . . for the Use of the Poor*, in *The Prose Works*, IV, p. 63.

25 Michael Hunter and David Wootton (eds), *Atheism from the Reformation to the Enlightenment* (Oxford, 1992), p. 11.

26 David Wootton, "New Histories of Atheism," in Hunter and Wootton (eds.), *Atheism*, p. 28.

27 In Francis Gastrell's *The Principles of Deism Truly Represented and Set in a Clear Light* (1708), for example, the debate has been rarified to the point that it now includes only a deist and a skeptic!

28 Jonathan Swift, *Preface to the Right Reverend Dr. Burnet, Bishop of Sarum's Introduction* (1713), reprinted in *The Prose Works*, IV, p. 84. On Tillotson as a Socinian, see Charles Leslie, *The Charge of Socinianism Against Dr. Tillotson Considered* (1694).

29 Anthony Collins, for example, coyly baits his exegetes into discussion of whether he was truly an atheist, a question to which Collins provides perfectly reasonable and often contradictory answers. For a specimen of this debate, see James O'Higgins, *Anthony Collins, The Man and his Works* (The Hague, 1970), and David Berman, *A History of Atheism in Britain from Hobbes to Russell* (London, 1990), pp. 70–92.

30 Most notable among these recent discussions of Augustan atheism, deism and freethinking are John Redwood, *Reason, Ridicule and Religion: the Age of Enlightenment in England, 1660–1750* (Cambridge, MA, 1976); Margaret C. Jacob, *Living the Enlightenment: Freemasonry and Politics in Eighteenth-Century Europe* (New York, 1991); *The Radical Enlightenment: Pantheists, Freemasons and Republicans* (London, 1981); *Deism, Masonry, and the Enlightenment*, ed.

J. A. Leo Lemay (Newark, DE, 1987); Champion, *The Pillars of Priestcraft Shaken*; and Hunter and Wootton (eds), *Atheism*.

31 *The New Eighteenth Century: Theory, Politics, English Literature*, ed. Felicity Nussbaum and Laura Brown (New York, 1987), pp. 3, 30.

32 Edmund Burke, *Reflections on the Revolution in France* (1790), in L. G. Mitchell (ed.), *The Writings and Speeches of Edmund Burke* (Oxford, 1989), VIII, p. 140.

33 *Jachin and Boaz: or the Stedfast and Unwavering Christian* (London, 1676), p. 10.

34 Anthony Horneck, *The Nature of True Christian Righteousness* (London, 1689), Sig. A3v.

35 Jonathan Swift, *A Tale of a Tub to Which is Added the Battle of the Books and the Mechanical Operation of the Spirit*, ed. A. C. Guthkelch and D. Nichol Smith, 2nd edn (Oxford, 1958), p. 5.

36 John Edwards, *Some New Discoveries of the Uncertainty, Deficiency, and Corruption of Human Knowledge and Learning* . . . (London, 1714), p. 19. No art form escaped suspicion. *The Gentleman Instructed*, part 3 (London, 1712) outlines ways in which music, vocal music in particular, could seduce one into error (pp. 31–33).

37 Alexander Pope, *Pastoral Poetry and An Essay on Criticism*, ed. E. Audra and Aubrey Williams (London and New Haven, 1961), l. 553; *The Dunciad*, ed. James Sutherland, 3rd edn. (London and New Haven, 1963), B, l. 212.

38 *Fog's Weekly Journal*, November 29, 1729. The contributors to the *Grub Street Journal* often seem preoccupied with the deists, Tindal in particular, whose exploits are described with all the lurid fascination of the modern tabloid press.

39 William Nicholls, *A Conference with a Theist* (1696), preface.

40 [Samuel Richardson], *The Apprentice's Vade Mecum*, ed. Alan Dugald McKillop (1734; rptd. Los Angeles, 1975).

41 *Representation of the Present State of Religion Among Us, with Regard to the Late Excessive Growth of Infidelity and Heresy and Prophaneness* (London, 1711), p. 1. Like so many of the works discussed in this collection, the *Representation* is not without its ironies. For while the Lower House felt comfortable with the role of Jeremiah, the Upper House, dominated by Whig bishops, refused to approve the document. Not surprisingly, there were those in the Lower House who suggested that the bishops' rejection of the *Representation* arose from their own complicity in the very infidelity they presumed to censure.

42 As Michael Hunter remarks, "the juxtaposition of an exaggerated 'atheist' stereotype with the sense of an inexorable continuum from mild to extreme infidelity had a wider significance. For it may be argued that through the concept of 'atheism' it was possible to express disquiet about tendencies in contemporary ideas and attitudes which were commonplace and which ultimately had irreligious implication, but which were rarely found in so extreme a form." ("The Problem of 'Atheism'," pp. 154–55).

43 David Berman has coined the phrase "theological lying," to describe a

particular kind of heterodox encoding. See, "Deism, Immortality, and the Art of Theological Lying," in Lemay (ed.), *Deism, Masonry, and the Enlightenment*. Citing research that Marlowe's atheist views can be "paralleled in writings against 'atheism'," Hunter suggests that "such books may well have helped to create the very phenomenon they sought to refute." It is likely that "the vocabulary of irreligion itself comprised commonplaces of heterodoxy picked up from orthodox sources," ("The Problem of 'Atheism'," p. 149.)

44 Swift, *The Prose Works*, III, p. 49.

45 Charles Leslie, *The Second Part of the Wold Stript of his Shepherd's Cloathing* (London, 1707), p. 2.

46 Father Simon had observed that the very notion of orthodox Protestantism as a safe passage between a Socinian Scylla and the Charybdis of Rome was a contradiction in terms. "There have . . . been very few Protestant Divines who have sufficiently answer'd the *Socinians*, who affirm that there can be no medium held betwixt their Religion, and the *Roman Catholick*; for if we take the Scripture, Reason, and Experience for our Rule, we must, say they, be of their Opinion, whereas if we follow the prejudices of Tradition, we must of necessity joyn with the Roman *Catholicks*." (Richard Simon, *Critical History of the Old Testament*, trans. Henry Dickinson [1682], III, p. 118.

47 *Representation*, p. 3. Swift traced modern heterodoxy to the "wild confusion" and regicide of the Interregnum. "To this rebellion and murder have been owing the rise and progress of Atheism among us. . . . And the same spirit of infidelity, so far spread among us at this present is nothing but the fruit of the seeds sown by those rebellious, hypocritical saints." (Swift, *The Prose Works*, IX, pp. 223–24.)

48 Nigel Smith has recently cited Christopher Hill for wanting, like the heresiographers of the seventeenth century, to "confuse heresy, unorthodox belief, and anticlericalism (but not unbelief) with atheism." Smith raises an important methodological issue, because in large measure any attempt to assess the impact of heterodox ideas in the seventeenth and eighteenth centuries must depend less upon the statements of belief issued by the heterodox themselves, than upon the critical responses of those who claimed to have been injured, since by definition writers engaging in esoteric and encoded discourse would offer little that could lead the modern historian of ideas to place them unequivocally in the heterodox camp. The result may be an unavoidable amplification of the danger. (See "The Charge of Atheism and the Language of Radical Speculation, 1640–1660," in Hunter and Wootton (eds.), *Atheism*, p. 131.)

49 Skelton, *Ophiomaches*, II, p. 222.

50 In Dryden's less sympathetic terms: "the *Common Rule* was made the *common Prey*; | And at the mercy of the *Rabble* lay. | The tender Page with horney Fists was gaul'd' | And he was gifted most that loudest baul'd." (John Dryden, "Religio Laici," [1682], in *The Poems and Fables of John*

Dryden, ed. James Kinsley [London, 1962], 11. 402–405.)

51 [Hare], *Difficulties and Discouragements*, p. 12.

52 Francis Atterbury, "A Scorner Incapable of True Wisdom" (1694), *Sermons and Discourses*, 2 vols. (London 1820), I, p. 85.

53 Champion, *The Pillars of Priestcraft Shaken*, pp. 9–10.

54 David Wootton, "New Histories of Atheism," in Hunter and Wootton (eds.), *Atheism*, pp. 47–48.

55 Edwards, *Some New Discoveries*, p. 94.

56 Samuel Parker, *A Discourse of Ecclesiastical Politie*, 3rd edn (London, 1671), p. xv.

57 Matthew Tindal, *The Rights of the Christian Church Asserted* (London, 1706), p. 16.

58 *Representation*, p. 5.

59 Hunter, "The Problem of 'Atheism'," p. 142.

60 John Leng, *A Sermon Preach'd Before the King at Newmarket* (London, 1699), p. 30.

61 In the Boyle Lectures for 1698, John Harris remarks that writers like Charles Blount "frequently disguise their true meaning; it is not the bare Words only, but the Scope of a Writer, that giveth the true Light by which any Writing is to be interpreted." (John Harris, *The Atheistical Objection Against the Being of God and his Attributes Fairly Considered, and Fully Refuted*, 2 vols. (London, 1698), II, p. 4.

62 Thomas Hobbes, *Leviathan*, ed. C. B. Macpherson (Harmondsworth, 1981), p. 332.

63 Parker, *A Discourse of Ecclesiastical Politie*, pp. xxxiv–xxxv.

64 *The Memorial of the Church of England* (London, 1705), p. 4.

65 Henry Sacheverell, *The Character of a Low Churchman* (London, 1702), p. 8.

66 A notable exception is David Berman, who treats Curteis at some length in his *History of Atheism*.

67 Champion, *The Pillars of Priestcraft Shaken*, p. 100. In 1686 Jean le Clerc remarked that the libertines of old had "attacked the Christian religion with nothing more than coarse humour that could only influence those whose hearts and minds were already debauched." But modern libertines had turned to the "weapons of philosophy and [historical] criticism to demolish our most sacred and unshakeable doctrines." (Jean le Clerc, *Defense des sentiments de quelques théologiens* [Amsterdam, 1686], pp. 219–20; quoted in Wootton, "New Histories of Atheism," p. 49.)

68 On Fielding's putative contempt of the clergy, see John Ogilvie, *An Inquiry into the Causes of the Infidelity and Scepticism of the Times* (London, 1783), pp. 263–326. See also Martin C. Battestin, *The Moral Basis of Fielding's Art: a Study of "Joseph Andrews"*.

69 Learning that he is about to die, Square confesses his mistreatment of Tom Jones and converts to Christianity. But Thwackum, spokesman for the Church of England, remains true to his clerical instincts and solicits Squire Allworthy for yet another, richer living.

I

The ideology and origins of heterodoxy

CHAPTER I

Within the margins: the definitions of orthodoxy

J. G. A. Pocock

It is an overstated half-truth that history is always written by the winners. From Thucydides to Clarendon, the great classical histories were as often as not written by losers, by supporters of the losing side concerned to answer the question "What went wrong?" In our own postclassical times, however, losers both conservative and radical have open to them a strategy in which they retreat into the gathering dusk, fit identification tags to the owl of Minerva, and release the bird in the misty air with the self-consoling and often arrogant cry, "History will prove us right!" – a pronouncement which has the advantage that it can never be deprived of its future tense and can never be proved true or false, with the consequence that one can always go on pronouncing it. As students of history – it is safer to speak of that than of literature – we are not concerned to verify predictions, and most of those made in the past will seem to us to have had outcomes that proved them neither true nor false because they were merely different. The heterodox of 1660–1800 would have found our world just as unimaginable as would the orthodox; this is true even of the United States, where the heterodoxies of the English-speaking world between those dates came nearer to being the orthodoxies of a new political culture than they did anywhere else.

Nevertheless it is an interesting paradox, another usable half-truth, that in our liberal culture history is very often written by losers who believe that they are really winners, that it is in some deep sense the losers who hold the keys to the future. It has been written very largely by nonconformists, or by those kindly disposed to nonconformity while remaining within the established structures, who have tended to regard the progress of society as running from orthodoxy to heterodoxy, from unity to plurality, from the sharing of beliefs to the distribution of opinions. Incidentally, the reduction of belief to opinion was, in the period covered in this volume, one of the cardinal strategies pursued by both the nonconformists and their conformist allies. In a further phase of the story the writing of history came to be practiced in large measure by agnostics, into whom the nonconformists and their allies had predictably enough developed; and by a concurrent, complicated and very interesting mutation, it came to be practiced by intelligentsias, that is to say by those who considered it the function of the intellectual to be progressive and alienated at the same time; critically discontented with the existing arrangements of society and perpetually imagining alternative possibilities with which, however, one would be equally discontented if they ever came to be actualities. He knew this, if he was a realist, because he knew that in history the achievement of goals always comes at high cost; if he was a moralist, because he knew that no moral purpose is ever more than relatively desirable. But one might know it without being either a realist or a moralist, being merely one who perpetually congratulated himself on the melancholy purity of his perceptions, retiring to dwell among the graves crying "Come not near me, for I am holier than thou!" It is a problem, though not an insoluble one, to maintain one's critical capacities without coming to be like that, and both the orthodox and the heterodox of the years 1660–1800 could see that the species was getting to be more common.

There is in consequence a dissentient as well as a Whig version of the paradigm of history as progress, a one-way road leading towards defeat in the place of victory. In Whig history the only intelligible process is that of explaining how the good guys win in the end; in dissentient history they always lose, being defeated or corrupted in the moment of victory by the irresistible success of the apparatchiks over the idealists. The apparatchiks erect a new orthodoxy, and perhaps most of the heterodox are seduced into joining them; but in due course a heterodoxy will be generated out of the orthodoxy, will rebel against it and the process will begin again. The apparatchiks triumph in this world; the heterodox triumph by maintaining the underground continuity of the church invisible, however they define it. The paradigm of progress is maintained, however, by maintaining the presupposition that the orthodoxy of the moment (whatever it may be) is dead and static, whereas the grain of mustard seed, the salt that has not lost its savour, is represented by the heterodoxy of the moment (whatever it may be) in which life and movement alone may be found, so that history conceived as process is to be found in the short-term subversion of the orthodoxy by the heterodoxy. As post-Protestant intellectuals in a liberal culture at the close of the twentieth century, we all live in some degree by this orthodoxy of heterodoxy – of which, by the way, what we call postmodernism is the latest version. Our writing, speaking, and thinking are all pervaded by its rhetoric, which not merely encourages but seeks to oblige us to take it for granted that the orthodoxy of the moment, whatever it may be, is static, so that the only movement going on is movement away from it; that it is always comfortable and self-reassuring, yet at the same time frightened and repressive; and – since the only theory and practice worth studying are those which lead away from it – once we have identified it as orthodoxy we have said all there is that needs saying about it, and nothing remains except to study the process of its destruction – with the aid of a theory of contradiction we may depict this as self-destruction – and replacement by something else.

We have a string of key words – "traditional" is one, "bourgeois" is another, and "orthodoxy" itself may be a third – which it is hard to exclude from our discourse or admit to it without finding that they have imported the whole of this paradigm with them, and of course the paradigm of heterodoxy can, like any other paradigm, be an orthodoxy in its own right. That belief systems may harden into armored shells of hollow authority it would not be reasonable to deny; but a good example would be, and has been, the growth of an automatic assumption that it is all they can do. I want in this chapter to advance the thesis that this assumption makes for an impoverished view of history; that it is not enough to view history as an unending series of butterflies bursting out of chrysalises; that we understand history better, and are more enriched by understanding it, when we understand that orthodoxy has its own history, is in history and has history in it. Orthodoxy is not a mere rejection of tensions or an attempt to freeze or deny them; it is a particular way of responding to tensions and seeking to recombine them, and this is no less so where it is conservative in the sense that it aims at maintaining durable and traditional positions. To anyone who suspects that I am trying to conserve some such positions, apologizing for the mind-set that conserves them, my reply is that I am trying to show that we understand history better when we understand the activity of orthodoxy within it.

Let us then consider orthodoxy, or what went on within the margins of orthodoxy, in the Anglo-American world between 1660 and 1800. (I say "Anglo-American" rather than "English-speaking" because there is little or nothing in this volume that seems to allude to what was going on in the Scottish, Scottish–Irish, or Scottish–American intellectual universes, although such universes did exist.) This has been to take our stand on one side of an important historical division, because when we look at the processes of enlightenment in Protestant cultures from the standpoint of what was going on in the Protestant Netherlands, Protestant Switzerland, and the Huguenot diaspora, we find that Enlightenment to have been very largely a continuation of the Synod of Dort:[1] that is, of the debate within Calvinism over the absolute decrees of grace, in which the Remonstrant side was capable of moving in the directions variously labeled Arminian, Socinian, and deist. But the Anglo-American world was predominately English, and in England after 1660 the ruling orthodoxy (and ruling certainly was what it aimed at) was not Calvinist but that of the Church of England, an orthodoxy that it is no light matter to define.[2] The Arminian debate had been vehement if unfocused before and during the civil wars, but the Church of England restored is largely defined by the debate for and against the absolute decrees of grace. We call it Anglican, though the term itself is an anachronism, by way of indicating that English orthodoxy, and the American as well as the English debate with it, have to be defined in terms appropriate to the Church of England. If enlightenment, of the kind of which Socinianism, deism, and Unitarianism were features, emerged from this debate as from the debate with the Calvinist churches – and it did so emerge – we find ourselves facing one more instance of the way in which English history converges with that of adjacent parts of Europe from a standpoint, and with enduring concerns, distinctively its own. The Scottish case is complicated by the fact that the beginnings of enlightened theology in Edinburgh and Glasgow appear to have arisen less from a Remonstrant movement, like that in French or Dutch Calvinism, than from elements of the English Latitudinarianism encouraged in Restoration Scotland by Alexander Leighton and Gilbert Burnet, though a collision with the high-flying Calvinism of the Popular party necessarily occurred sooner or later. Even in Scotland, perhaps, as in the American colonies certainly, our understanding of heterodoxy in 1660–1800 entails understanding of an orthodoxy which was that of the Church of England as by law established and as restored in the miraculous year 1660 and after.

Here I am aligning myself with the work of J. C. D. Clark,[3] who has outraged many people in many ways, not least by insisting on recounting the history of the eighteenth century with the established church at the centre of the stage, instead of making it a mummified presence in the wings like the dragon in *The Magic Flute* – with all the action taking the form of a procession away from it towards the temple of Sarastro. If we take it for granted that an authoritative religious structure is an inherently ridiculous and repressive construct, we will of course write Whig history of the kind Clark has condemned; but we write better history once we realize that there were those who did not consider it ridiculous, and both defended and endorsed it in word as well as deed. What, then, was the orthodoxy of the Church of England? It entailed the maintenance of two propositions: that the church in England was the church by law established, subject to the jurisdiction of the crown and established by the authority of statutes enacted by the king in parliament; and that the church was not thereby separated from the church that had been Christ's presence, and in some sense his body in the world since the ascension of his risen body into heaven, but continued to take part in that church's spiritual activity and its history as a human association. Between these two propositions there existed tremendous and tragic tensions, but if we call these tensions contradictions we may find ourselves conceding – whether as Catholics, as Unitarians, or as nonbelievers – that the enterprise of the Church of England was doomed from the start and that history can only be written as the record of its disruption; whereas if we call them tensions, we are in a position to see that there is a dynamic history to be written of the continuing attempts to resolve these tensions and to maintain the church's being and authority at the points where they all met. To borrow an image from that admittedly questionable source, the writings of G. K. Chesterton, the history of orthodoxy would resemble a chariot careering down the ages, always reeling wildly yet remaining upright and in motion. Whether the charioteer is still at the reins today is a question to which recent archbishops of Canterbury have sometimes sounded unsure of the answer, and I shall not attempt to resolve it.

The history of orthodoxy in the Church of England has not always – to put it mildly – been as exciting as that; there have been times when it has sought to maintain itself by lowering the key and discouraging debate. We may recall an episode in one of Anthony Trollope's novels when an imaginary Conservative prime minister – evidently Disraeli stealing clothes from Gladstone – proposes that the time has come for disestablishment; and within this fiction Trollope remarks: "Bishops as a rule say but little to one another, and now were afraid to say anything."[4] Under Victorian conditions the strategy would probably have carried them through the crisis Trollope imagined, which of course never arose in reality; and certainly there have from time to time existed bishops just like that, running the same risk that American politicians run today, that of turning off the public membership of their community because they think the best way of maintaining their position is never to discuss issues.

I intend to show that this was part of the orthodoxy of the long eighteenth century, but never was the whole of it; and behind its presence there could always be detected the presence of issues so explosive that it was dangerous to discuss them, with the consequence that they had to be discussed sometimes. These issues arose both formally and vitally from the tensions I have been indicating: those between the church as by law established and the church that was the continuing presence of Christ, promised to his Apostles at the Ascension and revealed to them on the Day of Pentecost. But we will never understand the long eighteenth century if we do not understand that the church thus dually established was essential to the structure of national sovereignty, part of the government of church and state established by the Tudors, torn apart in the civil wars and revolutions, and grimly reestablished at the Restoration. We shall not understand the long eighteenth century, in short, if we do not understand that it lived with the memory of the civil wars as the nightmare from which it was struggling to awake, or if you prefer, to go to sleep again. Its dullest complacency was a blanket spread over that memory, and even in the mid-Victorian period Bishop Stubbs – a great historian and not a very Trollopean figure – thought that seventeenth-century history should not be taught to undergraduates because it was too divisive.[5] But that did not mean that Stubbs thought there were no issues or that they did not have to be discussed; he was merely raising the question by whom they should be discussed and when. He was at the point of acknowledging that there were central issues in English life and history which were political because they were ecclesiological and that they were for the same reason theological. It was a matter of relating Christ to the crown and the church to the body politic; there was civil war and regicide in the memory of how these relations had been conducted; and the creed by which most of us live, that it is ludicrous as well as dangerous to suppose that these matters are related, is a radical solution which was found to the problem that they were related. It is an outcome of history, but a very poor way of understanding history.

I want here to endorse John Morrill's contentions that the English civil wars were wars of religion,[6] whether or not we think of them as the European wars of religion breaking out in a specifically English and Scottish form just as they were coming to an end on the adjacent continent. This does not have to mean that religious issues caused the outbreak of the wars or motivated all those who took part in them; it need only mean that once they were in the wars, they found that there were fundamental religious issues which affected them at every point and would have to be confronted if the wars were ever to be resolved. This occurred because the government of England was, by the definition laid down in the Act in Restraint of Appeals of 1533, the self-government of "empire," possessing an absolute jurisdiction over itself in spiritual as well as in temporal matters; so that when that government broke down, it broke down in church as well as in state and the two confusions could not be kept distinct from one another. We have to remember that this dissolution of authority, or dissolution of government, was the worst experience ever suffered by the governing structure of premodern England, and even by a large slice of those who were governed; some of the most radical things done were carried out in the attempt to restore authority in church and state, and there is hardly anything in the long eighteenth century which is not moved by the memory of these disasters and the knowledge that they could occur again. We need to linger a moment on the concept of authority. For one thing it was inseparable from the concept of law, even for those who thought the existing laws were unjust and placed authority in the wrong hands. For another, it is incredibly hard for us, raised as we are on the liberal presupposition that religion should have nothing to do with authority, to recapture the mentality of our predecessors to whom religion was an affair of authority and could not be otherwise. Christ, having come to earth to save humankind, had departed after authorizing certain persons and institutions to act for him; he had said he would be present in what he had left behind, so that contact with him was contact through those institutions which were his presence. To discover who were the persons so authorized, in what manner they had been authorized, what they had been authorized to do and say, and oblige us to say and do, was the necessary precondition of communicating with Christ and being saved through his merits; authority, in short, was the necessary condition of his continuing presence. The belief of the most radical congregations and individuals was the belief that this authority was reposed in themselves and in nobody else. To all others, who saw themselves as members or subjects of magisterial institutions exercising such authority, it followed not only that Christ's presence justified and rendered sacred those institutions of government, but that the existence of authority was the necessary condition of Christ's continuing presence in the world.

This is why there was so much that was sacred and divine about the governing institutions in church and state that underwent crisis in the seventeenth century; it was in the last analysis very hard to believe in Christ's presence, or his person, without them, unless one were willing to believe in the world turned upside down, by believing that Christ was represented only in one's own person and that of one's fellows. This, I suggest, explains why the actions and discourse of Englishmen in the seventeenth-century crisis are at once so conservative and so much more radical than can be found anywhere else in Protestant Europe. On the one hand William Lamont's studies[7] of such figures as Prynne and Baxter have shown us how it was possible to see the Ancient Constitution as the precondition of the Elect Nation: to see the maintenance of Tudor sovereignty, with all its historical pretensions, as the mode of England's independence of Rome and its capacity to act as the vehicle of Christ's presence and even his return. On the other hand, Lamont has also shown us how, if the king failed to act as the Godly Prince and the structure of the Elect Nation's sovereignty failed to maintain its unity, the authority to act in Christ's name reverted progressively (or regressively) to others and finally rested in Christ himself as conceived to be present in his people when all institutions had failed to act as his vehicle. Because this could not have happened if England the political entity had not claimed sovereignty – a political capacity that it claimed to exercise in Christ's name – the people in whom Christ was present might subvert all political institutions in the name of his presence, but could not do without political institutions as the vehicle of that presence. Failing to replace the Ancient Constitution, which they were predisposed to regard as sacred, with new institutions more sacred still, they brought back the Ancient Constitution, king, lords, forty-shilling freeholders and all, in 1659 and 1660. Milton and Harrington both understood that this was happening; but it is easier for us to understand than it seems to have been for them to anticipate, that the restoration of Tudor sovereignty would mean the restoration of the Church of England.

Nevertheless it had been claimed that Christ was in the people, the congregation or the individual, and it was against this Christian heterodoxy – which contained de-christianizing implications once it asserted that Christ was in them in the form of their reason – that the orthodoxy of the long eighteenth century was directed. It does not follow, however, that all the heterodoxies of 1660–1800 were derived from this source. Some were, but others were not. As Alan Kors is reminding us in his studies of the origins of French atheism,[8] heterodox doctrines are often invented by the orthodox or arise from the struggle to define orthodox positions; another reminder that orthodoxy is not a comfortable cessation of thought, but is produced in the course of an unending effort to achieve precision. Orthodoxy in the restored Church of England identified, as the immediate heterodoxy by which it was opposed, what it termed "enthusiasm": the belief that Christ or the Holy Spirit was directly and pentecostally present and active in the elect and empowered them to act in church or state; the orthodoxy of the long eighteenth century is very largely a polemic against this enthusiasm. But what the Church of England had to defend against enthusiasm – a defense which went on whether an attack was being mounted or not – was the institutional structure of the church in its alliance, or its unity, or its duality with the state, as defined by the Act in Restraint of Appeals and as by law established. It had therefore to be maintained that Christ did not activate his redeeming presence among people through any channels which were not those of the institutional church or in any way incompatible with the laws of civil government. Christ's presence was a structure of authority; the structure of existing authority was the form or mode of his presence. The enthusiast, taking Christ's presence to be in himself in a way which denied all authority, might well start as a fanatic and end as an atheist; this accusation is perfectly common and perfectly intelligible.

But the dual character of the Church of England – church in the apostolic succession, church as by law established – meant that there were two heterodoxies, as it defined them, which the mere statement of its position as orthodoxy necessarily brought before the defining mind. One was, or was taken to be, the Roman position: that authority in the church was exclusively apostolic, could be institutionalized only on apostolic premises, and was altogether independent of the authority of the civil magistrate. This was called the Popish danger, and the activities of the restored Stuart kings at times made it look much more dangerous than enthusiasm; the career of John

Dryden is that of a powerful mind which reached the conclusion that authority in church and crown alike could be secure only on the foundations of a Catholicism, which was as much Gallican as ultramontane. Just what kind of Catholic James II was has not been fully explained, though we know that the then Pope, Innocent XI, had reservations about him; he had one Gallican king on his hands already and may not have wanted another. But the Anglican clergy were in the difficulty that they needed to assert the apostolic sources of their authority, and the king, their supreme governor, needed to have it asserted; yet it could not be asserted without raising the accusation that they were seeking a micropapal authority in competition with that of the king himself – an accusation as likely to be levelled from within the Anglican lay community as from outside the church by law established. Here is another point at which we must decide whether to regard the history of the Church of England as that of an orthodoxy perpetually challenged or of a contradiction perpetually exposed. John Dryden was one who took the tension between clerical and lay authority to be irresolvable on Anglican terms, and became a Catholic; John Locke was one who came to the same decision and became, if not a Socinian, what was often taken to be such; the difference is that Dryden left the Church of England while Locke continued to be a communicant in it.

The second heterodoxy to be avoided was that generated by the doctrine of the church as by law established: the position that the church was not merely subject to but wholly the product of secular legislation. The civil wars had driven it into many minds that religious division was the principal cause of rebellion against civil sovereignty, and there were many within the religious establishment prepared to blame priests no less than enthusiasts for the existence of this threat. The anticlerical libertines studied by Mark Goldie[9] were often interested in maintaining civil order rather than the liberty of the mind; and chief among these was Thomas Hobbes, whose great image of Leviathan, with sword in one hand and crozier in the other, was accompanied by a rejection of all authority rooted in the spirit. This may have been aimed at Rome or at the sects, but the bishops and universities never forgave him for it. If the spirit had no authority it was because it had no substance, and if it had no substance what became of the person of Christ and his presence in the church? It was this grand subversion that the clergy detected in Hobbes's materialism and nominalism, his assault on all metaphysical realism and all scholastic theology; and if we look at the great Oxford book burning of 1683, the last *auto-da-fé* in English history, we shall find that half the propositions condemned justify resistance to kings and the other half condemn it on Hobbesian grounds. It is always worth keeping in mind the possibility that the orthodox are not stupid but know what they are up against. The historical situation was such that the Church of England had to steer its way between three menacing figures: Giant Pope, Giant Hobbes and Giant Enthusiast, the last a many-headed figure to be identified with no individual in particular, but with the individual himself or herself.

Hobbes was the enemy of enthusiasm in the sense that he denied the existence of any spirit that might pervade the material world; it would be hard to say of what nature he supposed Christ to be, and his atheism seemed to many to consist in his reduction of God to infinitely tenuous material substance. But this was not as far from enthusiasm as it might seem; if God, the mind, and material universe were all of one substance, thinking matter might have the weight of the whole universe behind its thoughts and authorizing its actions. Ralph Cudworth was at pains to distinguish between Hobbes, whom he supposed an atheist in the Democritean sense that he held the universe to consist in the free fall of atoms, and Spinoza, an atheist in the sense of a pantheist who held God and universe, mind and matter, to be of one substance and indistinguishable.[10] But the distinction did not always hold, and even when Giant Spinoza came to be considered the philosopher of atheism and enthusiasm, it was not Giant Hobbes who was mobilized to undo him but Giant Newton – that "mighty spirit leap'd from the land of Albion," in the words of William Blake, the last great poet of eighteenth-century enthusiasm.[11]

Margaret Jacob has described for us how the church's endorsement of Newtonian physics was part of the affirmation of a God who had created the universe and established the laws that governed its behavior while remaining personally and substantially distinct from it, so that he could never be confounded with it and the human intellect could discover him only through judicial reason, never sharing in either his knowledge or his substance.[12] In its implicit antipantheism, the alliance of orthodoxy with the new science was part of the critique of enthusiasm – hence Blake's hostile perception of Newton; but just how hard it was to prevent Newtonian reason from developing into enthusiasm along its own lines is revealed by the existence of the hidden Newton, prophet, alchemist, and antitrinitarian.

The alliance long antedates the *Principia*; it can be found in Cudworth's insistence that Platonism, properly understood, can be reconciled with atomism and theism, creationism and trinitarianism; and we can trace it back to the mid-1650s, in the activities of the group around Wilkins and Wallis at Oxford, who developed their own quarrels with both Hobbes and Harrington even as they were inaugurating the long polemic against enthusiasm. This group, as is well known, were embarked on mathematical studies and were active a few years later in the formation of the Royal Society; but in their pre-Restoration days they (and Cudworth too) were what were loosely termed "Presbyterians," in the sense that they could conform to the state-sponsored independence that was the ecclesiastical face of Protectoral government. They saw the Protectorate as a monarchy, not incapable of acting as the supreme governorship of a church, and after 1660 and 1662 they would be able to conform to the royal and episcopal Church of England, while accepting the view of the church's nature implicit in the readiness to redefine it. It was in this sense that they came to be defined, perhaps no less loosely, as "Latitudinarians"; but it is important to stress that in the 1650s, while the Oxford professors were quarreling with the materialist Hobbes and the quasi-Platonist Harrington over the epistemology of mathematics, their opponents were simultaneously quarreling over the nature of the apostolic succession with that refounder of Anglicanism, Henry Hammond.[13] The Church of England needed to maintain its pentecostal character along with its obedience to its lawful king; Hammond was keeping up the fight for a church of Christ and the Holy Ghost continued through the imposition of hands, whereas Hobbes and Harrington were joined in insisting on its political and civil character. Their aim was to destroy its claim to act as a vehicle of Christ's presence independent of the civil power; and if this entailed denying that the divine and human natures were compresent in Christ himself, Hobbes certainly and Harrington possibly were prepared to go the length of denying that he had been such a being as the Council of Nicea had declared him to be. Hatred of the clergy's claim to spiritual authority could arise from many sources, radical and conservative, and could move both princes and peasants to deny the clergy's view of Christ's nature and even his divinity; hence the convergence of antinomian radicalism with reason of state, and that of spiritualism with materialism. But the need to affirm the Church of England's subjection to royal authority could set up tendencies within that church itself of the kinds termed, once more loosely, "Hobbism" and "Socinianism"; and this is one of the most important tensions within orthodoxy and constituting its history.

The Cambridge Platonists – of which group Cudworth is regarded as having been one – held that to affirm reason to be "the candle of the Lord," implanted by God in man's nature, was to affirm the antidote to the intellectual malady, fever or hysteria, of enthusiasm. But if reason should appear to be of the substance of God, man would share in God's nature and the door to enthusiasm would be open once more. Hobbes had launched an indictment of the whole history of Hellenic philosophy, condemning both Plato and at least the scholastics' Aristotle as authors of the belief in real essences, from which had grown the doctrines of the real presence of spirit in matter underlying both Popish transubstantiation and sectarian enthusiasm. In the mid-1650s Samuel Parker, an Oxford Baconian and former Presbyterian turned persecuting Anglican, directed at least partly against Henry More a fierce assault on Plato as ultimately responsible for both priestcraft and enthusiasm.[14] In the place of such philosophy, basically the same as that condemned by Hobbes, he praised the experimental Baconianism of the Royal Society, which taught that the essences of things could never be known but only their behavior, and thus enjoined the vulgar to know their place and listen to their betters. Though running parallel with Hobbes this is not Hobbesian; Parker mistrusted Hobbes as a source of vulgar materialism in harness with vulgar spiritualism, and could have shared the perception of Hobbes's philosophy as a species of enthusiasm. The church was back on its *via media*, fighting off the attacks of Giant Pope and Giant Enthusiast, but the spectre of Giant Hobbes was harder to exorcise. The churchmen's insistence on obedience to civil authority brought down the accusation of Hobbism wherever the sovereign's loyalty to the church was suspect; and Parker, having denounced Plato as responsible for both Popery and enthusiasm, ended his own days as Bishop of Oxford a few months before the revolution of 1688, beset by enemies of whom some thought him a Hobbist, some a Papist, and some a mere rogue who would pretend to be either at need. Perhaps he was; but I find him held in respect some sixty years later by the great German historian Johann Lorenz von Mosheim,[15] who had been told about him by his Anglican correspondent Edward Chandler, Bishop of Durham. There is more in Parker than meets the eye; but the problems are likely to be Baconian rather than Hobbesian in character.

Parker was by no means the only churchman to applaud what Bacon, the Royal Society and Newton were doing because the experimental approach in natural philosophy could produce exactly the blend of confidence and humility needed to ensure the church's view of the universe and God's relation to it. It could discountenance enthusiasm by discouraging any belief that the mind could perceive the essences of things, the nature of the universe, and share in the being or substance of God himself. Instead, we could perceive only the behavior of things, and of persons including ourselves, and from these perceived regularities draw conclusions concerning the existence of God rather than his nature, and concerning his laws, of which we could perceive as much as the minds he had given us rendered us capable of perceiving. We move down the route thus signposted into the world of Locke, with which the church was happy enough insofar as it endowed us with confidence concerning the existence, goodness, and wisdom of God, and with humility concerning our capacity to understand either his essence or his ways. We might arrive at either a theology or an antitheology; similarly, at either a skeptical fideism or a rational, meaning a skeptical, theology intent on reducing the necessary component of dogma to those doctrines that the limited human intellect was capable of supporting. The Church of England had always rested itself on the proposition that things not necessary to salvation might be regulated by the magistrate, and had no aversion in principle to seeing the number of such things increased; to this extent skepticism, and what came much later to be known as liberalism, reinforced its authority and were part of its orthodoxy. But if a point were reached where there was nothing or next to nothing necessary to salvation, there would be no or next to no reason for the existence of a church which was the vehicle of salvation, or of a person communion with whom as present in his church was the means and meaning of salvation, and whose nature was defined as capable of being present in such a manner. The moment therefore arrived at which the process of skeptical fideism collided directly with the dogma of the Incarnation, and it was seen that Hobbes and Locke, declaring that the only article necessary to salvation was the profession that Jesus was the Messiah, had left unanswered the question as to who and what the Messiah was, and that there did not exist any neutral answer to that question. To leave it open to the formation of opinions was to declare that Christ was a being about whom one formed opinions, rather than a being who existed and was present to one and with whom one held communion, in whom one lived and moved and had one's own being. When an evangelical Hopkins undergraduate wrote in an examination paper that John Locke reduced faith to belief, that faith is reposed in persons and belief in propositions and opinions, he was drawing attention to an important historical (as well as theological) truth. It was hard to reduce the authority of the Spirit, whether for ecclesiastical or civil reasons, without reducing the authority of the church (and vice versa); and since the church claimed to represent Christ's person it was hard to do that without reducing the divinity of Christ, conceived as a person capable of leaving a church behind him in which he continued to be present. The Church of England, anxious to maintain its place in the structure of civil authority, found it hard to avoid reducing the authority of the Spirit, whether that were expressed in Roman or in dissenting forms, alike capable of challenging the authority of the state. With intentions often genuinely pious, it had allied itself with an experimental philosophy prepared to discuss everything except those things which could not be discussed; and this extension of the authority of discourse tended to reduce faith to belief, and belief to the discussion of debatable opinions. But the religion of free opinion could not be the Christian religion in the sense of the communion with a living Christ, even if one arrived at the opinion that Christ was a living presence; since Christ could not be present in the opinions people discussed about him, unless one held that the discussion of opinions was the activity of the Holy Spirit, which would be to readmit the enthusiasm that the reduction of faith to opinion had been designed to combat. The Church of England had gone far enough in this direction to set up movements of thought within its own community that tended to reduce not only the activity of the Spirit but the divinity of Christ; of this tendency, loosely termed "Socinian", John Locke was a leading if elusive exponent.[16]

Socinian or Unitarian theology was not a dissenting monopoly, and was probably more fiercely divisive within the Presbyterian connection than within the Church of England. Locke remained a communicant in that Church to his dying day; and his close acquaintance, Archbishop Tillotson – who had to clear himself of charges of Socinianism – must have known something about his theological positions, but must have regarded them as matters that convinced Christians could discuss among themselves. There was nothing necessarily hypocritical about this, nor was it primarily –

though it was incidentally – a question of censorship and freedom of speech. It was one thing to hold and discuss the opinion that Christ was a being divine in mission but not in nature, another to profess it publicly and offer to associate and communicate with others on its basis; that was to act on one's opinions, to perform an action designed to change the nature of the church. This was an important point behind the decision to refuse the benefits of the Act of Toleration to those who denied the doctrine of the Trinity. Without that doctrine the Two Natures might not be fully met in Christ; there might be no church that represented Christ's person, no person capable of exercising a divine presence; the Church of England would be separated from any action of Christ, and from the Catholic tradition that maintained the positions taken at Nicea and the other great councils, in the letters of Paul the apostle and the gospel attributed to John the apostle and evangelist. The Church of England as by law established had to endorse Nicea, or cease to be an apostolic church, thus yielding the position to Rome on the one hand and dissent and deism on the other; and this mattered to a realm still governed on the foundations laid down in the Act in Restraint of Appeals. Trinitarian dissenters might meet and worship publicly, and the Act of Toleration put all penalties on them into permanent suspension; even the division of English Presbyterians into Arians and Athanasians did not exclude them from the benefits of the Act; but Socinians and Unitarians were forbidden to congregate, associate and above all to incorporate – since incorporation, the act of forming a body, is close enough to incarnation to explain why religious bodies were forbidden to form corporations by the law of the state of Virginia. But the limits of toleration did not extend into the private realms of discussion and opinion. The Trinity, the Incarnation, the divinity of Christ were understood to be doctrines arrived at through dialectic and disputation; it was proper for persons of integrity to dispute them among themselves, as churchmen frequently did in print as well as in speech. Disputation was one thing and congregation was another; the latter was not merely the exercise of a civil right of meeting and speaking, but the act of forming not merely an association but a communion – alternatively, the act of departing from a communion, or of denying that communion with Christ was possible. If Locke did not believe that the Two Natures were met in Christ, and yet took communion in the Church of England on his deathbed, the question had to be asked with whom and through what medium he believed he was communicating. A number of answers were possible, and had been since the Reformation or before; several of them could claim to be orthodox, but either there was a debate about the content of orthodoxy or there was no such thing as orthodoxy at all. The implications of this extended beyond the church's interrelatedness with the civil power, but deeply affected the nature of the civil power as well.

There are two major points I would like to make in concluding this discourse concerning orthodoxy. The first is that there was a distinction between disputation and opinion. We can imagine Locke and Tillotson, Locke and Stillingfleet, Locke and Charles Leslie, holding a disputation – outside print, there is no record that any of them ever did – over the nature of Christ, finding themselves unable to agree, and resolving to respect one another's positions. But once they passed beyond respecting one another's sincerity and integrity and began to respect one another's opinions, they would approach the point of conceding that the differences between them could only be matters of opinion. This was a fundamental issue in the epistemology of the age; could the mind perceive things in their essences and natures, or could it only form opinions concerning them based on observation of the behavior? And this was a fundamental reason why the *Essay on Human Understanding* was perceived as a Socinian treatise; a Christ about whom one held opinions was removed from a Christ with whom one held communion. Every defense of religious freedom as the freedom to form opinions carried with it the implicit reduction of faith to opinion and communion to association, and thus entailed the holding of opinions inherently reductive of Christ's divinity. There was, to put it otherwise, an inherent quarrel between liberty and incarnation, and it reached further than the repressive or coercive authority of churches that claimed to be the institutionalized presence of Christ; it entailed the doctrine of Christ's nature as well as his presence, the doctrine of how he effected the salvation of those he redeemed. This quarrel reached further than the problem of authority in the church-state of England, and survived the American separation of church and state. The Virginia Statute of Religious Freedom[17] produced or was produced by an alliance between deists and Unitarians concerned with the liberty of opinion, and Baptists and revivalists concerned with liberty in Christ; and "liberal humanists" and "born-again Christians" have been in alliance and at strife in the United States ever since – a state of affairs that shows no sign of abating. Opinion was devised as the enemy of enthusiasm; but once opinion becomes the freedom of the spirit to seek Christ, it becomes enthusiasm once again. Edmund Burke and Josiah Tucker noted that this was happening in American religion in 1775,[18] and two and a quarter centuries have not diminished its effect. The sect as well as the church can affirm the living presence of Christ, and the relations of orthodoxy and heterodoxy are greatly complicated thereby.

The second point arises out of the first: it is that we should not overemphasize, but can never cease from emphasizing, the extent to which all discourse of toleration, liberty, and enlightenment was a polemic against the orthodox theology of Christ's divinity, against the Trinity and the Incarnation, the Council of Nicea, the Athanasian Creed – which got into the Thirty-Nine Articles of the Church of England – the Gospel according to St. John and the doctrine of the Word made Flesh. I have been trying to show why this had to be so, and one cannot cease from emphasizing it because it explains so much in the political, philosophical, theological, and historical controversies of the long eighteenth century; the danger of overemphasizing it arises because there was at the same time so sustained an endeavor to deemphasize it. The Church of England, on whose orthodoxy I have focused attention, contained strong tendencies in the very direction it was pledged to resist; with the aim of deflecting the spiritual certainties of enthusiasm, it had gone so far towards adopting the methodological cautions and skepticisms of Bacon and the Royal Society as potentially to increase the number of truths that were not necessary to salvation because they could not be known with certainty. The relations of doubt to consent, of skepticism to fideism, of confession to profession, were of genuine delicacy in the orthodox life, and could be kept delicate even in face of the robust positions which held that if a proposition could not be finally known, it was nonsense to hold and profess it or even to discuss it at all; orthodoxy was not committed to inquisition and authority, in any case where the civil law did not require it. But the wider there was extended the sphere of things in this sense indifferent, the greater there grew the tendency to substitute belief for faith and opinion for communion with the ecclesiological and christological consequences we have been noting. There had always been those in the Church of England whose caution in controversy led them in an antitrinitarian direction; and nearly a century and a half after Chillingworth and a century after Locke, these emerged from their Peterhouse closet and began campaigning for relief from the more Athanasian of the Thirty-Nine Articles, with no small consequences for church and state.[19] But while major set-piece battles between trinitarian orthodoxy and Unitarian heterodoxy can be found, the orthodox might also respond by playing down the significance of the whole debate, sometimes without considering whether they were not leaving the field to their opponents while so doing. This perhaps is the point of Trollope's joke about bishops disliking to say anything in particular; and I have not space to consider the strategy of diverting theology into morality, with the result that it would be possible to write the history of orthodoxy wholly in terms of the doctrine of eternal rewards and punishments, so largely the genesis of William Blake's Old Nobodaddy and Antichrist Creeping Jesus. The maintenance of orthodoxy can always be described in pretty cynical language, though this does not mean that orthodoxy is not maintained, or exhaust the ways in which it is significant.

I will conclude by pointing out that the conflict between orthodoxy and opinion provides the reason why the eighteenth century is a great age in the historiography of Christian doctrine. As orthodoxy came under the challenge of opinion, its defenders, like Bossuet, wrote great histories of orthodoxy conceived as the history of truth; but a wide variety of opponents both Christian and skeptical responded with histories of orthodoxy conceived as either definition or opinion. It was hard even for skeptics to write histories that were not histories of orthodoxy in its conflicts with heterodoxy; as Gottfried Arnold, and in our own day Christopher Hill, discovered, it is not easy to write history as that of an invisible church or radical underground perpetually repressed by the powers of this world, which make history as well as writing it. The skeptics, orthodox as well as heterodox, solved their problem by writing the history of orthodoxy conceived as opinion, which – as well as the theological consequences that by now should be obvious – had the effect of dissolving theology into the history of theology, the history of the human mind engaged in the formation of opinions, or more simply still the narrative of the history in which orthodoxy had come to be formed. The greatest history of this kind in English, in the judgment of John Henry Newman, was Gibbon's *Decline and Fall of the Roman Empire*; but Gibbon admired the Jansenist Tillemont, the Gallican Fleury, the Remonstrant Le Clerc, the Huguenot Beausobre and the Lutheran Mosheim a great deal more than he did the Unitarian Priestley, whose *History of the*

Corruptions of Christianity told essentially the same story as his own but led it to radical and millenarian conclusions where his were skeptical and conservative. Orthodoxy generates its own skepticism, and skepticism has its own relations with orthodoxy; this is part of the very complex history of the latter term.

NOTES

1 For this see various essays by H. R. Trevor-Roper, notably in *Religion, the Reformation and Social Change* (London, 1967) and *Catholics, Anglicans and Puritans: 17th-century Essays* (Chicago, 1988).

2 John Spurr, *The Restoration Church of England, 1646–1689* (New Haven, 1991); J. A. I. Champion, *The Pillars of Priestcraft Shaken: The Church of England and its Enemies, 1660–1730* (Cambridge, 1992).

3 J. C. D. Clark, *English Society, 1688–1832: Ideology, Social Structure and Political Practice During the Ancien Régime* (Cambridge, 1985).

4 Anthony Trollope, *Phineas Redux*, World's Classics edition (Oxford, 1983), p. 70.

5 J. W. Burrow, *A Liberal Descent: Victorian Historians and the English Past* (Cambridge, 1981), pp. 97, 99.

6 J. S. Morrill, "The Religious Context of the English Civil War," *Transactions of the Royal Historical Society*, 5th series: 34 (1984), 155–78; "Sir William Brereton and England's Wars of Religion," *Journal of British Studies*, 24: 3 (1985), 311–32. See further his *The Nature of the English Revolution* (London, 1993).

7 William M. Lamont, *Marginal Prynne, 1600–1669* (London, 1963); *Godly Rule: Politics and Religion, 1603–1660* (London, 1969); *Richard Baxter and the Millennium* (London, 1979).

8 Alan C. Kors, *Atheism in France, 1650–1729, Vol. I: The Orthodox Sources of Disbelief* (Princeton, 1990).

9 Mark Goldie, "The Civil Religion of James Harrington," in Anthony Pagden (ed.), *The Languages of Political Theory in Early Modern Europe* (Cambridge, 1987), pp. 197–222. See also Champion, *The Pillars of Priestcraft Shaken*.

10 Ralph Cudworth, *The True Intellectual System of the Universe* (London, 1678). See Richard Kroll, Richard Ashcraft, and Perez Zagorin (eds.) *Philosophy, Science and Religion in England, 1640–1700* (Cambridge, 1992); J. G. A. Pocock, "Thomas Hobbes Atheist or Enthusiast? His Place in a Restoration Debate," *History of Political Thought*, 11:4 (1990), 737–49.

11 William Blake, "Europe: A Prophecy" (1794) in *The Poetry and Prose of William Blake*, ed. David V. Erdman with commentary by Harold Bloom (New York, 1970) p. 63.

12 Margaret C. Jacob, *The Newtonians and the English Revolution, 1689–1720* (Ithaca, 1976); *The Radical Enlightenment: Pantheists, Freemasons and*

Republicans (London, 1981).

13 J. G. A. Pocock (ed.), *The Political Works of James Harrington* (Cambridge, 1977), pp. 90–96.

14 Samuel Parker, *A Free and Impartial Censure of the Platonick Philosophie* (Oxford, 1666). See Gordon Schochet, "Between Lambeth and Leviathan: Samuel Parker on the Church of England and Political Order," in Nicholas Phillipson and Quentin Skinner (eds.), *Political Discourse in Early Modern Britain* (Cambridge, 1993), pp. 189–208.

15 See Mosheim's preface to his Latin translation of Ralph Cudworth's *True Intellectual System of the Universe* (Leyden, 1768), pp. xxv–xxxi.

16 John Marshall, "John Locke and Latitudinarianism," in Kroll, Ashcraft and Zagorin, *Philosophy, Science and Religion*, pp. 253–82; and *John Locke: Resistance, Religion and Responsibility* (Cambridge, 1994).

17 J. G. A. Pocock, "Religious Freedom and the Desacralization of Politics; From the English Civil War to the Virginia Statute," in Merrill D. Peterson and Robert C. Vaughan (eds.), *The Virginia Statute for Religious Freedom: its Evolution and Consequences in American History* (Cambridge, 1988), pp. 43–73.

18 Edmund Burke, *Speech on Conciliation with America* (London, 1775); Josiah Tucker, *Letter to the Right Honourable Edmund Burke . . . in Answer to his Printed Speech* (Gloucester, 1775); J. G. A. Pocock, *Virtue, Commerce, and History: Essays on Political Thought and History, Chiefly in the Eighteenth Century* (Cambridge, 1985), pp. 164–66.

19 John Gascoigne, *Cambridge in the Age of the Enlightenment* (Cambridge, 1991).

CHAPTER 2

Freethinking and libertinism: the legacy of the English Revolution

Christopher Hill

Eighteenth-century infidelity – skeptical libertinism – goes back to what used to be called "the Puritan Revolution." Whether the one caused the other is a matter for discussion, but that eighteenth-century heterodoxy was anticipated during the English Revolution is easily demonstrated.[1]

First we must recall the circumstances of that revolution. England before 1640 was a society that had never known freedom of discussion. There had been censorship ever since the coincidence in time of printing with the Protestant Reformation and the translation of the Bible into English. Censorship was not always effective, but it was there as a deterrent, and it was tightened up as revolution approached in the 1630s. All English men and women were deemed to be members of the state church, legally bound to attend services in their parish church every Sunday; it was a legal offence to attend "conventicles," discussion groups not authorized by the national church.

Yet the Protestant Reformation and the availability of the Bible in English for an increasingly literate laity had intensified discussions over a whole range of subjects extending well beyond the narrowly theological. How should the church be governed? Should local congregations be subordinated to a national church? Was the English hierarchy of bishops, deans and chapters, and parish clergy authorized in the Bible? Why should all English men and women be legally compelled to pay tithes to a minister whom they had not chosen and whose personality or theology they might detest? Why might not congregations choose their own minister? Was the royal supremacy over the Church of England sanctioned in the Bible?

There was a third coincidence in time – the combination of the Copernican revolution in astronomy with the geographical opening up of America, Africa, and Asia. The world and the universe suddenly seemed very different places. Men became aware of other world religions that could not be dismissed as mere "heathenism"; and of the possibility that the earth was not the center of the universe, with all the questions which that raised.

These and related problems had been discussed long before the English government collapsed in 1640. The Protestant state church had always faced a dilemma. The basis of its rejection of Romish traditions had been the appeal to the Bible, the sacred repository of all truth that had at last been made available in print for all to read. But discussion of the Bible, especially by the uneducated, led to unorthodoxies that it was impossible to control. Illegal congregations sprang up which rejected the state church; significant numbers of persons emigrated to the Netherlands or to America, often because of dissatisfaction with the Anglican church. Many genuinely felt that "God was leaving England," his favored nation since the days of Wyclif and the Henrician reformation of Edward VI and Elizabeth. Charles I and his chief minister, Archbishop Laud, were believed by many to be betraying the Reformation, backsliding to Catholicism. The Thirty Year's War (1618–1648) was a catalyst here. There seemed a real danger in the 1620s and thirties that Protestantism on the continent might be destroyed, and England would not be safe if that happened. Catholic victories were accompanied by a resumption of church lands confiscated at the Reformation. So there were many reasons for opposing the pro-Catholic foreign policy of Charles I and Laud.

There was much to discuss when censorship and ecclesiastical controls broke down in 1640. Illegal congregations came up from underground, or formed themselves in the new freedom. In some areas parish churches were deserted. Discussion groups assembled under "mechanic preachers," artisans who worked six days a week and preached to voluntary congregations on the Sabbath. Discussion, both verbal and in print, was suddenly liberated. Ideas that had long been muttered in alehouses could now be freely aired; and as they were aired they were modified and refined by discussion, and other novelties suggested themselves. It must have been a very exciting time.

Initially discussion started from the Bible, which was agreed by nearly everyone to be the source of all wisdom. But once free discussion prevailed, men and women found that they disagreed in its interpretation. Inevitably the authority of the Bible itself came in question. Milton decided that "the entire Mosaic Law is abolished"; "the law is now inscribed on believers' hearts by the spirit." This licensed all individuals to interpret the Bible for themselves. "Attention to the requirements of charity is given precedence over any written law."[2]

Towards the end of Elizabeth's reign inquiring explorers and colonizers like Sir Walter Ralegh and Thomas Hariot were questioning the Bible's status because of its internal contradictions. Christopher Marlowe, with the widest historical and geographical imagination of any Elizabethan dramatist, was associated with their "school of night," whose members were accused of "atheism." ("Atheism" is used during this period to describe any deviation from "orthodoxy," or any readiness to tolerate.) Hariot said that belief in heaven and hell "worketh so much in many of the common and simple sort of people that it maketh them to have great respect to their governors."[3]

How could Cain say "every one that finds me shall slay me" when the only other man in the world was his father, Adam? Why should "the Lord set a mark upon Cain, lest any finding him should kill him?" Verses circulated suggesting that God, the afterlife, heaven and hell, were all "only bugbears," invented to "keep the baser sort in fear" and to defend the social order, especially property owners. Such ideas were not limited to intellectuals. A shoemaker of Sherbourne said men in his area (which was also that of Ralegh) thought that hell was poverty in this world. Similar ideas were to surface after 1640; Ranters and others followed Marlowe in arguing from the Bible that there had been men before Adam.[4]

There was much serious Biblical criticism from the early 1640s. John Wilkins, future bishop, decided that the "penmen of Scripture" might have been grossly ignorant. He thought the Biblical miracles could be explained by natural causes.[5] Lord Brooke in his *Discourse of the Nature of . . . Episcopacie* (1642) asked difficult questions about the authorship of books of the Bible.[6] There were also scholars who had not enjoyed a university education. Thomas Edwards in 1646 described how the radical minister William Erbery, *en route* for Wales, spoke at an informal meeting in Marlborough. He denied the divinity of Christ, and was taken up by a member of his audience who cited 1 John 5:7 and other texts against him. Erbery replied: "Those words were not in the Greek, but put in by some who were against the Arians."[7] That sort of exchange, we must imagine, was going on (usually unrecorded) all over the country as men found themselves newly liberated to discuss fundamentals without inhibitions. The Leveller John Wildman in the Putney Debates of 1647 argued that "it is not easy by the light of nature to determine there is a God. The sun may be that God. The moon may be that God."[8] The Arminian minister John Goodwin denied the literal authority of the Bible.[9] Before the poet Thomas Traherne went up to Oxford in 1653 he was a conscious skeptic, whose doubts extended to the authority of the Bible.[10]

Others went much further. The communist Gerrard Winstanley anticipated the idea that religion was the opium of the people. "While men are gazing up to heaven imagining after a happiness or fearing a hell after they are dead, their eyes are put out, that they see not what is their birthrights, and what is to be done by them here on earth while they are living" – as "indeed the subtle clergy do know." The Fall of Man, the Incarnation, Crucifixion, Resurrection and Ascension were all allegories for events that take place in the hearts and consciences of men and women. "The Scriptures were not appointed for a rule to the world to walk by without the spirit . . . for this is to walk by the eyes of other men." Of the Biblical narrative Winstanley coolly observed: "whether there were such outward things or no it matters not much." For Winstanley, as for Marlowe, heaven, hell and the devil have no existence outside human beings.[11]

The London merchant William Walwyn and the Wiltshire clothier Clement Writer used the internal contradictions and inconsistencies of the Bible to argue that it could not be the Word of God. "The Scripture reports the miracles," wrote Writer; "can the miracles reported by Scripture confirm that report?" Writer claimed to write for "the middle sort and plain-hearted people."[12] The radical John Webster wrote an influential book against belief in witchcraft in which he challenged Fellows of the Royal Society who thought skepticism about witches would lead to skepticism about the existence of God. Webster believed that the Bible had been deliberately mistranslated in order to support belief in witches.[13] Milton insisted that the Bible must be interpreted in accord with "the duties of human society." Divine ordinance, he said, "can bind against the good of man, . . . yea his temporal good not excluded."[14]

This skeptical discussion was summed up by the ex-Baptist Quaker Samuel Fisher in a massive tome published in 1660, *The Rusticks Alarm to the Rabbies*, whose title indicates that it represents a lower-class response to established religion. But it was also a serious scholarly work, though written in a rollicking, alliterative style. Fisher applied Renaissance standards of textual criticism to the Bible. He concluded that the Bible was "a bulk of heterogeneous writings, compiled together by men taking what they could find of the several sorts of writings that are therein, and crowding them into a canon or standard for the trial of all spirits, doctrines, truths; and by them alone."[15] Fisher treated the Bible as a book like any other. He thought it was read too much and quoted too often. That, after a century of Protestant bibliolatry!

Fisher was important because he wrote in the vernacular, in a racy popular style; and no one could accuse him of being an infidel. Only the shutdown of the censorship in the year in which his book was published prevented it from being widely discussed, but we know that it was widely read. Fisher's work became known to Spinoza, as Popkin has shown, and played no insignificant part in stimulating his critique of the Bible.[16] So through him the Biblical criticism of the English Revolution found its way into the European Enlightenment. Others who played a part in disseminating Fisher's ideas include Benjamin Furley, whose library at Rotterdam was at the disposal of scholars, and Anthony Collins, whose *Priestcraft in Perfection* (1710) and still more his *Discourse of Free-Thinking* (1713) incorporated Interregnum work on the contradictions and inconsistencies of the Bible.[17]

That religion was politics is very clearly recognized in the seventeenth century. Francis Osborn pointed out in 1656 that "the exploding of . . . belief [in heaven and hell] would be of no less diminution to the reverence of the civil magistrate than the profit of the priesthood."[18] By May 1661 Samuel Pepys was listening to a mathematician who did not so much "prove the Scripture false as that the time therein is not well computed or understood." Robert Boyle in 1663 said that anti-Scripturism "grows . . . rife, and spreads . . . fast."[19] Six years later John Owen thought that "no age can parallel that wherein we live" for atheism, unknown in "these parts of the world . . . until these latter ages."[20] That is the sort of thing old men say in every age; but an Italian traveler in England in the same year agreed that "atheism has many followers in England."[21] A few years later the author of *The Whole Duty of Man* recognized that atheism was fashionable, and called urgently for defense of the Bible against criticism.[22] The Boyle Lectures were founded for just such purposes. Swift no doubt exaggerated in 1708 when he said that the body of the people were freethinkers; but many similar remarks could be cited.[23]

So widespread was the radical idea that religion had been invented to keep the lower orders in place that defenders of Christianity took it over. Robert South, Bishops Samuel Parker and Gilbert Burnet, and Jeremy Collier all insisted that, irrespective of its truth or falsehood, belief in religion and in rewards and punishments in the afterlife was essential to the maintenance of social subordination. In 1664 Joseph Glanvill dedicated his *Scepsis Scientifica* to the Royal Society, stressing the Society's role in "securing the foundations of religion against all attempts of mechanical atheism."[24] In 1681 Bishop Parker, Andrew Marvell's butt, agreed that "plebeians and mechanics have philosophized themselves into principles of impiety, and read their lectures of atheism in the streets and highways."[25] Craftsmen and labourers were "able to demonstrate . . . that all things come to pass by an eternal chain of natural causes": human nature was a mere machine.[26] Bishop Burnet convinced the libertine peer Rochester on his death-bed that it was wrong to attack Christianity *publicly*.[27]

All this was part of a much wider movement of thought. D. P. Walker has analyzed the decline of belief in hell in this period, and Sir Keith Thomas the decline of casuistry.[28] Many other changes suggest a greater sensitivity to the pain and suffering in others. Torture ceased to be used in judicial proceedings; executions for witchcraft declined gradually as men and women ceased to believe in the direct intervention of the devil in human affairs. Providential history, in which God directly determined events, became old-fashioned even for a Royalist like Clarendon; Winstanley and Harrington related political to economic change. Calvinism, the dominant trend in English thinking for the previous century, lost its hold over intellectuals; with it declined the belief that the majority of the human race is condemned to spend all eternity in hell, and that there is nothing they can do about it.

The period also saw the end of many once-powerful religio-political myths. A scholarly consensus had expected the millennium to come in or around the 1650s; Milton's "shortly-expected king" of 1641 assumed this. George Fox had called on Oliver Cromwell to overthrow Antichrist – one of the necessary preludes to the end of the world – by invading France and Spain and going on to sack Rome, Antichrist's headquarters. Marvell urged the Protector to extend the British Empire in order to expedite the millennium. But later in the century, though Dryden and many other poets advocated imperialist expansion, the millenarian motive had disappeared. Antichrist had been a symbolic hate figure under which radicals subsumed everything which they detested in English society. By 1664 Henry More sneered

at "the rude and ignorant vulgar" who "have so fouled" the words
Antichrist and antichristian that they are now "unfit to pass the lips of
any civil person."[29] The rude and ignorant went on talking about
Antichrist at least until the time of William Blake.

In 1660 bishops and church courts came back; parsons were
restored to their parochial livings, and tithes were maintained to pay
them. "If there was not a minister in every parish," Robert South told
the lawyers of Lincoln's Inn in 1660, "you would quickly find cause to
increase the number of constables."[30] But it proved impossible to root
out dissent and maintain a single national church. Excommunication
ceased to be a serious punishment when men and women could
simply transfer to another congregation. Nottinghamshire employers
told their workers in 1675 that the worst penalty that church courts
could impose on them if they refused to pay tithes on their wages was
excommunication, "which was only their not going to church."[31]
Roger L'Estrange, the great harrier of Dissenters, had to admit by
1668 that juries would not convict the authors of what he regarded as
gross libels on the bishops and clergy of the Church of England.[32]
"The most effectual (not to say the most fashionable) argument for
liberty of conscience," Henry Stubbe suggested in 1673, was lack of
religious belief.[33] The Toleration Act of 1689 was the reluctant
recognition of this fact. Dissenters won freedom of worship, though
not political equality.

A different trend leading to skeptical libertinism was antinomianism.
The Protestant emphasis on the priesthood of all believers established
a direct telephone line between the faithful and God. During the
Interregnum this was extended to mean that whatever one's own
conscience told one to do must be God's will. In Milton's summary,
"the practice of the saints interprets the commandments." And, he
added, "we are released from the decalogue," which he did not believe
to be a faultless code. We ought "to believe what in our own consciences
we apprehend the Scripture to say, though the visible church with all
her doctors gainsay."[34] The Ranter Laurence Clarkson extended this
argument slightly but very significantly when he said, "no matter
what Scripture, saints or churches say, if that within thee do not
condemn thee, thou shalt not be condemned." Unlike Milton, Clarkson
suggests that the Bible does not matter. Other Ranters denounced the
Bible as the cause of all quarrels and bloodshed in the world. Thomas
Tany thought that there would never be peace till all Bibles were
burned. He burnt one in a public demonstration.

Clarkson used the supremacy of the individual conscience to legitimize sexual libertinism. "There is no such act as drunkenness, adultery and theft in God. . . . Sin hath its conception only in the imagination. . . . What act soever is done by thee in light and love, is light and lovely, though it be that act called adultery." "Till you can lie with all women as one woman, and not judge it sin, you can do nothing but sin. . . . No man could attain to perfection but this way."[35] Clarkson revealed that at one time or another God had told him to break all the commandments except "Thou shalt do no murder"; and he wondered whether and when that would be added to the list. Clarkson practiced what he preached, sleeping with any "maid of pretty knowledge" who was willing.[36]

The Ranter Abiezer Coppe agreed that "sin is finished." "Wanton kisses," he claimed, "have been made the fiery chariot to mount me into the bosom of . . . the King of Glory. . . . I can . . . kiss and hug ladies, and love my neighbor's wife as myself, without sin."[37] God's service, Coppe said, is "perfect freedom and pure libertinism." He was not using "libertinism" as a mere synonym for "freedom." He knew very well the specifically sexual sense that it could have. Coppe indeed went out of his way to shock the prudish. Being "dead drunk every day of the week" and lying "with whores 'i 'th' market place" were no worse sins than the clergy's grinding the faces of the poor by forcing them to pay tithes.[38] Coppe was not original: there had been "libertines" in Essex in 1551, and later men there who denied the existence of "sin."[39]

The legend of gloomy Puritans who hated pleasure dies hard. But nothing could be less true of the radical revolutionaries, whose maxim might have been "life, liberty, and the pursuit of happiness." Milton and the Leveller Richard Overton, like Thomas Hobbes and many others, believed that the soul was mortal; happiness was to be sought on earth – a doctrine that contemporaries associated with libertinism. The Diggers expected "Glory here!," heaven on earth and only on earth. Mortalism removed the fear of eternal torment in hell, which was one reason why it appealed to Lodowick Muggleton.[40] Milton believed that matter was good, since it had been created out of the substance of God; it and the pleasures of the senses were to be enjoyed. In *Paradise Lost* the angels eat, digest and excrete their food, and interpenetrate sexually, though in an appropriately angelic manner. Adam and Eve made physical love *before* the Fall – "whatever hypocrites austerely talk," Milton added, to show that he knew how unorthodox he was being. "The happier Eden" was Adam and Eve "emparadised one in another's arms." It was Voltaire who noted that Milton was the first to speak in favor of romantic love; Adam chose to fall because he could not conceive of living without Eve, even in Paradise. Hobbes believed that human actions were motivated by the pursuit of pleasure and avoidance of pain. Ranters thought sin was finished and ended, and Coppe conducted a campaign against sexual repression.[41] So radicals came to use the appeal to the individual conscience to justify what conservatives thought socially intolerable sexual conduct.

Ranters thought the Scripture a tale, a history, a dead letter. The Christ who died at Jerusalem was nothing to them: Christ is in all believers. Ranters were not isolated extremists. They won some sympathy by making themselves spokesmen for the poor. John Bunyan, always a passionate defender of the rights of the poor, was for a time under Ranter influence. They brought him to wonder "Whether the holy Scriptures were not rather a fable and cunning story than the holy and pure Word of God . . . " How could we know that the Bible was true and the Koran false? (The Koran had been translated into English in 1649.) The Bible might have been "written by some politicians, on purpose to make poor ignorant people to submit to some religion and government." "Paul . . . being a subtle and cunning man, might give himself up to deceive others with strong delusions." "How if all our faith, and Christ, and Scriptures, should be but a think-so?" And Bunyan had worse thoughts which even many years later he dared not utter.[42]

His Ranter friends condemned Bunyan as "legal and dark; pretending that they only had attained to perfection that could do what they would and not sin." (That, as we have seen, was Clarkson's doctrine; and Bunyan found it "suitable to my flesh, . . . I being but a young man, and my nature in its prime.")[43] Although Bunyan came to reject Ranter libertinism, it continued to haunt him. Many of the characters in *The Pilgrim's Progress*, *The Holy War* and *Mr. Badman* have recognizable Ranter characteristics. Bunyan was still arguing against the Ranter view that God had not created the world in a treatise on which he was working at the time of his death.

It is not surprising that the Blasphemy Act of 1650 was directed mainly against Ranters, as Coppe himself recognized. They advocated behavior that was disruptive of existing social norms and standards; even Milton, himself often described as a libertine, approved of the

Blasphemy Act. Ranters were suppressed, and Coppe was compelled to recant. Clarkson became a Muggletonian.

By 1660 the radical revolutionaries were hopelessly split among themselves, and exhausted by their failure to agree. In *Areopagitica* Milton had optimistically anticipated that free discussion would lead to agreement, consensus, on what the Word of God said. Alas. For Winstanley the Bible demonstrated the natural rights and natural equality of all men; recognition of that would – he thought – lead all to accept a communist society. Levellers agreed about natural rights, but thought that private property was sacred. Then the question arose whether the very poor could be trusted with the vote. Some radicals wanted the godly to rule; others addressed themselves to copyholders and artisans, regardless of their godliness. Bishops came back with the king in 1660 to restore order and discipline.

So after 1660 the Bible lost its overriding political authority as a book whose texts could solve all problems. God himself was on trial after the Restoration: Milton's task of justifying the ways of God to men was highly topical. An empiricist pragmatism fitted the state of affairs: the events of 1649 and 1660 seemed to have happened of their own accord. Harrington's political theory made better sense than that of the Levellers: the crude fact was that property ownership had been decisive over the wishes both of the majority and of the godly minority. Harrington's emphasis on the balance of property and Hobbes's emphasis on the brutal facts of power undermined radical democratic theories.

The Restoration of 1660 had been a compromise between Royalists and Parliamentarians in which many of the Revolution's achievements acceptable to conservatives had been preserved – Parliamentary control of taxation and the church, abolition of feudal tenures, confirmation of the Navigation Act and of the aggressive colonial foreign policy which it envisaged, continuity of the huge navy now financed by taxes voted by Parliament. Charles II and James II had tried to set back the clock to 1640, to destablize the settlement of 1660; 1688 confirmed that settlement, whilst establishing the legend that it merely restored the old English constitution.

As I have tried to show, the crucial significance of the events of the forties and fifties in establishing the post-1688 constitution was hushed up. Much literature was published in the 1690s and later dealing with party politics, political maneuvering, corruption, etc.; but those who mattered in politics after 1688 had no desire to revive the wider issues discussed in the forties and fifties. Protagonists of the eighteenth-century Enlightenment quoted the English constitution as interpreted by Locke rather than the ideas of the English Revolution. It was conservatives like Swift, Atterbury, and the Lower House of Convocation who kept insisting that 1688 was a pale reflection of 1641, and that the atheism and licentiousness of the Augustan Age derived from the radicals of the Interregnum.[44] Those contemporaries who stressed connections between the 1640s and 1690s were those who wished to denigrate radical ideas. When I use the phrase "hush up," I mean that whilst conservatives exaggerated and generalized wildly in smearing all republicans with "Enthusiasm" (irrational) or "extremism" (dangerous), radicals were too prudent to stress the origin of their ideas in the regicide republic. It would have been bad form and counterproductive.

Yet the ideas survived verbally. In 1709 Edward Ward's *History of the London Clubs* suggested that "the wicked seeds of sedition and dissension are speedily disseminated among the weaker brethren" in these clubs. "Nor . . . have there been any plots or conspiracies in any reign but what have been first hatched and nourished in these sorts of societies." According to Ward, "the Atheistical Club," whose members regarded themselves as "generous restorers of the people's liberty," urged "all men" to "set up to be their own master, and cast off the yokes of lawful authority."[45]

After 1660 slowly and reluctantly the religious sects abandoned the quest for political power and accepted the position of second-class citizens in return for religious toleration – intermittent until 1689. Quakers proclaimed the peace principle in 1661 and withdrew from direct political action. This had important consequences from our point of view. Henceforth Quaker writings were self-censored: the fierce demands of Fox and other Quaker leaders that Oliver Cromwell should lead his armies to conquer Rome disappeared. There is nothing about them in Fox's *Journal*: in the many reprints of Quaker writings in the late seventeenth and early eighteenth century their earlier bellicosity was suppressed. It has had to be rediscovered by modern scholars.

It was not only Quakers. When in 1698–99 John Toland printed Edmund Ludlow's *Memoirs* he carefully omitted the old republican's revolutionary millenarianism and hankering after a dictatorship of the godly, whilst retaining his critique of standing armies, so relevant to the politics of the 1690s. In Toland's version Ludlow seemed to be a

Williamite Whig. Toland may well have similarly bowdlerized Algernon Sidney's *Discourses Concerning Government* when he published them in 1698. Middle-of-the-road Parliamentarians, whose works had hitherto been suppressed, were printed or reprinted. But even the lapse of the Licensing Act in 1695 did not lead to republication of the writings of Levellers, Diggers, Ranters, or Fifth Monarchists. Publishers with an eye on the market censored themselves here: this was more effective than government censorship had ever been. In Toland's *Life of Milton*, for example, there is barely a hint of his very dangerous religious heresies; and his defense of regicide and his republicanism are played down. Together with Addison's deliberate sanitizing of Milton, this helped to create the image of Milton as the orthodox Puritan and radical Whig that confused critical views of him until relatively recently.[46]

Radical traditions survived but did not get into print. Benjamin Furley, freethinking Quaker heretic, friend of Sydney, Locke, and the Third Earl of Shaftesbury, who died in 1714, played a big part in Toland's intellectual development in the Netherlands in 1693. In Rotterdam Furley had a famous library of heretical books by most of the great English republicans and democrats, including two works by Gerrard Winstanley, and others by Lilburne, Clement Writer, Coppe and other Ranters, John Webster, Roger Williams, Sir Henry Vane, early Quakers, and Muggletonians.[47] Biblical criticism from the revolutionary decades survived through Fisher mediated by Spinoza, and was summed up by Toland's *Christianity not Mysterious* (1696) for which Toland was twice unsuccessfully prosecuted by the clergy.[48] In his last book, Edward Thompson has established the survival into the eighteenth century of political antinomianism: he lists many books by Ranters and Muggletonians which were reprinted in the mid- and later seventeenth century. Eighteenth-century antinomianism, he argues, was "an artisan or tradesman stance," nourishing a "robust anti-Court and sometimes republican consciousness."[49]

By the end of the century the Bible had lost its uniquely authoritative position as a guide to action in all spheres of life. Hobbes's skeptical attitude towards the Bible and religion in general contributed to the unbelief fashionable at the court of Charles II. "To say [God] hath spoken to him in a dream," Hobbes remarked, "is no more than to say he dreamed that God spake to him. . . . So that, though God Almighty *can* [my italics] speak to a man by dreams, visions, voice and inspiration, yet he obliges no man to believe that he hath so done to him that pretends it, who (being a man) may err, and (which is more) lie." Hobbes's wit was no less lethal, his use of brackets no less telling, when they were turned against the clergy's claim that they had a divine right to collect tithes from their flock: "Of the maintenance of our Saviour and his Apostles, we read only that they had a purse (which was carried by Judas Iscariot)." "The Apostleship of Judas is called (Acts 1.20) his bishopric."[50] Hobbes's conviction that belief in rewards and punishments in the afterlife destabilized society and the state perhaps contributed to the decline of this belief as a motive for political action towards the end of our period.

Restoration comedy took over, less seriously, much of the skeptical libertinism that had been so earnestly discussed in the forties and fifties. When Lady Brute in Vanbrugh's *The Provoked Wife* (1697) was told that the Bible said man must return good for evil, her reply came pat: "That may be a mistake in the translation." The former Royalist Samuel Butler denied the Scriptures to be the Word of God and used Hobbist arguments against miracles.[51] Rochester attacked the contradictions of the Bible even on his deathbed; he still thought that all came by nature. The stories of the creation and fall were parables. He had doubts about rewards and punishments after death and rejected monogamy.[52] We may also include Aphra Behn as a skeptical freethinker. Her *Oroonoko*, published in 1688 but written earlier, is one of the earliest noble savage stories, and perhaps the first significant English novel, if we except *The Pilgrim's Progress*. Oroonoko's honor and truthfulness are contrasted with the deceit and treachery of Christians (except for a Frenchman who was "a man of little religion, yet he had admirable morals and a brave soul"). The Trinity made Oroonoko laugh. To introduce Christianity into the West Indies, Aphra Behn wrote (and she had lived there), would "but destroy that tranquility they possess by ignorance; and laws would but teach 'em to know offences of which now they have no notion."[53]

In 1695 an Oxford Master of Arts published a letter to a nobleman in London in which he solemnly discussed "some errors about the creation, general flood and the peopling of the world." "The most rational way to examine these problems," he insisted, "is by the laws of gravity, or by the hydrostatics." The Biblical accounts are unacceptable: "the present age will not endure empty notions and vague speculations. . . . We presently call for clear proof or ocular demonstration." "The universal disposition of this age is bent upon a rational religion."[54] A century earlier the surreptitious discussion of such matters in Ralegh's circle was denounced as "a school of atheism." Now the Master of Arts did not even think them worth arguing about.

There was no English Enlightenment in the eighteenth century because the job had been done in the seventeenth century: the ideas of the European (and Scottish) Enlightenment derive from the biblically inspired discussions of the English Revolution, though by the end of the century its extremer ideas had been purged from printed memory. I stress *printed*. For what got into print depended on what publishers thought would sell. Unprintable, "extreme" ideas from the legacy of the Revolution were no doubt discussed in clubs like Toland's secret society, which "designedly shunned the multitude" and respected the laws that protected property. This was a select dining club as well as a conspiratorial society, whose credo and program were published *in Latin* in 1720, and in English translation only in 1751.[55] A more plebeian club was the Robin Hood Society, where tailors, bakers, butchers, and shoemakers met to air (among other things) their doubts about the Bible.[56] The radical Whigs, Thomas Hollis and Richard Baron, who in the mid-eighteenth century were accused of religious heterodoxy, were men steeped in the writings of the seventeenth-century English radicals. It was Catharine Macaulay's republican *History of England in the 17th Century* (8 vols., 1763–1783) that taught history did not begin in 1688.[57] But even at that late date there was irrational opposition to her case. Every opportunity was taken to insinuate either that a woman could not have written the *History*, or alternatively that she shouldn't have. Every opportunity was taken to stress the eccentricities of her private life rather than her very relevant message.

NOTES

1 See also my *The English Bible and the 17th-Century Revolution* (Harmondsworth, 1993) for further evidence of the many statements made here.
2 John Milton, "Of Christian Doctrine," in *Complete Prose Works* (New Haven and London, 1953–), VI: pp. 368, 521, 526, 537–41, 639–40; cf. "A Treatise of Civil Power," VII: p. 248; and *Paradise Lost*, XII: pp. 300–306, 523–24.
3 Simon Shepherd, *Marlowe and the Politics of the Elizabethan Theatre* (Brighton, 1986), p. 155.
4 See Christopher Hill, *The World Turned Upside Down* (Harmondsworth, 1975), pp. 144, 163, 174, 201, 205–207 *passim*.

5 John Wilkins, *A Discourse Concerning a New World and Another Planet* (London, 1641), pp. 10–14.

6 Lord Brooke, "*A Discourse opening the Nature of that Episcopacie which is exercised in England*" (1642), in *Tracts on Liberty in the Puritan Revolution*, ed. William Haller, 3 vols. (New York, 1934), II: pp. 119–20.

7 Thomas Edwards, *Gangraena*, 2 vols. (London, 1646), I, p. 78.

8 A. S. P. Woodhouse (ed.), *Puritanism and Liberty* (London, 1938), p. 161.

9 John Goodwin, *Divine Authority of the Scriptures Asserted* (1648), quoted in Haller, *Tracts on Liberty*, I: pp. 83–84.

10 G. Wade, *Thomas Traherne* (Princeton, 1944), pp. 43–44.

11 Hill, *The World Turned Upside Down*, pp. 144–45, 177–79, 262.

12 Clement Writer, *Fides Divina*, quoted ibid., pp. 265–66.

13 See Christopher Hill, *Religion and Politics in 17th-century England* (Brighton, 1986), pp. 333–34.

14 Milton, "Animadversions upon The Remonstrants Defence Against Smectymnuus" (1641), *Complete Prose Works*, I, p. 699.

15 Samuel Fisher, *The Rusticks Alarm to the Rabbies* (London, 1660), pp. 296–435; Hill, *The World Turned Upside Down*, p. 267.

16 R. H. Popkin, "Spinoza, the Quakers and the Millenarians, 1656–1658," in *Manuscrito VI* (Brazil, 1982), p. 132; "Spinoza and the Conversion of the Jews," in C. De Deugd (ed.), *Spinoza: Political and Theological Thought* (Amsterdam, 1984), p. 174.

17 Anthony Collins, *A Discourse of Free-Thinking* (London, 1713), especially pp. 14, 47–99, 169–70, 177; cf. Collins, *A Discourse of the Grounds and Reasons of the Christian Religion* (London, 1724). See also *A Complete Catalogue of the Library of Anthony Collins, Esq.*, ed. T. Ballard (London, 1731), parts 1 and 2, *passim*; *Biblioteca Furleiana* (Rotterdam, 1714).

18 Francis Osborn, "Advice to a Son", in *Miscellaneous Works*, 11th edn, 2 vols. (London, 1722), I, pp. 86, 99.

19 Robert Boyle, "Some Considerations Touching the Style of the Holy Scriptures", in *The Works of the Honourable Robert Boyle*, ed. T. Birch, 6 vols. (1773), II, p. 295.

20 John Owen, *The Works of John Owen*, ed. W. H. Goold, 24 vols. (1850–1853), XIII, p. 364. Cf. IX, p. 345 (1672); VIII, pp. 612–16 (1685).

21 *The Travels of Cosimo III, Grand Duke of Tuscany, though England* (London, 1821).

22 Richard Allestree, "The Ladies Calling", in *The Works of the Author of The Whole Duty of Man* (Oxford, 1704), pp. 109–10, 251–69.

23 Jonathan Swift, "An Argument to Prove, That the Abolishing of Christianity in England, May, as Things Now Stand, be attended with some Inconveniences,and perhaps, not produce those many good Effects proposed thereby", in *The Prose Works of Jonathan Swift*, ed. Herbert Davis et al., 16 vols. (Oxford, 1939–74), II, p. 26 *passim*.

24 Quoted in Christopher Hill, *Change and Continuity in 17th-Century England*, rev. edn. (New Haven and London, 1991), p. 259.

25 Samuel Parker, *A Demonstration of the Divine Authority of the Law of Nature, and of the Christian Religion* (London, 1681), pp. iii–iv.

26 E. N. Hooker, "Dryden and the Atoms of Epicurus," in H. T. Swedenberg, Jr. (ed.), *Essential Articles for the Study of John Dryden* (Hamden CT, 1966), p. 241.

27 Gilbert Burnet, "The Life and Death of . . . John Earl of Rochester", in *The Lives of Sir Matthew Hale, . . . Wilmot, Earl of Rochester; and Queen Mary* (1774), pp. 58, 76–79.

28 K. V. Thomas, "Cases of Conscience in Seventeenth-Century Europe," in J. Morrill, P. Slack and D. Woold (eds.), *Public Duty and Private Conscience in Seventeenth-Century England: Essays Presented to G. E. Aylmer* (Oxford, 1993).

29 Henry More, *A Modest Enquiry into the Mystery of Iniquity* (London, 1664), Sig. A3v.

30 Robert South, *Sermons Preached upon Several Occasions* (London, 1737), I, p. 131. South had previously written panegyrics upon Cromwell.

31 Christopher Hill, *Economic Problems of the Church* (London, 1968), p. 86.

32 Quoted by R. L. Greaves, *Enemies under his feet; Radicals and Nonconformists in Britain, 1664–1677* (Stanford, 1990), pp. 176–78.

33 Henry Stubbe, *A Further Justification of the Present War Against the United Netherlands* (London, 1673), pp. 70–71.

34 Milton, *Complete Prose Works*, VI, pp. 525–26.

35 Laurence Clarkson, *A Single Eye* (n.p., 1650), pp. 6–16.

36 Hill, *The World Turned Upside Down*, pp. 214–16, 315.

37 Ibid., pp. 210–13, 315.

38 Abiezer Coppe, "A Fiery Flying Roll" (1650), in *Abiezer Coppe: Selected Writings*, ed. A. Hopton (London, 1987), pp. 16, 22.

39 R. H. Hilton, *The English Peasantry in the Later Middle Ages* (Oxford, 1975), p. 24; J. B. Horst, *The Radical Brethren* (Nieuwkoop, 1972), p. 134.

40 Christopher Hill, *Milton and the English Revolution* (New York, 1978), pp. 317–23.

41 Ibid., pp. 456, 468.

42 John Bunyan, *Grace Abounding* (Oxford, 1977), pp. 16–17, 31–32; Christopher Hill, *A Turbulent, Seditious and Factious People: John Bunyan and his Church* (Oxford, 1988), pp. 75–77.

43 Bunyan, *Grace Abounding*, p. 17.

44 See, for example, Swift's "Sermon upon the Martyrdom of Charles I", *The Prose Works*, vol. IX; and the *Representation of the Present State of Religion Among Us, With Regard to the Late Excessive Growth of Infidelity and Heresy and Profaneness* (London, 1711).

45 Edward Ward, *The History of the London Clubs* (London, 1709).

46 Christopher Hill, *The Experience of Defeat: Milton and Some Contemporaries* (New York, 1984), pp. 164–69.

47 For Fisher's legacy see Popkin, "Spinoza, the Quakers and the Millenium," p. 174, and Hill, *The World Turned Upside Down*, chapter 11.

48 Margaret C. Jacob, *The Newtonians and the English Revolution, 1689–1720* (Ithaca, 1976), p. 216. Professor Jacob describes Toland as a Protestant for political reasons though not a Christian: cf. her *Living the Enlightenment: Freemasonry and Politics in Eighteenth-Century Europe* (New York, 1991), chapters 2 and 3. See also J. R. Jacob, *Henry Stubbe, Radical Protestantism and the Early Enlightenment* (Cambridge, 1983), *passim*.

49 E. P. Thompson, *Witness Against the Beast: William Blake and the Moral Law* (Cambridge, 1993). Thompson associated Blake with the antinomian tradition.

50 Hobbes, *Leviathan* (Everyman edn), pp. 411, 475, 564, 557.

51 Samuel Butler, *Prose Observations*, ed. Hugh de Quehen, (Oxford, 1979), pp. 85, 124.

52 Burnet, *Life of Rochester*, pp. 18–58.

53 L. P., "Two Essays," in *Somers Tracts* (1748–51), xi, pp. 291–308.

54 Aphra Behn, *Oroonoko, or the Royal Slave*, in *Works of Aphra Behn*, ed. Montague Summers (London and Stratford-on-Avon, 1915), v, pp. 157–66, 175, 196 *passim*.

55 John Toland, *Pantheisticon*, English translation (London, 1751), pp. 9–6, 57–59, 70, 95–107 *passim*; cf. Edward Ward, *The History of the London Clubs*, quoted above.

56 Richard Lewis, *The Robin-Hood Society: a Satire by Peter Pounce* (London, 1756), pp. v–vi, 19, 79.

57 Bridget Hill, *"The Republican Virago": The Life and Times of Catharine Macaulay, Historian* (Oxford and New York, 1992), chapters 3 and 8.

11

Locke and heterodox opinion

CHAPTER 3

Anticlericalism and authority in Lockean political thought

Richard Ashcraft

In this chapter I want to consider the problem of anticlericalism and ask, what does an understanding of that perspective contribute to our appreciation of Locke's conception of authority and the role played by that concept in his political thought, viewed as a whole? Anticlericalism is an understudied subject both with reference to the secondary literature on Locke and more generally as an aspect of the social consciousness of individuals living in seventeenth-century England. Such studies of anticlericalism as do exist have generally placed it within the political context of civic humanism, a paradigmatic framework that has become notorious for its exclusion of Locke and Lockean concepts.[1] Alternatively, when Locke's religious ideas are discussed they are placed within an intellectual context divorced from anticlericalism, where the preoccupation of interpreters lies in determining whether Locke was a Socinian or a deist or whether he should be aligned, intellectually, with the Dissenters or the Anglican Latitudinarians.[2]

Finally, of course, anticlericalism has most often been viewed as part of a larger process of secularization and an adjunct to the growth of a commitment to reason, science, and the emergence of modern society during the last half of the seventeenth century.[3] This perspective has also served as an interpretive framework for Locke's political thought, so that, for an older generation of scholars, Locke was honored as the first secular political theorist of the modern age.[4]

All of these presuppositions and categories, I shall argue, are inadequate not only in terms of understanding Locke's thought, but also as axes from which to view certain features of modern society. It is a major thesis of this chapter that there is a political meaning to anticlericalism that is grounded in religious belief, not rationalist skepticism, and that this political meaning cannot be confined to the discursive tradition of republicanism, unless that term is defined much more broadly than it is generally. As a secondary proposition, I suggest that rethinking the problem of anticlericalism from this standpoint will shed some light on certain features of modern society, as described, for example, by Karl Mannheim and Max Weber, without sacrificing the historical importance of religious belief to the imperatives of theorizing within the secularized framework of contemporary social science. Neither of these suggestions can be developed at length here; my intent is simply to open up lines of research for others to pursue, and, somewhat more self-interestedly, to establish a few of the connecting links between anticlericalism and Locke's political radicalism, a subject that I have discussed at length elsewhere.[5]

I

Locke's earliest writings express his opposition to the political role of the clergy, a view which he defended throughout his life. Writing as an opponent of toleration, Locke reflected upon the cause of the English Civil War, attributing it to the "ambition . . . pride and hypocrisy" of those "malicious men" – namely clerics – who employed the plea for toleration as a mask for their unleashing of the "destructive opinions that overspread this nation" and led to violent conflict.[6] Three decades later, in a work defending religious toleration, Locke is still berating "these incendiaries and disturbers of the public peace . . . [who] by flattering the ambition and favoring the dominion of princes and men in authority . . . endeavor with all their might to promote that tyranny in the commonwealth which otherwise they should not be able to establish in the church."[7]

Superficially these comments seem to point to the constancy of Locke's negative attitude towards the clergy, who are charged with the responsibility for fomenting revolution and/or promoting tyranny. Such a simplistic characterization, however, will not do. In the first place, as several commentators have noted, some of Locke's personal friends were clergymen. At the very least, therefore, Locke's negative remarks regarding the clergy have to be read within a context that allows for exceptions to be made. But this caveat does not go to the heart of the matter: anyone might criticize the misguided actions of clerics without necessarily endorsing anticlericalism as a general viewpoint. Thus a distinction must be drawn between the contingency of error and a failure to recognize a fundamental feature of social reality as the interpretive axis from which to assess the meaning of Locke's specific statements. Since the conceptual issue with respect to anticlericalism is one of authority, the question becomes, have the clergy misused their authority or do they have any authority?

The first set of Locke's comments occur in the unpublished two tracts on government he wrote between 1661 and 1662, which provide a defense of the civil magistrate's absolute authority over all the individual's actions. The clergy are thus denied an independent claim for authority on essentially Hobbesian grounds: all authority within society belongs to the sovereign.[8] By the time Locke made the second observation concerning the clergy, he did so in the context of having argued for limitations upon the magistrate's authority with respect to the indifferent actions of individuals. This limitation, however, was not made in favor of the clergy. According to Locke, they are still without authority. Rather Locke offers a decentralized claim for authority, based upon the individual's judgment, as a limitation upon the actions of either the civil magistrate or the clergy. The issue, as Locke put it in a manuscript of 1681 on toleration, was "how much is under the magistrate's authority, and how much is left to conscience?"[9] In short, whether Locke's anticlericalism is tied to an absolutist or a more democratic conception of politics cannot be determined merely from an examination of his references to the clergy. In a century in which religion and politics were deeply intertwined, this is hardly a surprising observation, but it does remind us that in considering the problem of anticlericalism we are not dealing with a single argument directed against the clergy's exercise of authority, but rather, with a network of interrelated arguments drawn from philosophy, history, and theology.

Let us begin with the relationship between the magistrate's authority and the individual's reliance upon the dictates of his or her own conscience, a relationship which, invariably, was accorded a place of prominence in any discussion of the problem of authority in late seventeenth-century England. Put simply the question was whether, in the event of a conflict between what the magistrate commanded an individual to do and what the individual's private judgment advised him or her to do, was it possible for the individual to substitute the authority of his or her conscience for the authority of the magistrate as a valid justification for his or her action (or inaction)? The orthodox answer to this question was an equally simple negative, which frequently incorporated the rhetoric of that otherwise "justly decried" book, Thomas Hobbes's *Leviathan*. For the individual to rely upon his or her conscience, Richard Allestree preached in the sermon "Of the Exercise of Conscience" would lead to a condition of anarchy because "this state of conscience is just the Leviathan's state of war."[10] Not only was this proposition a commonplace in Restoration England, but also Locke himself had made the same assertion in his two tracts on government, maintaining that "all authority will vanish from the earth" if appeals to private judgment or conscience are recognized as a valid source of authority.[11] Clearly this position had to be refuted if, as Locke later argued, an individual "has to be guided by his own conscience in things of faith and worship," and may refuse to obey what anyone else commands him or her to do with respect to matters of religion.[12]

Given the crucial importance of the issue of toleration to the structure of Locke's thought, it is worth considering the types of arguments that Locke believed would support an appeal to individual conscience. Only after such an examination will we be in a position to assess the relevance of these arguments to Locke's anticlericalism. Since the orthodox view assumed that individuals were generally directed by their passions towards actions that, in general, were contrary to the common good, the problem for Dissenters from this perspective was to provide a defense of the rationality of private judgment, both in terms of its formation and its social consequences.

We may distinguish analytically between the conditions under which a rational decision is made and a theory of rational action which places that decision within a framework where the freedom of the individual and the moral obligations which constrain or direct that freedom provide the substantive meaning of rationality. Once these structural features of Locke's theory of rational action have been delineated, we shall be in a position to assess the rationality of various claims for authority.

The extent to which, as a matter of ontological and sociological realism, Locke accepted the diversity and conflict of opinions as a structural feature of his theory of practical action has not generally been recognized by interpreters of his thought.[13] In the *Second Treatise of Government* he matter-of-factly refers to "the variety of opinions and contrariety of interests, which unavoidably happen in all collections of men."[14] In his lectures on natural law, he maintains that "this diversity among mortals, both in their manner of life and in their opinions" placed limitations upon the kinds of political or social institutions one might hope to establish.[15] In the *Essay Concerning Human Understanding* he argues that since "the mind has a different relish, as well as the palate," we may take it as a general proposition that individuals "pursue happiness by contrary courses" because "men may choose different things" as the "goods" that satisfy their desires.[16] Hence, he concludes, "there is nothing more common than contrariety of opinions."[17]

As Locke argues in the *Letter Concerning Toleration*, "it is not the diversity of opinions (which cannot be avoided)" that is the problem; rather, it is "the refusal of toleration to those that are of different opinions" which has produced a history of religious wars and persecution.[18] But, he insists, given "the variety and contradiction of opinions in religion" that exists in the world, it is unreasonable to suppose that individuals will "quit the light of their own reason . . . oppose the dictates of their own consciences, and blindly . . . resign themselves to the will of their governors."[19] In short, as a matter of practical policy it is foolish "to hope to cast all men's minds and manners into one mould."[20] Similarly, in the *Essay Concerning Human Understanding*, he advises that it would "become all men to maintain peace, and the common offices of humanity, and friendship in the diversity of opinions, since we cannot reasonably expect that any one should readily and obsequiously quit his own opinion, and embrace ours, with a blind resignation to an authority which the understanding of man acknowledges not."[21] In other words a realistic acceptance of diversity and conflict is, for Locke, a precondition for a tolerant attitude and a foundational assumption in his defense of the freedom of individuals to make rational choices.

Diversity of opinions, conflict of interests, and the uncertainty of outcomes are the contextual conditions for the exercise of rational judgment. Hence "the well management of public or private affairs" according to Locke, requires reasoning that relies upon "probability grounded upon experience" rather than "certain knowledge or demonstration."[22] Indeed Locke insists in the *Essay Concerning Human Understanding* that "most of the propositions we think, reason, discourse, nay act upon" rest upon probable beliefs.[23] Any theory of rational action, therefore, presupposes a set of conditions where uncertain outcomes are not antithetical to the concept of rational decision making, but are a constitutive feature of rational action.

Of course the freedom of individuals to exercise their rational judgment is not "a liberty for every man to do what he lists."[24]

Rather, Locke argues, freedom and rational action presuppose both a law of Nature and that an individual will "keep his actions within the bounds of it."[25] "For God having given man an understanding to direct his actions, has allowed him a freedom of will, and liberty of acting, as properly belonging thereunto, within the bounds of that law he is under."[26] Thus "the freedom then of man and liberty of acting according to his own will," Locke concludes, "is grounded on his having reason, which is able to instruct him in that law he is to govern himself by, and make him know how far he is left to the freedom of his own will."[27] Individuals, he maintains, must be "supposed capable of knowing the Law [of Nature]." When a person reaches a "state of maturity . . . he is presumed to know how far that Law is to be his guide, and how far he may make use of his freedom."[28] This presumption of rationality is not strictly speaking based upon an empirical observation of the behavior of human beings; rather for Locke it is a transcendental presupposition of any system of morality. "The idea of a supreme Being, infinite in power, goodness, and wisdom, whose workmanship we are, and on whom we depend; and the idea of ourselves, as . . . rational beings," according to Locke, supply the "foundations of our duty and rules of action."[29]

Locke believes that "God has made man such that these duties" prescribed by the Law of Nature "necessarily follow from his very nature," a nature which allows for "acting in conformity with reason."[30] Hence while "all obligation binds [the] conscience[s]" of individuals, it is "a rational apprehension of what is right" that guides the individual's conscience in determining what action to take or what claim for authority to accept.[31] At this point Locke's transcendental argument, as I have called it, becomes, when it is viewed as a reading of God's intentions, a fundamental axiom of his theology. For human beings are endowed with reason and freedom by their creator not only because God "could have none but voluntary subjects" as a feature of His plan for the salvation of mankind, but also, Locke insists, because "God, who knows our frailty . . . requires of us no more than we are able to do."[32] Within the structure of this moral universe there are only two sources of authority, namely a direct command from God, and what a rational person would consent to. Divine authority, however, requires a specific and literal directive in order to distinguish it from the divinely-structured conditions under which an individual acts upon his or her rational judgment. As we shall see, Locke employs this dichotomous conception of authority with considerable polemical skill against Filmer in the *Two Treatises of Government*, against Bishop Stillingfleet in the 1681 manuscript on toleration, and in the *Letter Concerning Toleration*.

Before turning to a consideration of Locke's anticlericalism, however, I want to briefly discuss a few of the ideas and arguments advanced by the Levellers. For, I shall argue, they provide a theoretical framework for anticlericalism, which in both its political and its religious dimensions is very close to the one developed in Locke's writings. In the secondary literature the Levellers have generally been characterized as the first secular political movement or party of modern society. Recent scholarship has exposed the inadequacy of this portrayal by demonstrating the importance of the religious beliefs of Baptists, Independents, and other sectarians in shaping Leveller political thought.[33] Indeed the latter, it is argued, must be understood in terms of the Levellers' commitment to "practical Christianity" as an inextricable mixture of religious and social duties.[34]

According to the Levellers "the meanest capacity is fully capable of a right understanding" of the essential tenets of Christianity.[35] This proposition provided the foundation for a fierce attack upon clerical authority. Not only do the clergy "darken the clear meaning" of the Bible with "their forced and artificial glosses" on its passages, but, William Walwyn argued, they purposely make the Scriptures appear to be difficult to understand in order to justify their own status and wealth in society.[36] The clergy's "pulpit-pratling," others insisted, had nothing to do with true religion. The clergy were nothing more than wolves in sheep's clothing who deserved to be exposed as deceivers of the people.[37]

But if "the meanest commoner" could understand the fundamentals of religion and hence meet his or her obligations with respect to the most important objective – personal salvation – there was no reason the same standard could not be applied to the law or to political duties. "The Levellers claimed that just as the clergy made religion difficult and uncertain in order to monopolize it and to dominate and exploit the people, so the lawyers made the law complex and confusing" in order to sustain their power and wealth.[38] Since the laws of society and the basic principles of politics were based upon and, the Levellers believed, ultimately reducible to "the essence of Christianity," political authority ought to be premised upon individual judgment.[39]

But while reliance upon individual judgment undermined political and religious claims to hierarchical authority, it did not lead, as many commentators on the Levellers have erroneously maintained, to either an atomistic or a possessive individualism.[40] "It is the command of God," Major Wildman declared, "that every man should seek the good of his neighbor." Or, as Richard Overton put it, "I was not born for my self alone, but for my neighbor as well, and I am resolved to discharge the trust which God hath reposed in me for the good of others." It is this sense of personal responsibility to act to promote the good of others – a sense of community – that "authorized" private individuals to engage in collective social action.[41] This authority was in turn grounded upon the precepts of natural law viewed as a codification of "practical Christianity." In a joint statement Lilburne, Walwyn, and Overton wrote that what they cared about was not "the formal and ceremonial" but rather "the practical and most real part of religion," that is to say, those actions which a true Christian was expected to perform.[42]

Hence the Levellers drew no distinctions between feeding the hungry or supporting the poor and relieving the oppressed or opposing tyranny. "I esteem it a high part of true religion," Walwyn declared, "to promote common justice." Lilburne and other Levellers echoed the point that freeing society "from all tyrants, oppressors and deceivers" was just as much part of practical Christianity as the "brotherly charity" God had commanded them to show to others.[43] In other words "true Christianity," as the Levellers understood it, authorized not only individual acts of charity, but also collective action against political oppression.

From the perspective that emphasizes the importance of religious beliefs to the Levellers, it is possible to understand why they espoused an individualism rooted in divine intentions and communal obligations, why they did not view political activity as a secular realm of social life, and why the demand for religious liberty – toleration – was central to the Leveller program.[44] Too little attention has been paid to this last point in the secondary literature on the Levellers in favor of an overemphasis upon their claim for manhood suffrage. But if as Colonel Rainborough argued, "the poorest he" had a moral right to participate in political decisions, it was because that individual was presumed to have the capacity to understand and perform his moral duties as set forth in the Scriptures and natural law. This presumption led even more directly to a defense of religious toleration, since reliance upon individual judgment necessarily defined a church as a voluntary society based upon the consent of its members, thus placing all churches upon an equal plane of authority. Included within the commitment to religious toleration was a defense of a free press, free speech, and free assembly as rights necessary to realize the objective of religious freedom.

In addition, however, "liberty of discourse" was defended by the Levellers as an independent contribution to the welfare of society because it was the means "by which corruption and tyranny would soon be discovered," whether they occurred in the church or the state. Thus freedom of the press, Lilburne wrote, was the means "whereby all treacherous and tyrannical designs may be the easier discovered, and so prevented."[45] It is worth repeating and emphasizing the point that while these democratic practices – free speech, free press, free assembly, extension of the franchise, and religious freedom – can be spoken of as natural rights, they are so for the Levellers only in the context of the assumption that they constitute the *means* whereby individuals are able to meet their communal obligations as set forth by God.

Like the Levellers Locke argues that the fundamental duties of Christianity are capable of being understood by everyone, and the exercise of this capacity with respect to religion is, in itself, sufficient to designate them as "rational creatures."[46] Locke's reasoning underlying this conclusion likewise develops the Levellers' argument that the essence of Christianity can be simplified to a few basic beliefs – the theme of *The Reasonableness of Christianity* – accessible to all, including the poor and the illiterate. Locke refuses to accept that "the greatest part of mankind (are) by the necessity of their condition, subjected to unavoidable ignorance in those things which are of greatest importance to them." "No man," he insists, "is so wholly taken up with the attendance on the means of living, as to have no spare time at all to think of his soul, and inform himself in matters of religion."[47] "I can see no reason," Locke writes, why anyone should conclude "that the meaner sort of people must give themselves up to brutish stupidity in the things of their nearest concernment," when it is obvious to him that there are sufficient examples of "very mean people, who have raised their minds to a great sense and understanding of religion."[48]

Not only is it the case, as Locke puts it in *The Reasonableness*, that every person must decide for himself what the fundamental tenets of Christianity are, but it follows from this, as Locke declares in the *Letter*

Concerning Toleration, that "those things that every man ought sincerely to inquire into himself, and by meditation, study, search, and his own endeavors, attain the knowledge of, cannot be looked upon as the peculiar profession of any one sort of men."[49] Reasoning about the Scriptures, Locke notes, is interpreted by his critics as "want of due respect and deference to the authority" of the clergy as "spiritual guides."[50] But the fact is, Locke argues, people are "hoodwinked" by the clergy and "a veil is cast over their eyes."[51] "The heads and leaders of the church, moved by avarice and insatiable desire of dominion," Locke declared in the *Letter*, have misused their power to promote persecution and tyranny.[52] In the 1681 manuscript on toleration Locke stated as a general maxim that "churchmen of all sects with power are very apt to persecute and misuse" that power against those who disagree with them.[53] If it is the case, as Locke insists, that "no man . . . has a right to prescribe to me my faith, or . . . to impose his interpretations or opinions on me," then the clergy, as a distinct group, is without "authority."[54] Neither Locke nor the Levellers denied that the Law of Nature obliged everyone to assist his neighbor, and, in the case of religion, this could be done through advice and persuasion, but this was a universal obligation laid upon all individuals without distinction. Moreover, as Locke elaborates, my "persuasion of truth" or "my orthodoxy gives me no more authority over [another], than his (for everyone is orthodox to himself) gives him over me."[55] In short, *The Reasonableness of Christianity* is a relentless critique of the clergy, philosophers, and any other social group who arrogates to itself the authority to instruct mankind in religious matters for which they have neither the authority nor the knowledge to do so.

Long before the *Reasonableness* denied the need or usefulness of clerical interpretations of the Bible, Locke had confronted clerical authority as a political problem in the *First Treatise of Government*. That work would not have been written, Locke explains in the preface to the *Two Treatises*, "had not the pulpit, of late years, publicly owned [Filmer's] doctrine, and made it the current divinity of the times." In doing so the clergy have "dangerously misled others" as to their political obligations. Locke not only attacks the dangerous consequences produced by the practical efficacy of sermons as the means for transmitting political beliefs to the populace, he also suggests that because Filmer's thought is internally inconsistent and, in places, absurd, this gives one "cause to suspect, that it's not the force of reason and argument" that leads the clergy to espouse Filmer's ideas, but rather, they do so because those ideas support their own ambitions and desire for temporal power.[56]

Filmer and the clergy who rely upon his ideas have made themselves vulnerable to this unmasking critique because their claims for authority cannot be substantiated. If a specific warrant of political authority based upon "a positive grant" from God cannot be discovered in the Scriptures – and it is Locke's argument at tedious length in the *First Treatise* that it cannot – then both the source of political authority and the interpretation of the Scriptures, Locke insists, must be left to a standard of what "any ordinary understanding" or "any sober man" would accept as reasonable.[57]

Similarly in the *Letter Concerning Toleration* Locke challenges his opponents to produce a warrant of authority for the exercise of force with respect to matters of religion. Locke repeatedly insists in the *Letter* that "the care . . . of every man's soul belongs unto himself, and is to be left unto himself."[58] And since "one man does not violate the right of another by his erroneous opinions, and undue manner of worship . . . the care of each man's salvation belongs only to himself."[59] God, Locke argues, has not given "any such authority to one man over another as to compel anyone to his religion." Nor, he adds, "can any such power be vested in the magistrate by the consent of the people, because no man can so far abandon the care of his own salvation as blindly to leave it to the choice of any other, whether prince or subject, to prescribe to him what faith or worship he shall embrace."[60] Thus in the absence of a specific grant of authority from God and the existence of an obligation laid upon the individual to care for his own soul, which he cannot renounce through consent or delegation, there are simply no grounds for a valid claim to authority for the exercise of force with respect to religious beliefs.[61]

The failure to put forward reasonable claims to authority again induces Locke to engage in ideological unmasking as to the true motives and purposes underlying the actions of the clergy. They are, he believes, "men striving for power and empire over one another."[62] When "zeal for the church [is] joined with the desire of dominion, how easily the pretence of religion, and of the care of souls, serves for a cloak to covetousness, rapine, and ambition."[63] In short, Locke concludes, "these incendiaries and disturbers of the public peace . . . by flattering the ambition and favoring the dominion of princes and men in authority, they endeavor with all their might to promote that tyranny in the commonwealth which otherwise they should not be able to establish in the church."[64]

Locke's reference to tyranny not only indicates the passionate depths of his anticlericalism, but also reminds us of the practical actions that might have to be taken in order to prevent this "striving for power" by clerics. Tyranny, Locke argued in the *Two Treatises*, is the exercise of "force without authority." Hence whoever "exceeds the power given him by the law, and makes use of the force he has under his command, to compass that upon the subject . . . [is] acting without authority, [and] may be opposed, as any other man, who by force invades the right of another."[65]

The implications of anticlericalism thus extend to a benevolent reading of divine intentions, universal access to the text of the Bible and a radical simplification of the essential doctrine of Christianity, a generalized claim for the reason of individuals in the context of their ability, as Locke argued in the *Two Treatises of Government*, to act for the common good because they understand themselves to be members of a "natural community,"[66] and a moral egalitarianism that challenges the exercise of tyrannical power by the church or by the state. In this world the clergy not only possess no specific or defensible claim to authority, they also, from a sociological standpoint, serve no functional purpose; that is, they have no social role.

Much more, of course, could be said regarding Locke's views, but I want to place the discussion of anticlericalism in the context of a tradition of discourse employing the notions of natural right, popular sovereignty, consent, and a defense of democratic practices that extends into the eighteenth century. These ideas were developed by Matthew Tindal, who was much influenced by Locke's writings. In *An Essay Concerning the Power of the Magistrate and the Rights of Mankind in Matters of Religion* (1697), Tindal begins with an acknowledgment that the subject has been virtually exhausted by the author of those "three incomparable Letters Concerning Toleration."[67] Yet this does not prevent him from restating Locke's argument – sometimes word for word without quotation marks. Since everyone is equal in the state of nature under the Law of Nature, the individual, Tindal writes, has a "sovereign right of judging" in matters relating to religion. Freedom of conscience is, as Locke claimed, a natural right.[68] Like Locke, Tindal insists that Christianity can be understood by "the simple and ignorant, the bulk of mankind," and, he argues, it is "the pride, ambition, and covetousness" of the clergy, and their instigation of the magistrate to employ force against dissidents that "has been the cause" of all mischief and disorder in Christian societies.[69] The clergy have attempted to make Christianity appear mysterious simply in order to preserve their authority over the laity.[70] The clergy engage in preaching "as a trade" to make a living, not as individuals in search for the truth. Moreover, Tindal argues, their compliance with the political whims of the magistrate makes them unreliable as guides with respect to any of the important questions of life.[71]

In *The Rights of the Christian Church Asserted* Tindal again begins with an unattributed citation from Locke, placing individuals in a state of nature and equality, where individuals possess the right to defend their natural rights, including liberty of conscience, by recourse to arms against anyone – clergy or magistrate – who exercises force against them.[72] Like Locke and the Levellers, Tindal recognizes no distinction between "ecclesiastical tyranny" and any other form of oppression. In a statement that could have come from Lilburne or Overton, Tindal maintains that individuals "are obliged by the common ties of humanity to assist one another in opposing tyrants," wherever they appear.[73] Tindal focuses upon the clergy's power, which he characterizes as "the most absolute, arbitrary, unlimited, uncontrollable power in the world," a power, he asserts, that is without foundation.[74] Thus, he concludes, there is in society "no room for the independent power of any set of priests."[75] Like Locke, Tindal's conception of the simplicity of Christianity, the equality of individuals, the church as a voluntary society founded on individual consent, and his reading of the history of Christianity leads him to deny a purposive social role to a distinct group of individuals. In effect we are all in a state of nature with respect to religion and politics, an argument certainly present in Locke's writings, but the concept of the state of nature is effectively made use of and emphasized by Tindal as the starting point for any discussion of religious authority.

What Locke claimed as the individual's "supreme and absolute authority of judging for himself" in matters of religion, Tindal characterizes as "the Protestant principle" or the essence of Protestantism.[76] Thus following a reference to Locke, Tindal describes his position as a defense of "Protestantism, the essence of which consists in everyone's having an impartial right to judge for himself, and which is the necessary consequence of it, acting according to that judgment."[77] By which Tindal means, as did Locke and the Levellers, the right to engage in collective action in defense of this right, as he makes clear in *The Rights of the Christian Church*.[78]

Finally, like the Levellers and the Dissenters of the Restoration,

Tindal argues that freedom of the press is inextricably linked to religious toleration.[79] But he also offers a more general defense, maintaining that "the more important any controversy is, the more reason there is for liberty of the press."[80] Moreover a free press is a weapon against tyranny, whether political or ecclesiastical.[81] And, as with individual judgment, Tindal makes a free press part of the essence of Protestantism. He asserts that "the Reformation is wholly owing to the press" and the discovery of printing.[82] Indeed, he argues, "the discovery of printing seems to have been designed by Providence to free men from the tyranny of the clergy," and he means both Catholic and Protestant clergy.[83] From this perspective what is only implied or hinted at in the writings of the Levellers is clearly and forcefully stated by Tindal, namely, that all the natural rights of the individual are theoretically defensible in terms of the essence of Protestantism, and historically these rights have become social practices within (seventeenth-century) society only as a consequence of anticlericalism, and the redefinition of authority in the wake of that phenomenon.

II

Finally, as I indicated at the outset of this chapter, I want to place this discussion of anticlericalism and political radicalism within a framework that encourages us to reexamine some widely accepted presuppositions concerning the origins of modern society and the social science concepts necessary to understand it. Consider, for example, the concept of ideology, whose emergence is generally traceable to the eighteenth-century Enlightenment, largely because of the linguistic association of the term with the work of Destutt de Tracy. Such an account, I suggest, divorces ideology from the specific sociological circumstances under which it emerged.

What Karl Mannheim attempts to show in *Ideology and Utopia* is that ideology as a process of unmasking an adversary's political argument in order to expose the connections between that argument and the interests or objectives of a particular social group is a distinctively historical and sociological phenomenon. In other words ideology as a social practice, according to Mannheim, emerges in historical time and under certain specific sociological conditions. Although the concept of ideology is not generally viewed from this perspective in the secondary literature, it should hardly come as a surprise that Mannheim, who learned a great deal from Max Weber, thought of ideology as being just as much a historical feature of Western society as Weber claimed for rationalization or as Marx claimed for capitalism.[84]

Mannheim describes his general approach – the sociology of knowledge – as an attempt "to comprehend thought in the concrete setting of an historical-social situation."[85] The question is, then, what is the concrete historical setting for the emergence of ideology as a special "type of thinking?" Since, Mannheim argues, "it is a specific social situation which has impelled us to reflect about the social roots of our knowledge," this "specific situation" can be investigated employing the methods of sociology. The sociological conditions that make possible the ideological unmasking of opposing views, according to Mannheim, is the collapse of "the internal unity of a world-view" as an authoritative standard of meaning for various social practices or cultural institutions, and its replacement by "a multiplicity of fundamentally divergent definitions" of social reality.[86] "In every society," Mannheim writes, "there are social groups whose special task it is to provide an interpretation of the world for that society," namely, the "intelligentsia." So long as that group enjoys "a monopolistic control over the molding of that society's world-view" – and here Mannheim offers the example of the medieval clergy – intellectual differences within the intelligentsia can be reconciled without altering its social status or role in society.

"From a sociological point of view," Mannheim observes, "the decisive fact of modern times . . . is that this monopoly of the ecclesiastical interpretation of the world, which was held by the priestly caste, is broken, and . . . a free intelligentsia has arisen." Thus "the fundamental questioning of thought in modern times does not begin until the collapse of the intellectual monopoly of the clergy." Only then can the "free competition" of ideas begin "to dominate the modes of intellectual production" in society.[87] This free competition, Mannheim argues, assumed "the form of religious conflict" because "many small sects arose," each with their intellectual defenders, in the wake of the collapse of the Catholic monopoly. Moreover Protestantism's doctrine "that each person should decide according to his own subjective conscience whether his conduct was pleasing to God and conducive to salvation," in effect insured, as a structural feature of modern society, a multiplicity of social groups with differing and opposing worldviews, that is to say, ultimate appeals to religiously grounded conceptions of the world. Indeed the collapse of the medieval clerical monopoly not only increased the religious diversity of the intelligentsia, it also encouraged the rise of a lay intelligentsia whose authority to write about religious or political issues has to be seen as part of what Mannheim calls "the democratic diffusion of knowledge."[88]

"Political discussion," Mannheim explains, "possesses a character fundamentally different from academic discussion. It seeks not only to be in the right but also to demolish the basis of its opponent's social and intellectual existence." Thus "political discussion is . . . more than theoretical argumentation; it is the tearing off of disguises – the unmasking of those unconscious motives which bind the group existence to its cultural aspirations and its theoretical arguments." Ideology, as a process of unmasking which moves beyond the boundaries of the substantive reasoning of the argument of one's opponent in order to attack "the social status of the opponent, his public prestige, and his self-confidence," is therefore, historically speaking, a distinctive product of the Reformation.[89] And in terms of the diversity of the intelligentsia, the democratic diffusion of knowledge, and the existence of a mass literate audience for political and/or religious tracts as sociological conditions necessary for the emergence of ideology as a specific form of thought, these were certainly features of seventeenth-century England.

Ideology, as a distinctive feature of modern political thought is not, I am arguing, the product of a rationalism, skepticism, or secularism characteristic of eighteenth-century Enlightenment thought.[90] Rather the meaning and the roots of ideology lie in the anticlericalism of the seventeenth century, in religious conflict amongst believers, and in the view, advanced by the Levellers, Locke, Tindal, and others, that there is no authoritative social status for the clergy as a distinctive social group in society; hence, their arguments must, ultimately, be assessed in terms of this existential fact. Whatever claims for authority are advanced by the clergy can, therefore, be unmasked in precisely the sense accorded to that term by Mannheim.

The second reconsideration of the origins of modern political thought to which I wish to direct attention concerns Max Weber's argument with respect to the importance of religious influences in shaping the practices and beliefs of modern society. In *The Protestant Ethic and the Spirit of Capitalism*, Weber maintained that "the rational ethics of ascetic Protestantism" supplied "the *ethos* of an economic system," namely capitalism.[91] Thus, Weber wrote, Puritanism "favored the development of a rational bourgeois economic life."[92]Now it is not my intention to discuss or to evaluate this well-known thesis here. Rather, I want to direct attention to a much less familiar and very different argument advanced by Weber with respect to the way in which religious beliefs shaped modern political thought. Shortly after his visit to America in 1904, Weber wrote an article entitled "'Churches' and 'Sects' in North America: an Ecclesiastical Socio-Political Sketch."[93] In this essay Weber explores the distinctive features of sectarian religion, by way of a contrast with the institutionalized, bureaucratic character of church-oriented religious activity. Sectarians – Baptists, Independents, Quakers – Weber maintains, were interested in the development of "ecclesiastical communal life" within the framework of an "anti-authoritarian climate."[94] These features of sectarian religious thought were crucial to the demand for religious toleration. Thus, Weber argues, "the demand that the state recognize 'freedom of conscience' as the inalienable right of the individual [was] conceivable from the position of the sect only as a positive *religious* claim." Weber means by this, as he explains, that "the autonomy of the individual . . . is anchored not to indifference but to religious positions; and the struggle against all types of 'authoritarian' arbitrariness is elevated to the level of a religious duty." Weber concludes that "the sects alone have achieved the combination of positive religiosity and political radicalism. They alone, on the basis of Protestant religiosity, have been able to instill in the broad masses, and especially in modern workers, an intensity for ecclesiastical interests" that can be translated into collective political action. Hence, in this feature of their thought, Weber observes, "the sects' importance extends beyond the religious sphere." And, specifically, he associates sectarian religion with the emergence of democratic institutions.[95]

Another feature of sectarian religion noted by Weber was its emphasis upon the importance of the "person" as the unit of "religious communal life," from which perspective sectarians opposed any claim for "knowledge" as the basis for legitimating "the leadership of the congregation." This presupposition constituted the foundation for a political struggle against paying tithes, against the claims of "office," and generally, against an "intellectually cultivated" elite with authority in religious matters.[96] In short, Weber has constructed an analysis linking sectarian Protestantism with a defense of individual rights rooted in religious communal obligations, political radicalism as a struggle through collective action to achieve religious toleration and various democratic practices related to that objective, and an attack upon clerical authority from the standpoint of a defense of personal responsibility. The sectarians, Weber argues, were able to channel the energy of the Reformation and to find meaning in the "calling" and the glorification of God not simply through the Calvinist disciplinary action of work, but also through engagement in collective action to secure radical political objectives.

Had Weber developed this line of argument, he would have bequeathed to modern social science not one, but two "Protestant Ethics," each with a very different relationship to the development of modern society. In addition to Calvinist worldly asceticism which finds the glorification of God through the calling of labor, market activity, and, ultimately, the accumulation of wealth, one could discern a sectarian Protestant ethos directed towards the glorification of God through collective political action directed against oppression and tyranny in defense of claims relating to the personal responsibility and salvation of the individual.

Unfortunately Weber subsequently revised his 1906 essay in the closing years of World War I and of his life, removing virtually all the features of the argument to which I have referred. When the revised version of the essay was translated as "The Protestant Sects and the Spirit of Capitalism," as it appears in the Gerth and Mills edition of *From Max Weber: Essays in Sociology*, Weber has dismissed the distinctive importance of sectarian religion, assimilating all dimensions of Protestantism to the Calvinist "bourgeois" ethic of market activity. "The whole typically bourgeois ethic," Weber writes in the revised essay, "was from the beginning common to all asceticist sects and conventicles" of Protestantism.[97] Or again, without distinction, Weber insists that all Protestant sects enforced "a certain methodical, rational way of life which – given certain conditions – paved the way for the 'spirit' of modern capitalism."[98]

Nevertheless Weber's friend Ernst Troeltsch recognized the importance of Weber's original insight, and in his own writings he cites this "justly famous" 1906 article innumerable times. In fact it is not claiming too much to say that *The Social Teachings of the Christian Churches* is structured around the distinction Weber draws between "church" and "sect" in his original article. However Troeltsch's two-volume work is so full of qualifications piled upon qualifications on the one hand, and a misguided methodological reliance upon a rigid employment of Weberian ideal types on the other, that the best one can say with respect to the *Social Teachings* as it relates to the discussion of this chapter is not that it elaborates and develops Weber's argument in a clear manner, but rather, that it at least preserves the insights advanced by Weber in his article. Troeltsch observes, for example, that Locke's ideas belong to the tradition of sectarian religion, not to church-type Calvinist Protestantism. "Locke," Troeltsch writes, "feared nothing so much as priestly domination, whether it be Catholic, Anglican, or Presbyterian in form," thus capturing the significance of anticlericalism to the structure of Locke's thought.[99] Troeltsch also recognizes the connection between the Levellers and sectarian religion, noting that with respect to their political and social demands, they "based their claims on religious grounds."[100] And more generally he reiterates Weber's general association of sectarian religion with the development of the practices and institutions of democracy.[101]

Anticlericalism, I have tried to suggest, was not only an important feature of Locke's political thought; it was also a significant historical phenomenon with respect to the emergence of modern democratic society. In both respects, however, it needs to be recognized how deeply rooted in religious belief anticlericalism was, for such a recognition affects the meaning and use of the concepts we employ in our theorizing about the beliefs and institutions that characterize modern society.

NOTES

1 J. G. A. Pocock, "Post-Puritan England and the Problem of the Enlightenment," in Perez Zagorin (ed.), *Culture and Politics: From Puritanism to the Enlightenment* (Berkeley, 1980), pp. 91–111. Others who have accepted Pocock's identification of anticlericalism with civic humanism include J. A. I. Champion, (*The Pillars of Priestcraft Shaken: The Church of England and its Enemies, 1660–1730* [Cambridge, 1992], pp. 170–195) and Roger L. Emerson ("Heresy, the Social Order, and English Deism," *Church History*, 37 (December 1968), 389–403; 399–400).

2 David Wootton, "John Locke: Socinian or Natural Law Theorist?" in James E. Crimminis (ed.), *Religion, Secularization and Political Thought* (London, 1989), pp. 39–67. For an exception to this generalization, see Mark Goldie, "John Locke and Anglican Royalism," *Political Studies*, 31 (1983), 61–85.

3 Margaret C. Jacob, *The Radical Enlightenment: Pantheists, Freemasons and*

Republicans (London, 1981); C. John Somerville, *The Secularization of Early Modern England* (Oxford, 1992); Franklin L. Baumer, *Religion and the Rise of Skepticism* (New York, 1960).

4 Harold J. Laski, *Political Thought in England: Locke to Bentham* (London, 1920), pp. 42, 47, 52; Sterling P. Lamprecht, *The Moral and Political Philosophy of John Locke* (New York, 1918), p. 21; George H. Sabine, *A History of Political Theory*, 3rd edn. (New York, 1961), pp. 518–19, 526.

5 Richard Ashcraft, *Revolutionary Politics and Locke's Two Treatises of Government* (Princeton, NJ, 1986).

6 John Locke, *Two Tracts on Government*, ed. Philip Abrams (Cambridge, 1967); "First Tract on Government," pp. 160, 162, 166, 170.

7 John Locke, "A Letter Concerning Toleration," in *The Works of John Locke*, 12th edn, 9 vols. (London 1824), v, p. 54.

8 "Second Tract on Government," p. 231. See also the introduction by Abrams.

9 Locke MS C34, fo.42 (Bodleian Library, Oxford).

10 Richard Allestree, "Of the Exercise of Conscience," in *Forty Sermons*, 2 vols. (London, 1684), II, p. 70; Philip Browne, *The Sovereign's Authority* (London, 1682); John Marshall, "The Ecclesiology of the Latitude-Men, 1660–1689; Stillingfleet, Tillotson, and 'Hobbism'," *Journal of Ecclesiastical History*, 36: 3 (July 1985), 407–27.

11 *Second Tract on Government*, pp. 226–27. See also Richard Harvey, "The Problem of Social-Political Obligation for the Church of England in the Seventeenth Century," *Church History*, 40: 2 (June 1971), 156–69.

12 Locke MS C34, fo.43; cf. fos.75, 120.

13 Susan Mendus, *Toleration and the Limits of Liberalism* (Atlantic Highlands, NJ, 1989), chapter 2 ("Locke and the Case for Rationality"), pp. 22–43.

14 John Locke, *Two Treatises of Government*, ed. Peter Laslett, 2nd edn (Cambridge, 1967); "Second Treatise," par. 98.

15 John Locke, *Essays on the Laws of Nature*, ed. W. von Leyden (Oxford, 1954), p. 203.

16 John Locke, *An Essay Concerning Human Understanding*, ed. Peter H. Nidditch, (Oxford, 1975), book II, chapter 21 sections 55–56.

17 Ibid., IV.20.1; Journal, 5 April 1677, MS fo.2; *Works*, v, p. 372.

18 *Works*, v, p. 53.

19 Ibid., p. 12.

20 "First Tract on Government," p. 146.

21 *Essay Concerning Human Understanding*, IV.21.4.

22 Journal, 26 June 1681, MS fo.5.

23 *Essay Concerning Human Understanding*, IV.15.2; IV.16.6. For a discussion of the relationship between probability and practical action in Locke's thought from a perspective different from the one presented here, see James Tully, "Governing Conduct," in Edmund Leites (ed.), *Conscience and Casuistry in Early Modern Europe* (Cambridge, 1988), pp. 12–71.

24 "Second Treatise," par. 57.

25 Ibid., par. 59.
26 Ibid., par. 58.
27 Ibid., par. 63.
28 Ibid., pars. 59, 60.
29 *Essay Concerning Human Understanding*, IV.3.18. Moreover, anyone "who would pass for a rational creature" must believe in God (Journal, 29 July 1676, Locke MS fo.1).
30 *Essays on the Laws of Nature*, pp. 199, 201.
31 Ibid., p. 185.
32 *Works*, VI, p. 235; V, p. 160; *Essay Concerning Human Understanding*, II, xxi, 54.
33 Brian Manning, "The Levellers and Religion," in J. F. McGregor and B. Reay (eds.), *Radical Religion in the English Revolution* (Oxford, 1984), pp. 65–90; J. C. Davis, "The Levellers and Christianity," in Brian Manning, (ed.), *Politics, Religion and the English Civil War* (London, 1973), pp. 224–250; Brian Manning, "Puritanism and Democracy, 1640–1642," in Donald Pennington and Keith Thomas, (eds.), *Puritans and Revolutionaries: Essays in Seventeenth-Century History Presented to Christopher Hill* (Oxford, 1978), pp. 139–160; James Fulton Maclear, "Popular Anticlericalism in the Puritan Revolution," *Journal of the History of Ideas*, 17: 4 (October 1956), 443–70; Lotte Mulligan, "The Religious Roots of William Walwyn's Radicalism," *Journal of Religious History*, 12: 2 (December 1982), 162–79.
34 Manning, "Levellers and Religion," p.73; Mulligan, "Religious Roots," 168–70, 175.
35 Manning, "Levellers and Religion," p. 65; Mulligan, "Religious Roots," 167.
36 Manning, "Levellers and Religion," pp. 66, 84; Mulligan, "Religious Roots," pp. 169,171.
37 Manning, "Levellers and Religion," p. 75.
38 Ibid., p. 67.
39 Ibid., p. 68; Mulligan, "Religious Roots," 169, 174.
40 C. B. Macpherson, *The Political Theory of Possessive Individualism*, (London, 1962).
41 Manning, "Levellers and Religion," pp. 70–71; Mulligan, "Religious Roots,' 168–70, 178.
42 Manning, "Levellers and Religion," p. 69; Mulligan, "Religious Roots," 170, 179.
43 Manning, "Levellers and Religion," pp. 71–73; Mulligan, "Religious Roots," 169–70, 173, 177.
44 Manning, "Levellers and Religion," pp. 78–82; Mulligan, "Religious Roots," 163, 173, 175; F. D. Dow, *Radicalism in the English Revolution, 1640–1660* (Oxford, 1985), pp. 35, 46.
45 Manning, "Levellers and Religion," pp. 82–83.
46 *Essay Concerning Human Understanding*, IV.20.6; *Works*, VI, p. 147.
47 *Essay Concerning Human Understanding*, IV.20.3; Journal, 20 March 1678, MS fo.3.

48 *Works*, II, pp. 342–43. For a more extended discussion of the social implications of this argument and a critique of Macpherson's interpretation of *The Reasonableness of Christianity*, see Richard Ashcraft, *Locke's Two Treatises of Government* (London, 1987), pp. 248–59.

49 *Works*, VI, p. 233; V, p. 25. The right a man has with respect to the care of his soul "is not annexed to his way of education, or acquisition in letters." Locke MS C34, fos.48–49.

50 *Works*, VI, p. 294.

51 Ibid., p. 297; V, p.26.

52 Ibid., V, pp. 23, 53–54; VI, pp. 290–92.

53 Locke MS C34, fo.11.

54 *Works*, VI, p. 359; "Toleration," (1679), Locke MS d.1, fo.125. "I affirm that it is out of the power of any man to make another a representative for himself in matters of religion, much less can another make one for him, since nobody can give another man authority to determine in what way he should worship God Almighty." Locke MS C34, fo.122.

55 *Works*, VI, p. 327.

56 *Two Treatises*, preface; "First Treatise," pars. 3, 13.

57 "First Treatise," par. 80; cf. Ashcraft, *Locke's Two Treatises*, chapter 3.

58 *Works*, V, pp. 23, 41, 43–4.

59 Ibid., p. 41.

60 Ibid., pp. 10–11.

61 Ibid., pp. 126, 153, 213, 495, 562, 565. Locke makes the same argument in the 1681 manuscript on toleration, maintaining that either God appointed the officers of the early Christian church, in which case, clerical authority is "unalterable" and "settled," or else, authority lies "wholly in the body of the church, as the like power is in other societies to constitute their officers with such powers as they think fit" (Locke MS C34, fo.18; cf. fos.71, 127–28). I have argued elsewhere for the importance of Locke's argument with respect to claims for authority as the interpretive framework for understanding Locke's perspective in the *Letter Concerning Toleration* (Richard Ashcraft, "John Locke and the Problem of Toleration," paper presented to the Conference on Discourses of Tolerance and Intolerance in the Enlightenment, at the William Andrew Clark Library, University of California at Los Angeles, May 20–22, 1994).

62 *Works*, V, p. 5.

63 Ibid., p. 36.

64 Ibid., p. 54.

65 "Second Treatise," par. 202.

66 Ibid., par. 128.

67 Matthew Tindal, *An Essay Concerning the Power of the Magistrate and the Rights of Mankind in Matters of Religion*, (London, 1697), p. 2; cf. p. 113.

68 Ibid., pp. 19–20, 24, 117–18; Locke, *Works*, V, pp. 41, 47–48.

69 Tindal, *Power of the Magistrate*, pp. 106–11, 141–42.

70 Ibid., pp. 112, 115.
71 Ibid., pp. 136, 139–40.
72 Matthew Tindal, *The Rights of the Christian Church Asserted*, 3rd edn (London 1707), pp. 2–3, 17, 19.
73 Ibid., pp. 26–27.
74 Ibid., pp. 32–3, 80.
75 Ibid., p. 81. This position was also taken by Walter Moyle in an *Essay on the Roman Government*, a manuscript copy of which Locke owned. Champion, *The Pillars of Priestcraft Shaken*, p. 188.
76 Locke, *Works*, v, p. 44; Matthew Tindal, *A Defence of the Rights of the Christian Church*, (London, 1707), p. 6.
77 Tindal, *Power of the Magistrate*, pp. 113, 117–18.
78 Tindal, *Rights*, pp. 17, 19, 26–27.
79 Matthew Tindal, *A Discourse for the Liberty of the Press in a Letter to a Member of Parliament*, (London, 1698; rptd. in *Four Discourses*, London, 1709), pp. 293–300, 313; idem, *Power of the Magistrate*, pp. 122, 184. Edmund Hickeringill, for example, who began as a Baptist chaplain in Robert Lilburne's regiment and later became a radical Whig and a deist, also drew this connection (Emerson, "Heresy," pp. 396–97; Manning, "Levellers and Religion," pp. 82–83).
80 Tindal, *Liberty of Press*, p. 307.
81 Ibid., p. 320.
82 Ibid., p. 303.
83 Ibid., p. 316.
84 For a further discussion of this point, see Richard Ashcraft, "Political Theory and Political Action in Karl Mannheim's Thought: Reflections upon *Ideology and Utopia* and its Critics," in *Comparative Studies in Society and History*, 23: 1 (January 1981), 23–50.
85 Karl Mannheim, *Ideology and Utopia* (New York, 1936), p.3.
86 Ibid., p. 6.
87 Ibid., pp. 11–12.
88 Ibid., p. 33.
89 Ibid., pp. 38–39. Franz-Xavier Kaufman, "The Sociology of Knowledge and the Problem of Authority," in *Authority in the Church*, ed. Piet F. Fransen (Leuven, 1983), pp. 18–31; Champion, *The Pillars of Priestcraft Shaken*, pp. 4, 10, 23.
90 For a thought-provoking article that challenges this orthodoxy along the lines suggested here, see Mark Goldie, "Ideology," in Terence Ball, James Farr, and Russell L. Hanson (eds.), *Political Innovation and Conceptual Change* (Cambridge, 1989), pp. 266–91.
91 Max Weber, *The Protestant Ethic and the Spirit of Capitalism* (New York, 1958), p. 27.
92 Ibid., p. 174.
93 Max Weber, "'Churches' and 'Sects' in North America: An Ecclesiastical Socio-Political Sketch," translated and introduced by Colin Loader and

Jeffrey Alexander, *Sociological Theory*, 3: 1 (Spring 1985), 1–13.
94 Ibid., pp. 7, 10.
95 Ibid., p. 10.
96 Ibid., p. 11.
97 Max Weber, "The Protestant Sects and the Spirit of Capitalism," in H. H. Gerth and C. Wright Mills (eds.), *From Max Weber: Essays in Sociology* (New York, 1958), pp. 302–22; p. 313.
98 Ibid., p. 321.
99 Ernst Troeltsch, *The Social Teachings of the Christian Churches*, 2 vols. (New York, 1931), II, pp. 637–38.
100 Ibid., p. 710.
101 Ibid., pp. 656, 688, 691.

CHAPTER 4

John Locke: conservative radical

G. A. J. Rogers

INTRODUCTION

There are many reasons why the interpretation of Locke remains a live issue. One is the wide range of his writings, another is the way in which he often so carefully covered his tracks in areas which he knew to be controversial. A third is a growing realization of the importance of reading his texts from within the context in which they were written and the increasing recognition, extending over at least some twenty years, of the central importance of Locke's religious commitments to a proper understanding of his thought. This chapter is concerned with some aspects of that relationship.

The relationship between Locke's religion and his philosophical thought obviously works two ways. Locke's theological beliefs are likely to impinge on his philosophy, indeed much more than some modern commentators, who have a tendency to read him as if he were some secular representative of twentieth-century philosophy, would allow. But here I also wish to lay stress on the converse relationship, on the way in which Locke's theological convictions are monitored by his philosophical principles, more specifically by his epistemology. Part of my objective is to show how this is true and to suggest that it was because of this rigorous discipline that Locke was sometimes taken to be either more of a skeptic in matters of religion than in truth he was, or that he was taken as more radical in his theology than was the case. None of this, however, will detract from the conclusion that Locke's intellectual position should, with some justice, be regarded as radical in its theological implications. On this matter I have much sympathy with Berkeley's worry that the new philosophy of Locke and Newton, albeit inadvertently, did indeed lay the groundwork for a secular outlook. For there were tendencies in Locke's thinking that appear to provide a basis for the deists to see him as their spiritual mentor. And the Unitarians, and even the Enlightenment materialists, could with reason find in his words a possible framework on which to construct their accounts of the world. How much Locke was himself one of any of their number, and whether he thought it any of our business whether he was or not, are large and important matters that I shall only touch on here.

Modern commentators rightly stress Locke's concern to map the limits of human knowledge and to note the dangers of claiming to cross those limits. On such a view Locke hovers on the edge of skepticism. But we must not fail to note that the identification of such boundaries itself presumes much about our abilities, a confidence in the human mind to be able to make sure judgments in such areas. And indeed the *Essay Concerning Human Understanding* offered reason why such judgments could be justified: substantially because Locke accepted the Cartesian criterion of clear and distinct ideas as providing a way of identifying what we could accept as certain. And to this criterion Locke added the vitally important ability to recognize (often with equal certainty) the *probable* truth of many claims.

Our ability to make such judgments, Locke tells us in the *Essay*, is a function of our faculty of reason, which he explains and carefully delineates:

The Word Reason in the *English* Language *has different Significations*: sometimes it is taken for true, and clear Principles: Sometimes for clear and fair deductions from those Principles: and sometimes for the Cause, and particularly the final Cause. But the Consideration I shall have of it here, is a Signification different from all these; and that is, as it stands for a Faculty in Man, That Faculty, whereby Man is supposed to be distinguished from Beasts, and wherein it is evident he must surpass them.[1]

So Locke the anti-Aristotelian (or so it is alleged) appears in this instance at least to be at one with the peripatetic philosophy.

This seems to me to be a matter of some importance for a proper understanding of the relationship between Locke's theology and his philosophy, and takes me to what amounts to my central claim about Locke: that, with minor qualification no doubt, he is always the philosopher in his theology, always the epistemologist in his assessment of the religious issues that came to play such a central place in his daily life. I say "came to play" not because there is any serious ground for believing that Locke was ever other than a committed Christian of the reformed church, but because religious thought, and specifically theology, seems to have come to occupy an increasingly important place in his life as he grew older, and particularly through his contacts in the years in Holland from the autumn of 1683. In Oxford, prior to moving to London in 1667, theology plays a comparatively small part in his reading.[2] But this was to change in the Dutch period as the balance of his interests (though not his interests themselves) came to center more on philosophy and theology and to move away from medicine and the natural sciences that had featured so powerfully before.[3]

That judgment accepted, we should not forget that religious issues were never far from Locke's mind or the routine of daily life in either Oxford or London. We may gain some insight into that centrality in the fact that whilst a member of the Shaftesbury household he was required to attend chapel three times a day.[4] If the attendance at church services of the general laity in England left the parish clergy with something to be desired, as was a common complaint, laxity in Locke's own practice would be difficult to substantiate.[5]

My central claim, then, is that insofar as Locke accepted or rejected any theological position it was because it either did or it did not meet the standards set by his philosophy for knowledge or probable opinion. The notion of what might be acceptable on grounds of faith was itself circumscribed by these other standards and could not override them. And, since the standards that Locke set were generally more demanding than those that had always or usually been applied before, there was inevitably a possibility that some of the theology that had until this time been accepted would fail to achieve the required level of proof or probability. Here indeed was scope for the radical and skeptical moves that others (and Locke himself) were encouraged to make.

There was another dimension to Locke's epistemology that was likely to encourage heterodoxy in religion: his generally minimalist theology. This was itself a product of his epistemological views, and we shall return to this.

Locke's thought developed and changed over his life. Besides the well-known shift on toleration from what is often seen as the near Hobbist position of the early *Tracts*, there were other amendments and modifications, sometimes of importance.[6] But for the most part these can be seen as part of the development of Locke's thought rather than as radical changes of outlook, at least from the time of his joining Shaftesbury's household in 1667. But his full theological position was, for the reasons already suggested, a product of his mature years. For this reason I shall focus mainly on Locke's views as they appear from the publication of his major works from 1689 until his death in 1704.

At the end of the seventeenth century there was no shortage of possible theological positions, and to which of them Locke subscribed remains a matter of debate. Arminian, Socinian, Calvinist, Unitarian, deist – to each of these in turn Locke has been assigned. How we should understand that difficulty of categorization will, I hope, be illuminated by what follows.

LOCKE AND THE INHERITANCE OF REASON

There is a basic distinction which needs to be remembered when considering Locke's religious position, the distinction between natural theology and Christian theology. Natural theology includes knowledge that God exists, and several other propositions such as that God is good, just, omnipotent and omniscient, and perhaps others such as that God is a spirit, eternal, unchanging, that He has created the world and us for some purpose, and so on. Christian theology includes all of these claims and in addition all the fundamental articles of revealed religion, for example those summarized in the Apostles' Creed.[7] Reason alone can lead to knowledge of natural theology but the knowledge of the fundamental articles was dependent on revelation. Though the balance in Locke's mind between these two kinds of religious knowledge may have tilted towards Christian theology in Locke's later years (as Arthur Wainwright suggests), both were always important for the Christian, whilst natural theology was in itself sufficient to justify theism in general.

My claim that the ground on which Locke built his theology was, first of all, epistemological requires his belief that he was able to square his commitment to the Christian faith (or at least his version of it) with his epistemological certainties. Outside of these there were a number of claims made by many Christians that could not be shown to be certain, and others that were not even probable on Locke's epistemic premises. It was Locke's recognition of the low epistemic status of the latter especially, that in the eighteenth century would allow deists and freethinkers to see Locke as their mentor.

Locke's point of departure, I have suggested, was his commitment to reason. In this he was hardly the first nor was he alone in the seventeenth century. He shared totally, for example, Whichcote's view, perhaps heard from Whichcote himself from the pulpit of St. Lawrence Jewry, that "there is nothing proper and peculiar to man, but the use of reason and the exercise of virtue" and "to go against *Reason* is to go against God".[8] In the *Essay* Locke was to write: "*Reason must be our last Judge and Guide in every Thing*" (IV.19.14; p. 704). Of course this is not to suggest that Locke was totally successful in expunging all his prejudices. But it is to lay stress on his highly successful commitment to the elimination of unwarranted beliefs: a determination to scrutinize those propositions that he did accept, and to allocate them to the appropriate epistemic categories: those of certainty and varying degrees of probability, through improbability and absurdity, to those that could be totally rejected as involving contradiction.

The precise place of reason within theology and its relationship to revelation was a matter of considerable disagreement in the seventeenth century. Some of this disagreement arose from a failure properly to distinguish within the Christian religion the propositions of natural theology from those that depended on revelation. But much also arose from a clash between those who accepted direct revelation, who, in Baxter's phrase (referring to the Ranters), "called men to hearken to Christ within them,"[9] and those, like Whichcote and his fellow Cambridge Platonists, who saw all sound judgment as monitored by reason.

It might be doubted that all the Cambridge Platonists were as wedded to reason as was Whichcote. The mysticism of the young Henry More, which took its departure from the *Theologia Germanica*, and that of the sadly short-lived John Smith, might suggest that reason and sense experience was always subordinate to "that brighter Eye of our Understandings, that other Eye of the Soul,"[10] the mystical apprehension of the Godhead. Earlier, Smith had appeared to reject reason as a path to knowledge: "We must not think we have attained to the *right knowledge* of Truth, when . . . by a *Logical Analysis* we have found out the dependencies and coherences of [words and phrases] one with another."[11] But if the Cambridge Platonists would all have agreed with Smith that the effect of religion is "That it Spiritualizes Material things, and so carries up the Souls of Good men from Earthly things to things Divine, from the Sensible World to the Intellectual,"[12] they never abandoned the general position so strongly advocated by Whichcote that "Religion is most Rational." "I conceive Christian Religion rational throughout," wrote Henry

More in a general preface to his *Collection of Several Philosophical Writings*, "and I think I have proved it to be so in my *Mystery of Godliness*."[13] It was the supremacy of the rational intellect in man, God, and the universe that Cudworth saw as the supreme truth which alone could account for the world as we find it.[14] Despite attempts to disparage reason by individual clergymen in the Restoration, the Cambridge Platonists were very far from being alone in their commitment to it. In that commitment they were following a well-established tradition, which in the late sixteenth century had received strong backing from Richard Hooker's *Of the Laws of Ecclesiastical Polity*.[15]

Another important figure in this tradition was Joseph Glanvill, who in several ways bridged the divide between the rationalist tendencies of the Cambridge Platonists and the empiricist leanings of the Royal Society. Glanvill drew a line between fundamental and "accessory" principles of religion similar to that between natural and revealed religion. Amongst the fundamental principles was the being of a God and the perfection of his nature; knowledge of his providence and of moral good and evil. These, Glanvill held, are absolutely necessary to religion. The assisting principles, on the other hand, such as that God will pardon us if we repent and that we will be punished in another world if we do not, are not in the same degree as absolutely necessary.[16]

The Cambridge Platonists had supported their commitment to reason with a commitment to some, not altogether clear, notion of innate knowledge. Cudworth, for example, wrote that "the Soul is not a mere *Ras Tabula*, a naked and Passive thing, which has no innate furniture and activity of its own, nor anything at all in it, but what was impressed upon it from without."[17] In this the Cambridge Platonists were in agreement with many others, of whom Glanvill, perhaps surprisingly, was one. The principles of reason are, he wrote, "those inbred *Fundamental Notices*, that God hath implanted in our Souls; such as arise not from external Objects, nor particular Humours or Imaginations, but are immediately lodged in our Minds."[18] One of Locke's important departures from this tradition was to hold onto the central place of reason but to combine it with a rejection of the doctrine of innate ideas and thereby to place reason and religion unequivocally under the umbrella of empiricism.

LOCKE'S INTELLECTUAL CERTAINTIES

The deep commitment to reason, which as we have seen is central to Locke's position, required of him the subordination of faith itself. It has even led some commentators to argue that his commitment was strong enough to prevent him seeing the moral issues that toleration or, alternatively, intolerance raise. Although it is possible to defend Locke against this charge, it is certainly the case that the place of reason is so central to his analysis that there is an important sense in which all is held as subordinate to it. Indeed, it is recognition of that fact which takes us to a proper appreciation of his position.

For Locke the first test that any claim to faith must meet is its compatibility with reason. For reason is the faculty that enables us to establish the certainty or probability of propositions by deduction from the ideas furnished by sensation or reflection. Reason contrasts with faith, which is the acceptance of a proposition as coming from God "in some extraordinary way of Communication" that we call revelation (IV.18.2, p. 689). Whether any putative revelation is indeed the Word of God must, he insists, itself be subject to the tests of reason. And "*no Proposition can be received for Divine Revelation,* or obtain the assent due to all such, *if it be contradictory to our clear intuitive Knowledge*" (IV.18.5; p. 692).[19]

This authority of reason has an unambiguous political message: "*Nor can we be obliged, when we have the clear and evident Sentence of Reason, to quit it,* [i.e. our commitment to that truth] *for the Contrary Opinion, under a Pretence that it is a Matter of Faith*; which can have no Authority against the plain and clear Dictates of *Reason*" (IV.18.6; p. 694).[20] We cannot, that is, ever be justifiably required by some agency – state, church, or monarch – either to hold onto a claim on the ground that it is a matter of doctrine or faith, that we ourselves see as running contrary to reason. Nor, on the other hand, can we be required to give up what we see as justified by reason on the grounds that it conflicts with some matter of faith.

The matter is otherwise, however, when the dictates of reason generate other than certainty. There are many things about which we have imperfect ideas, which can only be, when revealed, a matter of faith. Locke gives us two examples: first, the belief that some part of the angels rebelled against God. And second, the belief that the dead shall rise and live again. Reason alone can settle the truth of neither. And where we have only probable conjectures, then revelation "where God has been pleased to give it" must prevail (IV.18.8; p. 694). Even when the event is an unlikely one "an evident *Revelation* ought to determine our Assent even against Probability" (IV.18.9; p. 695).

On this basis Locke was able to draw what for him was an important conclusion with strong implications about the limits of political interference by church or state with matters of personal faith: "*Nothing that is contrary to, and inconsistent with the clear and self-evident Dictates of Reason, has a Right to be urged, or assented, as a Matter of Faith, wherein Reason has nothing to do*" (IV.18.10, p. 696). The implications of these distinctions and priorities are obvious enough. Reason itself imposes limits on what any earthly power should (and no doubt any heavenly power would) require us to accept.

Two central Christian doctrines that might be open to challenge on Locke's principles were those of transubstantiation and the doctrine of the Trinity. The first of these – transubstantiation – Locke, from within the Anglican church, has no difficulty in dismissing. He does so precisely on the basis of that distinction which he has just drawn: "we can never receive for a Truth any thing that is directly contrary to our clear and distinct Knowledge," he writes, and this he holds to be true of the doctrine of transubstantiation. For he believed that it required Christ's body to be in two places at once (as the mass may obviously be celebrated at two distant places at the same time). But "The *Ideas* of one Body, and one Place, do so clearly agree; and the Mind has so evident a Perception of their Agreement, that we can never assent to a Proposition, that affirms the same Body to be in two distant Places at once, however it should pretend to the authority of a divine *Revelation*" (IV.18.5, p. 692). If Locke had wished to spell the argument out in detail, then no doubt he would have appealed to his account of the conditions required for bodily identity in what was to become book 2, chapter 27 of the second edition of the *Essay*. (Though in parentheses it must be said that the argument Locke requires is less straightforward than this brief nod towards it suggests.[21])

The doctrine of the Trinity was too complex and, perhaps more importantly, too sensitive a matter to discuss in print. But it was one that troubled Locke on at least two counts. First, because it was debatable whether it was indeed clearly stated in the Gospels, and therefore unambiguously a revelation. And second, it remained a matter of contention as to whether it was possible to understand the claim in ways that did not violate our clear and distinct ideas.

LOGIC TEXTBOOKS AS THE TOUCHSTONE
OF REASON AND FAITH

By the mid-eighteenth century Locke's *Essay* was to become the logic textbook at Oxford. The nature of Locke's commitment to reason, and its implications for wider issues including that of religion, can be appreciated by contrasting the *Essay* with its immediate predecessors as a university textbook. Those that Locke displaced embodied a view of the relationship between faith and reason totally alien to that of the *Essay*. The most widely used logic text in the seventeenth century was Sanderson's *Logicae artis compendium*. Locke owned the first edition of 1615. Sanderson, like many other Puritan logicians of the century (and, as we shall see, some Catholic logicians as well) included discussion of faith and certainty in his text. The position that he adopted contrasts strongly with that of Locke. For Sanderson, divine testimony gives *scientia*, and we have such testimony in the Scriptures.[22]

There is a sense in which Locke does not dissent from this at all. But there is for him an important addition to the Sanderson claim. It is that the decision to accept something as divine testimony or not should itself be a product of reason. Locke expressed his position clearly in the chapter on enthusiasm. He does so in language that highlights the religious foundation for his understanding of the centrality of reason:

Reason is natural *Revelation*, whereby the eternal Father of Light and Fountain of all Knowledge communicates to Mankind that portion of Truth, which he has laid within the reach of their natural Faculties. (IV.19.4; p. 698)

Revelation, on the other hand, is:

natural *Reason* enlarged by a new set of Discoveries communicated by GOD immediately, which *Reason* vouches the Truth of, by the Testimony and Proofs it gives, that they come from GOD.

The consequence is that

he that takes away *Reason*, to make way for *Revelation*, puts out the Light of both, and does much what the same, as if he would perswade a Man to put out his Eyes the better to receive the remote Light of an invisible Star by a Telescope. (Ibid.)

The sharp contrast that Locke makes between the clear light of reason and the remote light of an "invisible" star should not go unnoticed. It was, of course, invoked to support Locke's strong attack on the supposed "immediate revelation" that the enthusiast so often claimed, "a much easier way for men to establish their Opinions than the tedious and not always successful Labour of strict Reasoning" (IV.19.5; pp. 698–99).

It has often rightly been noticed that Locke's logical doctrines are importantly indebted to Port Royal. But the debts should not blind us to the differences. The Port Royal logicians could write: "It is certain that divine faith ought to influence us more than our own reason."[23] It is a sentence that Locke could never have let escape his pen. Whether consciously or not Locke's earlier cited example, the elliptical reference to the Eucharist, is anticipated in a contrary sense by Arnauld when he writes:

Reason . . . shows us that one body cannot at the same time be in different places nor two bodies in the same place. We should realize, however, that this is merely the *natural* condition of bodies; it would be a defect of reason to believe that our finite minds can understand the extent of the power of an infinite God.

Arnauld concludes: "Heretics, who attempt to destroy the mysteries of faith – such as the Trinity, the Incarnation, and the Eucharist – by criticizing them in the light of truths about the natural conditions of bodies obviously stray from reason in this attempt to make the effects of the infinite power of God commensurate with man's reason."[24] They are words that Locke could have read as if they were directed at him personally. He would certainly have rejected them as standing for all that he opposed in matters of reason and religion.

CERTAINTY AND ITS LIMITS

So far I have concentrated on showing that Locke's use of reason, although sharing many aspects with some of his immediate predecessors, both Puritan and Catholic, stands in marked contrast to them in at least one important respect. Whereas his predecessors were prepared to fudge the issue as to whether it could ever be right to accept propositions contrary to reason (matters above reason Locke was always willing to allow), Locke was quite unwilling to do so and held out for a quite unequivocal position: the certainty of reason could not be compromised.

I wish now to briefly touch on some other certainties, and their limits, in Locke's theological landscape, many of them well acknowledged by scholars. The first certainty is the most important and the most obvious: Locke's conviction that we can know that there is a God, or perhaps we should say we can know that God exists. There is a demonstration that leads us by clear and distinct ideas to the conclusion that it follows necessarily that there is a deity. Locke briefly summarizes his argument in the *Essay* thus:

> *something* necessarily must *exist from Eternity*, 'tis also as evident, that *that Something must* necessarily *be a cogitative Being*: For it is as impossible, that incogitative Matter should produce a cogitative Being, as that nothing, or the negation of all Being, should produce a positive Being or Matter. (IV.10.11; p. 625)

It is not my intention to examine Locke's proof of a deity. It is a causal proof and similar to others offered by earlier thinkers. It is, however, worth noting that it is hardly one that fits with a reading of Locke that makes him a closet materialist. And it is important to remember that Locke's proof of a deity, in common with the moral knowledge that we are capable of attaining, is one of the very few areas of human inquiry where Locke holds that we are capable of reaching certainty or knowledge, in contradistinction to merely probable belief. He puts this all succinctly and clearly in the posthumously published *Conduct of the Understanding*, written in 1697[25], a work that remains a rich source for an appreciation of Locke's position. Theology, where it is not corrupted by faction and secular interest, he says, is that one science incomparably above the rest, which contains "the knowledge of God and His creatures, our duty to him and our fellow creatures, and a view of our present and future state." It is thus "the comprehension of all other knowledge directed to its true end, i.e. the honour and veneration of the Creator and the happiness of mankind."[26]

Locke's use of the words "science" and "knowledge" (twice) in these passages should be taken seriously. The *Conduct* was written as an intended chapter of the *Essay*, and the contrast between knowledge and science on the one hand, and probable belief on the other, is well to the fore in Locke's mind. Theology is that science, Locke goes on to tell us, that "every one that can be called a rational creature is capable of." And it is everybody's responsibility to engage in it. We can all come to know enough theology and attain to enough moral knowledge to be aware of our duty: "The works of nature and the words of revelation display it to mankind in characters so large and visible, that those who are not quite blind may in them read and see the first principles and most necessary parts of it."[27] It is worth recalling that, although Locke does not say it here, he has made it clear in other places in the *Essay* that we can all know what is required for our main purpose here on earth, namely our salvation. But, and this is important, our theological knowledge is strictly limited. Granted that we can all attain to the limited amount necessary for our purpose on earth; there are, nevertheless, "infinite depths filled with the treasures of wisdom and knowledge," the more abstruse parts that can be reached only by those that have time, industry (and presumably, though Locke does not say it) the intellectual ability to master them.

These more obscure areas are necessarily much more contentious and require the proper disposition of intellectual skills that are not always manifest. To flourish, the theology of which Locke here speaks requires an environment that is unfortunately not always available. "This is the science" he tells us, and in so doing underlining what was for him a central political point, "which would truly enlarge men's minds, were it studied, *or permitted to be studied*, [my emphasis] everywhere with that freedom, love of truth and charity, which it teaches, and were not made, contrary to its nature, the occasion of strife, faction, malignity, and narrow impositions."[28] And Locke finishes as his epistemology requires: "it is undoubtedly a wrong use of my understanding to make it the rule and measure of another man's; a use which it is neither fit for nor capable of."

Locke's message would appear to be clear. The central truths of theology and morality are available to all through the use of natural reason. But it is never right to try to force people to accept what I take those truths to be. In fact Locke entered into a long and quite important debate on just that point with Jonas Proast in the four "Letters Concerning Toleration", the last of which he was engaged in completing at the time of his death. Constantly through that debate Locke emphasizes what should for us now be a familiar theme, the crucial distinction between knowledge and belief. As Locke puts it in the fourth "Letter": "Believing in the highest Degree of Assurance is not Knowledge. That whatever is not capable of Demonstration, is not, unless it be self-evident, capable to produce Knowledge,"[29] and popular ways of talking, he goes on to say, which allow matters settled on well-grounded arguments of probability to be called knowledge, should not be allowed to confuse the crucial distinction.

THE IMPLICATIONS

We are, I hope, now in a position to draw some preliminary conclusions that we may use to address my original claims about the extent and nature of Locke's radical theology. The central thesis I offer is that Locke divides theology into exoteric and esoteric knowledge. The exoteric is available to all, though even here we have to make a further distinction. Although all human beings may reach central theological truths by the application of their natural faculties – the truths of natural theology – only those who have had access to the specific Christian teachings will be in a position to know the full Christian exoteric truths. Access granted, all human beings are capable of comprehending them. It is just these truths that Locke himself undertook to expound in the *Reasonableness of Christianity*. But he was very careful, in that exposition, always to emphasize that there was no substitute for the individual's own careful study of the biblical text, both for knowledge of theology and of morality. Demonstration by reasoning alone could be at most only for a few, whilst the "Instruction of the People were best still to be left to the Precepts and Principles of the Gospel."[30] For the Gospels are suited to the capacities over the whole range of human intellectual abilities, and cannot but be accepted by all as having both attestation of miracles and reason in their support.

What precisely has to be accepted theologically is, however, minimal. Locke argues that all which is required of the Christian is that he accept that Jesus is the Messiah "together with those concomitant Articles of his Resurrection, Rule, and coming again to judge the World."[31] These are fundamental and all that faith requires. As for the remaining truths revealed in the Gospels: "a man may be ignorant of [them]; nay, disbelieve, without danger to his Salvation."[32]

So we can see that there are three reasons why doctrines of the Christian religion may be open to debate, discussion, and dispute without in any way threatening the moral or theological integrity of the disputants. First, it may be a genuine intellectual issue as to which way the text should be interpreted, and we should recognize that neither side may have clear demonstration, and therefore, knowledge to settle the matter. Or, secondly, it may be that no right answer to some question has actually been revealed in the text, and the question must remain open. Or, finally, it may be that in addition to the text not revealing any settled conclusion, reason itself may be incapable of reaching an answer. That these difficulties exist should not in itself prevent anyone attempting to seek answers for himself either from the text or from his own intellectual resources, so long as we always remember that where no demonstration can be given we may not demand acceptance of the proposed solution from others.

On this view, to make claims of certainty in matters that are clearly contentious becomes a major fault on several counts. In a telling phrase in his early (1667) "Essay on Toleration," Locke, whilst listing opinions and actions that he sees as "absolutely destructive to society" includes amongst these holding that "one is bound to broach and propagate any opinion he believes himself."[33] In other words, Locke saw it as a serious political and indeed moral error to hold that one had a duty always overtly to propagate one's beliefs without due regard for the likely social consequences. A decent silence was often not just prudentially but *morally* the right policy. To publicly pronounce one's views might be regarded as the intellectual equivalent of engaging in malicious gossip. This stands in strong contrast to the right to *hold* speculative opinions (without proselytizing them), which all should have as an unlimited freedom. We must underline that these are *opinions*, not matters of knowledge. Locke's examples of such issues are revealing: "the belief of the Trinity, purgatory, transubstantiation, antipodes, Christ's personal reign on earth."[34] We of course know Locke's view on some of these, but the consideration he wishes to insist on is that we shall sometimes have a duty arising out of the social context in which we find ourselves to refrain from giving public expression to those views.

We now have two separate but related bases for supposing that Locke would believe it right not to claim knowledge on a particular theological or philosophical issue. The first reason is Locke's contention that the issue was not a matter of knowledge, but of opinion. Such would be all those esoteric matters of theology to which I have already referred, including, famously, the issue of the Trinity, which I shall take as an example.

Many scholars (including Locke's contemporaries) have noted that Locke never asserts the truth of the trinitarian doctrine. He also never denies it (as he himself often pointed out). On my analysis, we do not have to suppose on this basis that Locke was a closet Unitarian (as many Unitarians have supposed) to explain this lack of public commitment. Rather, we can see the controversy of the Trinity as an issue about which Locke recognized there to be difficult argument and interpretation of Scripture, with no certain knowledge available to us. It is quite compatible with this hypothesis that Locke himself, as I suspect, believed the balance of evidence to be against the doctrine. But it is quite likely that as he struggled to interpret the texts (perhaps in the company of Newton) he knew he did not have sufficiently strong a case to warrant bringing the matter to the bar of learned opinion. This, of course, was not sufficient to prevent it being read into the *Essay*, most famously by Stillingfleet and Edwards.[35]

Another issue, with strong theological implications, where Locke did venture an opinion was one onto which Stillingfleet also fastened and which was to remain a matter of debate well beyond his death. This was Locke's suggestion in book IV, chapter 10 of the *Essay* that matter might think. Locke's protestation that all he had ever claimed was that "for all we know" it was not beyond God's power to superadd to matter a power of thought, that is to say that there was no incoherence in the supposition of thinking matter, was continually twisted by his opponents into a positive claim designed to support the covert materialism to which he was allegedly secretly wedded. In the formidable hands of Leibniz, as Nicholas Jolly has demonstrated, the issue was construed as the great matter of disagreement between himself and Locke. For Leibniz was, as he wrote "above all concerned to vindicate the immateriality of the soul which Mr Locke leaves doubtful."[36] Without entering into an examination of the many sides of this major issue, we can say that it is perfectly consistent for Locke to hold that we do not *know* that matter could not think, but to *believe*, as he says he does on other grounds, that it in fact does not.

We may also note that we may hold beliefs with varying degrees of certainty, and with varying matches between the evidence that we have for them and the strength of our personal conviction. Locke was well aware – only too aware – that there was often no connection at all between the conviction with which a belief is held and the evidence available for it. All of these considerations would provide grounds for withholding public expression of one's convictions even if privately our persuasions were strong, though clearly many such beliefs could be regarded only as examples of prejudice, a subject, under the category of "partiality," to which Locke gave special attention in sections 22 and 24 of the *Conduct of the Understanding*.

Locke's second ground for holding it right not to make public claim to knowledge, or we must add, even belief, on some topic was because he judged some issues too contentious to be aired as they were liable to lead to harmful social and political consequences, for example, we might suppose, to riot and other disorder. It is sometimes at least a duty to remain silent about our opinions, even if we are very confident indeed about them. Locke might have even said *especially* when we are very confident about them. It is easy enough to think of examples, especially in the area of religious beliefs. It is important to see that this is not just a matter of personal prudence with which it may easily be confused. Still less is it an example of moral cowardice. I think Locke would have included the issue of the Trinity as one example falling within this category, as well as in the one earlier mentioned. He might have come to classify the supposition of the possibility of thinking matter as similarly unnecessarily contentious if he could have foreseen the controversy it was to generate, which John Yolton has so ably documented.[37]

Finally, for completeness, we should note a third reason for not making public claims to knowledge: prudence. On some issues we may think it worth remaining silent merely because it is too risky to express our opinions. No doubt some of Locke's political and theological beliefs fell into this category.

CONCLUSIONS

We can now finally turn to the issue with which we began. In what sense was Locke a conservative? In what sense was he a radical? Clearly some of Locke's most strongly held philosophical claims, of which the denial of innate ideas was probably the most important, alone had implications enough to justify Locke's contemporaries seeing him as a radical. But my argument is that Locke's writings provided a starting point for much other radical theology that he may never have wished to set in motion. Thus although he was seen by James Martineau in 1840 no doubt in some sense correctly as the founding father of Unitarianism,[38] there is no reason to suppose that Locke sought such a position in history, and he may well have been intellectually genuinely undecided about the matter. Alternatively, I suggest, he may have become a Unitarian, but believed that the argument was so difficult and problematic that it would have been wrong to make his commitment public. A radical by intellectual conviction, he was not prepared to make his convictions public because of his desire not to be the cause of undesirable social consequences. It is certainly an understanding of the role of the responsible intellectual in society that cannot just be dismissed, though I shall not attempt to defend it here.

And the same general position, I venture to suggest, is true of his alleged materialism. So, for example, we can scarcely recognize Locke's philosophy in William Carroll's fantastic reinterpretation of him as a subtle propagandist for materialism in *A Dissertation Upon the Tenth Chapter of the Fourth Book of Mr Locke's Essay Concerning Human Understanding*, published in 1706, just two years after Locke's death.[39]

Similar remarks might be made about his relationship to deism. As John Biddle has argued, we cannot read back into Locke's theology and philosophy the doctrines of Toland. For in rejecting the suggestion that anything could be above reason, Toland was also rejecting the central place allocated by Locke to Revelation. Locke explained his position in the *Reasonableness of Christianity*:

> A great many things we have been bred up in the belief of from our Cradles, (and are Notions grown Familiar, and as it were Natural to us, under the Gospel,) we take for unquestionable obvious Truths, and easily demonstrable; without considering how long we might have been in doubt or ignorance of them, had Revelation been silent.[40]

Reason alone, then, would at best be an unlikely source for all religious knowledge. And therefore the deist's program, or Toland's version of it, was yet another example of hope exceeding experience. Locke's position here is very similar to that which he adopted concerning morality. Just as Locke held that there was a practical impossibility in our deriving all of the propositions of ethics by demonstration,[41] so, *contra* Toland, and in line with the position I have been urging in this chapter, Locke was not keen to encourage the deist's overconfident expectations about the power of reason alone to serve man's religious objectives.

The history of Locke's thought in the eighteenth century is, I am suggesting, an example of the way in which a philosopher's uncertain conjectures on religious questions can be taken and used to support positions probably much more radical than their author ever intended.

Whether a parallel interpretation to that offered here for Locke's religious beliefs is also appropriate for Locke's political ideas is of course another question, but one, I would venture to suggest, that is worthy of scrutiny.

NOTES

1 John Locke, *An Essay Concerning Human Understanding*, book IV, chapter 17, section 1. All references to this volume will be by book, chapter and

section number, and to the Clarendon Edition, edited by Peter H. Nidditch (Oxford, 1975). The quotation cited is on p. 668.

2 On Locke's early intellectual interests, see John Milton, "Locke at Oxford," in G. A. J. Rogers (ed.), *Locke's Philosophy: Content and Context* (Oxford, 1994), pp. 29–48.

3 Cf. John Marshall, "John Locke and Latitudinarianism," in Richard Kroll, Richard Ashcraft and Perez Zagorin (eds.), *Philosophy, Science and Religion in England, 1640–1700* (Cambridge, 1992), pp. 253–74.

4 Cf. Maurice Cranston, *John Locke: A Biography* (London, 1957) p. 148. I was reminded of this point whilst reading John Marshall's "John Locke in Context: Religion, Ethics and Politics" (Ph.D. dissertation, Johns Hopkins University, 1990). This work and discussions with John Marshall have been important for my understanding of Locke's religious position.

5 For an assessment of piety amongst the laity in the Restoration period, see John Spurr, *The Restoration Church of England, 1646–1689* (New Haven and London, 1991), especially pp. 353–75.

6 For an alternative reading, see P. J. Kelly, "John Locke: Authority, Conscience and Religious Toleration," in John Horton and Susan Mendus (eds.), *John Locke, A Letter Concerning Toleration, in Focus* (London, 1991), pp. 125–46.

7 The obvious sources for Locke's account of the fundamental articles of the Christian religion are the *Reasonableness of Christianity* (1695) and the first and second *Vindication* (1695 and 1697). For some discussion of their place in Locke's theology, see Arthur W. Wainwright's introduction to his edition of Locke's *A Paraphrase and Notes on the Epistles of St Paul* (the *Clarendon Edition of the Works of John Locke*, 2 vols., [Oxford, 1987], I, pp. 28–59).

8 Benjamin Whichcote, *Moral and Religious Aphorisms*, ed. Samuel Salter (London, 1753), aphorisms 71 and 76.

9 Richard Baxter, *Narrative of His Life* (1696) I, p. 76, quoted in R.A. Knox, *Enthusiasm* (Oxford, 1950), p. 141.

10 John Smith, *Select Discourses. 1. Of the True Way or Method of Attaining to Divine Knowledge*, 2nd edn. (Cambridge, 1673), I, p. 16.

11 Ibid., p. 8.

12 John Smith, "The Excellency and Nobleness of True Religion," *Select Discourses*, p. 419.

13 Henry More, *A Collection of Several Philosophical Writings of Dr. Henry More*, 4th edn (London, 1712), p. iv.

14 Although this theme runs right through Cudworth's *True Intellectual System of the Universe* (1678) it emerges, in many ways most clearly in his posthumous *A Treatise Concerning Eternal and Immutable Morality* (1731).

15 For a good recent survey of the issue in the period, see W. M. Spellman, *The Latitudinarians and the Church of England, 1660–1700* (Athens, GA, and London, 1993), chapter 4.

16 Cf. Joseph Glanvill, "The Agreement of Reason and Religion" in *Essays on Several Important Subjects in Philosophy and Religion* (London, 1676), especially pp. 4–5. (The essays are separately paginated.)

17 Cudworth, *A Treatise Concerning Eternal and Immutable Morality*, p. 287.

18 Glanvill, "The Agreement of Reason and Religion," p. 5.

19 We should remember that each of these last three words – "clear, intuitive knowledge" – is, for Locke, a precise technical term within his philosophy, whose meaning has been spelt out in early sections of the *Essay*.

20 It is not clear from the text whether this obligation is a logical or a moral point. Is it as a matter of logic that obligation cannot arise here because obligation can only occur if there is the possibility of our being able to do what is required of us, and we have no power to believe things against the dictates of reason? Or would it always be morally wrong for any power to try by force to make us accept what we hold to be contrary to reason? From other sources we know that Locke would have wished to assent to both these interpretations.

21 It must be remembered that Locke distinguished between the criteria that had to be satisfied for something to be the same material nonorganic object and those required to be the same living thing. In the former case, it was numerical identity of the material parts that was essential. For the latter, it was "participation in the same life" without any strict requirement of "same parts." Cf. II.27. especially 1–5.

22 Sanderson, *Logicae artis compendium* (1615) III.17.1–4. I am grateful to Rick Kennedy for drawing my attention to Sanderson's discussion of faith in a paper he gave at the British Society for the History of Philosophy's "Descartes" conference in Reading, September 1991: and to his paper, "The Alliance between Puritanism and Cartesian Logic at Harvard, 1687–1735," *Journal of the History of Ideas*, 51 (1990), 549–72.

23 Antoine Arnauld, *The Art of Thinking*, trans. James Dickoff and Patricia James (New York, 1964), p. 339.

24 Ibid.

25 For the date of composition, see Locke, *Correspondence*, Clarendon Edition of the Works of John Locke, ed. E. S. de Beer, 9 vols. (Oxford, 1976–) VI, p. 87, letter 2243, Locke to William Molyneux, April 10, 1697.

26 *Conduct of the Understanding*, with introduction and notes by Thomas Fowler, 3rd edn. (Oxford, 1890), p. 50.

27 Ibid.

28 Ibid.

29 "A Fourth Letter for Toleration," *The Works of John Locke*, 2nd edn, 3 vols. (London, 1722) III, p. 461.

30 *Works* (1722), II, p. 535.

31 Ibid., p. 538.

32 Ibid., p. 539.

33 Published in H. R. Fox Bourne, *The Life of John Locke*, 2 vols. (London, 1876; reprinted Bristol, 1991), I, p. 186.

34 Ibid., p. 176.

35 Locke, in his reply, did not openly state that he supported the doctrine but attempted, quite successfully, to defend himself by showing that because Toland rejected the doctrine, even though Toland saw himself as arguing from Lockian principles, it did not follow that Locke accepted Toland's argument. See especially *Locke's Second Reply to the Bishop of Worcester*. For Edwards, see especially his *Socinianism Unmasked* (London, 1696).

36 Quoted in Nicholas Jolley, *Leibniz and Locke: A Study of the "New Essays on Human Understanding"* (Oxford, 1984), p. 102.

37 See especially Yolton's *Thinking Matter: Materialism in Eighteenth-Century Britain* (Oxford, 1983), and, most recently in its French context, *Locke and French Materialism* (Oxford, 1991).

38 Cf. H. McLachlan, *The Unitarian Movement in the Religious Life of England* (London, 1934), p. 240.

39 Now republished with an introduction by John W. Yolton (Bristol, 1990).

40 *Reasonableness of Christianity* (1695) pp. 277–78, cited in John C. Biddle, "Locke's Critique of Innate Principles and Toland's Deism," *Journal of the History of Ideas*, 37 (1976), p. 421.

41 Cf. *Essay*, IV.3.18–20; pp. 549–52.

III

Policing the margins

CHAPTER 5

Samuel Parker, religious diversity, and the ideology of persecution*

Gordon Schochet

Samuel Parker, ardent Interregnum Presbyterian turned persecuting Restoration divine and briefly – at the end of his life – Bishop of Oxford, had a deep and profound understanding of the intimate relationship between the civil and religious institutions that defined Stuart England.[1] He appreciated, as did few of his contemporaries, the heterodox, sectarian threat to that relationship which the future might hold. His view of that future was not unlike the hell that Plato derisively called "democracy" in the *Republic* – a world of isolated, undisciplined individuals in which the "Wild and Fanatique Rabble" would run free, and the interests of "proud, ignorant, and supercilious Hypocrites" would replace the temperate judgment, wisdom, and order of traditional authority.[2]

That was Parker's view in 1669. By 1681 the deterioration of English Protestantism was well under way. "The general Term of Protestancy," he said then, "is an indefinite thing."

> ... there are *Hobbian* Protestants, *Muggletonian* Protestants, *Socinian* Protestants, Quaker Protestants, Rebel Protestants, Protestants of 41, and Protestants of 48. All or most of which are as different as Popery it self from the true Protestancy of the Church of *England*. And therefore it is necessary to stick close to that, both as it is established by the Law of the Land, and by the Law of Christ. For unless we limit it to the Law of the Land, we may in time have a Church consisting of nothing but Protestants dissenting from the established Religion, that is, a Church not only without, but against it self. And ... we may quickly be (as we are in a fair way to be) a Reformed Church of Protestant Atheists, that is, a Church without Religion.[3]

For more than twenty years Parker defended the orthodox, Anglican establishment with an ideological vehemence and fervor and a volume of writings that were equaled by few if any of his peers. He met the liberty of conscience and toleration that nonconformists sought with calls for magisterial imposition and justifications of religious persecution. His was perhaps the most extreme view in late seventeenth-century England. Although Parker's position found favor among some members of the High Church hierarchy, it was never adopted, and apologists for Parker are difficult to find. Nonetheless, he did have the peculiar virtue – along with Edward Stillingfleet and a few others – of incorporating a conception of the absolute power of the sovereign into Anglican doctrine and thereby lending a kind of respectability to this aspect of the otherwise shunned Hobbesian theory. In the end he may have been partially responsible for hastening the advent of the heterodox future he dreaded by giving his opponents so clear and stable a target and by unwittingly driving some Anglicans away from his outrageous railings.

For all that Samuel Parker is virtually unknown today outside a relatively small but growing circle of scholars.[4] What lingers of his fame is due to his having goaded the poet Andrew Marvell into writing one of his earliest self-consciously political works, *The Rehearsal Transpros'd* (1672),[5] and, according to Richard Ashcraft, to his having written a work that was the very essence of the doctrines that John Locke and his political allies spent the 1670s and 1680s combatting.[6] That book, *A Discourse of Ecclesiastical Politie*, was an intemperate and hostile attack on nonconformists. Its subtitle announced it as a defense of "The Authority of the Civil Magistrate over the Consciences of Subjects in Matters of External Religion."[7] It was the third of Parker's attacks on nonconformity and was followed by many more. One of them, his anonymous "Preface Shewing What Grounds There Are of Fears and Jealousies of Popery" of 1672 prefixed to Bishop John Bramhall's posthumous *Vindication of Himself and the Episcopal Clergy from the Presbyterian Charge of Popery*, was the work that ultimately attracted Marvell's attention.[8] And as Jonathan Swift observed about that exchange barely twenty-five years after Parker's death, "*we still read* Marvell's Answer to Parker *with Pleasure, tho' the Book he answers be sunk long ago.*"[9]

Because he had the misfortune to be on the wrong side and defended the persecution of religious dissidents, Parker was consigned to infamy and eventually forgotten. But his modern obscurity is not exclusively due to his having lost his battle to the emerging "Whig/liberal" ideology; aside from Marvell and Locke, who achieved fame in other arenas, few of his opponents are much better remembered. Perhaps ever more important is an historiographic indifference toward the issues themselves. Parker engaged in a protracted debate that, for all its importance in Restoration England, has long since been incapable of exciting the passions.

Religious persecution, as Mark Goldie has recently reminded us, was the order of the day throughout the Restoration.[10] Although hardly ended, these policies were softened with the passage of the so-called Act of Toleration in 1689. Their aim had been to eliminate at least Protestant challenges to the established Anglican uniformity of late Stuart England, and in that they utterly failed. Such persecutorial practices and attitudes, nurtured and encouraged as they were by Samuel Parker, were an important if unlikely source of modern religious liberty; they remind us of the ambiguous fragility of that liberty and may motivate us to consider more seriously than is our current practice the place of religion in a secular society.

This chapter is concerned with Parker's opposition to the Dissenters, which it approaches from the perspective of the religious politics of Restoration England and the controversies over toleration in which Parker engaged, with occasional looks at the doctrines of persecution, toleration, and religious liberty themselves and their ideological and conceptual sources and consequences.

I

The demise of the Protectorate and the consequent reestablishment of the monarchy and the traditional, episcopal hierarchy of the Church of England created a religious muddle unlike anything in previous English history. It left England a sharply divided nation and provided the legal basis for the sectarian conflicts and parliamentary and church policies of persecution that characterized the reigns of Charles II and James II. These conflicts, and the official exclusion of all non-Anglicans from public and corporation offices, would not be fully ended until the nineteenth century.

The religious strife of the late seventeenth century in many respects marks the conclusion of the peculiarly *English* Reformation: it was during this period both that the civil character of the Church of England and its relationship to the political nation were firmly established and that the existence of heterodox Protestant sects was given legal acknowledgment as policy toward them changed from persecution to the initially grudging and eventually indifferent indulgence that has come to be called "toleration." This transformation was not due to a principled shift in attitudes toward Dissenters or to the new political importance of them or their supporters as a result of the Glorious Revolution of 1688–89. Quite the contrary; its sources lay rather more in political maneuvering, a recognition that persecution had been unsuccessful, and the belief that a limited "toleration" that did not convey new political entitlements to nonconformists might accomplish the same ends.[11]

Samuel Parker did not participate in the development of the new policy toward Dissenters; he died before James II fled England and abandoned his throne. Had he lived, as Bishop of Oxford – a position to which James had appointed him over the objections of the Archbishop of Canterbury, William Sancroft, and as an apparent reward for services to be rendered – Parker would have been a member of the House of Lords when it considered the Indulgence Bill. Although he was among the few officials of the church who endorsed James's 1687 Declaration of Indulgence and wrote a tract in defense of the king,[12] his overt support was limited to advancing the interests of Roman Catholics. He was silent about indulgence for Protestant nonconformists, which he had spent the entirety of his adult, literary life attacking.

He was raised as a Presbyterian and spent his student years at Oxford as an enthusiastic and devoted member of that faith, so there was more than a touch of irony to his bitter attacks on his former co-religionists, describing the "Geneva *Faction*" in 1672 as a "*Waspish Sect*" whose members were "*moderate* [and] . . . *lukewarm men*" who "*prepare the ways for* . . . [the] *man of Sin*."[13] As Marvell reminded him,[14] his father, a judge under Cromwell, had published a defense of the Commonwealth's Engagement in 1650, arguing, "that if any King or Queen did command or prohibit any thing, or in any other manner than the Laws directed, it was void, and the people were not bound to obey."[15] He insisted that "all Government is in the people, from the people, and for the people, touching altering or abrogating of Lawes, or making of new, which none can doe without them" and "that the Pretended Negative Vote of both King and Lords" thwarted the people's entitlements and wills as expressed by their representatives in Parliament. "Our present age," he said, "hath been more straining of the [royal] Prerogative, than of hundreds of yeares before," but Parliament has "Cured" these "distempers" and "Gangrenes." "Behold then, O *England*," he concluded, "and consider thy Governours; the Lawes of this Nation, free from passion, ambition, and all other exorbitant affections, yet willing to be reformed by your selves for your good."[16]

It was precisely these doctrines that the younger Parker would spend his professional life refuting. It would be tempting to speculate about the influence of his father's views on his own unrelentingly bitter assaults on nonconformists. That temptation is increased by the fact that Parker apparently did not suffer for his Presbyterianism. In the absence of evidence, however – Parker is not known to have left any manuscripts other than an unrevealing *History of His Own Time*[17] – any such comments could never be more than mere speculation. More to point, the intention here is not to *account for* Parker's views – which in any event certainly sprang from multiple sources, including his ambitions for office in the Church of England – but to *situate* and *explain* them in terms of the religious politics of Restoration England.

II

The long-term religious legacy of the Interregnum was sectarianism and diversity ("pluralism"). The Act of Uniformity had divided the political nation into an established church and nonconformists. There were also Roman Catholic recusants, whose devotion to the religion of their ancestors made them feared and reviled by nonconformists and some Anglicans. Charles and James, some High Churchmen, and numbers of political figures on the other hand were sympathetic to Roman Catholicism, which was played by all sides as something of a wild card throughout the Restoration.

The immediate source of the difficulties was Charles II's now famous Breda Declaration, issued on the eve of his restoration. Charles committed himself, with some qualifications, to guarantee "a liberty to tender consciences."[18] In obvious recognition of Interregnum sectarianism he promised that "no man shall be disquieted or called into question for differences of opinion in matter of religion which do not disturb the peace of the kingdom" and affirmed his readiness "to consent to such an Act of Parliament as upon mature deliberation shall be offered to us for the full granting that indulgence."[19]

The Cavalier parliament was in no mood to accommodate either Papist or Dissenter, and its response to the king's concern for "tender consciences" was the Clarendon Code. The Act of Uniformity, which reestablished the Church of England as it had existed before the Revolution and laid down legal regulations concerning the form of worship, was made law by Charles's assent in May 1662. It was the cornerstone of the parliamentary policy; more than any other post-Interregnum official pronouncement, it was the source of Restoration sectarianism. The Act drove out of the established church all ministers, teachers, and other holders of religious offices who could not by oath affirm that they would "conform to the liturgy of the Church of England as it is now *by law established*."[20] What that law "established" was "the uniformity in the public worship of God," brought about, *inter alia*, by the universal adoption of *The Book of Common Prayer* and the exclusion of all ministers who had not been "ordained priest or deacon according to the form of episcopal ordination."[21] This last requirement mandated the reordination of Presbyterians and Independents who wished to retain their ministerial positions.

But these concessions, especially reordination, were too high a price for most of them to pay. They were thus forced into nonconformity, many taking their congregations with them. It is impossible to determine the number of congregants who followed their departing ministers,[22] but it is evident that the prevention of "disorders and disturbances" in the church that Samuel Parker celebrated as one of the primary effects of the Act of Uniformity left some numbers of what he called "factious men"[23] free to wreak their havoc in society at large. Somewhat more soberly, perhaps, he observed in 1666 that if the common people are "suffered to run without restraint, they will break down all the banks of Law and Government."[24]

The problem, in Parker's terms as well as those of the establishment, was to make sure that these Dissenters were not allowed to remain free from order and discipline. Ideally they should have been reunited with the Church of England – "comprehended" in the terminology of the day – which would have eliminated the divisive effects of their heterodox, erroneous, and possibly schismatic separation. Failing that they would have to be persecuted, punished for their deviations from the established practice and hounded until they ceased to exist or were driven into the established church. From the Dissenters' perspective, however, it was the Church of England that was in error, and so long as it refused to change its practices, reconciliation was impossible.

The picture was rather more complicated than this, for there were two distinct types of nonconformists: Presbyterians who wished to rejoin the establishment once it made the necessary modifications, and intentionally separating sects – Independents, Quakers, Baptists, and a handful of others – to whom the episcopal hierarchy and parish churches that constituted the organizational basis of Anglicanism were anathema. The Presbyterians, on the other hand, had always accepted the inclusiveness of the parish, the members of which they often likened to a "flock" that needed its ministerial "shepherd." In this respect, they departed from the stricter Calvinism of the Independents and were already on the road to Arminianism in the sixteenth century. Even though they called for parish discipline and wanted to loosen the episcopacy, their standard remained that of a unified, national church.[25]

The separating denominations viewed religious organization as "gathered churches" of believers. This conception was a harbinger of the transformation of religious groups into genuinely "voluntary associations";[26] it precluded the possibility of an established, "national" church, membership in which was coextensive with membership in the civil society. These separatists could not accept the structure either of a national episcopacy or of ruling synods – to say nothing Anglican doctrines – and wanted legal recognition without penalties for their status outside the official church.

The responses appropriate to these groups were radically different. As Edward Polhill put it in 1682, "There are Two sorts of *Nonconformists* we know; The *One* who do allow of a *Liturgy*, and our Parochial Churches, and these may be all *Comprehended* upon very reasonable condescensions: The *Other* who do not allow of either, and these must be *Indulged*, or destroyed."[27] This distinction was lost on most officials of the established church, to whom the only difference between Presbyterians and Independents was that the former claimed they wanted to rejoin the church but were unwilling to make any concessions, whereas the separatists were at least honest in their rejection of Anglican discipline. Coercion of some sort thus was the appropriate treatment for the Presbyterians; the others required persecution. Although the penal law provisions of the Clarendon Code were the only available legal remedies for both groups, it is important to maintain the differences between coercion and persecution.

The Biblical roots of coercion were to be found, in part, in Christ's words in the fourteenth chapter of Luke (verse 23): "Go out in the highways and hedges, and compel *them* to come in, that my house may be filled." Using this text, St. Thomas Aquinas, following St. Augustine, concluded that "unbelievers who at some time have accepted the faith, and professed it, such as heretics and all apostates . . . should be submitted even to bodily compulsion, that they may fulfil what they have promised, and hold what they, at one time, received."[28]

The justification of religious coercion, then, was the opportunity it afforded to engage in persuasion – to reason with and educate the Dissenters. A policy of coercion thus rejected all compromise; Presbyterian demands that the church's practices be altered to make them more acceptable were not even to be considered. To the extent that it is part of a *theological* policy and not merely a policy of suppression pretending to be based in religion, coercion presupposes the unique and unquestioned *validity* of the religion in whose behalf it is exercised. It is part of a religious discourse that is concerned with orthodox purity and salvation and with the elimination of heresy and schism.

Persecution differs from reincorporation in that its end is "punishment" for outsiders. Its aim is to eliminate heterodoxy by destroying schismatics or driving them back into the church; its method is to make the costs of separation too high. In these respects persecution is rather more political than religious; it is certainly more political than genuine religious coercion, which continues to hold out the possibility of a single, unified church.

Comprehension is related to coercion, which it resembles, but as advocated by seventeenth-century English Presbyterians, it was predicated on changes that would make the established church acceptable to divergent groups. While the Presbyterians talked of compromise on both sides, their complaints could have been addressed only by the alteration of Anglican rituals and practices. Comprehension was also a goal of moderate Anglicans – often called "Latitudinarians" – who spent much of the Restoration period in unsuccessful searches for compromises that both sides could accept. Advocates of comprehension usually argued that the penal statutes should remain in place as protection against Roman Catholics.

Toleration or "indulgence" was the goal of the Independents and the other separating denominations; it would have allowed them to remain outside the establishment without incurring serious penalties. From the vantage of the Church of England, toleration would have been an appropriate way of dealing with those whom it wished to *exclude* but was not willing to persecute.

In the absence of comprehension, indulgence – which in practice was similar to toleration – would have relieved Presbyterians, along with other nonconforming Protestants, from the strictures of the

Clarendon Code even though it would not restore them to membership in the Church of England. On three occasions, Charles – in 1672 – and James – in 1687 and 1688 – used their prerogative powers to "suspend" the operation of the penal laws as a means of courting the support of Dissenters and of assisting Roman Catholics, to whom their indulgences were also extended. Charles was forced by strenuous parliamentary objections to withdraw his indulgence, and James's declarations were among the immediate precipitants of the 1688–89 revolution.[29]

As the repeal of or granting statutory exemption from the anti-Protestant parts of the Penal Statues (in contrast to their being merely "set aside" by an "indulgence"), toleration was rarely advocated as an end in itself within either the parliament or the established church. Rather it was almost always tied to proposals for comprehension for Presbyterians, who usually supported it. Independents, Quakers, and other sectarians did call for toleration, fearing that they would ultimately be suppressed once the Presbyterians – who were presumed to be more desirable from the Anglican perspective – had been reabsorbed into the church.[30]

On all sides the word *toleration* itself tended to be used somewhat loosely and in ways that rendered it close to indulgence. When it was given a distinct and more precise meaning by John Locke, its sense was close to what we mean today by the *religious liberty*. But genuine religious liberty of the sort enjoyed by citizens of the United States by virtue of the First Amendment to the Constitution was not an option in seventeenth-century England. As I have argued elsewhere, it was not advocated until very late in the period by John Locke in his *Letter concerning Toleration*, and even then, the advocacy was muted.[31]

All these options were conceptually in place, politically available, and well enough known and understood by the time that Parker launched his first attack on Dissenters. Of the three, persecution is the most difficult for the modern, secular mind to grasp; ideologically at least, it is so unredeemably objectionable that it is hard to imagine what sort of case could be made for it. "Toleration" is familiar as a twentieth-century policy, but it is frequently discussed in ways that makes it indistinguishable from "religious liberty." "Comprehension" and "indulgence," having long since disappeared from the political landscape, are sufficiently remote to be made historically intelligible without the intrusion of modern ideology. The conceptual elusiveness of persecution must be overcome if the origins and nature of the relations between church and state, of "pluralism," and of what is called "cultural diversity" in the twentieth century are to be understood. The sources of much that is vital – as well as problematic – in the modern and "postmodern" worlds are to be found in the overthrow of the mentality of persecution and in the subsequent workings out of the logics of toleration and religious diversity and in their extensions beyond the confines of what we think of as church/state relations.[32]

III

Religious persecution has a long and to Parker – if not to all his contemporaries – venerable history. In fact, a number of Parker's later tracts were written expressly to demonstrate its long-standing validity as a Christian practice, which had been a constant theme of his earlier works.[33] Conceptually and psychologically persecution has been a response to the breakdown of orthodoxy and the rise of heterodox and, hence, heretical sectarianism. Politically it reflects the failure of coercion as the means of maintaining religious uniformity. Almost invariably it is a consequence of that failure and is dependent upon the close association of civil and sacred authority. A policy of persecution, in other words, presumes that religion is of vital importance to the achievement of whatever the public good and the ends of civil society are taken to be, and that religion is not a matter of personal or narrowly private concern.

From the perspective of the late twentieth-century Western mind, religious persecution is precisely the sort of practice that distinguishes "traditional" from "modern" societies. It rests upon the denial of the pluralism and diversity that characterize the modern state. In these terms an important part of the history of that state is to be found in the long and painful process by which the orthodoxy of established religious uniformity gave place to officially recognized heterodoxy.[34] And the understanding of that process requires an understanding of both the politics and the mind-set of religious coercion and persecution.

Religions are not generally open or forgiving (neither, for that matter, is politics). Religions and the people who construct and use their vocabularies have been forced, over time, to learn to share physical as well as conceptual space. Religious talk concerns itself classically with divine intention and human salvation and the relation between the two; structurally, religion is about order, rule following, and the accommodation if not explanation of the mysterious. From the internal perspective of any religion, it is difficult to conceive how there could be room in the universe for contrary or alternative accounts of these things. Religions aspire to be hegemonic, and when they encounter rival doctrines, they become defensive in protection of the territories they have claimed. That is to say, if they have not done so already, they seek the shelter of and sometimes even take over the political order.

This relationship is no less beneficial to the polity, which is even more concerned with order and rule following than is religion. The yoking of divine mystery and political power affords secular force to one and spiritual sanction to the other, and the resulting union is a most formidable orthodoxy regardless of whether ultimate authority resides in the temporal or the sacred arm of the society. From the vantage of another religion, so long as potential conflicts between what we today call "state" and "church" are satisfactorily resolved, the orthodoxy remains unbreachable, and its policy toward those who challenge or otherwise do not subscribe to its tenets remains oppressive.

None of this is intended as a *reduction* of religion and theology to politics and ideology; the point, rather, is to underscore the closeness of those two realms in what we might label the "preheterodox" world. At the same time, however, the irreducible nature of traditional theology should be kept in mind. That same "modern" conceit – especially in its academic form – that is conceptually troubled by the mere existence of religious orthodoxy, stumbles even more over the place of sincere religious conviction in the world of our forebears. Service to God and the seeking of salvation were, and remain, matters of overwhelming importance in traditional societies as well as to people who hold deep religious convictions in the diverse, technological societies of the late twentieth century. Piety of all sorts continues to provide succor and sustenance to those who take it seriously; such people go to great lengths in pursuit of their theological objectives and in defense of their chosen ways.

This has the twin consequences of making challenges to religious views assume momentous status as psychological threats and of calling for and legitimating extreme actions in defense of the religion. Where religion is important in itself, it becomes the irreducible and independent basis for much else, and can simultaneously sanction aggressive challenges to an establishment and equally aggressive defenses against such threats. The roots of all this are in some combination of political power, fear of heterodoxy, conceptions of religious purity, and even downright mean-spiritedness, all of which can be found in the religious debates of Restoration England.

IV

Within the larger context of the persecution/toleration debates there were two separate but related controversies to which Parker contributed. One was a debate over indifferency (or *adiaphora*), the other was concerned with the place of conscience in the politics of religion.

The discussion of indifferency was nearly as old as Christianity itself; it dealt with the distinction between those things that were *necessary* for salvation because they were *required* by Scripture and those about which God had been silent and so had been left to human discretion.[35] Disagreement over such matters is the stuff of which accusations of heresy, religious reformations, and schism are built. And in mid-seventeenth-century England it was a series of indifferency disputes that provided the religious grounds that kept Presbyterians and Independents out of the Church of England.

No one questioned the distinction, but there was considerable disagreement over what was indifferent and what was required, and over the extent to which subjects were bound to obey magisterial impositions on matters indifferent. John Locke's oldest surviving political work, his manuscript essays of 1660–61 – published in 1967 as *Two Tracts on Government* – were a contribution to the indifferency debate on precisely this issue.

In 1660 Edward Bagshaw's anonymous *The Great Question Concerning Things Indifferent in Religious Worship* argued that the realm of indifferency was beyond the legitimate reach of the magistrate. "It is an infinite Trouble and matter of Disquiet to the Party imposed upon, because he is thereby disabled from using his *Liberty*, in that which he knows to be *Indifferent*," Bagshaw insisted against the orthodox claim that if something was indifferent the magistrate was *therefore* entitled to regulate it.[36] Locke replied that precisely *because* of their indifferent status, these practices could be regulated and *imposed* by the civil magistrate.[37] In this respect, he was at one with the reply Parker would make to this same general argument. Parker held that a permissiveness on indifferency would create a diversity of practices destructive of the civil order that was necessary for peace and stability.[38]

Parker had little more to say on the subject at this point in his life. Despite its importance in Restoration politics, indifferency as such does not appear to have been a matter of great moment to him. Others completed the story for him, but – as we shall see – he returned to the subject briefly in one of his later works.

God's having left the determination of indifferent practices to human choice, anti-Dissenter writers argued, vested the power of choice in each civil society, not each person, congregation, or sect. Nonconformists obviously could not accept this claim and were unwilling to concede that matters such as the organization (parishes or congregations) and structure (episcopal hierarchy or synods) of the church were indifferent. Because there were no shared *theological* grounds on which they and their Anglican adversaries could even frame the argument, these disputes were effectively irreconcilable and therefore became political. Accordingly they were given over to the magistrate for resolution, a solution that Dissenters could hardly have accepted.

An illustration of all these issues is provided by Edward Stillingfleet's *Irenicum*, apparently written on the eve of the Restoration and published six months later. Nonconformists argued that because the primitive church had been organized congregationally, the intrusive episcopal hierarchy of the Romanist church should not be perpetuated by the Church of England. To this Stillingfleet had an ingenious answer. Claiming to have discovered the ancient status of bishops as well as of synodical rule, he concluded that the very structure of church government was a matter of indifference and, therefore, was legitimately subject to magisterial regulation. Because history and practice demonstrated the preferability of the episcopate in England, Presbyterians were *obliged* to accept episcopacy and could do so without offending or fettering their consciences, which remained free even though "authority" over them was necessarily surrendered.

Stillingfleet professed his support for toleration and actually began the *Irenicum* with a plea for the toleration of indifferent practices that were not necessary for salvation.[39] It was this position, in all likelihood, that has earned him a place among Latitudinarians, for the toleration he advocated was to take place *within* the established church. Stillingfleet was assertively antagonistic to nonconformist separatism on the grounds of indifferency. Separation was only lawful when "communion becomes sin," not upon "supposition of corruption."[40]

It was on this issue that Parker again took up indifferency in 1681. In a work that was designed in part to demonstrate the divine origins of episcopacy he refused to adopt Stillingfleet's formula but instead argued that the structure of the church was not indifferent:

if the Form of Government in the Christian Church be not setled by the Founder of it, that then we are at a loss to know by whom it may or ought to be determined. For the Society of the Church being founded upon an immediate Divine Right, no Person can justly challenge any Authority in it as such, unless by vertue of some Grant or Commission from the divine Founder of it.[41]

It was a difficult and contentious argument that forced Parker to acknowledge a few pages later that non-episcopal Protestant churches were in error. But all this, he claimed, "concerns only those that either are, or ought to be members of the Church of *England*." Other churches that "deviate from the Primitive Institution" had to "stand and fall to their own Master." Certainly he, Parker, was not going to "be so uncharitable as to go about to un-church them, or to renounce brotherly communion with them."[42]

V

Parker more than made up for his relative silence about *adiaphora* by his seemingly unending tirades about conscience, which were the basis on which much of his politics doctrine was built. Uprooting appeals to "conscience," showing their invidious relationship to doctrines of toleration, and banishing them from religio-political discussions seem to have been his major conceptual preoccupations. He spent much of his life in distrustful fear of the masses, who were waiting "*to fall into the snare of an abused and vicious Conscience*" prepared for them by the dissenting ministers.

There is no Observation in the world establish'd upon a more certain and universal Experience, than that the generality of mankind are not so obnoxious to any sort of Follies and Vices, as to wild and unreasonable conceits of Religion; and that, when their heads are possess'd with them, there are no principles so pregnant with mischief and disturbance than they. And if Princes would but consider, how liable mankind are to abuse themselves with serious and conscientious Villanies, they would quickly see it to be absolutely necessary to the Peace and Happiness of their Kingdoms, that there be set up a more severe Government over men's Consciences and Religious perswasions, than over their Vices and Immoralities.

It followed, then, that *"Indulgence and Toleration is the most absolute sort of Anarchy."*[43]

After lengthy discussions of the origin and nature of civil and ecclesiastical power, the necessity of sovereign authority in religious matters, and the differences between inward liberty of conscience and the outward liberty of action, Parker attacked Hobbes's conceptions of obligation and the state of nature and his doctrine of the liberty of conscience.[44] He then defended religious persecution as the only way to ensure that the attachment people have to their "parties" did not erupt into civil strife:

for the godly Party not to be uppermost, is, and ever will be Persecution. For nothing [is] more certain, than that all men entertain the best opinion of their own Party, otherwise they had never enrolled themselves in it: and therefore if the State value them not at as high a rate as they do themselves, they are scorn'd and injured, because they have not that favour and countenance they deserve. . . where-ever there is *difference* of Religion, there is *opposition* too; because men would never divide from one another, but upon grounds of real dislike; and therefore they are always *contrary* in those Differences that distinguish their Parties.[45]

Government, he insisted, was absolutely necessary, and religion was no less important to the smooth conduct of human affairs; it was the best source of stability:

For 'tis the Church that is the best part of every Commonwealth; and when all Projects are tried, Religion is the best Security of Peace and Obedience: The Power of Princes would be a very precarious thing, without the Assistance of Ecclesiastics, and all Government does and must owe its quiet and continuance to the Churches Patronage; 'tis the Authority that it has over the Consciences of Subjects, that chiefly keeps the Crown upon the Prince's Head, and were it not for the Restraints of Conscience, that are tied on by the Hands of the Priest, and the Laws of Religion, Man would be a monstrously wild and ungovernable Creature.[46]

But as "harmless and peaceable" as religion is in itself, "when mixt with the Follies and Passions of men, it does not usually inspire them with overmuch gentleness and goodness of Nature." Therefore it is essential that religion "submit to the same Authority, that commands over the other affections of the mind of man."[47] Religious dissent or schism was equivalent to "rebellion," he said in an implicit attack on the appeal to indifferency:

to quarrel with those forms of Publick Worship that are establish'd by [lawful] Authority, only because they are *Humane Institutions*, is at once notorious Schism & Rebellion: For when a Religion is Establish'd by the Laws, whoever openly refuses Obedience, plainly rebels against the Government, Rebellion being properly nothing else but an open denial of obedience to Civil Power. Nor can Men of this Principle live Peaceably in any Church in Christendom, in that there is not a Church in the World, that has not peculiar Rites and Customs, and Laws of Government and Discipline.[48]

The true evil for Parker was "*the Pretense of a Tender and unsatisfied Conscience*" pleaded in response to the "*Commands of Publick Authority*."[49] Transforming "tender" into "weak," Parker asserted that "Weakness of Conscience always proceeds in some measure from want of wit," and what could be more ludicrous than using that witlessness to discipline political superiors. It "is just as if a Child in *Minority* should reject the advice of his *Guardians*, because he has not wit enough to know, when he is well advised."[50] In the end, "it gratifies their [i.e., people's] pride & vanity, to seem more knowing than their Governours in that part of wisdom, that they think most valuable," and it is a rejection of "the common interests of Humane Society" for anyone to deny that "power over men's outward actions, . . . as far as it concerns all publick affairs . . . of necessity must pass away to the Rulers of that Society he lives in." Such a person will "live not under Government, but in a state of *Anarchy*," a condition that, as Parker described it, sounded strikingly like the Hobbesian state of nature: "where men will be the absolute Masters of their own actions, it is not the freedom of Conscience, but its power and sovereignty, for which they contend."[51]

These were themes that ran through all his polemical writings, but what Parker meant by "conscience" was never entirely clear.[52] At times he seems to have intended something like the Hobbesian notion of conscience as the irreducible "Private Judgment" or "opinion" of an individual that, by its nature, could not be coerced or fettered and therefore had no place in civil society.[53] This position allowed Parker the luxury of simply dismissing nonconformist appeals to conscience because of their utter irrelevance to government. But it would not free them from their necessary obligations to the sovereign; that was to be found in some other source. As he said in reply to Marvell, conscience might be "unlimited," but it is not "unhoopable."[54] At other times, however – and often within a few pages of his Hobbes-like declarations – Parker described conscience as rather more tractable and legitimately subject to external impositions. He insisted that there had to be a "*Supreme Authority over the Conscience in Matters of Religion*,"[55] and said in response to John Owen that conscience had to be more than "our secret thoughts," for if a law does not oblige the conscience, "it obliges nothing."[56] Owen complained that the only argument Parker ever made for the power of the magistrate over conscience was that it was necessary for the peace and tranquility of the community. Marvell made a similar observation and added that "Necessity" was a vague term that justified nothing.[57] Parker did not reply to either critic on this score.

All this, as I have said, was part of a continuing and ultimately unresolved seventeenth-century debate. It was generally agreed that while conscience was sacrosanct, it could err, and it could be informed without being violated. Accordingly a frequent Anglican claim was that nonconformists who pleaded scruples of conscience as the reasons for their rejections of the Church of England were – if not dissembling[58] – in error and that their consciences needed to be better educated. In fact, Restoration theorists usually recognized the irreconcilability of conflicts of conscience. The way around the claim that the imposition of religious practices interfered with conscience was through the distinction between *conscience* and *will*. The latter had to do with outward behavior and conformity alone and could be ordered, engaged, and even coerced without touching conscience.[59]

VI

Parker basically had no *theological* position. He was much more concerned with political power and the preservation of stability than he was with religious *principles*. To the extent that he actually talked about "schism" and "heresy," he did so in terms of politics and the need for order rather than from a theological perspective. There were theological and religious arguments against toleration and in support of persecution available to Parker, as well as arguments about the teachings of Christ, the nature and form of the primitive church, and heresy. These are arguments that a high-ranking Anglican clergyman might have been expected to have used – in addition to psychological, political, and ideological attacks on dissent – but there is virtually nothing of them in his writings.

By the same token Parker ignored by silence theological arguments in support of toleration that looked to education and conversion as the principal means of reuniting Christianity. He was deaf to the insistence that the punishment and deprivation he advocated were powerless to change people's minds and that, at best, he was calling for insincerity and hypocrisy in the name of order and stability, or, as Marvell put it, the *"Whipping-Post"* and *"Pillories"* will hardly convert anyone.[60] In fact there is strikingly little conventional and traditional theological concern in any of Parker's publications. There is nothing in his voluminous writings about the character of the "true" church, although he certainly regarded the nonconformists as the source of potential error and, presumably, of corruption. Salvation and the state's place in it were of passing interest to him, and even his limited discussions of Christian redemption tended to be couched more in moral than in theological terms and looked to moral behavior, not divine grace.[61]

VII

Parker's debate with Marvell carried little of principled, theoretical, and theological note. With one series of significant exceptions, Marvell's substantive contributions were even slighter than those of Parker's. His books are filled with wit, cleverness, innuendo, well-turned phrases, ridicule, nastiness, sarcasm, and dazzling displays of literary allusions and apparent commentary on much classical and contemporary literature.[62] The latter are so frequent and often obscure that it is difficult to know whom Marvell intended as his audience. Parker – who was likened by Marvell to Hobbes,[63] and Manwaring, Sibthorpe, and Laud[64] – for all his own invective talent, was no literary match for Marvell. The two volumes of the *Rehearsal Transpros'd* were more polemical than theoretical and constructive, and they contain little that moved the *political/religious* debate along.[65]

The claims of Parker that Marvell rejected and refuted with invective and *reductio* arguments, were rarely replaced by coherent statements of the poet-essayist's own doctrines. He provided no sense of what he thought conscience was and did not talk about the extent of the entitlements (let alone "rights") of the Dissenters *vis-à-vis* the established church; nor did he, as Locke would do later, talk about the undesirability of an established church. Marvell attacked Parker's factual assertions from time to time, but he had little himself to say about the nature of government, the limits of authority, and the whole question of indifferency.

Toward the middle of his second volume, however, Marvell briefly departed from literature and insult and seriously and perceptively considered a number of vital and theoretically interesting political issues that were designed to undermine Parker's absolutism. A discussion of the relevance of a state of nature and its origins to princes and to priesthood – designed to show that Parker had contradicted himself rather than to demonstrate anything about the nature of government in the seventeenth century[66] – was followed by a Harrington-like and possibly republican constitutionalist insistence on the importance of reforming government from time to time. It is in the nature of all governments and human societies – political as well as ecclesiastical – "in the process of long time [to] gather an irregularity, and wear away much of their primitive institution." Humanity has learned over the ages "to review at fit periods those errours, defects or excesses, that have insensibly crept on into the Publick Administration; to brush the dust off the wheels, and oyl them again, or if it be found advisable to chose a set of new ones." This oversight, he said, "is most easily and with least disturbance to be effected by the Society it self," just as individuals "amend their own manners" from time to time.[67]

If the government fails to accomplish these reforms, the people, for better or worse, will do it themselves. Marvell's argument contained the germ of a modern doctrine of consciousness that grew out of shared oppression:

if Princes shall not take advantage of their errours to reduce them to reason; this work, being on both sides neglected, falls to the Peoples share, from which God defend every good Government. For though all Commotions be unlawful, yet by this means they prove unavoidable. In all things that are insensible there is nevertheless a natural force alwayes operating to expel and reject whatsoever is contrary to their subsistence. And the sensible but brutish creatures heard [*sic*] together as if they were in counsel against their common inconveniences, and imbolden'd by their multitude, rebel even against Man their Lord and Master. And the Common People in all places partake so much of Sense and Nature, that, could they be imagined and contrived to be irrational, yet they would ferment and tumulate at least for their own preservation. Yet neither do they want the use of Reason, and perhaps their aggregated Judgment discerns most truly the errours of Government, forasmuch as they are the first to be sure that smart under them. In this only they come to be short-sighted that though they know the Diseases, they understand not the Remedies, and though good Patients, they are ill Physicians.[68]

A few pages later Marvell showed a deep understanding of what was at stake for the nonconformists in their conflict with the English church and state. Dissenters, he observed, asserted the authority of Scripture against the innovations that the Church of England

defended on grounds of political practice and historical sanction. All
this would have been settled, Marvell believed, had the civil
magistrate stayed out of it; the cause of the present tumult was
precisely that magisterial meddling:

it is yet to me the greatest mysterie in the world how the Civil Magistrate
could be perswaded to interess himself with all the severity of his power in a
matter so unnecessary, so trivial, and so pernicious to the publick quiet. For
had things been left in their own state of Indifferency, it is well known that
the *English* Nation is generally neither so void of Understanding, Civility,
Obedience, or Devotion that, but that they would long ago have voluntarily
closed and faln naturally into those reverent manners of Worship which
would sufficiently have exprest and suited their Religion.[69]

Parker had put forth a series of empirical hypotheses about human
nature as well as ideological claims about the need for order. The best
sort of response would have been a set of equally empirical
counterassertions about the possibilities of cooperation without harsh
impositions. Presbyterian claims about their desires to live peaceably
within the Church of England were dismissed as lies, and protestations
made by Independents and Quakers were ignored. Appeals to
principle and commitments to establishing social cooperation in the
midst of religious diversity were simply out of the question. "Rights"
and "liberties" and the sanctity of personal "conscience" were the
stuff on which the late Revolution had been built; they were the
appeals of "Levellers," "Ranters," and now Quakers to which no
opponent of toleration would listen.

John Locke had made precisely the appropriate empirical observations in 1665 while on a diplomatic mission to the Continent. While
visiting Cleves he had the opportunity to see religious toleration in
practice. As he wrote to Robert Boyle:

The town is little, and not very strong or handsom; the buildings and streets
irregular; nor is there a greater uniformity in their religion, three professions
being publickly allowed: the Calvinists are more than the Lutherans, and
the Catholicks more than both (but no papist bears any office) besides some
few Anabaptists, who are not publickly tolerated. But yet this distance in
their churches gets not into their houses. They quietly permit one another to
choose their way to heaven; for I cannot observe any quarrels or animosities
amongst them upon the account of religion.
This good correspondence is owing partly to the power of the magistrate,
and partly to the prudence and good nature of the people who (as I find by
enquiry) entertain different opinions, without any secret hatred or rancour.[70]

But these were private reflections that – so far as we know – influenced no one but Locke himself.

Marvell, as we have just seen, had made a similar point in part 2 of *The Rehearsal Transpros'd*. So Parker had to have been aware of the argument, but it was another of those issues to which he never responded.

VIII

At least since scholars began to pay attention to Alexis de Tocqueville's *Democracy in America*, the "voluntary association" has been among the hallmarks of modern society. And it is among the (largely unexamined but not apparently unreasonable) presumptions – if not conceits – of Western modernity that voluntarism is at least *preferable* and probably *superior* to coercion.[71] This voluntarist ideology is increasingly extended into various aspects of life; it builds upon and carries along with it the doctrines of "rights" and "liberty," both of which ascribe some degree of autonomy to individuals and ultimately look to the will and self-commitment as the justifying sources of obligations, duties, and, in some cases, responsibilities. Behind all this is an often unspoken (or unconscious) presumption that most of our social institutions are "artificial" or "conventional" rather than "natural" and that they are therefore subject to human control and manipulation. And in something of an ironic working out of Tocqueville's insight, law and litigiousness in general increasingly have become the vehicles for settling the disputes that arise within these voluntary associations.

Among the most important and irreducibly voluntary of the institutions of modern society are those associated with religion. Beliefs – especially religious beliefs – are regarded as "private" and personal and are therefore not subject to public scrutiny. The religious liberty to which all this is a kind of a societal sidelight, is a relatively new institutional establishment. It did not exist in the seventeenth and eighteenth centuries but is a long-term response to (and consequence of) the denominational sectarianism and heterodoxy that became the legacy of the Reformation. Among its numerous facets, religious liberty means that the state is regarded as *conceptually* incompetent to regulate religious practices, that the members of society have the *right* to determine for themselves their religious affiliations, and that no civil penalties may be attached to those choices.

All this is a far cry from the world of Restoration England where the hegemonic orthodoxy of the established Anglican church was being challenged. By today's standards assertions of the *right* of religious choice and of the *inability* of the political order to regulate religious practices were conspicuously absent from that world. Not until the publication in 1689 of John Locke's *Letter Concerning Toleration* – with its insistence that the "business of true religion is something quite different" from that of the state[72] – was the basis of what was to become the modern doctrine of religious liberty forcefully asserted, but even then it was with some hesitancy and caution. And, as if to confound the entire matter, Locke consistently spoke of "toleration" where modern usage would seem to require "liberty."[73]

IX

Throughout the period – and well into the eighteenth century – the continuing presumption was that in the realm of religion, states *can* and, unless legitimately restricted, are entitled to do what they will. The debate, accordingly, was about what they *should* and *should not* be doing and why; it was about the theory that we now call "constitutionalism" and would ultimately become an argument between the normative perspective of Locke's "Second Treatise" and the empirical claims of Hobbes's *Leviathan*. Among the central issues in that continuing controversy was the political and legal status of religious heterodoxy; at stake were the very survivals of the separate churches of the Protestants who dissented from the Church of England. And at this stage the argument was not so much about intrinsic *entitlements* to rights and liberty as it was about instrumental *grants* or *privileges* of toleration and comprehension.

The rhetoric of rights and liberty is somewhat peculiar, for the verbal assertion of one or the other usually takes the form of a claim to a natural and conceptually irreducible possession. But the argument itself – like all political argument – is designed to justify and persuade. Nonconformists in late seventeenth-century England tended not to use this vocabulary. Instead they asked for relief from the oppressive restrictions of the Clarendon Code. Presbyterians wanted to reunite with the Church of England but required that it modify some of its practices first; separatists sought a toleration that would not penalize them for continuing to stand apart from the established church.

These intentional nonconformists thus were asking for legal approval of their heterodoxy; their goal was governmental policies that would acknowledge they could not, without violating their deeply held convictions about what God required of them, do the state's bidding in religious matters. They were asking that *privileges* be granted to them, not that their asserted *rights* be recognized.

All this is clear enough in the case of toleration, and comprehension comes to the same thing. Presbyterians claimed to have been driven into heterodoxy by the refusal of the established church to compromise on matters that the Church of England called indifferent but which they, no less than their separating brethren, regarded as incompatible with the express will of God. The Church of England, in effect, responded. "We conduct our business in this manner, are within our legal and religious rights in doing so, and require these things of our members. If you will not conform, you cannot be a member; if you wish to be a member, you must conform."

The modern understanding of the nature and place of religion in public life would find nothing wrong with the Anglican position so long as three conditions obtained: that those who (for whatever reasons) did not conform were given leave to establish and follow their own institutions and practices; that they could do so without penalty; and that they suffered no other public or political loss as a consequence of their nonconformity. That they could not – because, from their perspective, they were not permitted to – join the church of their choice might be unfortunate, but in light of these three provisos, it could have no effect on their conceptual standing. People are not necessarily *entitled* to join voluntary and wholly private associations for which they are not qualified. Presbyterians would enjoy the same status as the Independents.

In the end nothing quite like this occurred. It is true that with the passage of the so-called Act of Toleration in the spring of 1689 and the failure of comprehension plans by early winter,[74] Presbyterians were rendered politically indistinguishable from other nonconformists, some trinitarian Protestant sects were given permission to meet for prayer so long as they satisfied certain conditions, and the sanctions of some parts of the Clarendon Code were suspended by parliamentary act. But the penal laws were not repealed; the Church of England retained its privileged position as the established church; and the restrictions that the Corporation and Test Laws placed on non-Anglicans remained in effect.

While all this amounted to something of a first step toward making religious membership voluntary, toleration was far from the *liberty* that genuine religious voluntarism entails. The operating presumption was still that full, participating membership in the civil society was coincident with membership in the established confession; as J. C. D. Clark has put it, England continued to be a "confessional state"[75] through the eighteenth century. Until that was changed, religious liberty would remain an unattainable goal.

NOTES

*The research on which this chapter is based has enjoyed the generous support of both the research and fellowship divisions of the National Endowment for the Humanities, the Center for the History of Freedom of Washington University, the Folger Institute of the Folger Shakespeare Library, and the Research Council of Rutgers University. It is a pleasure to record my gratitude to all these sources as well as to Roger Lund for his saintly patience and friendly advice.

1 For an account of Parker's career and a summary analysis of his writings, see Gordon J. Schochet, "Between Lambeth and Leviathan: Samuel Parker on the Church of England and Political Order," in Nicholas Phillipson and Quentin Skinner (eds.), *Political Discourse in Early Modern Britain* (Cambridge, 1993), chapter 9.

2 [Samuel Parker], *A Discourse of Ecclesiastical Politie* (1669), 3d edn (London, 1671), preface, pp. ii, iii. This edition retains the pagination of the original, from which it differs only in the occasional correction of errors.

3 S[amuel] P[arker], *The Case of the Church of England, Briefly and Truly Stated* (London, 1681), pp. 263–4.

4 For references and discussion, see my "Between Lambeth and Leviathan." To the works cited there should be added N. H. Keeble, *The Literary Culture of Nonconformity in Late Seventeenth-Century England* (Leicester, 1987), pp. 114–18 *passim*, and pp. 247–50; and Isabel Rivers, *Reason, Grace, and Sentiment: A Study of of the Language of Religion amd Ethics in England, 1660–1780*, vol. 1, *Whichcote to Wesley* (Cambridge, 1991), pp. 124, 128, both of which have interesting things to say about Parker's comments on the literary style of his opponents.

5 See Andrew Marvell, *The Rehearsal Transpros'd* and *The Rehearsal Transpros'd, The Second Part* (1672 and 1673), ed. D. I. B. Smith (Oxford, 1971), editor's introduction, pp. xi–xv. (All subsequent references will be to this edition, with the two works cited separately as I and II even though Smith's pagination is continuous.) Parker is mentioned in much of the Marvell literature, but he is rarely discussed in detail. And while Parker replied to *The Rehearsal Transpros'd* in his anonymous *A Reproof to the Rehearsal Transprosed, in a Discourse to Its Author* (London, 1673), he somewhat uncharacteristically did not reply to Marvell's *The Rehearsal Transpros'd, The Second Part*, which was a response to *A Reproof*.

6 Richard Ashcraft, *Revolutionary Politics and Locke's Two Treatises of Government* (Princeton NJ, 1986), especially pp. 41–54.

7 [Parker], *Ecclesiastical Politie*, title page.

8 Cited as [Parker], "Preface to Bramhall."

9 Jonathan Swift *A Tale of a Tub to Which is Added The Battle of the Books and the Mechanical Operation of the Spirit* ed. A. C. Guthkelch and D. Nichol Smith, 2nd edn (Oxford, 1958), p. 10.

10 Mark Goldie, "The Theory of Religious Intolerance in Restoration England," in Ole Peter Grell, Jonathan I. Israel, and Nicholas Tyacke (eds.) *From Persecution to Toleration: The Glorious Revolution and Religion in England* (Oxford, 1991), chapter 13.

11 For the claims that politics and interest rather than principle were the primary motivating factors, see Gordon J. Schochet, "The Act of Toleration and the Failure of Comprehension: Persecution, Nonconformity, and Religious Indifference," in Dale Hoak and Mordechai Feingold (eds.), *The World of William and Mary* (Stanford, 1995); and "From Persecution to 'Toleration'," in J. R. Jones (ed.), *Liberty Secured? Britain Before and After 1689* (Stanford, 1992). The best and fullest account of the political and religious debates of the period is now John Spurr, *The Restoration Church of England: 1646–1689* (New Haven, 1991), but Roger Thomas, "Comprehension and Indulgence," in G. F. Nuttall and O. Chadwick (eds.), *From Uniformity to Unity, 1662–1962* (London, 1962), remains important.

12 Samuel Parker (signed the last page), *Reasons for Abrogating the Test, Imposed on all Members of Parliament* (London, 1688). For discussion of that work, see Schochet, "Between Lambeth and *Leviathan*," pp. 192–93 and 206–208.

13 [Parker], "Preface to Bramhall," sigs. a4v and a5r.

14 Marvell, *Rehearsal Transpros'd*, II, pp. 205–206.

15 [John Parker], *The Government of the People of England Precedent and President the Same* (London, 1650), p. 2 (Thomason's copy is dated March 5, 1649: Thomason Tract E594.19).

16 [Parker], *The Government of England*, pp. 7, 16, 17, and 18.

17 *Reverendi amodum in Christo Patri, S. Parker . . . de rebus sui temporis commentariorum libri quatuor* (London, 1726) – not seen; title from British Library *Catalogue* – twice translated, with minor textual differences, as *Bishop Parker's History of His Own Time* (London, 1727 and 1728). The narrative stops in 1680 and was more of a commentary on the times than an account of Parker's life, but it does reveal his animus toward Dissenters. Parker was chaplain to the Archbishop of Canterbury Gilbert Sheldon from 1667; his *History* is used in Victor D. Sutch, *Gilbert Sheldon, Architect of Anglican Survival, 1640–1675* (The Hague, 1975), which has little to say about Parker.

18 While Charles was not the first person to employ this phrase, he certainly popularized it. Occurring in Civil War and Interregnum tracts, it was

frequently used in writings by and about Dissenters during the Restoration. Usually there were no overt references to the Breda Declaration, but the intention was probably to remind readers of Charles's unkept promise, however unreasonable it may have been.

19 The text is available in Andrew Browning (ed.), *English Historical Documents*, 1660–1714 (London, 1954), document 1, pp. 57–58, from which this quotation is taken.

20 Act of Uniformity, 1662 (14 Car. II, cap. 4), article 6, as printed in Browning, *Historical Documents*, document 137, p. 379.

21 Act of Uniformity, arts. 2 and 9, in Browning, *Historical Documents*, pp. 378, 380.

22 The Act of Uniformity caused 1,000 Protestant clergymen to be deprived of their pulpits; more than half of them were Presbyterians. To that number should be added approximately 630 more, not all Presbyterians, who had been forced out of their positions in 1660 either because they could not satisfy parliament's demands or because they were replaced by "sequestered" Anglican ministers who were restored to their posts. Michael R. Watts, (*The Dissenters: From the Reformation to the French Revolution* [Oxford, 1978], I, p. 219) says that a total of 2,029 clergymen, lecturers, and fellows were deprived between 1660 and 1662.

23 Parker, *History of His Own Time*, (1727 edition), trans. Thomas Newlin, pp. 32 and 33.

24 Samuel Parker, *An Account of the Nature and Extent of the Divine Dominion and Goodness* (1666), 2nd edn (Oxford, 1667), p. 219. An earlier work – to which the *Account* was something of a supplement – *A Free and Impartial Censure of the Platonick Philosophie* (Oxford, 1666; 2nd edn, 1667), was riddled with Parker's hatred of Enthusiasm and the Cambridge Platonists, and his contempt for the common people.

25 Although their doctrines went back at least to the reign of Elizabeth I, the English Presbyterians remained within the Church of England. Their organizational identity emerged during the religious conflicts of the 1640s, but it was the ejection of their ministers from parish pulpits at the Restoration that marks their initial visibility outside the established church. My understanding of the history of English Presbyterianism is very much indebted to C. G. Bolam, Jeremy Goring, H. L. Short, and Roger Thomas, *The English Presbyterians: From Elizabethan Puritanism to Modern Unitarianism* (London, 1968); and of Arminianism, to Nicholas Tyacke, *Anti-Calvinists: The Rise of English Arminianism, c. 1590–1640* (Oxford, 1987).

26 The larger history of all this – going back to the earliest days of Christianity – is discussed in a number of contributions to W. J. Sheilds and Diana Wood (eds.), *Voluntary Religion*, Studies in Church History, XXIII (Oxford, 1986), but the volume as a whole has little to say about *what* voluntary religious associations are and is disappointing in this theoretical and conceptual silence.

27 [Edward Polhill], *The Samaritan: Shewing that Many and Unnecessary Impositions Are Not the Oyl that must Heal the Church* (London, 1682), p. 114. (I am indebted to Henry Horwitz of the University of Iowa for having called this interesting and important work to my attention.) See also John Spurr, "The Church of England, Comprehension, and the Toleration Act of 1689," *English Historical Review*, 104 (1989), 927–29. (In *The Restoration Church*, p. 202, Spurr identifies Polhill as a "Nonconformist" – which he certainly seems to have been – but the title page of *The Samaritan* says of the author that he "goes to *Common-Prayer*, and not to *Meetings*.")

28 Thomas Aquinas, *Summa Theologiae*, II–II, Q. 10, art. 8, text from the Christian Classics Edition, 5 vols. (Westminster, MD, 1981), III, p. 1213. This Biblical passage was used by St. Augustine to the same effect in his 93rd and 185th epistles, both cited by Aquinas. Although he does not distinguish between "coercion" and "persecution," Goldie ("Theory of Religious Intolerance," *passim*), provides an excellent discussion of the importance of Luke 14.23 in Restoration England. More generally, see John Kilcullen, *Sincerity and Truth: Essays on Arnauld, Bayle, and Toleration* (Oxford, 1988), especially chapters 2 and 3.

29 See Frank Bate, *The English Indulgence of 1672: A Study in the Rise of Organized Dissent* (London, 1908) – a work that very much needs to be updated – and Richard E. Boyer, *English Declarations of Indulgence, 1687 and 1688* (The Hague, 1968).

30 See in general Spurr, "The Church of England," *passim*.

31 See Gordon Schochet, "John Locke and Religious Toleration," in *The Revolution of 1688–89: Changing Perspectives*, ed. Lois G. Schwoerer, (Cambridge, 1992).

32 For a fuller statement of this claim, see my "Why Should History Matter? Political Theory and the History of Political Discourse," in J. G. A. Pocock, Gordon J. Schochet, and Lois Schwoerer (eds.), *The Varieties of British Political Thought, 1500–1800* (Cambridge, 1993), chapter 10.

33 Specifically P[arker], *The Case of the Church of England*; Samuel Parker, *Religion and Loyalty: Or, A Demonstration of the Power of the Christian Church within It Self* (London, 1684); and Samuel Parker, *Religion and Loyalty: The Second Part* (London, 1685).

34 See for instance Judith N. Shklar, "Facing up to Intellectual Pluralism," in *Political Theory and Social Change*, ed. David Spitz (New York, 1967); and Quentin Skinner, *The Foundations of Modern Political Thought*, 2 vols. (Cambridge, 1978), II, p. 352 *passim*. (Skinner, it is worth noting, seems to use "toleration" and "religious liberty" almost interchangeably. See, for example, II, p. 244.)

35 See in general and for the earlier sixteenth century, Bernard J. Verkamp, *The Indifferent Mean: Adiaphorism and the English Reformation to 1554* (Athens, OH, 1977). There is no comparable work for later periods.

36 [Edward Bagshaw], *The Great Question concerning Things Indifferent in*

Religious Worship (London, 1660), p. 6.

37 The entire tenor of this work is generally taken to vary considerably from Locke's later writings. See Philip Abrams's introduction to his edition of John Locke, *Two Tracts on Government* (Cambridge, 1967), for historical details, an excellent presentation and analysis of the entire question, and the standard interpretation of the *Tracts*. For an interpretation that stresses continuities between this and Locke's later works and minimizes their differences, see Gordon J. Schochet, "Toleration, Revolution, and Judgment in the Development of Locke's Political Thought," *Political Science*, 40 (1988), 84–96.

38 [Parker], "Preface to Bramhall," sigs. b2v–b4r.

39 Edward Stillingfleet, *Irenicum. A Weapon-Salve for the Churches Wounds: Or, The Divine Right of Particular Forms of Church-Government Discussed and Examined* (1661), 2nd edn (London, 1662), preface, sig (a2)r.

40 Ibid., chapter 6.

41 P[arker], *The Case of the Church of England*, p. 243.

42 Ibid., p. 268.

43 [Parker], *Ecclesiastical Politie*, preface, pp. xlii–xliii and lxv. Italics in original.

44 In "Between Lambeth and Leviathan," I argue that while much of his *Ecclesiastical Politie* was an attack on Hobbes's conceptions of natural law and morality, Parker's own conceptions of politics and sovereign authority were at least "Hobbesian" if not drawn directly from the *Leviathan*.

45 [Parker], *Ecclesiastical Politie*, pp. 168–69.

46 [Parker], "Preface to Bramhall," sigs. c7r–c7v. Italics in original.

47 [Parker], *Ecclesiastical Politie*, p. 217.

48 Ibid., p. 105.

49 Ibid., p. 265, chapter title.

50 Ibid., pp. 279, 281.

51 Ibid., pp. 310, 315, 318.

52 A complaint made by [John Owen], *Truth and Innocence Vindicated: In a Survey of a Discourse concerning Ecclesiastical Politie* (London, 1669), p. 88.

53 Thomas Hobbes, *Leviathan: or, The Matter, Forme, and Power of a Commonwealth, Ecclesiastical and Civil* (1651), chapter 29. For Parker's concurrences, see, for example, *Ecclesiastical Politie*, pp. 89–93 and 283–84; and "Preface to Bramhall," sigs. a8v–b1r and d2r–d2v.

For further discussion of this aspect of Hobbes, see Gordon J. Schochet, "Intending (Political) Obligation: Hobbes and the Voluntary Basis of Society," in Mary G. Dietz (ed.), *Thomas Hobbes and Political Theory* (Lawrence, KS, 1991).

54 [Parker], *Reproof*, p. 13.

55 [Parker], "Preface to Bramhall," sig. b1r.

56 [Parker], *Reproof*, p. 32, citing [Owen], *Truth and Innocence*, p. 215.

57 [Owen], *Truth and Innocence*, p. 140, and Marvell, *Rehearsal Transpros'd*, II, pp. 230–31.

58 See [Parker], *Ecclesiastical Politie*, pp. 268-70, 283-84.
59 This was Hobbes's position in the discussion in *Leviathan* (chapter 29) cited above. Locke also made this distinction in his *Two Tracts*, pp. 238–39. Abrams cites Robert Sanderson, *De Obligatione Conscientiae, Praelectiones Decem* (1660), book 6, §§ iv, v, and Jeremy Taylor, *The Liberty of Prophesying, Ductor Dubitantium* (1648), iii, p. i, for parallel statements and as possible sources for Locke.
60 Marvell, *Rehearsal Transpros'd*, ii, pp. 202–203.
61 See [Owen], *Truth and Innocence*, pp. 10 (cf. p. 44), 181, and 244, who complained that Parker reduced religion to morality. This aspect of the dispute is put into context in Dewey D. Wallace, Jr., *Puritans and Predestination: Grace in English Protestant Theology, 1525–1695* (Chapel Hill, 1982), pp. 166–70. See also Rivers, *Reason, Grace, and Sentiment*, i, chapter 3, and Schochet, "Between Lambeth and *Leviathan*."
62 The editor's textual notes to the modern edition of *The Rehearsal Transpros'd* are nearly as overwhelming in this respect as is the text itself.
63 Marvell, *Rehearsal Transpros'd*, i, pp. 6, 47, and ii, p. 214.
64 Ibid., i, pp. 129-30, 133-35, and ii, pp. 223, 313.
65 Cf. John M. Wallace, *Destiny His Choice: The Loyalism of Andrew Marvell* (Cambridge, 1968), pp. 184–207, which is the only extensive analysis of the politics of Marvell's *Rehearsal Transpros'd*.
66 Marvell, *Rehearsal Transpros'd*, ii, pp. 207–209.
67 Ibid., ii, p. 239.
68 Ibid., ii, p. 240. Marvell's conceptualization neatly and intriguingly blended an Aristotelian argument with a constitutionalist doctrine that anticipated Locke's understanding of the way in which the prerogative was limited and his notion of the probability of resistance when things had gone too far.
69 Ibid., ii, p. 242.
70 Locke to Robert Boyle, 12/22 December 1665, *The Correspondence of John Locke*, ed. E. S. de Beer (Oxford, 1976–), i, p. 228. The argument about indifferency in his manuscript essays of 1660–61 had turned, in part, on a belief that people could not live at peace in a world of religious diversity. By 1667, however, he had changed his mind; that year, in an "Essay on Toleration" – which was also unpublished – he argued for a limited degree of religious freedom. His experiences in France seem to have been decisive in framing that new outlook. See Schochet, "Toleration, Revolution, and Judgment," for a full statement of this argument and further references.
71 For general and theoretical discussions see *NOMOS XI: Voluntary Associations*, ed. J. Roland Pennock and John W. Chapman (New York, 1969). Despite its importance the subject does not appear to have generated much scholarship.
72 Text from John Locke, *Epistola de Tolerantia: A Letter on Toleration*, ed. Raymond Klibansky, trans. J. W. Gough (Oxford, 1968), p. 61.

73 For a full statement of the claim that Locke's concern was religious "liberty" rather than "toleration" despite his having talked of the latter, see Schochet, "John Locke and Religious Toleration."

74 See Schochet, "The Act of Toleration and the Failure of Comprehension," and, more generally, "From Persecution to 'Toleration.'" Also relevant is J. W. Martin, "Toleration 1689: England's Recognition of Pluralism," in *Restoration, Ideology, and Revolution*, Proceedings of the Folger Institute Center for the History of British Political Thought, ed. Gordon J. Schochet 4 (Washington, DC, 1990).

75 J. C. D. Clark, *English Society 1688–1832: Ideology, Social Structure and Political Practice During the Ancien Régime* (Cambridge, 1985).

CHAPTER 6

The Societies for the Reformation of Manners: between John Locke and the devil in Augustan England

Shelley Burtt

Over the past several decades historians of political thought have offered quite contrasting accounts of the persistence in eighteenth-century England of an *ancien régime* in church and state, especially as regards the extent and strength of religious orthodoxy. In the 1960s and seventies, most historians placed England's decisive break with *ancien régime* in the events following upon the Glorious Revolution. The repudiation of divine right ideology and the extension of tolerance to Dissenters suggested the demise of the "confessional state," both constitutionally and ideologically. Isaac Kramnick's early work *Bolingbroke and His Circle* is typical of this tendency. The authors he discusses inhabit a largely secular world and are more concerned with matters of finance than of religion. His subtitle, *The Politics of Nostalgia in the Age of Walpole*, implies the conclusion that those defending the old order had already been passed by.[1]

The Pocockian moment in historical scholarship reinforced and extended this view of an *ancien régime* come to grief earlier rather than later in the century's span. Court and country spoke the same language of civic humanism; while those of either party who sought alternative conceptual resources with which to make sense of the postrevolutionary polity turned to an equally secular language of manners and politeness. Religious self-understandings, while occasionally acknowledged, were accorded little enduring significance.[2] During the 1980s a number of revisionist histories have challenged this historical consensus, emphasizing among other things the vitality of both religious and High Tory (even Jacobite) conceptions of political order long past the consolidation of William and Mary's rule. Thus J. C. D. Clark assembles a diverse body of evidence and polemic for "the continued cultural dominance of Anglican and aristocratic ideals and norms" up to the passage of the first Reform Bill. And a more recent monograph emphasizes the religious (if heterodox) character of even republican challenges to England's continued existence as a "Christian confessional state." This body of work argues for a magnificently resilient *ancien régime*, one which held English society in its thrall through the long eighteenth century.[3]

Whether one sees religious and political orthodoxy undermined as early as 1688 or as late as the 1830s, the imagery called to mind by virtually all histories of the period is that of a battle – a battle between new and old, fought by opponents with distinct and antagonistic political, intellectual, and economic allegiances: Anglicans and Dissenters; Tories and Whigs; Jacobites and freethinkers; gentry and merchants. Clark in fact chooses this precise trope as a fitting conclusion to his introductory chapter:

> How such a [aristocratic] social order disintegrated is an underlying theme of this study. Far from the "old society" steadily declining in effectiveness, petering out in bumbling incompetence . . . the *ancien régime* became steadily stronger in its own terms in the half century after the American revolution. Events therefore led to a decisive conflict with those elements in society which brought to the national arena fundamentally different terms of reference. The defeat of the "old society," in and after the events of 1828–32, cannot be pronounced objectively more necessary or more inevitable than the outcome of any other battle; it was no more foreordained than Napoleon's defeat at Waterloo.[4]

In this matter the works of Kramnick and Pocock make common cause with Clark, giving the general impression that the challenge to orthodoxy comes from without.[5] The opposing forces – Anglican uniformity versus Protestant pluralism; aristocratic oligarchy versus egalitarian democracy – square off; each levels its practical and ideological ammunition; the battle is engaged. When the smoke clears one side or the other is victor. Either the forces allied with the *ancien régime* have beaten off (for the moment) the modern renegades, or the heterodox faction has succeeded in putting paid to the outdated designs of the *ancien régime*.

Explaining political or ideological change in this manner involves a particular claim about the beliefs and commitments of the losing side that I am concerned to challenge. To pursue the martial metaphor: in an actual military skirmish or engagement, victory depends on inflicting sufficient losses or injuries on an enemy to bring about withdrawal or surrender. Armies win by killing their opponents, not by converting them. Similarly, historians tend to describe political or ideological change as occurring when representatives of the new order mass sufficient force in the realm of politics or ideas to drive the old guard off the field. The beliefs and commitments of the defeated party remain the same as before, but they no longer possess the same degree of authority or legitimacy.

These images may accurately reflect the historical process at certain dramatic moments of social change. But other moments in history require other metaphors. In particular the image of conflict sketched above tends to obscure the possibility of what might be called "transformation from within." The old, in its effort to meet the challenge of the new, may gradually or rapidly adjust its commitments, its approaches, its concepts and language. It may attempt to coopt the new or sidestep its challenges. In so doing it may prepare the way for, or inch towards, the new order to such an extent that explaining change solely in terms of a "challenge from without" no longer makes sense. As Pocock points out in the opening chapter of this volume, "orthodoxy is not a mere rejection of tensions or an attempt to freeze or deny them; it is a particular way of responding to tensions and seeking to recombine them." While political and religious heterodoxy eventually wins out, we are no longer dealing with simple victory for an upstart and defeat for an old standby. The *ancien régime*, the reigning orthodoxy, is itself implicated in its own demise.

The case of the Societies for Reformation of Manners (SRMs), active in England from about 1690 to 1740, can both clarify this idea of "transformation from within" and give evidence for the existence of this process in eighteenth-century England.[6] The Societies were perhaps the most prominent and controversial arm of what one scholar has called "the moral revolution of 1688," and as such their campaign against public immorality and vice has received a fair amount of scholarly attention. I do not pretend here to add to these studies of the SRMs' structure, ideology and history. What I do want to examine is what the mixed fortunes of this religiously oriented moral reform movement might teach us about the nature and scope of early challenges to England's *ancien régime*. For readers unfamiliar with the organization, I briefly describe the Societies' goals and operation, before turning to the central question of how SRM supporters defended their much-criticized campaign.

Open to Dissenters as well as Anglicans, the Societies broke new ground in what had been, since the Puritan experiment in social control, a largely hortatory effort at moral reform. Contemporary records offer competing accounts of the Societies' origins, although it

now seems clear that the idea of a private, voluntary association
devoted to "promoting the Execution of the Laws, against Prophaneness
and Debauchery" was taken up by a number of different sets of
reformers at once.[7] Although both more energetic and more long-lived
in the capital, the movement for reformation of manners spread,
unevenly, to the provinces as well.[8]

Legislation had long regulated the manners and morals of English
citizens. A 1643 pamphlet, for example, listed sixteen laws useful for
"the better suppressing of unlawful pasttimes, swearing and cursing,
drunkenness, [and] . . . unlawful games."[9] Yet since government
officials had neither the energy nor interest to prosecute such lapses
from virtue, the enjoyment of private vices proceeded apace despite
the law's injunctions. The result was the not infrequent complaint
that "England has the best laws the worst obeyed of any civilized
nation."[10] The Societies for Reformation of Manners were organized
to remove this discrepancy, operating as a sort of citizens' vice squad
to assure the vigorous execution of laws that had, in their opinion, for
too long "lain asleep."

In pursuing this end the SRMs relied on the right of English
subjects to prosecute criminal offenders. By swearing out a warrant
and having the local constable serve it, any citizen could send an
offender before a justice of the peace. The Societies streamlined this
system by printing and distributing packets of blank warrants;
messengers were hired to deliver the completed versions to the
magistrates and follow up on their disposition. In London sympathetic
officials were recruited to give special attention to the SRMs' charges.
With this infrastructure in place the Societies urged their members
"as their leisure should permit, to go out into the streets and markets,
and public places on purpose, and to observe the people's behavior
there." Those who violated both the law and the SRMs' canon of
respectability were to be reported and prosecuted. The Societies
pursued such offenders with enthusiasm, securing the convictions of
almost 100,000 citizens during their forty-year crusade.

The task the Societies set themselves was immense; the range of
behavior they sought to eliminate, daunting. One tract of 1695
condemned "swearing, cursing, drunkenness, revelings, lasciviousness,
whoredoms, riot, gluttony, blasphemies, gamestering, and such-like
wickedness."[11] Another, three years later, targeted a similar list of
unlawful – and immoral – activities: "idleness, profaneness, drunkenness,
houses of unlawful games, profane swearing and cursing, speaking or

acting in contempt of the holy sacrament, disturbing ministers, absenting from church, profanation of the Lord's Day, debauched incontinency, and bastard-getting."[12] But the stakes themselves were high. Consider, for example, the following passage praising

those worthy Persons who . . . have brought so many thousands to Justice, and convicted them of Swearing, Drunkenness, Lewdness, Profanation of the Lord's Day, &c. in order to prevent the Judgments which are so solemnly denounc'd against those Sins . . . By this Means they have very much cleans'd our Streets of the lewd Night-walkers, other publick Places of detestable Gangs of Sodomites, and many Parts of the Town of notorious Bawdy-houses.[13]

This brief text pithily captures the twin concerns of those pursuing moral reform in the manner endorsed by the SRMs. Most importantly, English men and women had urgently to forswear immoral and ungodly behavior or risk punishment by Him whom they thus dishonored. Yet this providential rationale was linked almost seamlessly to a more immediate and direct benefit: public order. The Societies detailed the number and kind of arrests and prosecutions they effected first in irregular "Black Lists" and then in annual "Accounts" appended to SRM sermons. These records allow us to see the focus of their activities. Thus the account published for 1717 showed 1,927 prosecutions for lewd and disorderly practices (the common law offense under which prostitution was punished), 524 for trading on Sundays, 400 for profane swearing and cursing, 33 for keeping bawdy or disorderly houses and 25 for drunkenness. For 1723/24, the figures were: 1,951 for lewd and disorderly practices, 600 for Sunday trading, 108 for profane swearing, 29 for keeping bawdy or disorderly houses, and 12 for drunkenness; the report also indicates that the SRMs assisted in the prosecution of 21 common gamesters and 2 gaming houses. The number of prosecutions dropped precipitously through the 1730s, the "Fortieth Account" for 1732/33 recording only 170 cases of lewd and disorderly practices and 240 sabbath breakers. The "Four and Fortieth Account" set the total number of prosecutions since the inception of the SRMs at 101,683.[14]

From the beginning, the Societies' methods provoked controversy and opposition. The sermons preached on a quarterly basis to the Societies and related pamphlets produced by the Societies' supporters spoke glowingly of the range of benefits to be reaped by a more zealous execution of the laws against vice. But the Societies' plan to accomplish the nation's reformation by bringing petty morals offenders to book elicited only "the furious opposition of Adversaries and neutrality of Friends."[15] High Church Anglicans shunned the organization because of its ecumenical cast; Henry Sacheverell's notorious assizes sermon of 1709, "The Communication of Sin," is perhaps the most perfervid example of High Church obloquy. Low Church clerics, while willing at times to make common cause with Dissenters, worried about the choice of civil courts to pursue an essentially religious reformation (a concern manifest for example in Edmund Gibson's 1713 work on ecclesiastical law).[16] Detractors in both Anglican and dissenting camps accused the Societies not only of intruding impolitically on the populace's "necessary liberties," but also of ignoring the real source of Britain's moral decay: corruption among the nation's political elite.[17] The Societies' annual reports always took care to list the names of peers and bishops who endorsed their efforts. But their plan to promote morality by enforcing England's morals legislation found few enthusiastic supporters outside the intensely religious and moralistic middle class milieu from which most of the Societies' active members were drawn.

This reluctance to endorse the Societies' activities requires explanation. Given the widespread concern for the supposed decline in public and private morality, why *not* support an earnest effort to restore good order, good citizenship, and good morals through the better execution of existing laws? The answer, I think, has to do with an aspect of the Societies' philosophy that receives little attention in the secondary literature. Whether the preferred alternative is a renewed church discipline, better moral examples from the gentry or simply tolerance of the people's foibles, those objections to the Societies' methods are united in disputing the Societies' understanding of how and why the civil magistrate ought to effect moral reformation.

It is possible to argue that here we have a classic case of a "challenge from without," the rout of the old (in this case, a traditional understanding of the civil magistrate as auxiliary church officer) by the new (an understanding of the government's role that drew much sharper lines between the sacred and secular domains). If this account were correct one would expect the Societies to justify their program of prosecution in language reminiscent of the Puritans, characterizing secular authority as working conjointly with spiritual powers to reform sinners, prevent offense to religious morality and generally uphold the church's conception of proper religious and political order. Reformers' difficulties would then follow quite straightforwardly from their attachment to this outdated understanding of the role and responsibility of the civil magistrate. A polity increasingly geared towards facilitating the success of large-scale commercial endeavors, and governed by individuals increasingly attracted by liberal characterizations of state authority, could be expected to resist the effort of religious reformers to recall the state to its traditional role of partner with the church in excoriation of vice.

The reality, I think, is quite a bit more complicated than this hypothetical account suggests. A careful consideration of the arguments used by supporters of the SRMs to defend their program of arrest and prosecution reveals little difference between reformers and their opponents on the crucial question of the nature and scope of the civil magistrate's authority. The problem for the SRMs, then, was not one of doing ideological battle with obsolete weaponry, for they willingly took up the conceptual armory of their opponents. In place of a Puritan vision of political authority in which temporal authorities are pious partners with the church in advancing religious ends, eighteenth-century reformers stressed the explicitly temporal benefits of a moral populace. Most friends of the SRMs defended their enforcement of penal laws against immoral conduct on relatively uncontroversial utilitarian grounds. My argument is that this calculated self-transformation succeeded too well. By defending their moral reform efforts in terms that accorded comfortably with contemporary visions of political authority and responsibility as well as with their own evolving understanding of state power, they invited and received a devastating criticism of their work on purely secular grounds.

To make this case I begin by constructing a rough typology of the differing strategies chosen by moral reform movements, ranged along two axes: institutional affiliation (church or state) and method (coercive or persuasive/regulatory). These categories are deliberately broad. "Institutional affiliation," for example, covers both private, voluntary associations that make use of church or state resources (the Society for Promoting Christian Knowledge [SPCK], for example, or the SRMs) and reforming activity directly sponsored by either church or state (presentments before ecclesiastical courts by church-wardens or a royal proclamation against vice and immorality). The distinction between "coercive" and "persuasive/regulatory" methods is meant to focus attention on the choice for or against a punitive response to immoral behavior. A reformation of manners affiliated with either church or state that chooses *coercive* methods will opt to

Table 6.1.

| Method | Institutional affiliation | |
	Church	State
Persuasive/Regulatory	SPCK	Gin laws
	Charity schools	
Coercive	Ecclesiastical courts	Justice Court (Scotland)
	(Anglican) Scottish kirk	SRMs (England)
	sessions (Presbyterian)	

Note: The examples given are meant to be representative, not comprehensive.

punish individuals for breaking laws meant to establish behavioral norms, enforcing this punishment with the coercive authority of church or state. A "persuasive" method prefers education to incarceration, seeking to accomplish the same end of moral regeneration through preaching, charity, and private moral instruction. By "regulatory" I have in mind laws such as the Gin Acts of 1729 and 1736 that attempt to control a problem in public morals (in this case, drunkenness) through nonpunitive means. As Lee Davison has recently argued, parliament's attempt to reduce gin consumption through prohibitive duties and licensing fees is an example of direct state involvement in moral matters, but it does not qualify as "coercive," as that term is used here.[18]

Using this schema moral reform efforts of the seventeenth and eighteenth century fall into the categories defined in table 6.1.

As table 6.1 indicates, a religiously inspired reformation of manners could pursue its goals in one of two ways. It could disdain the strong arm of the state or church, seeking to effect its ends through less coercive means: education, preaching, private moral instruction and persuasion. Or it could invoke the "terror of the magistrate's sword" and seek a reformation of manners through prosecution and criminal punishment, a strategy chosen by the Puritans of the seventeenth century as well as by the SRMs. (A note on the placement of ecclesiastical courts: since the idea is to enforce behavioral norms by punishing deviance from them, an appeal to church courts involves more than persuasion or regulation. On the other hand by the beginning of the eighteenth century, the sanctions of penance and excommunication were largely symbolic. One could therefore make a case for placing recourse to ecclesiastical courts at the top of the right-hand column of the table.)[19]

The decision to turn to the civil magistrate to effect moral reform could itself be grounded in two ways. On the one hand, reformers could offer a religious or theocentric rationale for using the state's penal laws to enforce religiously inspired behavioral norms. In this view the civil magistrate properly acts as "handmaiden" to the church, punishing the sins of drunkenness, profanity, fornication, and gaming precisely because they are sins, prohibited by God and condemned by the church. Few eighteenth-century reformers absolutely repudiated this theocentric case for the magistrate's role in cultivating virtue. But what I find particularly striking about those writing and preaching in defense of the SRMs is the alternative, secular rationale they give for loosing the state's coercive authority against "the corrupt viciousness of degenerate men."[20]

Certainly the explicit and enthusiastic desire of the SRMs to promote more moral behavior by a strict enforcement of existing morals legislation reminded many wary observers of the unwelcome Puritan regime of the past century.[21] But between the reforming endeavors of the seventeenth century and those of the eighteenth, there was a significant shift in the way this activity was justified. Puritans articulated a cohesive view of church and state in which criminal prosecution of morals offenses was part of a civil magistrate's God-given duty, aimed both at securing the sinner's salvation and at protecting the "community of true believers from contamination."[22] The rationale for reform was essentially religious, directed at achieving a godly commonwealth. Thus, Luther's disciple, Melanchthon, asserted: "worldly power serves above all to enforce the two commandments to maintain morality and peace. It is obliged, with all earnestness, zeal and determination, to punish adultery, incest and impurity contrary to nature, even though these depravations do not concern the peace."[23] The sermons preached to the SRMs defended a similar recourse to the civil magistrate's coercive powers in secular rather than religious terms. Execution of the laws against vice was justified precisely *because* such "depravations" concerned the peace.

I have elsewhere argued that certain distinctive features of seventeenth-century Anglican theology helped to promote this preference for a primarily secular language of justification that emphasized the material and temporal benefits of reformation of manners.[24] Their understanding of sin as lawlessness, the Thomistic heritage of Anglican political theory (which encouraged a distinction between the ends of church and state), the pragmatic cast of Latitudinarian moral theology – all these made it easier for Anglican clerics supportive of the Societies to stress the practical political benefits of a religiously inspired moral reform than for first and second generation Protestants. Recent work on the Societies suggests two other considerations that may have helped to tug Augustan moral reformers away from a strongly religious account of the state's role in moral reform: the concern to reestablish public order and an interest in reviving "primitive Christianity."[25] But, as in my book *Virtue Transformed*, I want here to propose a further factor shaping the nature of the Societies' argument for state involvement in the reformation of manners: the new account of the ends of magistracy gaining ground outside the church.

Following the Revolution of 1688, accounts of the origin and end of civil government increasingly accepted temporal welfare as the primary aim of the political community, citing the protection of individuals' prosperity and safety as the first responsibility of the civil magistrate.[26] Rather than maintain against this view a more theocentric account of the ends of civil society and the responsibilities of the civil magistrate (as responsive above all to God's will), supporters of the SRMs began to shape their case for moral reform to this secularized understanding of the scope of political action. This was true both within and without moral reform societies.

A 1720 sermon by Benjamin Ibbot, Chaplain-in-Ordinary to George I, suggests the extent to which some Anglicans at least embraced this new view of the civil magistrate's role. Ibbot's discussion of the proper province of state authority begins with a Lockean account of the ends of civil government. Since the only reason men "enter into Societies [is] for the mutual Security and Defence of their Person and Proprieties . . . [t]he proper Business of the Magistrate is to preserve the external Peace of the World, and the temporal Good of the Community." As Ibbot goes on to argue, this account of the end of government means that immoral behavior should be publicly prosecuted only if it impinges upon the temporal concerns of the magistrate. Vices "fall under his Cognizance, as they are injurious to Mens Civil Interests, and destructive of the good Order and Government of the World; and not as they have an inherent Turpitude in them." A typical Augustan moralist, Ibbot is confident all "Violations of the Divine Law are also prejudicial to Human Society." Still he insists the magistrate must abstract vices from their status as "Transgressions of the Laws of God" and consider them solely as disruptive political acts. On this basis alone he may punish them. "If the ill Influence which these Vices have upon the Peace and Welfare of Human Society, could be separated from their Immorality . . . the Magistrate could have nothing to do with them."[27]

In accounting for the origin of government without reference to the will of God, Ibbot admittedly outstrips many of the Anglican clergy. Nor, preaching to the Lord Mayor of London on election day, is he specifically concerned to defend the reforming efforts of the SRMs. However in firmly circumscribing the magistrate's role – even in moral matters – to the advancement of temporal interests alone, this sermon suggests the conception of state authority with which even religiously minded moral reformers had to grapple if they were to make a convincing case for using the powers of the civil magistrate to round up and punish offenders against religious morality.

I am not arguing here for a full-blown conversion among Anglican clerics or dissenting ministers to the most radical or controversial elements of Lockean social contract theory. Rather, I am suggesting in its account of the ends of political society and the proper role of the civil magistrate (although not necessarily in its account of contract and rebellion), that Locke's *Second Treatise* gave sophisticated philosophical expression to a view of government to which more and more persons in Augustan England were attracted. In defending the prosecution of moral offenders, both lay and religious supporters of the SRMs appealed to political conceptions of this sort rather than the theocentric accounts of the civil magistrate's role prevalent among Puritan moral reformers. When Daniel Williams, for example, argued that a reformation of manners was "the surest way to revive our Trade, prolong our Peace, and recover England's glory," he offered purely temporal reasons for pursuing the fundamentally religious task of reforming sinners.[28] Another reformation of manners booster admitted, "If ungodly Persons did hurt only themselves, there might be some pretext for indulging, and conniving, at them." Compare this suggestion that the civil magistrate's authority might not extend to correcting purely private immoral behavior with Melanchthon's explicitly theocentric account of temporal laws. Fortunately (for the SRMs), this minister concludes confidently, "but the case is otherwise, they do a real harm to the Community, of which they are Members."[29] On this thoroughly modern, Millian basis, moral offenders might be informed upon and punished.

John Disney's scholarly compendium *A View of Antient Laws against Immorality and Prophaneness* (1729) provides an especially good example of this newly secular cast in the reforming divines' arguments. Disney, a onetime justice of the peace, devoted much of his efforts to the moral reform movement, although he was never explicitly associated with the SRMs. The first sentence of the book's introduction states plainly his rationale for reformation.

If Impiety or Vice were to be considered only with regard to their Consequences in another World, it might be tolerable to leave it to Mens private Reflexion, and to the care of Divines . . . but since they affect the *public* and *present*, as well as *personal* and *future* Interests of Mankind, 'tis fit the Civil Authority should exert itself, in a way of Coercion to suppress such practices.[30]

Disney then proceeds to demonstrate the "public and present" interests at stake in every form of immoral behavior from blasphemy to drunkenness and sodomy. Most eighteenth-century jurists condemned profanity and sabbath breaking as offenses against God, a category that in itself explained their criminalization. Even in this case, Disney offers primarily secular reasons to justify laws against such behavior.

There's a political reason too . . . to preserve the Honour of the Lord's Day; for Atheism would soon be the Consequence of a general Neglect of it, and Barbarism would not be far behind. . . . The political Reason, why Magistrates are highly concerned to suppress Common Swearing, is, that it naturally leads to Perjury; which is destructive to the Safety, and all the Interests of Mankind.[31]

Disney sets out the dangers of most other vices in the same way. While drunkenness "is a Sin by the Law of God . . . the Arguments most proper here are of another kind; drawn from the vice itself, and the ill consequences of it [personal and political] in this life."[32] Disney's account of why immoral behavior deserves criminalization thus emphasizes its impact on the temporal welfare of society. Although the impulse behind his hefty folio volume, detailing the morals legislation enacted by past civilizations, is broadly religious, the arguments he advances to support his aims are not. They represent rather an effort to show that "the end of Government being the general Safety, Good Order, and Prosperity of the Subjects, there can be no just and careful Government . . . without care for the Suppression of Vice."[33] Other proponents of moral reform followed

Disney in staking their case for the reformation of manners on the claim that the cultivation of personal morality was a "Matter of human Policy."[34]

This was true even in the way SRM supporters talked about what seemed to them the very real possibility of providential punishment leveled at their sinful nation. As Richard Smalbroke explained, the vicious "contribute to the Ruine of their Country" in two ways: "both by the natural Consequences of their Vices and by provoking God to send down his Judgements on a sinful Nation."[35] This concern with God's righteous wrath drew on the familiar Christian teaching that, although God balanced an individual's moral account in the afterlife, governments paid for the toleration of their citizens' sins within human history. Seventeenth-century cries for reform and repentance made much of the imminence of this cosmic justice, warning of God's impending judgment on a covenanted nation.[36] But Smalbroke and his compatriots shared none of these millenarian expectations. Instead they used the possibility of national judgment to appeal to the magistrate's temporal priorities, arguing that there is "not a Maxim more just in any Politicks [than that] Profanity and Debauchery are the worst Enemies to a State." The reason: "the Prosperity of States and Kingdoms depends entirely upon the Favour of . . . God . . . and that therefore a profound Contempt of Him . . . Lewdness and other Vices, suffered without Restraint, draw down the divine Judgments upon them."[37] Ministers thus cast even the prospect of divine retribution as a secular concern, making it a matter of political expediency to punish citizens' lapses from virtue.

In sermon after sermon, then, ministers supportive of the SRMs claimed that the civil magistrate had a responsibility, indeed an obligation, to enforce religious standards of moral behavior – not only or merely on the basis of Biblical accounts of God's will, but as a consequence of the magistrate's primary civil duty: the maintenance of temporal peace and order. They contended that the promotion of popular morality served the explicitly temporal interest of English society and, for *this* reason, lay well within the legislative province of the civil authority. George Smyth's sermon summarizes this approach to the magistrate's authority in moral matters. "Vice and Immorality are faulty every way . . . offensive to God, Prejudicial to the Sinner's Personal Interests, and Injurious to Society . . . [But it is] upon this latter Account principally, if not only, that they are punished by the civil Magistrate; and that you are justifiable in Detecting and

Informing against them."[38] Or, as another minister had it, vice and immorality "may and ought to be restrained by the Magistrate's Coercive Power . . . because they have an evil Aspect upon Civil Government."[39]

Other sermons to the Societies rely on secular arguments to defend the SRMs' work. Matthew Heynes argues: "The Immoralities of a Nation strike at that society which Government was design'd to cement . . . it necessarily follows, that the Reasons of Government, even in its Original Design, require that open Vices and Immoralities, should be restrained." Samuel Smith concurs: although Christianity provides no "Precedent for enforcing Religion by the Civil Sword," the magistrate may still suppress sin given his "prior Engagements . . . to advance the common Welfare for Vice, if suffer'd to spread . . . will soon bring on a total Dissolution of any form of government."[40] Richard Smalbroke goes farther than most in suggesting a political rationale for suppressing sodomy: "But as the Good of Society is the particular care of the Magistrate, whatever has a direct tendency to lessen the Number of Subjects, and to weaken and dishonour the Government . . . falls under his immediate Cognizance."[41]

The discussion so far suggests the following conclusion. Stalwarts of the moral reform movement in the early eighteenth century almost certainly valued the Societies' activities for specifically religious reasons. They might even have believed that it was as much the business of the state as of the church to make citizens more godly, less sinful. But as Ibbot's sermon illustrates, both lay and religious audiences were increasingly unlikely to understand the magistrate's role in these religious terms. To the extent the moral reformers wanted a convincing justification for using the coercive authority of the state to advance the reformation of manners, they needed to find other grounds for public action. So they turned to the argument that reformation of manners served ends which everyone could agree were politically appropriate: the protection of life, liberty, property, prosperity, and order.

But this strategic decision had important and ironic consequences. Adopting the newly secularized language of Augustan politics in the service of orthodox religious ends, the reformers found themselves trapped, one might say, between John Locke and the devil. In establishing a link between religious codes of personal morality and the public good, the SRMs sought to ground their case for moral reform in a political goal agreeable to the devout and skeptical alike: furthering the temporal welfare of the state. But this effort to strengthen their case actually exposed their assumptions to an empirical scrutiny harsher than they could bear. While hardly anyone would think to challenge the ministers' claim for the sinfulness of, say, prostitution, all sorts of people could and did dispute the argument that whipping prostitutes and jailing drunkards substantially advanced the commonweal.

Perhaps the most notorious attack against the SRMs' efforts came in Henry Sacheverell's 1709 assizes sermon, "The Communication of Sin." Labeling moral reformers as "troublesome Wasps," he criticized their determination to punish public immorality as "the unwarranted Effects of an Idle, Incroaching, Impertinent, and Medling Curiosity . . . the base Product of Ill-Nature, Spiritual Pride, Censoriousness and sanctified Spleen." Sacheverell's complaints were prompted primarily by the Societies' tolerance of Dissenters among their ranks. Like most High Church clerics, Sacheverell considered the correction, not accommodation, of such schismatics to be the first step in the restoration of moral order. However he chose to frame his attack on the Societies in political rather than religious terms: reformers' activities "arrogantly intrench upon Other's Christian Liberty, and Innocence," and interfere with "our Neighbor's Proceedings, that don't belong to us."[42] Such criticisms bluntly reject the Societies' contention that the cultivation of personal morality makes an important contribution to national welfare. Those truly concerned about the morals of Englishmen and the welfare of the community would prod Dissenters back into the Anglican communion.

Clerics supporting the SRMs had to admit that not even the justices of the peace (the officials charged with enforcing morals legislation) saw the profound political dangers of personal immorality. "'Tis shocking," complained one minister, "to hear such a one [a local magistrate] say, with an Air of Indifference, 'tis but Swearing, but Drunkenness, but Sabbath-breaking, and ranging them under the Head of Necessary Liberties, which the common People must be allowed."[43] Yet reformers invited just this response by suggesting that the reformation of manners be pursued precisely for its public benefits. If the Societies had continued to justify their cause as did earlier reformers – in terms of the magistrate's religious responsibility to exterminate vice, or his right to correct moral failings regardless of their public impact – then the contention that immoral behavior must be tolerated as "Necessary Liberties" would have lost much of its force as a convincing rejoinder.

Although differences in temperament, religion, and political allegiance usually put Daniel Defoe and Jonathan Swift on opposite sides of any social issue, these two authors respond in a remarkably similar way to the SRMs' reforming campaign. Thus Jonathan Swift, in *The Advancement of Religion and Reformation of Manners* (1709), dismisses the SRMs as "factious Clubs . . . grown a Trade to enrich little knavish Informers." Far more effective and lasting moral reform would come, Swift argues, were the government to draw men to a personal and public virtue through the persuasion of political and economic patronage. The queen herself should begin this transformation by establishing "Piety and Virtue . . . [as] Qualifications necessary to Preferment," seeing that her deputies and subordinates do likewise. By requiring good moral character of all potential employees, the queen and her court can make it in "every Man's Interest and Honour to cultivate Religion and Virtue."[44]

Like Swift, Daniel Defoe mocks the reforming pretensions of the Societies for Reformation of Manners, although with a more pronounced concern for the organization's class bias. "They were Zealous against the poor Drury Lane Ladies of Pleasure; and the Smithfield Players and Poets were sensible of their Resentments . . . but Cheating, Bribery and Oppression found no zealous Reformer." To secure its safety and welfare, Great Britain needs a reformation not in "private Vices . . . [but] in the Public and Political Vices of a People . . . Avarice, blind Ambition and Luxury."[45] As with Swift, the key to moral reform lies in "examples, not penalties."[46] Securing the reformation of leading citizens would remove the need to "push on the Laws" against their social inferiors. Since a remoralized gentry would seek out only sober and honest friends and employees, "Interest and Good Manners would Reform us of the poorer sort."[47] Neither Defoe nor Swift disagreed with the Societies' claim that the nation's welfare depended importantly on a reformation of its citizens. But this common conception did not translate, for either author, into support for the SRM's particular policies. Policing of the poor's morals simply did not count for them as an effective method of national regeneration.

Even more devastating in its application of the Societies' logic is Bernard Mandeville's caustic satire *A Modest Defence of Publick Stews* (1724), which is dedicated to "the Gentlemen of the Societies." In this work Mandeville uses the moral reformers' own utilitarian principles to argue for the establishment of state-run brothels. Setting up cheap, clean and accessible bordellos would "prevent most of the mischievous

Effects of this Vice, [and] even lessen the Quantity of Whoring in general."[48] Properly regulated, public brothels would prevent theft and other crimes related to prostitution, end the spread of venereal diseases, and assure the safety of bastard infants. They would spare men the financial expenses of maintaining private mistresses, and by satisfying men's natural urges, protect the wives and daughters of the upper classes from seduction and debauchery.[49] Thus "few or none of [these Evils attributed to prostitution] are the necessary Effects of Whoring consider'd in itself, but only proceed from the Abuse and ill Management of it."[50] From the standpoint of public welfare, a judicious accommodation of the business of prostitution makes as much if not more sense than a program of prosecution. Mandeville, then, is the extreme example of contemporary critics of the SRMs who meet and best the Societies on their own ground.

Mandeville's rhetorical triumph neatly illustrates the dilemma that confronted the supporters of the SRMs. On the one hand, these individuals made a genuine effort to justify their program of moral reformation in a way that fitted contemporary sensibilities. On the other hand by framing their case for the coercive enforcement of personal morality in pragmatic, political terms, the Societies initiated a debate that they would ultimately lose. Critics like Defoe, Swift, and Sacheverell all too willingly challenged their claim that punishing individual lapses in personal morality made a valuable contribution to the nation's welfare. I think we can now see the problem with any effort to explain the failure of the Augustan moral reform movement by reference to some sort of face-off between old (religiously oriented views of the civil magistrate) and new (more secular worldviews). Far from adhering rigidly to increasingly outdated notions of political authority and moral virtue, the SRMs made a genuine effort to engage the modern concerns of their coreligionists, to update their arguments for moral reform for contemporary consumption. This effort should not be seen as hypocritical or disingenuous, but rather as a salutary effort to adapt to changing political circumstances, one prefigured institutionally by their ecumenical membership. But while the SRMs' persuasives spoke properly to the concerns of the modern polity, these arguments shifted the terms of public debate in a way that actually disadvantaged their reform proposals.

Since rehashing traditional theocentric rationales for the reformation of manners would not have made political sense, moral reformers emphasized the secular advantages of their program. This shift from a religious to a political rationale was intended to shore up the old order by finding a new, more convincing way of validating the traditional involvement of the civil magistrate in the enforcement of religious standards of personal morality. But instead it had the unintended consequence of hastening the demise of the *ancien régime* – helping to legitimate the modern Lockean assumption that temporal benefit rather than spiritual welfare should be the only measure of the legitimacy of the civil magistrate's acts.

To return to the problem of the images we use to make sense of political and ideological change. The experience of the Societies suggests that instead of, or along with, a "challenge from without" to traditional modes of thought and political action, we have a "transformation from within," a process whereby an old order is itself implicated in the transition to the new. The grounds on which the claims of the Societies were ultimately rejected – that reformation of manners served above all temporal welfare – were chosen first of all by the Societies' supporters themselves.

NOTES

1 Isaac Kramnick, *Bolingbroke and His Circle: The Politics of Nostalgia in the Age of Walpole* (Cambridge, MA, 1968). See also, among others, J. P. Kenyon, *Revolution Principles: The Philosophy of Party, 1689–1720* (Cambridge, 1977); H. T. Dickinson, *Liberty and Property: Political Ideology in Eighteenth-Century Britain* (New York, 1977); Reed Browning, *Political and Constitutional Ideas of the Court Whigs* (Baton Rouge, 1982) and most recently, Isaac Kramnick, *Republicanism and Bourgeois Radicalism: Political Ideology in Late Eighteenth-Century England and America* (Ithaca, 1990).

2 See especially the later chapters of J. G. A. Pocock's *The Machiavellian Moment: Florentine Political Thought and the Atlantic Republican Tradition* (Princeton, 1975); "Early Modern Capitalism: the Augustan Perception," in Eugene Kamenka and R. S. Neale (eds.), *Feudalism, Capitalism and Beyond* (Canberra, 1975); and *Virtue, Commerce, and History: Essays on Political Thought and History, Chiefly in the Eighteenth Century* (Cambridge, 1985). On politeness, see also Lawrence Klein, *Shaftesbury and the Culture of Politeness: Moral Discourse and Cultural Politics in Early Eighteenth-Century England* (Cambridge, 1994).

3 J. C. D. Clark, *English Society, 1688–1832: Ideology, Social Structure and Political Practice During the Ancien Régime* (Cambridge, 1985), p. 77; J. A. I. Champion, *The Pillars of Priestcraft Shaken: The Church of England and its Enemies, 1660–1730* (Cambridge, 1992), p. 7. See, also, Linda Colley, *In Defiance of Oligarchy: The Tory Party, 1714–60* (Cambridge, 1982); and for a critical assessment of the revisionist claims, J. Innes, "Jonathan Clark,

Social History and England's '*Ancien Régime*,'" *Past and Present*, 115 (1987). Champion, chapter 1, provides a useful review of the literature.

4 Clark, *English Society*, p. 7.

5 This is less true of Pocock's recent work; see, especially, the chapter in this volume.

6 Much of the material that follows appears in somewhat different form and context in Shelley Burtt, *Virtue Transformed: Political Argument in England, 1688–1740* (Cambridge, 1992), chapter 3.

7 Francis Grant (Lord Cullen), *A Brief Account of the Nature, Rise, and Progress of the Societies, for Reformation of Manners* (Edinburgh, 1700), p. 8. On the Societies' genesis and membership, see especially Robert B. Shoemaker, "Reforming the City: The Reformation of Manners Campaign in London, 1690–1738," in Lee Davison et al. (eds.), *Stilling the Grumbling Hive: The Response to Social and Economic Problems in England, 1689–1750* (New York, 1992).

8 See, most recently, Mary E. Fissell, "Charity Universal? Institutions and Moral Reform in Eighteenth-Century Bristol," in Davison et al., *Stilling the Grumbling Hive*; and T. C. Curtis and W. A. Speck, "The Societies for the Reformation of Manners: A Case Study in the Theory and Practice of Moral Reform," *Literature and History* 3 (1976), 45–64.

9 *A Collection of Certain Statutes in force . . . for the better Caution of such as are inclinable to Delinquency* (London, 1643).

10 John Heylyn, *A Sermon Preached to the Societies for Reformation of Manners . . .* (London, 1721). See also Edward Fowler, Bishop of Gloucester, *A Vindication of a Late Undertaking of Certain Gentlemen, In Order to the Suppressing of Debauchery, and Profaneness* (London, 1692) for similar sentiments.

11 *Proposals for a National Reformation of Manners* (London, 1695).

12 George Meriton, *Immorality, Debauchery and Profaneness Exposed to the Reproof of Scripture and the Censure of the Law* (London, 1698).

13 From the *Observator*, November 12–16, 1709, cited in William Bragg Ewald, *Rogues, Royalty and Reporters: The Age of Queen Anne Through Its Newspapers* (Westport, CT, 1978), p. 136.

14 These figures are found respectively in Thomas Hayley, *A Sermon Preach'd to the Societies for Reformation of Manners* (London, 1718); Edward Chandler, *A Sermon Preach'd to the Societies for Reformation of Manners* (London, 1724); Robert Drew, *A Sermon Preach'd to the Societies for Reformation of Manners* (London, 1735); and Samuel Smith, *A Sermon Preach'd to the Societies for Reformation of Manners* (London, 1738).

15 Grant, *Brief Account*, p. 8.

16 Edmund Gibson, *Codex Juris Ecclesiastici Anglicani* (London, 1713).

17 Prominent examples of criticism of this sort come from both Jonathan Swift, *A Project for the Advancement of Religion and the Reformation of Manners* (1709) in Herbert Davis et al. (eds.), *The Prose Works of Jonathan Swift*; and Daniel Defoe, *Poor Man's Plea to all the Proclamations, Declarations, Acts*

of Parliament, etc. . . . .for a Reformation of Manners (London, 1698). The reference to "necessary liberties" is from Thomas Newman, *Reformation, or Mockery . . . A Sermon Preach'd to the Societies for Reformation of Manners at Salter's Hall* (London, 1729), p. 28.

18 Lee Davison, "Experiments in the Social Regulation of Industry: Gin Legislation, 1729–1751" in Davison et al., *Stilling the Grumbling Hive*.

19 On the decline of ecclesiastical courts, see John Addy, *Sin and Society in the Seventeenth Century* (London, 1989), chapter 14, as well as The Reverend M. G. Smith, *Pastoral Discipline and the Church Courts: The Hexham Court, 1680–1730* (York, 1982). For more on the Scottish examples, see Gordon DesBrisay, "Fornication, Illegitimacy and Godly Discipline in the Early Modern Scottish Town," unpublished paper, 1991.

20 Thomas, Earl of Stamford, *Speech at the General Quarter-Sessions Held at Leicester* (London, 1691).

21 Tina Isaacs, "The Anglican Hierarchy and the Reformation of Manners, 1688–1738," *Journal of Ecclesiastical History*, 33 (1982), 391–411.

22 Patrick Collinson, *The Elizabethan Puritan Movement* (London, 1967), p. 40.

23 Philip Melanchthon, *Selected Writings*, ed. E. E. Flack and Lowell Satre, trans. C. L. Hill (Minneapolis, MN, 1962), p. 335.

24 See Burtt, *Virtue Transformed*, pp. 53–57.

25 See respectively, Shoemaker, "Reforming the City" and Fissell, "Charity Universal?" both in Davison et al. *Stilling the Grumbling Hive*.

26 See for example the primary and secondary works cited in Richard Ashcraft and M. M. Goldsmith, "Locke, Revolution Principles, and the Formation of Whig ideology," *The Historical Journal* 26 (1983), 773–800. Of course, to say these themes were increasingly present is not to say they predominated.

27 Benjamin Ibbot, *The Nature and Extent of the Office of the Civil Magistrate* (London, 1720), pp. 4–7.

28 Daniel Williams, *A Sermon Preach'd at Salter's Hall to the Societies for Reformation of Manners* (London, 1698), p. 53.

29 John Spademan, *A Sermon Preach'd November 14, 1698 and Now Publish'd at the Request of the Societies for Reformation of Manners* (London, 1699), p. 36.

30 John Disney, *A View of Antient Laws against Immorality and Profaneness* (Cambridge, 1729), p. i.

31 Ibid., pp. 234, 198. On the political danger of profanity see also Gilbert Burnet, *Charitable Reproof. A Sermon Preached to the Societies for Reformation of Manners* (London, 1700), p. 22; M[atthew] Heynes, *A Sermon for Reformation of Manners, Preach'd . . . at the Assizes* (London, 1701), p. 13; Edward Cobden, *The Duty and Reward of Turning Others to Righteousness. A Sermon Preach'd to the Societies for Reformation of Manners* (London, 1736), p. 17.

32 Disney, *View of Antient Laws*, p. 257.

33 Ibid., p. iii.

34 George Stanhope, *The Duty of Juries. A Sermon Preach'd at the Lent-Assizes, holden at Maidstone, in Kent* (London, 1703), p. 13.

35 Richard Smalbroke, *Reformation Necessary to Prevent our Ruine. A Sermon Preach'd to the Societies for Reformation of Manners* (London, 1728), p. 6.

36 John Wilson, *Pulpit in Parliament: Puritanism during the English Civil War, 1640–48* (Princeton, 1969), pp. 199–200; William Lamont, *Godly Rule: Politics and Religion, 1603–1660* (London, 1969), chapter 4.

37 *A Representation of the State of the Societies for Reformation of Manners, Humbly Offered to his Majesty* (London, 1715), p. 4. For similar fears, see Spademan, *Sermon* ("Wicked men are certainly Enemies to the public Good by provoking God to withdraw his protection"); Samuel Freeman, *A Sermon Preach'd at the Assizes, held at Northampton* (London, 1690); Edward Calamy, *A Sermon Preach'd to the Societies for Reformation of Manners* ... (London, 1699); Fowler, *Sermon*; William Colnett, *A Sermon Preach'd to the Societies for Reformation of Manners* (London, 1711); Joseph Rawson, *Righteousness the Exaltation, and Sin the Reproach of a People. In a Sermon Preach'd at the Lent Assizes* (London, 1714), p. 8; Thomas Coxe, *A Sermon Preach'd at the Assizes held at Bedford* (Oxford, 1730).

38 George Smyth, *A Sermon Preach'd at Salter's Hall to the Societies for Reformation of Manners* (London, 1727), p. 12.

39 Thomas Troughear, *The Magistrate's Duty to Honour God, Set Forth in a Sermon Preach'd at Southampton* (Oxford, 1733), p. 14.

40 Heynes, *Sermon*, p. 6 and Smith, *Sermon*, pp. 15–16.

41 Smalbroke, *Reformation Necessary*, p. 22.

42 Henry Sacheverell, *The Communication of Sin. A Sermon Preach'd at the Assizes held at Derby* (London, 1709), pp. 20–21, 15, 20, 21. This account of the SRMs' critics closely follows Burtt, *Virtue Transformed*, pp. 58–62.

43 Newman, *Reformation*, p. 28.

44 Jonathan Swift, *A Project for the Advancement of Religion and Reformation of Manners* (1709), reprinted in Herbert Davis et al. (eds.), *The Prose Works of Jonathan Swift*, II, pp. 57, 48, 47.

45 Daniel Defoe, *Les Soupirs de la Grande Britaigne: Or, the Groans of Great Britain* (London, 1713), pp. 14, 15.

46 Daniel Defoe, *An Essay upon Projects* (London, 1697), p. 4.

47 Defoe, *Poor Man's Plea*, pp. 23, 24.

48 Bernard Mandeville, *A Modest Defence of Publick Stews* (1724), ed. Richard I. Cook (Los Angeles, 1973), p. 11.

49 Ibid., pp. 17–22, 25, 26, 50–1.

50 Ibid., p. 6.

CHAPTER 7

Irony as subversion: Thomas Woolston and the crime of wit

Roger D. Lund

As the first work of British philosophy to fully exploit the subversive potential of irony and ridicule, Hobbes's *Leviathan* was also the first to be reviled for a brilliance of style and subtlety of wit that made it seem virtually "unanswerable."[1] Deists and freethinkers were quick to find in *Leviathan* a rhetorical model for their own assaults on priestcraft and political tyranny, abandoning more conventional modes of argumentation for the strategic indirection of irony and wit. The adaptation of irony to the demands of religious and philosophical controversy inspired the systematic defense of ridicule as a test of truth given its most memorable form in Shaftesbury's *Essay on the Freedom of Wit and Humor* (1708) and Anthony Collins's *Discourse of Irony and Wit in Writing* (1729). The efflorescence of heterodox wit also elicited angry rejoinders from critics as various as Lord Clarendon, Richard Blackmore, and Mary Astell, all of whom recognized the power of wit to undermine orthodox assumptions.[2]

Treatments of eighteenth-century wit have been limited almost exclusively to discussions of its aesthetic significance, but as we shall see, much of the critical and philosophical debate over the "decorum" of Augustan ridicule disguised a much more fundamental struggle over the very means by which power was to be defended or assailed. This chapter briefly traces the process by which wit first came to be associated with heterodox assaults on established institutions of religion and government, and recounts subsequent attempts to proscribe all forms of rhetorical indirection, including ridicule, innuendo, and wit, as essentially subversive modes of discourse. I focus on the case of Thomas Woolston, whose conviction for blasphemous libel in 1729 crystalized the conflict between orthodox power and heterodox wit, a case in which not the matter of the argument but the witty manner of its presentation provided the grounds for legal prosecution.

I

Responding to the challenge of *Leviathan*, Isaac Barrow was one of the first who attempted to define the appropriate limits on jesting, a resolution that seemed

especially needful in . . . (this pleasant and jocular age,) which is so infinitely addicted to this sort of speaking, that it scarce doth affect or prize any thing near so much; all reputation appearing now to vail and stoop to that of being a wit. . . Many at least, to purchase this glory, to be deemed admirable in this faculty, and enrolled among the wits, do not only make shipwreck of conscience, abandon virtue, and forfeit all pretences to wisdom; but neglect their estates, and prostitute their honour.[3]

Over the next half century Barrow's complaints regarding the dangers of unrestrained wit would be elaborated and embellished by a variety of writers, all of whom shared the settled conviction that as modes of argumentation or philosophical discussion, wit and ridicule were fundamentally unfair, inherently impious, and uniquely dangerous. To quote Joseph Glanvill, "Philosophy can shame, and disable all the reasons that can be urged against it . . . jests and loud laughter are not to be confuted; and yet these are of more force to degrade a thing in the esteem of some sort of spirits, than the most potent demonstration."[4] Glanvill's response to Hobbes finds an echo in William Warburton's riposte to Shaftesbury: "RIDICULE having from the hands of a skillful disputant, the same effect in barbarous minds, with the new invented darts of Marius, which, though so weak as to break in the throw, and pierce no farther than the surface, yet sticking there, they more intangle and incommode the combatant, than those arms, which fly stronger, and strike deeper."[5]

Although otherwise an ill-matched pair, Glanvill and Warburton share one fundamental certainty: that ridicule is inherently more dangerous than reasoned argument. The implications of such logic were as far-reaching as they were seductive: since the liberty of wit led inevitably to witty libertinism, wit, irony, and ridicule were rhetorical forms that called for suppression, by violence if necessary. For Jeremy Collier, that stalwart champion of theatrical probity, witty writing was simply too dangerous to be tolerated, in part because wit had become the hallmark of the atheistical libertine. "One would think Atheism and Lewdness were some very useful Discoveries," he writes, since "they are so carefully cultivated and improved. With what Magnificence of Art are these Things set off? With what affecting

Ideas, points of Wit, and pompous Descriptions? As if it was a glorious Exploit to sap the Foundations of Justice, to strike at the Vitals of Religion, and Debase Mankind into Brutes." Collier's diagnosis is common enough; his prescription is not. For he recommends that nothing short of the outright cultivation of dullness can indemnify the age against the dangers of atheistical wit:

What then; must fine Thoughts be stifled, and all the range of Fancy check'd? Is not this to cramp our Understandings, and impose Dullness on the World? Yes, such Restraints without question are great Grievances: If a Man did not Murther now and then, he might possibly forget the Uses of his Weapon. Well, if Sense be so ill Natur'd a Quality, I wish we had less on't. What if some People have Wit? Must we therefore have no Religion, must the Scriptures be ill Treated, the noblest Professions ridiculed, and the Dignity of Things made an Argument for Contempt? . . . To be Museridden at this rate is somewhat hard. If these Outrages are repeated, we must think of reprisals.[6]

Modern scholars have often dismissed Collier as a pious crackpot, but his apprehensions as to the dangers of wit were widely shared, as were his calls for official reprisal. Decrying the flood of "Socinian books and pamphlets" that appeared upon the lapse of the Licensing Act in 1695, the Convocation of the Church of England complained bitterly that

Books [previously] written, in an argumentative way, against the Divinity of our blessed Lord, did, in a little time, produce others of a worse spirit and Tendency; wherein the Doctrines, by him reveal'd, were Spoken of with Profane Levity and Contempt, his Humiliation and Sufferings were derided, his Person was blasphem'd, and treated with as Great Indignity and Scorn, as when he stood at the Judgment Seat of Pilate.[7]

Like Collier or Glanvill, the Convocation asserts the necessary relationship between heterodox ideas and the "profane levity" that had come to mark heterodox style. They indicate as well their growing conviction that where philosophical or theological arguments were concerned, the rules of engagement had somehow been altered by the introduction of wit.

Writers like Blount and Shaftesbury celebrated the change, defending the role of ridicule and wit in serious discourse and denying that wit was a legitimate cause for official concern.[8] But they were oddities in an age when Collier and the Convocation seemingly defined popular frustration with the misuses of wit. As one might expect, the most strident demands for legal action against licentious and heterodox writers came from those High Churchmen who controlled the Lower House of Convocation. But even Dissenters like Defoe argued that something needed to be done, so great was the threat of libertine wit. "'Twould be endless to examine the Liberty taken by the Men of Wit in the World," he writes, "the loose they give themselves in Print, at Religion, at Government, at Scandal; the prodigious looseness of the Pen, in broaching new Opinions in Religion, as well as in Politicks, are real Scandals to the Nation, and well deserve a Regulation."[9]

Regulation perhaps, but of what sort? Merely restoring the Licensing Act (a proposal forwarded by some) was clearly no answer, since it served only to censor those who were out of power.[10] And yet, there was a widespread feeling something needed to be done to suppress rhetoric that defied open and direct refutation. As a result defenders of the faith resorted to increasingly strident, if frequently ill-focused, demands that the civil authorities prosecute witty and heretical writers whom they were seemingly unable to confute directly. While few clergymen were as bloodthirsty as Charles Leslie, who suggested that execution was the only appropriate punishment for witty blasphemy, there was general agreement that the government needed to intervene in some fashion to punish those modern infidels who now sat in the seat of the scorner.[11]

In the course of the seventeenth century charges of outright blasphemy (with its embarrassing reminders of the *auto-da-fé*) had gradually given way to trials for seditious or blasphemous libel. Successful prosecution of "contumelious reproaches" against God or the established church seemed far more likely once blasphemous wit had been redefined as a form of sedition that somehow threatened to undermine the foundations of the constitution itself.[12] Such linkage of religious ridicule with presumptive political subversion was one product of a growing concern that the government's "good name should be maintained, and that the limits of legitimate criticism should be drawn within a narrow compass."[13] Still smarting from his own misadventures with irony in the *Shortest Way With Dissenters*, Defoe would write: "Governments will not be jested with, nor reflected upon, nor is it fit that they should always lye at the mercy of every pen."[14] During the trial of John Tutchin in 1704 Chief Justice Holt argued: "if people should not be called to account for possessing the people with an ill opinion of government, no government can exist."[15] In other words ridiculing the government or its officers made

it contemptible in the eyes of the people and as such weakened its
authority. It was an easy step to extend such logic to the ridicule of
divine government as well. In Barrow's terms ridicule

proportionably groweth more criminal, as it presumeth to reach persons
eminent in dignity or worth, unto whom special veneration is appropriate.
. . . It is not only injustice, but profaneness to abuse the gods . . . their defects
are not to be seen, or not to be touched by malicious or wanton wits, by
spiteful or scornful tongues; the diminution of their credit is a public
mischief, and the state itself doth suffer in their becoming objects of scorn.[16]

Barrow gives voice to an increasingly popular argument that the
ridicule of religion was a threat to government as well. Since bishops
and clergymen were in effect officers of the crown, ridicule of the
clergy was also a libellous assault on the very foundations of the
constitution. Legal precedent had been clearly established in *Rex* v.
Taylor [1675] (27 Car. 2.), a case in which Justice Hale had argued
"that *Christianity* is Parcel of the Laws of *England*; and therefore to
reproach the *Christian Religion*, is to speak in Subversion of the Law."[17]
The Taylor case significantly expanded the prerogatives of the
criminal courts. It was a decision by which "the court of the King's
Bench invented a new crime," establishing the precedent that "the
common law had jurisdiction over the expression of unorthodox
religious opinion,"[18] a precedent that was to have profound implications
for the trial of Thomas Woolston. Indeed the equation of the
established version of Christianity with the English constitution itself
would serve clerical defenders of various kinds of official persecution.
Warburton argues that the abuse of the clergy of the sort found in
Tindal's *Rights of the Christian Church* and *Christianity as Old as the
Creation* is "not only an affront to Religion . . . but likewise, an insult to
civil liberty. For while there is such a thing as a Church established by
law, its Ministers must need bear a sacred, that is, a public character
. . . to abuse them, therefore, as a body is insulting the State which
protects them."[19]

Of course had it been the case that those guilty of religious ridicule
were *actually* undermining the stability of the government, penalties
for treason might have been more appropriate. Such an argument
had been advanced by Sir George Mackenzie, Supreme Justice of the
Scottish criminal courts, who in 1678 had defined blasphemy as
"divine lease majesty, or Treason," a decision that eased the process
by which Thomas Aikenhead was tried and executed for blasphemy

in 1698. Characteristically the legal arguments asserting Aikenhead's guilt stressed his "scoffing, ridiculing, railing against and cursing the Bible."[20] However, nettled as they were by the outburst of Socinian pamphleteering that marked the 1690s, even the most vindictive of prelates south of the Tweed were hesitant to demand the ultimate penalty for scoffing at religion, choosing instead to prosecute heterodox texts as forms of seditious or blasphemous libel, a charge sufficiently amorphous to include works of wit. Originally the province of the Star Chamber, responsibility for ferreting out seditious and blasphemous libels after the Restoration devolved variously on the Stationers' Company, the Houses of Parliament and the courts of common law, most notably the court of the King's Bench.[21] The common law courts assumed the jurisdiction of the Star Chamber as a "censor morum," punishing indecency, ribaldry, and blasphemy. The common law courts also assumed the jurisdiction of the ecclesiastical courts and punished the publication of heterodox ideas as tending to sedition and as undermining the "foundations of the Christian faith."[22]

The publication of Matthew Tindal's *Rights of the Christian Church Asserted* (1706) reignited the controversy over attempts to suppress wit through civil prosecution. Tindal was vilified as one of those "Libertines" who had attacked the clergy with "the most scurrilous Contempt and scornful Disdain that Profane Wit and Malice could invent." And he was instantly linked with writers like Blount and Toland, whose works were "fullest of Scandalous Reflections and Profane, Scornful, Impious, Blasphemous Revilings of the Blessed Son of God Christ Jesus and his Religion."[23] Like his fellow deists Tindal was condemned as a wit whose works cried out for civil prosecution specifically because of their "contumelious" character. Although his book was presented to the Middlesex grand jury and attempts were made to prosecute those who sold the *Second Defence* of the *Rights*, Tindal remained largely unmolested by the secular arm.[24] While the Convocation of the Church of England sought to censure Toland's *Christianity Not Mysterious* (1696), they found themselves constitutionally incapable of censuring any book without license from the king, a license that was never forthcoming.[25] Traditionally, public burning had been the punishment reserved for outrageously heterodox texts like Blount's *Two First Books of Philostratus* (1680) and Arthur Bury's *The Naked Gospel* (1690), and it was a fate meted out to a variety of works in the eighteenth century.[26] As a means of limiting the spread of heterodox wit, however, public burning proved less than perfect. In 1720 a committee of the House of Lords found Joseph Hall's antitrinitarian tract *A Sober Reply to Mr. Higgs' Merry Arguments*, "a mixture of the most scandalous Blasphemy, Profaneness, and Obscenity; [which] does, in a most daring, impious Manner, ridicule the Doctrine of the Trinity, and all Revealed Religion," and consigned it to the flames. Ironically, burning books often served as a form of advertisement, and two days after Hall's book was burned by the common hangman a complaint was made that "a great Number of Books, the same with that ordered to be burnt Yesterday, were dispersed and publickly sold in Westminster Hall, and other Places."[27]

II

While the record for successful prosecution of heterodox works was uneven at best, the threat of civil punishment was nonetheless sufficient to convince many writers that their survival depended on the perfection of a new form of indirect and ironic discourse custom-made to undermine established pieties in religion and government while frustrating the prosecutorial zeal of those determined to eliminate such indirect attacks.[28] Paradoxically, the more assiduously authorities sought to eradicate irony and wit as modes of public criticism, the more firmly entrenched those modes became. Some, like the licenser Sir Roger L'Estrange, argued that forcing heterodox writers to resort to innuendo and witty indirection was actually a good thing. Because they are expressed in a more cautious vein, he argues, modern pamphlets have in fact been rendered less dangerous than controversial works published during the Interregnum. From the standpoint of spreading the gospel of sedition,

the *Old Ones* have a great Advantage of the *New*; for being Written in times of *Freedom*, and Menag'd [*sic*] by great *Masters* of the Popular Stile, they speak *playner*, and stike *homer* to the *Capacity* and *Humour* of the *Multitude*; whereas they that write in the fear of a *Law*, are forc'd to cover their Meaning under *Ambiguities*, and *Hints*, to the greater Hazzard of the *Libeller* than of the *Publique*.[29]

For L'Estrange this was a great step forward, but for heterodox writers themselves, the necessity to encode their arguments was a fact to be lamented. Blount mordantly remarks: "'Tis a thing of most Dangerous Consequence to Oppose any Doctrine that is publickly receiv'd, how sottish soever it be." Although Blount had quite cheerfully roasted a glebe-full of sacred cows, beneath his bravado one detects a real fear that "it might fare with me as it did with poor *Esop*, Who . . . only speaking against Priests of *Delphos*, cost him his Life." At one point he recommends the five-year silence of Apollonius. "Words make all men our Enemies, and none but Fools our Friends; therefore, *Vir sapit, qui pauca loquitur*. He that makes others afraid of his wit, ought himself to be afraid of their memory; for as much as I have known many men, who (though they could not break a jest) could break a head."[30] Blount was not alone. As John Toland remarks, "Daily experience sufficiently evinces, that there is no discovering, at least no declaring of TRUTH in most places, but at the hazard of a man's reputation, imployment, or life."[31] Toland complains that "Such is the deplorable Condition of our Age, that a Man dares not openly and directly own what he thinks of Divine Matters . . . if it but very slightly differs from what is receiv'd by any Party, or that is establish'd by Law; but he is either forc'd to keep perpetual Silence, or to propose his Sentiments to the World by way of Paradox under a borrow'd or fictitious Name."[32]

In response to this state of affairs Toland worked out an elaborate rhetoric of encoding and indirection, subdivided into esoteric and exoteric forms – esoteric writing directed to the initiated, exoteric designed for public consumption. Shaftesbury had predicted that such esotericism would become necessary, pointing out that such strategies of indirection were the natural by-products of political repression:

If men are forbid to speak their minds seriously on certain subjects, they will do it ironically. If they are forbid to speak at all upon such subjects, or if they find it really dangerous to do so, they will then redouble their disguise, involve themselves in mysteriousness, and talk so as hardly to be understood, or at least not plainly interpreted by those who are disposed to do them a mischief.[33]

Even Warburton, no supporter of Shaftesbury's defense of ridicule, nonetheless agrees that "a RESTRAINT on free inquiry, will force writers into this vicious manner . . . the only way men have to escape persecution being to cover and intrench themselves in obscurity."[34]

Reviewing this controversy from mid-century, Philip Skelton remarks that the deists' claims of persecution were grossly overstated, as was their defense of disguise, irony, and innuendo. "If you will believe them," he writes, "they are under a necessity of using stratagem and cunning for these purposes, to prevent the prosecutions to which an opener conduct might expose them in this age of bigotry." Skelton falls back on a familiar tautology: that deists and freethinkers resorted to rhetorical subterfuge not because they had been forced to do so, but because their arguments would not bear exposure. If they would only argue in an open, decent and manly fashion, Skelton argues, deists and freethinkers would be answered with equivalent civility.[35] Writers like Toland were not convinced. "Nay, I have read of invitations to Heretics, Deists, and Atheists, to speak above-board; and heard it much lamented, that the books of such were formerly destroy'd, or that they are not suffer'd now to write; because Truth wou'd thereby triumph the more, and these unfortunate men be the more easily reclaim'd." Now, he argues, "if it be a desirable thing to have the Truth told without disguize, there's one method to procure such a blessing. *Let all men freely speak what they think, without being ever branded or punish'd but for wicked practises, and leaving their speculative opinions to be confuted or approv'd by whoever pleases; then you are sure to hear the whole truth, and till then but very scantily, or obscurely, if at all.*"[36] Skelton blithely ignores the force of such arguments: "I can hardly think of a jury capable of frightening these souls of the first magnitude," he writes, "for not one in ten of them hath been ever prosecuted at law for his book; and such as were, made twice as much by the retail of their counterband wares, as they lost by the prosecution."[37]

Thomas Woolston, of course, was that "one in ten," first prosecuted for his *Moderator Between An Infidel and An Apostate* (1725) and then again for *Six Discourses of the Miracles of Our Saviour* (1727–30). Woolston portrays himself as a writer forced to employ irony and innuendo and he evinces great sympathy for writers like Anthony Collins, whose *Discourse on the Grounds and Reasons of the Christian Religion* (1724) and *Scheme of Literal Prophecy Considered* (1726) were currently under attack. "I was afraid the Prosecution of the *Moderator*, would have deterr'd you from the Press," Woolston writes of Collins. "Go on then . . . and if you are deny'd the Liberty of the Press, and public Sale of your Books, I hope you'll for all that, as occasion offers it self, oblige the Learned and Curious with some more of your bright Lucubrations, tho' you print them, and dispose of them in this clancular and subtil Method."[38]

This "clancular and subtil Method" posed unique problems for those attempting somehow to discourage such works through legal prosecution. For whatever the venue, parliament or King's Bench, trials for libel increasingly turned on questions of how ironic or indirect argument was to be treated by the court. What had begun with Glanvill and Barrow as an attempt to establish the decorum of wit and ridicule, had become by the early eighteenth century a struggle to define indirect or encoded discourse in such a way that it might be successfully prosecuted. According to *A Digest of the Law Concerning Libels*, "It seems to be now agreed, that not only Scandal expressed in an open and direct manner, but also such as is expressed in Irony amounts to a Libel."[39] Another anonymous jurist cites a case under James I, tried in Star Chamber, in which it was established that "ironical Words in Writing, are adjudged libellous; open and sarcastical Reproaches, are allowed, on all Hands to be so. Nothing then remains which may by any Possibility evade the Law, but Writing in *Allegory*, or . . . *Descriptions and Circumlocutions.*"[40]

The truth of Glanvill's warning about the irrefutability of jests and loud laughter grew increasingly evident as attorneys for the crown struggled to demonstrate the presence of an actionable irony in the descriptions and circumlocutions of heterodox texts. How was a prosecutor, or a jury for that matter, to determine what was actually meant by particular veiled references in a controversial pamphlet? How were they to determine whether irony was actually present? Whether the works under indictment seemingly attacked the settled principles of Anglican Christianity or British government, prosecutors found themselves uncomfortably circumscribed by the hermeneutic circle. Everyone presumably "knew" what innuendos meant, but how was one to prove that such meanings necessarily inhered in particular utterances, or that they were even intended by the author? In the Sacheverell trial, for example, many of whose arguments turned on such questions of interpretation, Sergeant Parker, one of Sacheverell's accusers, complained of the difficulty of unraveling indirect rhetoric that everyone understood intuitively, but whose meaning was not otherwise demonstrable.

This is an extraordinary step, that, let a Man cause never so many scandals and reproaches on the government, though in never so public a manner, yet if it be done by way of suggestion and insinuation, and the charges not expressly maintained and avowed, there is no crime in it, nor any high one: That is, in short, sedition and exposing the Government is lawful; only the manner is to be taken Care of. Do not do it directly and avowedly, for that would be dangerous; but do it by suggestions that every body will

Understand, and which will have their full Effect, and all's safe; for those who come to judge you are not to understand you, though every body else does.[41]

As we shall see it was precisely the question of the *manner* of presentation that would prove so damning in the Woolston case.

However tangled such interpretive knots might appear, they were presumably not beyond the ingenuity of the court to untie. Indeed, argues the author of *State Law*, it is within the power of the court to penetrate those veiled suggestions that "everybody understands" and thus determine the true intention of the author.

From the Reasons of Law, a Libel in Hieroglyphicks, is as much a Libel, and as highly punishable, as an open Invective. If it be really unintelligible to any one, it will pass for Nonsense with every one, and, as such, meet with Impunity; But if there be only a thin Veil, or aukward Disguise thrown over it, thro' which those who can see and observe may perceive the lurking Satyr within, a Court of Law will examine it narrowly, and judge of it according to the Intention of the Maker, and the Influence it may have upon the injured Party's Reputation.[42]

This version of the court's prerogative, that it had the power to expose the "lurking Satyr within" esoterically encoded discourse, was by no means adopted unanimously, however. Critics of attempts to prosecute libellous innuendo pointed out that it set a dangerous precedent when officers of the court were allowed to become juridical interpreters of literary texts. Archibald Hutcheson writes that "all the senses clapt upon all heathen authors by their scholiasts, and all the tenets charg'd upon the Inspired Writings by Dutch commentators, were not so wild, absurd, and arbitrary, as what the single force of an innuendo can fix upon any passage, when play'd *secundum artem*, in the hands of a nice state empirick."[43] The *British Journal* argues that any prosecution based upon the interpretation of ironic innuendo poses a greater hazard to British liberty than anything (no matter how offensive) the writer might suggest. "When words used in their true and proper sense, and understood in their literal and natural meaning, import nothing that is criminal, then to strain their genuine signification to make them intend sedition . . . is such a stretch of discretionary power, as must subvert all the principles of free government, and overturn every species of liberty."[44] The problem of determining an author's meaning was further clouded by the effort to divine his intentions. Theoretically, authorial intention was not relevant to one's guilt or innocence of the charge of libel. But as *State*

Law makes clear, the court might well seek to demonstrate the "lurking Satyr within" an allegedly libellous text by presuming to elucidate the intentions of its author.[45]

III

In a legal climate supercharged with fears of esoteric and hermetic meanings in heterodox texts it was perhaps no accident that Thomas Woolston would be tried for blasphemous libel. Certainly no work of eighteenth-century heterodoxy was more custom-tailored to test the patience and ingenuity of the court than was Woolston's *Six Discourses of the Miracles of our Saviour* (1727–30). At the level of literal exegesis, Woolston argues that "the History of *Jesus's* Life, as recorded in the *Evangelists*, is an emblematic Representation of his spiritual Life in the Soul of Man; and his Miracles are Figures of his mysterious Operations. The four Gospels are in no Part a literal Story, but a System or mystical Philosophy of Theology" (I, p. 65). In practice, however, Woolston's tracts provide an unrelenting burlesque of the Scriptural account of Jesus' miracles. His sober protestations notwithstanding, Woolston's true intentions seemed clear, and such intentions were radical enough to

prove that the literal Story of many of *Jesus's* Miracles, as they are recorded in the *Evangelists*, and commonly believed by Christians, does imply Improbabilities and Incredulities, and the grossest Absurdities, very dishonourable to the Name of Christ; consequently, they, in whole, or in part, were never wrought, but are only related as prophetical and parabolical Narratives of what would be mysteriously and more wonderfully done by him. (I, pp. 19–20)

Woolston's paradoxical defense of Christ's Messianic authenticity – by debunking his miracles – struck his critics as completely disingenuous. Indeed, so telling is Woolston's irony that even a hardened old agnostic like Leslie Stephen dismisses him as a "mere buffoon jingling his cap and bells in a sacred shrine."[46] Woolston certainly dons an antic disposition. He remarks that gold, frankincense, and myrrh were no proper gifts for either Mary or her child, arguing that if they had brought soap, candles, and sugar instead, the Magi had acted "as wise as well as good Men" (I, p. 56). Such irreverence was bad enough, but worse still was the fact that most of Woolston's allegorical readings of Scriptural miracles involved ridicule of the church and its hireling clergy. Thus Woolston's version of Christ's cleansing of the temple becomes an allegory of the corruptions of the Anglican priesthood. Even the woman with an issue of blood (described by Woolston as a possible nosebleed!) becomes an emblem of the diseases of the church. Worst of all, Christ himself is treated with a witty familiarity that strays well beyond the boundaries of decorum. Woolston's comparison of Jesus on the Mount of Transfiguration with a theatrical "*Posture-Master*," transforming himself into a "Calf, a Lyon, a Bear, a Ram, a Goat, an Hydra, a Stone, a Tree etc." (I, p. 42), simply beggared rational refutation.[47]

One might multiply instances of Woolston's wit, but his version of the story of the Gadarene swine will serve by way of example. Woolston raises numerous questions about Jesus' presumed transference of a legion of devils to a herd of swine, which, according to him, wouldn't have been in the neighborhood in the first place.

If any Historians but the *Evangelists* had said so, none would have believed it. The *Jews* are forbidden to eat Swine's Flesh; what then should they do with Swine . . . who eat neither *Pig, Pork*, nor *Bacon?* Some may say that they were kept there for Use of Strangers: but this could not be; because that after Time of *Antiochus*, who polluted the Temple with the Sacrifice of an Hog, the *Jews* forbad, under the Pain of an *Anathema*, the keeping of any *Swine* in their Country. Perhaps it may be said, that the *Gadarens*, so call'd from the Place of their Abode, were not *Jews*, but neighbouring *Gentiles*, with whom it was lawful to eat, and keep *Swine*. We will suppose so, tho it is improbable; but then its unlikely (without better Reason than at present we are apprised of) that our Saviour would permit the Devils to enter into a Herd of them to their Destruction. (I, pp. 33–34)

According to the church Jesus' miracles were all said to be innocent, but where was the goodness of this miracle; what was the use of it? "The Proprietors of the Swine were great Losers and Sufferers; and we don't read that *Jesus* made them amends, or that they deserv'd such Usage from him" (I, p. 34). At the very least, Woolston suggests, the Gadarenes might well have sued Christ for damages – and collected.

I know not what our *Divines* think of this Part of the Story, nor wherefore Jesus escaped so well; but if any *Exorcist* in this our Age and Nation, had pretended to expel the Devil out of one possess'd, and permitted him to enter into a Flock of Sheep, the People would have said that he had bewitch'd both; and our Laws and Judges too of the last Age, would have made him to swing for it. (I, pp. 34–35)

Whatever its exegetical merits, Woolston's offhand suggestion – that in the real world Christ would have been hanged for sheepstealing and witchcraft – was guaranteed to offend his readers, and he knew it.

Although Woolston suffered throughout his life from varying degrees of madness, there can be no question that he understood exactly how his works would be received.[48]

The reading of this Head will, I doubt not, strike with Horror some of our squeamish *Divines*, who, notwithstanding they will sacrifice almost any Principles to their Interest, will not bear that our literal evangelical History of such renown'd Miracles should be thus called in Question, and contemptuously spoken of. What does this *Author* mean, will some say, thus to do Service to Atheism and Infidelity? Away with him! Our Indignation is moved against him! NO Censure and Punishment can be too severe for such Impiety, Profaneness, and Blasphemy, as is aim'd at, and imply'd in this Proposition. (I, p. 20)

Although Woolston was himself an ordained priest of the Church of England, this was hardly the language of one seeking merely to clarify vexed and obscure passages of Scripture. Woolston all but sticks his tongue out at the "little *Whisslers* in Divinity" (Defence, p. 3), dedicating each of the individual *Discourses* to one of the bishops who had attacked him: "Use me as roughly in Print as you think fit, I'll not take it ill. . . . I desire nothing more than to be furiously attack'd from the Press, which, if I am not much mistaken, would give me a long'd for Opportunity to expose your Ignorance to more Advantage" (I, pp. 64, 65).

No other heterodox writer went out of his way so to provoke prosecution as did Thomas Woolston. And there is clarity in his purpose, a design to force his critics either to accept his literal argument or to prosecute him on grounds derived largely from an ironic interpretation of his text. Woolston got his wish; he was set upon by such clerics as Edmund Gibson, Bishop of London, who found "the *Blasphemous Manner* in which [Woolston] has taken the liberty to treat our Saviour's Miracles and the Author of them" an epitome of all that was most dangerous in heterodox wit. Gibson wishes to make it clear that it is not the substance of Woolston's argument that offends, however, but the style. "I am far from contending, that the Grounds of the Christian Religion, and the Doctrines of it, may not be discussed at all times, in a calm, decent, and serious way," Gibson remarks. And he reiterates the common assertion that all Christian practices and beliefs are open to discussion;

indeed so powerful and self-evident is the case for Christianity that such discussion must necessarily strengthen the orthodox position. Still, he draws the line at ridicule, and "cannot but think it the Duty of the Civil Magistrate at all times, to take care that Religion be not treated either in a *ludicrous*, or a *reproachful* manner."[49]

Matthew Tindal responded immediately to the glaring contradictions in Gibson's argument. Can the Bishop, he asks, "be for punishing a Person, whom he dares not say is in his right Senses, as a Blasphemer, only for the Manner of expressing himself, where the Matter may be lawfully discuss'd?"[50] Tindal points out that were Gibson consistent, he should have thanked Woolston for providing an occasion for Christianity to triumph yet again over the specious assertions of heterodox wits. And he points out the dubious legality of Gibson's insistence that Woolston be punished for the style, not the substance of his argument.

Since the Crime of this Clergyman wholly consists, not *in discussing the Miracles of our Saviour* (for *That,* 'tis granted, *helps to strengthen Christianity*;) but in the Manner of doing it; by which he can only have prejudic'd his own Cause, and not That of Christianity; ought not this *Writer* to have shewn, how That can make the Doing a lawful Thing become not only unlawful, but even blasphemous?[51]

Tindal's argument goes to the heart of the matter. And no one who recommended the prosecution of heterodox wit ever answered his question regarding the miraculous transformation by which the superaddition of a particular rhetorical form could somehow turn an acceptable argument into an actionable offense.

Such subtleties were wasted on Bishop Gibson, who insisted that the civil magistrate prevent all offenses against Christian sensibility, that he effectually "discourage such Books and Writings, as strike equally at the Foundation of all Religion, and of Truth, Virtue, Seriousness, and good Manners; and by consequence, at the Foundation of Civil Society."[52] One might reasonably question a recommendation that the magistrate punish breaches of "good manners," yet such was the panic engendered by heterodox wit that otherwise reasonable persons lost all sense of proportion in the face of it. As Tindal points out, Gibson was asking for nothing less than the prosecution of writers for violations of decorum! Anthony Collins, who was equally sensitive to the sweeping implications of this argument, points out the difficulty that must attend any effort to legislate style or manners.

When you draw up your Law, you will find it so very difficult to settle the Point of *Decency* in Writing, in respect to all the various kinds of *Irony* and *Ridicule*, that you will be ready to lay aside your Project; and that you will be no more able to settle that *Point of Decency*, than you would be to settle by Law, that *Cleanliness* in Clothes, and that Politeness in Dress, Behaviour, and Conversation, which become Men of Quality and Fortune in the World.

Collins immediately recognizes the ideological agenda at the heart of calls to legislate decorum, suggesting that even if you could determine what constituted a legal standard for good manners, "you will find it very difficult to engage the Lawmakers in your Project. For I am persuaded, that if our Lawmakers were, out of a rational Principle, disposed to give Liberty by Law to a *serious* Opposition to publickly receiv'd Notions, they would not think it of much Importance to make a Law about a Method of *Irony*."[53]

But that is precisely what was called for by critics like Richard Smalbroke, Bishop of St. David's (translated to Lichfield and Coventry in 1731), who sought to "invigorate the Zeal of the Magistrate, in putting the laws in Execution against so flagrant a sort of Profaneness . . . and to convince the World that the *Minister* of that *God*, who is so highly Affronted, *bears not the Sword in vain*."[54] Here Smalbroke performs the rhetorical hat trick so common to Anglican clerics of the age, simultaneously insisting that ridiculing the church is affronting God directly, that affronting God is endangering the civil polity, and that demanding prosecution is in no wise an infringement of the English liberty from which that polity derived. Of course, no one calling for the suppression of heterodox texts or the punishment of Woolston ever confessed to a persecutorial motive. Instead, they attempted to redefine irony and ridicule as rhetorical modes fundamentally unlike other forms of argumentation and therefore susceptible to peculiar penalties. Like Gibson, Smalbroke is more than willing to consider the objections against Christianity "when proposed with Decency, or indeed with Indecency in the Present Instance." But he "cannot be induced to think that there is no real Difference between Arguments and buffoonery, or that licentious Invectives against the Founder of our Religion, and a professed Ridicule of those *Miracles* that Confirm the Truth of it, are any part of the *Liberties* of a *Christian* Nation, or are the only Libels that are not Cognizable by a *Christian* Magistracy."[55] So pernicious is ridicule that its very presence signals wicked intentions. To quote Bishop Gibson: "*When you meet with any Book upon the Subject of Religion, that is written in a ludicrous or unserious manner; take it for granted that it proceeds from a* deprav'd *mind, and is written with an irreligious design."*[56] If another of his gentle critics is to be credited, Woolston's wit was like the mark of Cain: an invitation to persecution. "If I am grosser in my Expressions, than seems consistent with Christianity, or good Manners," he argues, "let the Provocation be considered: He can have no Claim to civil Treatment, who runs so foul a Riot on God and Men; and as he has divested himself of all Consideration and Respect of Persons, there can be no Terms too severe for so abominable a Fellow."[57]

There was a specious charm in such arguments that allowed clerics like Gibson and Smalbroke simply to dismiss Woolston's rights as an Englishman since he had apparently resigned those rights when he chose to be witty. Smalbroke is pleased to explain in detail why punishment for wit ought to be considered fundamentally unlike other forms of prosecution. He argues that Woolston

has, with other Patrons of an *Unbounded* Liberty, so far abused the true and Legal Notion of Liberty, as to introduce a *Licentiousness* . . . a Liberty to be avowedly Profane and Irreligious, to Deride whatever is Sacred, and blasphemously to Revile the Founder of the Religion which is Professed and Established in these Your Kingdoms: A sort of Liberty, that is so great an Insult on the National Settlement, as to make it evident to all Unprejudiced Persons that *Liberty* itself ought to have its just Bounds, in order to render it a Blessing to Mankind.[58]

Smalbroke argues that since the true ends of government require an established religion, and since established religion becomes thereby part of the constitution, all attempts to bring contempt on that religion promote "the Disturbance of the Peace."[59] Such is the process, then, by which religious ideology comes to be translated into law; such is the curious chain of argument by which Woolston's admittedly ludicrous treatment of Scriptural miracles is transformed into a criminal denial of the Act of Settlement.

Of all those clerics who weighed in for the Woolston bout, only Simon Browne was willing to argue that the civil magistrate had no business interfering in cases of religious ridicule. Unlike Shaftesbury, however, Browne makes no case for ridicule as a test of truth. Rather he shrugs it off as an irritating but essentially harmless misuse of rhetoric. He agrees with Gibson and Smalbroke "that there is a vast difference between . . . *ludicrous insult* and *scurrilous invective*, and *grave reasonings* and *manly decent talk*." Yet he is not convinced that laughing at religion does it any "real harm," or that religion be made "*absurd* and *ridiculous*, by senseless cavils, empty jests, and rude invective."[60] Browne is contemptuous of the argument that Woolston's ridicule of religion somehow threatened the constitution. "*Magistrates* may indeed think their *wisdom* affronted, and *their authority* despised, who have thought meet to profess and countenance this religion, if it be reproached; and may resent this, and by prosecutions shew their resentment; but this is really a meer *human concern* for their own honour, not a *Christian concern* for the honour of *Jesus's* religion." In fact, Browne argues, magistrates are not directly affronted at all, but only "by *implication* and *innuendo*, as far as the reproach of the religion they profess and countenance, involved *theirs* in it."[61]

Browne was spitting against the wind, for Woolston's enemies would argue that implication and innuendo were affronts in themselves that could only be controlled with civil prosecution. Upon the publication of Woolston's *Fifth Discourse*, Secretary of State Townshend (with the gentle coaxing of Bishop Gibson?) signed a warrant for Woolston's arrest. And on March 4, 1729 he stood trial at Guildhall on charges of blasphemous libel.[62] Woolston was convicted and sentenced to a year's imprisonment, with a fine of £100 (£25 for each of the four *Discourses* under indictment) and "then to continue in prison for life unless he himself should be bound in a recognizance for £2000, and two others for £1000 each, or four for £500 each, with condition for his good behaviour during life."[63] Given the nature of the offense, such penalties were stiff indeed. But if they were intended to insure Woolston's silence – one function of the heavy bond requirements – they failed miserably. While in prison, Woolston produced yet another *Discourse* and two *Defenses* of what he had already written.

Woolston was certainly incorrigible, his *Discourses* undeniably offensive to most sensibilities, but it was necessary to argue that he was dangerous as well. The facts in the case were not in dispute, since Woolston readily admitted to having written the *Discourses*. And when counsel attempted to move in arrest of judgment in the court of King's Bench, Chief Justice Raymond answered that the court "would not suffer it to be debated, whether to write against Christianity in general was not an offence punishable in the temporal courts."[64] Citing the precedent of *Rex* v. *Taylor* (1675), Raymond reminded Woolston's counsel that "Christianity is a parcel of the common law of England . . . now, whatever strikes at the very root of Christianity, tends manifestly to the dissolution of civil government."[65]

As the trial proceeded Attorney General Yorke argued that the *Discourses of the Miracles of Our Saviour* was "the most Blasphemous Book that ever was Publish'd in any Age whatsoever, in which our Saviour is compared to a Conjurer, Magician and Imposture, and the Holy Ghost, as wrote by the Blessed Evangelists, turn'd into Ridicule and Ludicrous Banter."[66] The defense responded that the *Discourses* revealed no such intention. Indeed the outcome of the trial turned on the question of whether or not Woolston had actually *intended* to ridicule the Gospels. Mr. Birch, Woolston's counsel, said "He should not dispute that Mr. Woolston did publish this Book, but he could not agree it was done with a Blasphemous Intent, to bring our Religion into Contempt, but to put Our Religion upon a better Footing, and shew, That the Miracles of Our Saviour were to be understood in a Metaphorical Sense, and not as they were Literally Written." Birch was answered that "If Mr. Woolston's Intent was to do so, he would not have turn'd the Miracles of Our Saviour into Ridicule, and Proceeded in so Ludicrous a Manner, as he has done, but to have endeavour'd to prove, They were not to be taken as they are Litterally Wrote, by a Serious Discourse and Sound Argument."[67] The Attorney General's argument seems to echo the sentiments of Bishop Gibson, that heterodox writing was acceptable only if pursued in a sober and genteel fashion. The court having accepted the argument that ridicule was itself proof of depraved intent, Woolston's conviction rested largely on the construction of his irony, and innuendo. Had it been concluded that he was indeed serious about his attempts to put religion on a better footing, Woolston would have been vindicated. But as the prosecution argued, the mere fact of their being witty was prima facie evidence of the libellous intent of Woolston's *Discourses*. This is certainly the construction that Woolston himself placed upon his conviction. As Henry Stebbing, one of Woolston's critics, recounts the trial, Woolston was "prosecuted, he tells us, for the *Style and Strain of his Writings*, that is, I suppose, for burlesquing and ridiculing the Miracles of our Blessed Saviour."[68]

Woolston was absolutely right; the court had responded to calls for a peculiar vengeance like those issued by Bishop Smalbroke, who argued that such is the threat posed by ironic discourse, that it ought to be answered with the most draconian penalties. "And tho' all such Attempts, whether *Serious* or *ludicrous*, are punishable by Common-Law," argues Smalbroke, "yet they are not, as is pretended by Mr. W. all *equally* punishable; since *Ludicrous* Attempts of that kind, and especially as attended with those that are *Serious*, which explain the Design of the *Ridicule*, carry with them a greater *Contempt* of the Authority of the *Constitution*, and therefore *a fortiori* Demand a proportionable Punishment."[69] In other words, because they pose a more serious threat to the constitution, witty libels deserve more severe punishment than do libels presented in a more sober fashion.

If nothing else, Woolston's conviction offered a clear warning to other heterodox writers that ridicule and burlesque would not be tolerated.[70] Although prosecutions for blasphemous libel were infrequent for the rest of the eighteenth century, they tended to follow the precedents laid down with the Woolston case. Indeed by the first decade of the nineteenth century it had become a settled conclusion that "blasphemy against the Deity in general, or attack upon the Christian religion individually, for the purpose of exposing its doctrines to contempt and ridicule, is indictable."[71] In 1841 a Royal Commission claimed that "all the recorded instances of prosecution for blasphemy, subsequent to Woolston's case, have been publications of indecent and opprobrious language." As a result all sentences were based "entirely upon the offensive *manner* of writing."[72] We begin in the seventeenth century with the argument that jests and loud laughter are not to be confuted and conclude with a legal consensus that religious ridicule is a fit object for civil prosecution. So threatening was wit that the preservation of orthodoxy required not only the control of heterodox ideas but the proscription of the rhetorical modes in which those ideas were embodied. While the Augustans may have released the genie of wit, they found it more difficult to restrain him when he proved unruly or even dangerous. But, the argument went, if you couldn't coax the genie back in the lamp, at least you could try to put him in jail, which is where, in 1733, Thomas Woolston died.[73]

NOTES

1 The phrase is that of John Dowel, *The Leviathan Heretical* (1683), but of the contemporary attacks on *Leviathan* listed in the bibliography to S. I. Mintz's *The Hunting of Leviathan* (Cambridge, 1962), some two dozen pamphlets complain of Hobbes's wit, ambiguity, trickery, and entrapment.
2 See Mary Astell, *Bartlemy Fair; Or, An Enquiry After Wit* (1709). Richard Blackmore, *A Satyr Against Wit* (1700). Edward Hyde, Earl of Clarendon, *A Brief View and Survey of the Dangerous and Pernicious Errors to the Church and State in Mr. Hobbes's Book Entitled Leviathan* (1676).
3 Isaac Barrow, "Against Foolish Talking and Jesting," (1678) in *The*

Theological Works of Isaac Barrow, D. D., ed. Alexander Napier, 9 vols. (Cambridge, 1859), II, p. 3.

4 Joseph Glanvill, *A Blow at Modern Sadducism in Some Philosophical Considerations About Witchcraft* (London, 1668), p. 152.

5 William Warburton, "To the Free-Thinkers," *The Divine Legation of Moses*, rptd. In *The Works of the Right Reverend William Warburton*, 7 vols. (London, 1788), I, pp. x–xi.

6 Jeremy Collier, *Miscellanies Upon Moral Subjects, The Second Part* (London, 1695), epistle dedicatory.

7 *Representation of the Present State of Religion with Regard to the Late Excessive Growth of Infidelity, Heresy, and Profaneness* (London, 1711), p. 4.

8 On Shaftesbury's defense of wit, see A. O. Aldridge, "Shaftesbury and the Test of Truth," *PMLA*, 60 (1945), 129–56. Charles Blount had preceded Shaftesbury in his insistence that wit and ridicule ought not to be censored. Blount argues, for example, that he cannot find any censorship among the ancients. "Neither do we read of any Decree against the Satyrical sharpness of *Lucilius, Catullus, or Flaccus.*" Indeed as if meeting the enemy on his own terms, Blount denies the common argument that the sentence of death against Socrates was facilitated because Aristophanes had first made him ridiculous. "We do not find amongst the Greeks, that their *Vetus Comedia* (which was so much censured for Libelling and Traducing Men by Name as to be prohibited Acting on the Stage) was ever supprest from being read, but rather the contrary; for that Plato himself recommended the Reading of *Aristophanes* (the loosest of all those old Comedians) to his Royal Scholar *Dionysus.*" (Charles Blount, *A Just Vindication of Learning and the Liberty of the Press* (1695), rptd. in *Miscellaneous Works* [London, 1695], pp. 5–6).

9 Daniel Defoe, *An Essay on the Regulation of the Press* (1704), ed. John Robert Moore (Oxford, 1948), pp. 3–4.

10 Indeed as Charles Blount would remark, any return to a system of licensing would almost certainly strike hardest at the wits of the age. "Heaven grant," Blount writes, "that in time, there be not the same Restraint and Monopoly over Witty Discourse, as there is now over Ingenious Writing." *Vindication*, pp. 15–16.

11 Charles Leslie, *A Supplement Upon Occasion of A History of Religion* (1694), rptd. in *The Theological Works of the Rev. Charles Leslie*, 7 vols. (Oxford, 1832), II, p. 661. A few, like the author of the *Memoirs of the Life and Writings of Matthew Tindall, LL.D.* (1723), saw both the savagery and silliness of demands for civil prosecution. For "whenever Church Power, or the Church Interest, is attacked, all Ecclesiastics in the Universe are in a high Delirium, and Inquisitions and Bulls, in Romish Countries; the Power of the Kirk, in Scotland, and Crown Informations in England, are the constant Caustics which are applied to the poor Laity. While the Priesthood aloud continually do cry, *the Secular Arm! the Secular Arm!* in that alone, is our Refuge" (p. 12).

12 Leonard Levy, *Treason Against God: A History of the Offense of Blasphemy* (New York, 1981), pp. 314–16.

13 Laurence Hanson, *Government and the Press 1695–1763* (Oxford, 1936), p. 17.

14 Daniel Defoe, *The Review*, 1: (August 12, 1704).

15 *A Complete Collection of State Trials*, ed. T. B. Howell, 33 vols. (London, 1812), XIV, p. 1127.

16 Barrow, "Of Foolish Talking and Jesting," II, p. 3.

17 *A Digest of the Law Concerning Libels* (London, 1765), p. 57.

18 G. D. Nokes, *A History of the Crime of Blasphemy* (London, 1928), p. 49.

19 Warburton, "To the Free-Thinkers," I, p. xxiii.

20 Levy, *Treason Against God*, p. 327. For the most complete account of the Aikenhead trial see Michael Hunter, "'Aikenhead the Atheist': The Context and Consequences of Articulate Irreligion in the Late Seventeenth Century," in *Atheism from the Reformation to the Enlightenment* (Oxford, 1992), pp. 221–54.

21 The line between outright blasphemy and seditious libel was blurry at best. For a history of the prosecution of blasphemous libels, see Levy, *Treason Against God*, pp. 297–330, and Donald Thomas, *A Long Time Burning: The History of Literary Censorship in England* (London, 1969), pp. 63–73. See, also, Nokes, *Crime of Blasphemy*; William Holdsworth, *A History of the English Law* (London, 1938), VIII, pp. 333–78; James Fitzjames Stephen, *A History of the Criminal Law in England* (London, 1883), II, pp. 397–497.

22 Holdsworth, *English Law*, VIII, p. 407.

23 John Turner, *A Vindication of the Rights and Privileges of the Christian Church* (London, 1707), preface, pp. xxii, v.

24 On the rather slipshod procedure by which works were singled out for prosecution, see Samuel Hilliard, *A Narrative of the Prosecution of Mr. Sare and His Servant, for Selling the Rights of the Christian Church* (London, 1709).

25 Thomas Lathbury, *History of the Convocation* (London, 1853), pp. 348–51.

26 For a full inventory of all those works burned, see Charles Ripley Gillett, *Burned Books: Neglected Chapters in British History and Literature*, 2 vols. (New York, 1932), II, pp. 667–702.

27 Ibid., II, p. 590.

28 For a record of prosecutions of blasphemy at common law, see Nokes, *Crime of Blasphemy*, pp. 147–67.

29 Roger L'Estrange, *Considerations and Proposals in Order to the Regulation of the Press* (London, 1663), pp. 9–10.

30 Charles Blount, *Two First Books of Philostratus Concerning the Life of Apollonius Tyaneus* (London, 1680), p. 55, preface.

31 John Toland, "Clidophorus," *Tetradymus* (London, 1720), p. 67.

32 John Toland, *Christianity Not Mysterious* (London, 1696), preface, pp. 4–5.

33 Shaftesbury, *Characteristics of Men, Manners, Opinions, Times* (1711), ed. John M. Robertson 2 vols. (1900; rptd. Indianapolis, 1964), I, p. 50. For a fuller analysis of the mechanics of indirection in heterodox texts, see

David Berman, "Deism, Immortality, and the Art of Theological Lying," in J. A. Leo Lemay (ed.), *Deism, Masonry, and the Enlightenment,* (Newark, DE, 1987), pp. 61–78; and "Disclaimers as Offense Mechanisms in Charles Blount and John Toland," in Michael Hunter and David Wootton (eds.), *Atheism from the Reformation to the Enlightenment* (Oxford, 1992), pp. 255–72.

34 Warburton, "To the Free-Thinkers," I, pp. xxvi–xxvii.

35 Philip Skelton, *Ophiomaches: Or, Deism Revealed* ed. David Berman 2 vols. (1749; rptd. Bristol, 1990), II, p. 373.

36 Toland, "Clidophorus," pp. 95–96.

37 Skelton, *Ophiomaches*, II, pp. 373–74.

38 Thomas Woolston, *Six Discourses of the Miracles of Our Saviour, and Defences of His Discourses* (1727–30; rptd. New York and London, 1979), first discourse, p. 68. All quotations from Woolston are taken from this edition and are quoted in the text by discourse and page number.

39 *A Digest of the Law Concerning Libels,* p. 6.

40 *State Law, or the Doctrine of Libels Discussed and Examined* (London, 1729), p. 58.

41 *State Trials,* xv, pp. 183–84. In *Vindicius Liberius* (1702) Toland lays out his own strategy for interpreting ambiguous but potentially heterodox texts: "We are . . . oblig'd to make the most candid Construction of their Designs, and if their words admit of a double sense, (which is hard to be always avoided in any Language) we ought to allow the fairest interpretation of their Meaning" (p. 6); quoted in Berman, "The Art of Theological Lying," p. 64.

42 *State Law,* p. 74. This pamphleteer further argues that "Courts of Justice may be directed by the received Opinion, by the Sense of the World, and not stick to the literal Sense of Words," since "Words have been adjudged scandalous, which, from the bare Meaning, no Scholar could find any harm in" (p. 59).

43 *The Freeholder's Journal,* 36 (September 1722).

44 *British Journal,* 6 (October 27, 1722). For Defoe as well the importance of innuendo as a determinant in libel verdicts was worrisome, particularly when there was no case law outlining exactly what constituted libel in the first place. "The crime of an Author is not known; and I think verily no Book can be wrote so warily, but that if the Author be brought on his Tryal, it shall be easy for a cunning lawyer, ay for a Lawyer of not great Cunning, to put an innuendo upon his meaning, and make some Part of it Criminal" (Defoe, *Essay,* p. 20).

45 Nokes, *Crime of Blasphemy,* pp. 67–69.

46 Leslie Stephen, *History of English Thought in the Eighteenth Century,* 2 vols. (1876; rptd. New York, 1949), I, p. 232.

47 For a survey of the arguments in the *Discourses,* see William H. Trapnell, "What Thomas Woolston Wrote," *British Journal for Eighteenth-Century Studies,* 14 (Spring 1991), 13–30.

48 William Trapnell, "Who Thomas Woolston Was," *British Journal for*

Eighteenth-Century Studies, 11 (1988), 143–58.

49 Edmund Gibson, *The Bishop of London's Pastoral Letter to the People of his Diocese* (London, 1728), p. 35.

50 Matthew Tindal, *An Address to the Inhabitants of the Two Great Cities of London and Westminster in Relation to a Pastoral Letter Said to be Written by the Bishop of London* (London, 1729), p. 25.

51 Ibid., p. 20.

52 Gibson, *Pastoral Letter*, p. 35.

53 Anthony Collins, *A Discourse Concerning Ridicule and Irony in Writing* (London, 1729), p. 26.

54 Richard Smalbroke, *A Vindication of the Miracles of Our Blessed Saviour*, vol. I (London, 1729), dedication to the Queen Regent.

55 Richard Smalbroke, *A Vindication of the Miracles of Our Blessed Saviour*, vol. II (London, 1731), dedication, A4.

56 Gibson, *Pastoral Letter*, p. 8.

57 *For God Or the Devil, Or, Just Chastisement No Persecution* (London, 1729), p. 17. The claim that Woolston had run "riot" was one which came easily to those involved in suppressing nonconformity of various kinds. In 1673, leaders of a Jewish synagogue in London were indicted for a "riot" that had consisted of praying in their synagogue (Levy, *Treason Against God*, p. 319). For other attacks on Woolston's style, see Nathaniel Lardner, *A Vindication of Three of Our Blessed Saviour's Miracles* (London, 1729); *An Expostulary Letter to Mr. Woolston, on Account of His Late Writings, By a Clergyman in the Country* (London, 1730); Thomas Ray, *A Vindication of Our Saviour's Miracles, in Answer to Mr. Woolston's Five Last Discourses* (London, 1730).

58 Smalbroke, *Vindication*, II, dedication.

59 This was an expansive but thoroughly dubious legal claim. Writing long after the issue had ceased to inspire such fierce passions, a jurist reminds his readers of Coke's early argument that "slanderous words are not a breach of behaviour, for tho' such words are motives and mediate provocations for breach of the peace, yet tend they not immediately to a breach of the peace like a challenge." (*A Letter Concerning Libels, Warrants, the Seizing of Papers and Sureties of Behaviour*, 3rd edn [1765], p. 40).

60 Simon Browne, *A Fit Rebuke to a Ludicrous Infidel: In some Remarks on Mr. Woolston's Fifth Discourse on the Miracles of Our Saviour*, (London, 1732), p. iii.

61 Ibid., p. v.

62 On the conduct of Woolston's trial, see Trapnell, "Who Woolston Was," 149–51.

63 Hypatia Bonner, *Penalties Upon Opinion* (London, 1943), p. 35.

64 Nokes, *Crime of Blasphemy*, p. 63.

65 Holdsworth, *English Law*, VIII, p. 408.

66 *An Account of the Trial of Thomas Woolston, B.D.* (London, 1729), p. 1.

67 Ibid., p. 1.

68 Henry Stebbing, *A Defence of the Scripture History* (London, 1730), p. v.

69 Smalbroke, *Vindication*, pp. x–xi.
70 Certainly the prosecutor's summary of the case leads toward the conclusion that because they undermine the Civil Constitution, innuendos against God deserve peculiar punishments. "The Laws of God, as was observ'd by the Council, are a Part, and the Chief Part of the Laws of this Kingdom; and if a Man, who should write against our stated Laws, or but to turn them into Burlesque and Ridicule, cannot escape with Impunity, what can he expect, who shall strike at the Root of Christianity, and bring into Contempt the Author and Finisher of our Faith." *Account*, p. 6.
71 Charles Bradlaugh, *The Laws Relating to Blasphemy and Heresy: An Address to Freethinkers* (London, 1878), p. 19.
72 Levy, *Treason Against God*, p. 335.
73 Incarcerated "within the rules" of King's Bench prison, Woolston actually had considerable freedom of movement, and did not die in close confinement. On the conditions of Woolston's imprisonment, see Trapnell, "Who Thomas Woolston Was," 151–52.

CHAPTER 8

The limits of moderation in a Latitudinarian parson: or, High-Church zeal in a Low Churchman discover'd

Jeffrey S. Chamberlain

I

In the political and religious turmoil of the late seventeenth and early eighteenth centuries some clergymen began to urge "moderation." By this they meant comprehension of orthodox Dissenters within the Church of England. Dissenters were persecuted in the Restoration period, and many clergymen felt that this persecution was too extensive and too severe. They proposed to "widen the Terms" under which nonconformists could be comprehended by the church.[1] The proposal for greater latitude within the church by these divines led many others to fear for the purity of the church, and soon reactionaries applied the pejorative "Latitude-Men," or "Latitudinarians", to the advocates of a policy of moderation.[2] These "Low Churchmen," as they were also called, were frequently branded as trimmers who sold their birthright in the Church of England for a mess of pottage. As one of their opponents wrote, "the common Notion of a moderate Minister is . . . one that will comply with the humours and fancies of all Parties, and oblige them by condescentions of this nature."[3] They were perceived as traitors to the church who would tolerate or compromise with anything, even deism and atheism. For this reason Henry Sacheverell, after the defeat of the Occasional Conformity Bill, lashed out and called all such Latitude-Men "False Brethren" because they were allowing a pure church to become defiled.[4]

In Sacheverell's time these "Latitude-Men" were also politically linked to the Whig party, a linkage with apparent origins in the debates surrounding the Popish Plot and the Exclusion Crisis.[5] But whatever the origin was, in the late seventeenth and early eighteenth centuries Latitudinarians were identified with Whiggish belief in the Protestant succession. They were less concerned about the hereditary line of succession than they were that the monarch would preserve true religion and protect the freedoms of the people.[6] This blatant disregard for tradition and procedure, not to mention God's ordained pattern, elicited contempt from High Churchmen who believed that the entire constitution was in danger of being destroyed. They feared that any diminution in the power of the king would lead to antimonarchalism or republicanism, which would erode the church even further. Church and state were inextricably linked, and any change in either would lead to disaster.[7]

Though few historians accepted the wild exaggerations of Sacheverell and his ilk, many, if not most, tended to adopt the High Church characterization of Latitudinarians – that they were tolerant to the point of indifference and moralistic (or rationalistic) to the point of theological negligence. The Latitudinarians were thought to have "preached up" reason and natural theology until the distinction between them and the deists was trivial. As such they were portrayed, sometimes positively, as forerunners of modern liberalism.[8] Recently however some historians have been writing to demonstrate that there were limits to the moderation of the Latitudinarians and that they were not so different from High Churchmen as was thought.[9] In fact there is as much confusion as ever about the nature of Latitudinarianism because historians are saying very different things.[10] Some have gone so far as to suggest that Latitudinarians either did not exist, or that they were indistinguishable from other clergymen,[11] while others continue to maintain that Latitudinarians had changed in significant ways from earlier Anglicans.[12]

Part of the difficulty in isolating the phenomenon comes from the lack of profiles of individual Latitudinarians.[13] Most studies of Latitudinarianism have focused on the intellectual implications of debates, controversies, and principal writings of the higher clergy.[14] This chapter will take a different tack. Rather than address the issue of Latitudinarianism from the top down, it will examine it from the bottom up. It will explore the life and thoughts of one eighteenth-century Latitudinarian parson – Thomas Curteis, Rector of Wrotham and Sevenoaks, Kent – as a case study. This portrayal of Curteis's background and sympathies will help to shed light on what it meant to be a Latitudinarian, and it will demonstrate that though Latitudinarians *were* more moderate than many parochial clergymen, they were limited in their moderation. In fact at times their zeal matched that of the High Churchmen, only it was directed not at Dissenters, but at deists.

Thomas Curteis's[15] background is sketchy. Born sometime in either 1665 or 1666,[16] he was undoubtedly heir to the gentry family that settled in the Weald of Kent in the late medieval period.[17] Though there were many Curteises that were Anglican churchwardens and minor government officials, Thomas's branch of the family must have been influenced by Dissenters, since Thomas himself was one. But other than this and the fact that his first vocation was practicing physic, we know very little of his early years. Sometime in the first decade of the eighteenth century, he decided to conform and become a priest in the established church. When in 1716 the Bishop of Norwich wrote to Archbishop Wake to introduce Curteis to him, he observed that Curteis "was Ordain'd Deacon & Priest by me at your predecessors [Thomas Tenison's] desire who had, and I think justly, a good opinion of him, tho' he was reproach'd for the favour he shewed him," most likely because of Curteis's reputation for nonconformity.[18] Nevertheless, the bishop maintained, "I believe [he] went into orders with a very Christian intention." "He is," Norwich continued, "a good scholar, and entirely well affected to the Constitution in Church and State."[19]

Curteis was indebted to Tenison for much, because it was Tenison who in 1714 presented him to the Vicarage (and afterwards Rectory) of Wrotham, in west Kent. In 1716 he was granted in addition the nearby Rectory of Sevenoaks. Curteis settled comfortably into these livings, and is said to have been very wealthy, reaping as much as £3,000 per annum. He also founded a clerical dynasty, since his son and grandson followed in his footsteps and became parsons in west Kent and east Sussex (the Rectory of Sevenoaks remained in the family until 1907).[20]

Though many converts to the established church became reactionary churchmen, Curteis adopted a Latitudinarian stance.[21] Politically he was a Whig. On the day of thanksgiving for George I's arrival upon the English throne Curteis preached a thanksgiving sermon that resounded with praise and gratitude for the "safe, peaceable, and happy accession of his present Majesty, King George." Further, he spoke of the "Happy Act of Settlement" that had made it possible, and deplored the "arbitrary power" that resulted from unmitigated royal prerogative. Though this sermon was not a full-fledged apology for Whig ideology, Curteis was still afraid that it would earn him reproach from High Churchmen. In preaching the sermon and having it published he had "suffer'd it to run the Gantlet at a Time when I am sure nothing of mine will escape the severest Lashes." And in true Latitudinarian style he made a plea for tolerance and understanding. Since the Church of England was full of "Charitable Principles, and ennobling Latitude," its members should bury "in Eternal Oblivion all our Party-Quarrels, invidious Characters and reproachful Names of Distinction." Rather they should turn "the sad Distinction of *High* and *Low*, into a pious Unanimity" and support king and church.[22]

Curteis was more explicit in his Whiggery just a year and a half later. In a sermon to condemn the Jacobite uprising he argued that though government was a human convention, kings should be honored and obeyed when their commands were "consistent with the indispensable Dictates of Natural and Revealed Religion, and the respective Laws of each Civil Constitution." Since King George's government clearly was consistent with such "Dictates," any and all who rebelled were traitors and "the vilest Miscreants."[23]

Curteis and his family were committed Whigs at a time when the majority of parochial clergy were staunchly Tory.[24] By the 1720s Curteis was to be found zealously campaigning for the Whig candidates put forward in Sussex by the Duke of Newcastle and in Kent by the Duke of Dorset. He not only voted for the Whigs, he also pressured his tenants to do so as well, and even set up his son with a freehold in Sussex for the purpose of supporting the candidate of the Duke of Newcastle in that county.[25] He also wrote propaganda at the time of elections that was classically Whig in content.[26]

Curteis constantly found it necessary to struggle against Toryism and Jacobitism among his neighboring clergymen, and even discovered discontent with Whig principles in his subordinates. In 1722 he reported to Archbishop Wake a "disagreeable incident." He discovered, to his dismay, that his own curate was tainted with High Church and Jacobite ideas, and he felt constrained to persuade him away from them, and failing that, to restrict his ministrations. As he told Wake,

My Curate, Mr. Drake, on the last 5th of Nov. came to me and told me that he could not read the Service of the Day, as it stands with the Additions since the Revolution.[27] After reasoning with him on the proceeding Danger [of not reading the prayer], together with the Necessity Justifiableness and Advantages of that Happy Turn, and the shocking consequence of His Sentiments (sc. that then we must be suppos'd in a State of Usurpation) I still found him inflexible; and therefore did not suffer him to go into the Desk that Day.[28]

Curteis's curate had been influenced by John Johnson, a vocal High Churchman in the county[29] who had written a pamphlet with Jacobite overtones that Curteis considered "audacious."[30] Curteis called for legal proceedings to be instigated against Johnson for his treachery, but was dismayed with the lack of action taken.[31] Johnson "had dispers'd Transcripts of the Chief Materials [of the pamphlet] among the County Clergy (doubtless to spirit them into the same Obstinacy)," one of which had come into Drake's possession and had convinced him not to read the 5th of November prayer as it stood in the revised liturgy. Though Curteis regretted this development, since "in other respects I have a true value for Him," he thought that he would have to "part with" his curate.[32] Curteis simply could not allow that kind of treasonous obstinacy in his parish. Curteis was loyal to the house of Hanover out of Whiggish principle (not just convenience), and he would not countenance those who refused to acknowledge their right to the throne.

Politically therefore Curteis was a Low Churchmen, and he also fit that characterization when it came to his attitudes of churchmanship. The whole of the Curteis family, apparently, deplored the extremes to which High Churchmen went in their zeal to keep the church safe and pure. Curteis's son William included "Sacheverels" in his list of "Malcontents" and "Fools."[33] To Thomas Curteis and his kin, High Churchmen were not conscientious, they were captious and fearful of the slightest challenges. They would never, he lamented, "think the Church out of Danger so long as their great Grievance, the Toleration Act is subsisting."[34] Fear and anxiety drove High Churchmen to suppress dissent even after it was proven that Dissenters were no threat to the church. For this reason Curteis maintained that High Churchmen were those who had a particularly "Narrow, Rigid, and Censorious Temper." They were propelled by "the Warmth of a Mis-guided Zeal for some Unhappy Distinctions, Groundless and Unwarrantable in themselves." Their fears and apprehensions were whipped up to an unnatural and unreasonable frenzy, and they fought for unnecessary distinctions and absurd minutiae. He hoped that they would come to their senses and stop contending for the "Unhappy" and "groundless . . Distinction of High and Low." Curteis advised his son to keep well clear of High Churchmen, since they evinced the very opposite of "the Extensive Charity of our Blessed Saviour's Great Example." And he advocated Latitudinarianism, since it was the "Ennobling Latitude" of the Church of

England that caused it "to surpass all other National Churches in the world."[35]

As a man of latitude, Curteis encouraged his family, friends and countrymen to extend charity and moderation to nonconformists. He could adopt this tolerant view, no doubt because of his own personal experience of dissent – he knew firsthand that most nonconformists were pious and conscientious believers, not perverse and obstinate miscreants as high churchmen portrayed them. Curteis exulted in the Toleration Act, which he called "that most just, that truly reasonable, and Christian Law," since he felt that Dissenters should be granted the same rights as other Englishmen. "Liberty of Conscience in Religious Matters" was to Curteis the "indefeazable [sic] Right of Every Man, both by the Law of Nature, and by the peculiar precepts of Christianity."[36] This was a perspective completely opposite to that of High Churchmen, who were still calling for persecution of dissenters to safeguard the church from danger.[37]

Curteis even sized up other people according to their attitudes towards Dissenters. In 1723 he apologized to Archbishop Wake for opposing a candidate that the prelate had put forward for an ecclesiastical post. Had he been more aware of the man's "prudent Behaviour towards All, even to Dissenters," he said, he would have been much quicker to back him.[38] He advised his son to "Endeavour, therefore, as far as is Practicable, to live Friendly, as well as Peacably with all Men." Curteis advocated a course of "Prudence, Charity, and Good Nature" in dealing with individuals who had different views, and he encouraged the "Laying aside all manner of Rash Censures" on fellow Christians, even if they were not of the same communion.[39] He also published a couple of books that were intended to "soften the unreasonable prejudices among too many of Us" about Dissenters. Unfortunately, neither his *Unity of the Catholic Church* nor *The Preference of Charity to Knowledge and Faith* appear to have survived,[40] but the intent of the works is clear: they were calls for toleration and for goodwill towards Dissenters.

This temperate attitude was more than rhetoric. Curteis was willing to compromise on some matters for the sake of peace and the hope of reunion with nonconformists. In 1729 he wrote Edmund Gibson, Bishop of London, with a scheme of modifying the liturgy so as to "remove the scruples" which kept Dissenters from rejoining the established church. They were minor points in his mind, and he could not "apprehend, in those Alterations, any thing parted with, that bears proportion to so desireable an effect" of bringing many of the

Dissenters "over to us." He advocated, first of all, allowing communicants to stand rather than kneel at the Sacrament if they so desired. He thought, secondly, that it would be well to abolish the practice – or, at least, the mandatory use – of signing the cross in baptism.[41]

These concessions may seem minor or even trifling to moderns, but they were major issues to High Church Anglicans who felt that giving in to Dissenters on these points was a signal of defeat. All through the Restoration and well into the eighteenth century High Churchmen argued that these were things "indifferent," and were therefore not issues which individuals could legitimately use as obstacles to communion.[42] Curteis's High Church contemporaries campaigned zealously against just such concessions as Curteis advocated, on the basis that they were unnecessary and that they would impoverish worship.[43] Curteis's revisions were, therefore, precisely the sorts of Latitudinarian compromises that High Churchmen considered treasonous.

In addition Curteis had no qualms about supporting Lord Middlesex, the Duke of Dorset's son, when he stood for parliament (in Kent in 1733/34 and in Sussex in 1741), though other clergymen were against him because of his reputation as a member of the "Calve's-Head Club," which was thought to be a nefarious organization that was bent on subverting established religion and government through republicanism and Presbyterianism.[44] But Curteis does not seem to have been dismayed by Middlesex's reputed attachment to the Calve's Head Club – he wholeheartedly supported him anyway, and lent his assistance in the campaigns in whatever ways he could.[45] Curteis was broad enough in his churchmanship and secure enough in his faith that he did not let rumors and allegations against Middlesex affect his determination to support him. The High Church clergy campaigned against Middlesex both because of his reputation, and because he was known to have voted to repeal the Test Act (another reason he had a reputation as a Presbyterian).[46] But because of Curteis's moderation towards Dissenters, this was no obstacle to his endorsement of the candidate.

High Churchmen certainly thought that moderation such as Curteis's was trimming and inherently detrimental to the church. But despite these High Church allegations, Curteis's moderation should not be interpreted as indifference in his attachment to the Anglican church or languidness in his devotion to it. It must be remembered, first of all, that he had converted from nonconformity to Anglicanism, and that was not a move motivated only by self-interest or hope of material gain or status. As he told his son, rather, he had come to the conclusion that "the Reform'd Episcopal Church, Establish'd in this Nation, and of which you are a Member, is the Best-Constituted of any National Church upon the Earth, and most agreeable to the Ages of Purest Antiquity."[47] In fact Curteis had moved so far from the Presbyterianism in which he was reared, that he was an ardent episcopalian. In 1717 he complimented Archbishop Wake on a book he had written which affirmed that bishops were of apostolic origin, and not a later convention as Edward Stillingfleet had maintained (in his *Eirenicum*). The latter, Curteis thought, granted too "large Concessions" to the Presbyterians.[48] He also advised his son to never "be wanting in a Due Reverence and Orderly Subjection to those Proper [governors]" of the church, since they were "of Divine Institution."[49]

Though critics tried to tar Low Churchmen with the brush of indolence in religious duties, and latter-day commentators have frequently mirrored that opinion,[50] Curteis defied that caricature. He was not negligent when it came to his responsibilities as a rector, and he was not cavalier in his usage of the canons or liturgy. In fact his letters reveal that he carefully and conscientiously went about doing his business, adhering as closely as possible to the written prescriptions of the church. He considered whether or not a contemplated act was in keeping with the rubrics of the church, and he proceeded only if he was sure it was.[51] And when he delegated his responsibilities he was diligent to make sure his curates were attentive to their duties.

Curteis, then, was a Latitudinarian in his attitude towards dissent, but this tolerant spirit did not make him spiritually weak, lazy, or uncritical. He was a "man of latitude," but his latitude did not bring with it indifference or carelessness in the Faith. Curteis aligned with the Whigs politically, but that did not make him a theological trimmer as High Churchmen charged. In fact the only differences between Curteis and High Churchmen were that Curteis was more tolerant and accommodating, and that he espoused Whig ideology. Other than that, his churchmanship could not be faulted, even by his high-flying colleagues.

III

But for all Curteis's Latitudinarian moderation and generosity of spirit towards Dissenters, in some things he was resolute and unyielding. In his reaction to heterodoxy, for instance, he displayed very high-churchmanlike attitudes. Curteis published more works against deism and infidelity than on any other single topic. He wrote at least three book-length apologetic treatises and one extended poem "design'd to excite an awful sense of religion both in the indolent and the unbelieving part of mankind," and preached a number of sermons countering the threat of infidelity to the Faith [52] and contending for historic Christianity.

Although he wrote against Matthew Tindal and Anthony Collins, he did not really address their arguments. He did not have to, he felt, for two reasons: first of all, other capable apologists had countered them cogently, and, secondly, Tindal, Collins, and the other deistic agitators would not honestly weigh the orthodox arguments, since they were obstinate, rebellious, and were not really looking for the truth. Curteis, therefore, wrote mainly for the benefit of his parishioners and others who might be influenced by the principal deist authors.[53]

His arguments were neither unique nor remarkable, but they certainly reflected the mood of clergymen of the day, and undoubtedly carried influence with at least some of his readers. He built his case step by step, beginning with the existence of God and culminating with special revelation and the reliability of the Scriptures. In proving the existence of God, he began with the need of man. He argued, in true Pascalian form, that humans were born with an innate sense of God which would be purposeless and absurd if no God existed. God's presence was "legibly written in every Man's Heart" no matter what country or culture that man called his own. Further, God could be clearly seen in nature, as the Apostle Paul had claimed in Romans 1.20. For these reasons God's existence could be considered a "self-evident Principle."[54] Without God man was simply adrift in the universe, a sensible being searching for completion and meaning which was not there. Without God man's yearning for the divine would be absurd and his moral sense futile and out of place. Even reason made no sense in a cosmos that was not reasonable.[55]

Though Curteis acknowledged that reason (or natural theology) could lead men to the belief that there was a God and that there was an afterlife where men's deeds would be judged, he felt that it could not communicate any adequate scheme of salvation. Natural theology could convince a person of God's existence and of the need for morality, but it could never carry that individual to the safe harbor of redemption. Morality was not all there was to Christianity – revelation was needed as the "only Medium" of "Reconciliation and Acceptance with God." Thus the deists, in trusting the "dim Light of Nature," cut themselves off from the only thing that would truly show them the way to salvation.[56]

The deists, Curteis maintained, seriously overestimated the capabilities of unaided reason. Tindal, for example, in his *Christianity as Old as the Creation*, argued that the faculty of reason was adequate to discover all that was necessary for redemption. But, Curteis charged, "if he would think aright, he must be sensible of its [Reason's] present Corruption and Degeneracy in most Men, so as to need a superior Guide."[57] Curteis did not flinch when it came to the doctrine of original sin. Sin had distorted man's reason and conscience such that he needed a reliable and perfect guide to pull him from the mire in which he was wallowing: "shall we be so vain as to think that we can perfectly trace the deep and latent Corruption, Obliquity and Deceitfulness of our own Hearts; or that we are, of ourselves, sufficient to find out and apply an effectual Remedy against it?"[58] To prove the point Curteis brought up the illustration of the heathen: "In those unhappy Places, where this Divine Light [of Revelation] has never dawn'd, how gross and unbecoming have Mens notions been." The human soul, defiled by sin, did not naturally seek the truth. Rather, "under the palpable Degeneracy of Human Nature, the Weakness and Imperfection of its Rational Powers," human beings could not, or would not, come to the Light in all its brightness. Without Revelation, without some initiative by God, men would hopelessly and perversely wander in darkness.[59] Reason could lead a person to some knowledge, but it was inadequate in and of itself because it was debased from the effects of the Fall of Man. Though a Latitudinarian, Curteis was very far from being a Pelagian, or even a semi-Pelagian.

Though Curteis acknowledged natural religion and spoke highly of it, he did not make the same mistake as Tindal in claiming that Christianity was merely a republication of natural religion. Curteis had no doubts that revealed religion was absolutely necessary, because natural religion was limited and, when it came to appropriating truths necessary for redemption, beggarly. Curteis had not let his orthodoxy slip at this point: he believed in human depravity and felt that the only solution to it was the grace revealed through revelation. This was the real danger of deism – it lured men into accepting the Light of Nature as the whole authority of religion, which would "at once Divest them of those strong and invaluable Consolations, arising from the Discovery of the blessed Means of their Reconciliation and Acceptance with God; from the choicest Supports under all Evils of this Life; and from the Glorious Hopes, and the lively Anticipations of the World to come."[60] In short, without revelation there was no salvation.

Curteis proceeded to recite the standard litany of proofs for the Bible and the supernatural history of Christianity. He marveled at the precision and accuracy of Old Testament prophesy and its New Testament fulfillment; he remarked upon the purity and supernaturalness of Christ's life and testimony; he called attention to the extraordinary feat of the Resurrection, and observed that there were many unimpeachable eyewitnesses to that event; he noted the sensational and startling conversion of the Apostle Paul and other disciples; he commented on the many miracles accompanying the apostles' preaching; and he waxed eloquent on the superb order, method, and beauty of expression of Scripture itself.[61] All of these things, he felt, were clear and indubitable proofs of the truth of Christianity. Anybody who did not acknowledge them was simply blind or obstinate.

At this point Curteis turned the tables on the deists, and charged that though they claimed to be operating from a standard of reason, they were, in fact, the most unreasonable of men. "The most dangerous Inroads to *Atheism* and Irreligion, have been in all Ages made by the greatest Pretenders to Reason, and never in Any, more than the Present." The reason to which deists "pretended" was not true reason, but a perversion and corruption of the real thing. Deists reasoned only with "the most palpable Abuse of that very Reason which they so much pretend to."[62] They admitted the existence of God and the reality of judgment, but denied their own need of redemption. How reasonable was this? "How abandon'd then, to the worst of Impiety; how utterly destitute of all Reason and Goodness, of every spark of Humanity and Gratitude, and of all Sense of Duty and Interest, must *they* be, who contemptuously vilify and reject the Free Offers of such inestimable Benefits!"[63] Deists ignored what their own reason should have taught them: that they were needy and helpless without revelation and grace. "Every One, therefore, who will fairly consult the Dictates of his own Reason, must acknowledge, that under the palpable Degeneracy of Human Nature, the Weakness and Imperfection of its Rational Powers . . . such a gracious and supernatural Revelation was highly necessary and desireable."[64]

For this reason Curteis could not believe that deists were honest in their doubts. On the contrary they were restless and "open Enemies to all Religion, both Natural and Revealed, who, by Rambling and inconsistent Notions, empty Quibble, palpable Malice, and wicked Arrogance, instead of their boasted Freedom, betray a wild Licenciousness of thought: not to instruct, but to perplex the World."[65] Collins and Tindal alike received nothing from Curteis but opprobrium and censure, as those who were "capable of doing real Service to Mankind," but chose rather "to destroy the true Ground of all Happiness in this Life, and the only comfortable Prospect into Eternity!"[66] Over and over he marveled at their obstinacy and perversity in defying God and his revelation.

It is clear from such arguments, therefore, that Curteis treated the deists in almost the exact same manner as high churchmen treated Dissenters. Though Curteis was charitable to nonconformists, he could see nothing but danger in tolerating the deists. Though he could chide the high churchmen for believing the church in danger from dissent, he himself feared for the security of Christianity if heterodoxy persisted unchecked. Curteis was intimidated by the threat of deism, and when he was, he unleashed the same vocabulary of dread and consternation that had animated High Churchmen. His alarms were shrill and his caveats dire: "If we should be so infatuated, as to fall in with the present Stream of Infidelity," he warned, "what will there be left, that can denominate our Condition easy, safe or promising? And what can preserve the very Name of Christianity from being either lost, or treated with Contempt, in the Rising Generation?"[67] Deists struck at the foundation of the faith. The very survival of Christianity was at stake, and Curteis was unnerved by the prospect of deist victory.

England, Curteis maintained, had been far too lenient with these would-be destroyers. After all, no other "Nation under Heaven had ever suffer'd what they esteem'd most Sacred and Inviolable, to be so wickedly trampled on."[68] Deists had no excuse for their infidelity and perversity, and Curteis was just as happy to exclude them from society as High Churchmen were to bar Dissenters, since the infidels had only brought such ostracism upon themselves. "Such men," he said, "having made themselves the Bane of Human Society, have no Injustice done them, if they become the general Scorn and Aversion of Mankind."[69] They were rightfully shunned and excluded from society because of their self-conscious design of destroying it. Pastors like Curteis felt beleaguered by those who were always railing against Christianity. Agitators seemed to be everywhere employing their "vile Excrements of Wit and infernal Sophistry . . . in Burlesquing the Divine Oracles, and turning the most Sacred things into Ridicule."[70] Almost all parish clergymen complained about the lack of respect they received, and they were quick to attribute their slipping authority to the diabolical plot of deism and infidelity.[71] Clergymen felt that they were persecuted and oppressed, and they needed an explanation and a scapegoat at which to direct their frustration and rage. Therefore deists, skeptics, and infidels became targets of their ire. Even those like Curteis who were otherwise moderate, feared that the "Sacred Ministerial Function" (and therefore their own authority) was being torn apart, and they lashed out in fury at those who appeared to be causing the damage.

But despite Curteis's fears of deism and despite his fulminations against the "despicable Sett of Men" who championed it, the Rector of Wrotham could be charitable to those who suffered doubts. In 1724 he wrote to Archbishop Wake and informed him that he had performed the burial office for a known deist. He was careful, first of all, not to violate the rule of the church in so doing, but he came to the conclusion that there was no impediment. The "unhappy" man he buried was not an agitator. In fact, "he was so far from vilifying the Establish'd Church, that He always spoke well of it." Curteis, with naive confidence in his own cogency, believed that the doubter had even been moved by a sermon he once gave on the divine authority of Scripture. "Nonetheless, His Doubts recurr'd," and Curteis had "reason to think He persisted in his diffidence." But he was not a rabble rouser: when the Rector admonished him not to spread his doubts among his neighbors, "He gave me His Word & Honour that He would not, adding that he should rather encourage both them and His Domestics in frequenting the Publick Worship, & wish'd he could bring Himself to the same satisfaction."[72]

This anecdote illustrates an important point. Curteis felt no animosity towards this particular deist and was even saddened by his plight, but only because he did not perceive any danger or threat from him. He was not publicly defaming the church or its ministers, or goading others to do so; on the contrary, he actually encouraged his friends and servants to pursue a life of piety. And Curteis hoped that he himself had found faith. Since there was some question, Curteis decided to be merciful: "As it often happens (which was now the case) that we cannot have a certain knowledge of the thoughts & Dispositions of Men in their Last Hours, it seems best, not to limit the Mercy of God, but rather to err on the Charitable Hand than otherwise."[73] However, if the man had been an agitator, it is doubtful that Curteis would have been so compassionate in his attitude or benevolent in his actions. Given his remarks about Collins, Tindal, and the other "vile despisers" of the Faith, it is unlikely that he would have given them the like consideration. These latter were menaces to Curteis's faith and authority, and he refused them any privilege or favor. Curteis's Latitudinarian moderation and indulgence had definite limits.

IV

Curteis's case is instructive. He was one of those clergymen whom High Churchmen condemned as "traitors" and "false brethren" because they seemed to be so compromising that the church was in danger of subversion and attrition. And indeed Curteis for his part accused the High Churchmen of being too rigid and censorious. Yet when he felt a similar danger, he reacted in exactly the same way as High Churchmen had. Low churchmen obviously still had many of the same fears and insecurities as High Churchmen. The only distinction was that they had different boiling points.

There are some significant conclusions to be drawn from this portrait of Thomas Curteis. First of all it should be noted that Curteis, as a Latitudinarian, had a clear difference of opinion with the deists over the extent to which reason and natural theology could be authorities. Curteis believed in natural theology and he preached on the topic, but for him it was very limited in what it could achieve. Revelation was far more important for him because it alone could apprehend God and communicate the plan of redemption. Though Curteis is only one individual, his example should be enough to make us cautious of overemphasizing the rationalism of Latitudinarian theology.

Curteis's reaction to heterodoxy may also help explain why High Churchmanship declined so rapidly in Hanoverian England. The

Latitudinarians and High Churchmen were agreed in their disdain of heterodoxy. When the threat of deism and atheism became so prevalent that it overshadowed the threat of dissent, the High Churchmen readily joined with the Low Churchmen in defense of their common faith. The peril posed by heterodoxy galvanized the church to a unified defense. This is precisely what Curteis pleaded for in the conclusion to his *Reflexions on Natural and Reveal'd Religion*. He appealed to Anglicans of every stripe, and even Dissenters, to "lay aside their private Animosities, harsh Censures, and uncharitable Provocations, and sincerely unite, as with one Heart and Soul, in vindicating their common Christianity."[74] And to a great degree that is exactly what happened: the divisions and parties within the church were knit together once again in order to fight the common foes of heresy, infidelity, and unbelief.

If the Restoration church was insecure because of the threat of nonconformity, the Hanoverian church was insecure because of the threat of heterodoxy. The church had certainly progressed in terms of moderation and toleration, but it had not progressed to the point that anything was acceptable. As one clergyman towards the end of the century succinctly put it, the Latitudinarians could easily live in peace "with all serious & conscientious Christians of all Denominations who dissent from" the Church of England. But "it will be found impossible to maintain Peace & Amity" with the "prophane Hypocrite," "the professed Libertine," and the "Seducer to Irreligion."[75] Latitudinarians had learned to live with differences in doctrine and polity, but they still could not live with those who threatened Christianity itself. Low Churchmen were certainly more tolerant and moderate than High Churchmen, but they were not ready to compromise with anybody. They too wanted to retain a controlled religious environment in the state. The difference was that they perceived the threat not from dissent, but from heterodoxy. The fear and insecurity which animated High Churchmen could also animate Low Churchmen – they could demonstrate the same type of zeal when the church was "in Danger."

NOTES

1 Edward Pearse, *The Conformists Plea for the Nonconformists* (London, 1681).
2 W. M. Spellman, *The Latitudinarians and the Church of England, 1660-1700* (Athens, GA, and London, 1993), pp. 11-32; Martin I. J. Griffin, Jr.,

Latitudinarianism in the Seventeenth-Century Church of England (Leiden, 1992), pp. 3-13.

3 John Evans, *Moderation Stated* (London, 1682), pp. 40-41. See also *The Distinction of High-Church and Low-Church Distinctly Consider'd and Fairly Stated* (London, 1705) and Henry Sacheverell, *The Character of a Low Churchman* (London, 1701).

4 Henry Sacheverell, *The Perils of False Brethren, both in Church and State* (London, 1709).

5 See J. R. Jones, *Country and Court: England 1658-1714* (Cambridge, MA, 1978), pp. 197-216; Geoffrey Holmes, *Politics, Religion and Society in England, 1679-1742* (London and Ronceverte, 1986), p. 196; John Spurr, *The Restoration Church of England, 1646-1689* (New Haven, 1991), pp. 75-82; Robert Willman, "The Origins of 'Whig' and 'Tory' in English Political Language," *Historical Journal*, 12: 2 (1974), 247-64; and John Kenyon, *The Popish Plot* (London, 1972). Though few doubt that the political and ecclesiastical parties coalesced during this period, there is considerable recent discussion about how and precisely when they emerged, and even what the parties signified. See, for example, Jonathan Scott, *Algernon Sidney and the Restoration Crisis, 1677–1683* (Cambridge, 1991), pp. 1–49; Tim Harris, *Politics Under the Later Stuarts: Party Conflict in a Divided Society* (London and New York, 1993), pp. 52–75; and the debate among Gary De Krey, Richard Greaves, Tim Harris, James Rosenheim, and Jonathan Scott in *Albion*, 25: 4 (Winter 1993).

6 Though Tim Harris is undoubtedly correct that Tories argued "their position by appealing to the middle ground" during the Exclusion Crisis – that is, downplaying the absolutist strain and appealing to law – they, unlike the Whigs, were nevertheless willing to accept a Catholic monarch who acceded through divinely-ordained hereditary right. The Whigs would not hear of such talk, and they planned to exclude James II and all other Catholic monarchs by a law restricting the succession to Protestants. See Tim Harris, "Party Turns? Or, Whigs and Tories Get Off Scot Free," *Albion*, 25:4 (Winter 1993), 582–90.

7 Sacheverell, *Perils of False Brethren*, pp. iii, 19-25; Daniel Lafite, *No Lawful Ministry Without a Divine Mission* (London, 1713), pp. 3, 19.

8 Edward A. George, *Seventeenth-Century Men of Latitude* (London, 1908); John Tulloch, *Rational Theology and Christian Philosophy in the Seventeenth Century* (Edinburgh, 1872); R. N. Stromberg, *Religious Liberalism in Eighteenth-Century England* (Oxford, 1954), pp. 9-13.

9 William Spellman has demonstrated that few if any Latitudinarians compromised with Socinianism or deism. *Latitudinarians*, pp. 54-131.

10 For a very good summary of the issues see John Walsh and Stephen Taylor, "Introduction: The Church and Anglicanism in the 'Long' Eighteenth Century," in John Walsh, Colin Haydon and Stephen Taylor (eds.), *The Church of England c.1689-c.1833: From Toleration to Tractarianism* (Cambridge, 1993), pp. 35-45.

11 John Spurr has argued that since the term "Latitudinarian" was a pejorative, it cannot be used as a term of distinction. ("'Latitudinarianism' and the Restoration Church," *Historical Journal*, 31 [1988], 61-82.) Richard Ashcraft has gone so far as to argue that Latitudinarians were nearly as critical of Dissenters as High Churchmen, and that the comprehension scheme for which Latitudinarians fought was really "an attempt to defeat the policy of toleration, while legitimating the prosecution of religious dissent." ("Latitudinarianism and Toleration: Historical Myth Versus Political History," in Richard Kroll, Richard Ashcraft, and Perez Zagôrin [eds.], *Philosophy, Science and Religion in England 1640-1700* [Cambridge, 1992], p. 154.) As to the theological issues, Alan Clifford has reached the astounding conclusion that the Latitudinarian John Tillotson was, in reality, a devoted follower of John Calvin. (Alan Clifford, *Atonement and Justification: English Evangelical Theology 1640-1790* [Oxford, 1990].)

12 Griffin, *Latitudinarianism*; Gregory Scholtz, "Anglicanism in the Age of Johnson: The Doctrine of Conditional Salvation," *Eighteenth-Century Studies*, 22:2 (winter 1988/89), 182-207; Neil Lettinga, "Covenant Theology Turned Upside Down: Henry Hammond and Caroline Anglican Moralism: 1643–1660," *Sixteenth Century Journal*, 24 (fall 1993), 653–69.

13 One of the few such profiles is Norman Sykes's portrayal of James Woodforde. Though fascinating, it is sketchy because it is based upon very few sources. For this reason it is highly questionable as an outline of a representative Latitudinarian parson. It is also, of course, quite late in the century. *From Sheldon to Secker* (Cambridge, 1959), pp. 177-87.

14 Walsh and Taylor, "Introduction," pp. 41-42.

15 Note: his surname was probably pronounced *ker'tis*, since those whose spelling tended to be more phonetic than proper, frequently spelled it "Curtis."

16 We only know this because he reported to the Duke of Newcastle in 1740 that he was at that time seventy-four years of age. June 21, 1740, BL Add. MS 32, 693 f. 406. This makes the assumption in *Alumni Cantabrigienses* (1, part 1, p. 434) that he matriculated at Corpus Christi College, Cambridge, in 1676 extremely unlikely, for he would only have been ten years old when he entered (the average was sixteen to seventeen). Further, it is very doubtful that he conformed this early since he still had a reputation as a Dissenter in the early eighteenth century.

17 Nigel Yates, "A Kentish Clerical Dynasty: Curteis of Sevenoaks," *Archaeologia Cantiana*, 108 (1990), 1-2.

18 Tenison himself had a reputation for Latitudinarianism that was not appreciated by his High Church subordinates. *DNB* vol 19: 537–40; Sykes, *From Sheldon to Secker*, pp. 47-57 *passim*.

19 C. Norwich to Wake, February, 9 1716, Arch. W. Epist. 7, fo. 56, Christ Church, Oxford.

20 Yates, "Kentish Clerical Dynasty," pp. 1-2.

21 Many Dissenters complained that those who conformed at the Restoration
    became vehement, persecuting Episcopalians. See Neil Caplan, "An
    Outline of the Origins and Development of Nonconformity in Sussex:
    1603-1803," (unpublished typescript in the British Library, Dr. William's
    Library, and the library of the Sussex Archaeological Society, Lewes,
    1965), p. 46 ff. See also the sermons (especially the sermon of January 30,
    1678) of Richard Ireland, ESRO AMS 2276.

22 Thomas Curteis, *Thankfulness and Unanimity the Proper Returns of National
    Blessings. A Sermon Preach'd on the late Day of Thanksgiving for his Majesty's
    Safe and Peaceable Accession to the Crown* (London, 1715), preface, pp. 10,
    13, 24. I am grateful to Peter Lefevre for providing me with a copy of this
    sermon.

23 Thomas Curteis, *Religious Princes the Greatest Blessing and Safety to the Church
    and State. A Sermon Preach'd in the Parish Church of Wrotham in Kent, on
    Thursday the 7th of June, 1716. Being the Day appointed for a Publick
    Thanksgiving to Almighty God, for the Suppression of the Late Horrid and
    Unnatural Rebellion* (London, 1716), pp. 10-12, 23, 25.

24 Geoffrey Holmes estimated that in the years immediately preceding the
    Hanoverian accession some eighty per cent of the clergy were associated
    with extreme Toryism. (Geoffrey Holmes, *Politics, Religion and Society in
    England 1679-1742* [London and Ronceverte, 1986], p. 211.)

25 See letters to the Duke of Newcastle, BL Add. MSS 32, 688 ff. 246, 336,
    393; 32, 693, f. 406; 32, 698 f. 371 and letters to the Duke of Dorset, Kent
    Archives Office, Sackville of Knole Papers, U 269/C 148/2, 8, 10, 18.

26 "An Appeal to the Reason and Consciences of all True Englishmen,
    concerning their Unhappy Prejudices, and the Fomenters of them: But
    more particularly with regard to the Next Election of the Representatives
    in Parliament. By an Impartial Hand," unpublished manuscript, 1733,
    BL Add. MS 33, 344 ff. 70-90.

27 The 5th of November service was originally a celebration of thanksgiving
    for James I's deliverance from the gunpowder plot of Guy Fawkes. After
    the Revolution of 1688, it was extended to include thanksgiving for
    deliverance of the church by William of Orange. As the new prayer read:
    "Accept also, most gracious God, of our unfeigned thanks for filling our
    hearts again with joy and gladness, after the time that thou hadst
    afflicted us, and putting a new song into our mouths, by bringing his
    Majesty King WILLIAM upon this Day, for the Deliverance of our
    Church and Nation from Popish Tyranny and Arbitrary Power."
    Jacobites and extreme high churchmen could countenance neither the
    references to William as deliverer nor the implicit Whig ideology.

28 Curteis to Wake, November 29, 1722, Arch. W. Epist. 9, fo. 232, Christ
    Church, Oxford.

29 Johnson was the Rector of Cranbrook, Kent (some fifteen miles southeast
    of Wrotham), and was known for his High Church writings, such as *The*

Clergyman's Vade-Mecum: or, an Account of the Ancient and Present Church of England; the Duties and the Rights of the Clergy; and of their Privileges and Hardships (3rd edn, London, 1709), and *The Unbloody Sacrifice, and Altar Unvail'd and Supported; in which the Nature of the Eucharist is explain'd according to the Sentiments of the Christian Church in the Four First Centuries* (London, 1714).

30 This was probably *The Case of Occasional Days and Prayers: containing a defence for not solemnizing the Accession-Day . . . and for not using occasional prayers* (London, 1721).

31 Johnson was ultimately called to account. He was apparently given an ultimatum: either issue a complete retraction or face prosecution. Johnson chose the former. In a statement made on March 3, 1723, he wrote: "Now know all Men by these presents that I the sd J. J. do acknowledge and confess myself sorry for having given offence in the matters contained in the said Articles & do hereby retract the negative Issue given by me to them & do confess the said Articles in all and every part thereof & submit myself in all things to the Rt. Revd the Archdeacon." (Arch. W. Epist. 9, fo. 277, Christ Church, Oxford.)

32 Curteis to Wake, November 29, 1722, Arch. W. Epist. 9, Christ Church, Oxford.

33 William Curteis to Joseph Tucker, October 20, 1715, ESRO Fre. 5368.

34 "Appeal to the Reason and Consciences of all True Englishmen," BL Add. MS 33, 344 ff.

35 Thomas Curteis, *Advice to a Son at the University, Design'd for Holy Orders. By a Clergyman* (London, 1725), p. 80.

36 "Appeal to the Reason and Consciences of all True Englishmen," BL Add. MS 33, 344 ff. 86-87.

37 See, for instance, the attitudes of the High Church Frewens on this issue in Jeffrey S. Chamberlain, "Portrait of a High-Church Clerical Dynasty in Georgian England: The Frewens and Their World," in Walsh et al. *The Church of England*, pp. 299-316.

38 Curteis to Wake, September 21, 1723, Arch. W. Epist. 9, fo. 273, Christ Church, Oxford.

39 Curteis, *Advice to a Son at the University*, p. 83.

40 Curteis informed Bishop Gibson in 1729 that he had "lately" published these essays. But he also noted that he "took the strictest care to be concealed," which makes identifying them difficult even if they are still extant. Lambeth Palace Library, MS 1741, fos. 57-61. The *Eighteenth-Century Short Title Catalogue* contains no references to works with the titles Curteis mentioned, but he may well have been taking liberties of paraphrasing which were so frequent among eighteenth-century bibliographers.

41 Curteis to Gibson, April 12, 1729, Lambeth Palace Library, MS 1741, fos. 57-60.

42 See for example [Robert Grove], *A Perswasive to Communion with the Church of England* (London, 1683).

43 Note, for example, the preaching of John Frewen in Chamberlain,

"Portrait of a High-Church Clerical Dynasty," pp. 300-303.

44 Lionel Cust and Sidney Colvin, *History of the Society of Dilettanti* (London, 1914), pp. 36–37.

45 KAO, U 269/C 148/2, 8, 10. BL Add. MS 32, 698 f. 371. Curteis's son, Thomas, and brother, John, also supported Middlesex. KAO, U 269/ C 148/18/1 and 3.

46 The Tory/High Church coalition in Sussex in 1741 argued against supporting him because he "eminently distinguish'd Himself" in his personal behavior and in his "conduct in Parliament, in voting for the Convention, Repeal of the Test, &c&c." *An Address to the Freeholders of the County of Sussex* (n.p., December 1741). Thomas Frewen, a Sussex High Churchman, wrote to his cousin Thankful in 1741 that "I think the clergy who vote for Ld Middlesex, are beyond all others the most inexcusable; because He voted for repealing the Test Act, besides his being obnoxious upon other accounts." December 5, 1741, ESRO Fre 1301.

47 Curteis, *Advice to a Son at the University*, p. 85.

48 Curteis to Wake, November 23, 1717, Arch. W. Epist. 7, fo. 53, Christ Church, Oxford.

49 Curteis, *Advice to a Son at the University*, p. 85.

50 *The Distinction of High-Church and Low-Church, Distinctly Consider'd and Fairly Stated. With Some Reflections upon the Popular Plea of MODERATION* (London, 1705), pp. 29-30; J. H. Overton and F. Relton, *The English Church from the Accession of George I to the End of the Eighteenth Century* (1896); J. H. Overton, *The English Church in the Eighteenth Century*, 2 vols. (1878); Horton Davies, *Worship and Theology in England* (Princeton, 1965), III.

51 Curteis to Wake, October 31, 1724, Arch. W. Epist. 10, fo. 92, Christ Church, Oxford.

52 Thomas Curteis, *Essays Moral and Divine, . . . Design'd to illustrate the Necessity, Authority, and Amiableness of Revealed Religion*, 2nd edn, (London, 1715); *A Dissertation on the Unreasonableness, Folly, and Danger of Infidelity; Occasion'd by a late Virulent Book [by Anthony Collins], intitul'd A Discourse on the Grounds and Reasons of the Christian Religion* (London, 1725); *Reflexions on Natural and Reveal'd Religion: Design'd as a Preservative against the Growing Scepticism of the Present Age: and Particularly against the Subtil Insinuations in a late Book [by Matthew Tindal], intitul'd, Christianity as Old as the Creation* (London, 1733); *Genethlia: A Poem on the Blessed Nativity. Design'd to excite an Awful Sense of Religion both in the Indolent and Unbelieving Part of Mankind* (London, 1727); *The Harmony between Natural and Revealed Religion, Asserted. In a sermon preached before the Worshipful the Master, Wardens, and Company of Apothecaries, in London, on the 23rd of September, 1731* (London, 1731); and *Christianity, in its Nature and Design, Offers no Violence to the Reason or Conscience of Men. A Sermon preach'd in the Chapel at Tunbridge-Wells, on Sunday, the 31st of August, 1735* (London, 1735).

53 *Dissertation*, pp. 17-18; *Reflexions*, p. v.

54 *Dissertation*, pp. 22–25.
55 Ibid., pp. 28-34.
56 Ibid., p. 46. See also his *Harmony between Natural and Revealed Religion*. I am indebted to Peter LeFevre for providing me with a copy of this sermon.
57 *Reflexions*, pp. iii-iv.
58 Ibid., p. 12.
59 Ibid., p. 13.
60 Ibid., p. v.
61 *Dissertation*, pp. 89-179.
62 Ibid., pp. 14-15.
63 Ibid., p. 67.
64 *Reflexions*, p. 6.
65 Ibid., p. ii.
66 Ibid., p. xi.
67 *Reflexions*, dedication.
68 *Dissertation*, p. 16.
69 Ibid., p. 68.
70 *Dissertation*, p. 14.
71 As John Veneer, Rector of St. Andrew's in Chichester, lamented, "The most dangerous restless, and insolent Enemies that we have now, are a numerous and increasing Party of Apostate Infidels, carrying on their Cause, some of them, in a sly and crafty, others with a most unheard-of Degree of Insolence and Audaciousness." (*An Exposition on the Thirty Nine Articles of the Church of England*, 2nd edn, 2 vols. [London, 1724] 1, pp. xvi–xvii. See also Walsh and Taylor, *The Church of England*, "Introduction," pp. 21–22.)
72 Curteis to Wake, October 31, 1724, Arch. W. Epist. 10, fo. 92, Christ Church, Oxford.
73 Ibid.
74 *Reflexions*, p. 113.
75 Stanley Burroughs, Rector of Sapcote, Leicestershire, c. 1780. ESRO Fre. 736.

IV

Orthodox defenses, heterodox results

CHAPTER 9

Deists and Anglicans: the ancient wisdom and the idea of progress

Joseph M. Levine

I

For much of the early modern period it was a commonplace to say that all true knowledge and wisdom had come from the East, and in the course of centuries had made its way by degrees to Europe and even to America. Typically, for James Howell in 1642, the transit of the arts and sciences was like the movement of the sun, traversing the world from East to West in endless cycles. The ancient wisdom, "budded first among the Brachmans and Gymnosophists in India, then blossom'd amongst the Chaldeans and Priests of Egypt, whence it came down the Nile, and crossed over to Greece . . . and bore ripe fruit." Afterwards it found its way to Italy, and "then clamber'd over the Alpine hills to visit Greece and France, whence the Britaines and other North West Nations of the Roman World fetch'd it over." Nor was it impossible, Howell concluded, "that the next flight it will make, will be to the Savages of the newly discovered World in America, and so turn round, and by a circular perambulation visit the Levantines again." Not everyone was so optimistic, although the philosopher, George Berkeley, certainly held out the prospect for America when he set out for Bermuda in 1721.[1]

The career of the ancient wisdom is, of course, much too vast a subject to attempt in this space. Indeed, it is a story that in its fullness still remains to be told.[2] During the seventeenth century it proved a convenient notion to all sorts of people, from historians, like Walter Ralegh, who sought a beginning to human history; to natural philosophers, including astrologers and alchemists and even the great Newton himself, who found comfort in the thought that they had been anticipated in antiquity; to the theologians of almost all parties who were committed to finding an historical authority for their partisan convictions. Needless to say there was much disagreement about the content of the ancient wisdom as well as its transmission through the ages, but there were hardly any doubters, except perhaps for a few recalcitrant Puritans, who thought the Scriptures were endangered by the idea, and a few of the new philosophers, who felt they had to wipe the slate clean before they could proceed. It was natural that the subject should come up for dispute in that great quarrel between the ancients and the moderns that came to a climax in the last decade of the century: the notorious "battle of the books." What I should like to do here is describe one crucial intersection between that controversy and another bitter quarrel that was going on more or less simultaneously between deists and Anglicans, and that involved many of the same people. And I would like to suggest a somewhat paradoxical conclusion: that it was the proponents of the "modern" cause who chose to lead the onslaught against the deists, and it was the deists who were, in this respect anyway, decidedly more backward than their orthodox opponents.[3]

A word first about the battle of the books.[4] The chief proponent of the ancients was Sir William Temple, whose little essay in 1690 began the quarrel. There Temple argued simply and forthrightly that what was oldest was best and that the ancients had excelled the moderns in every human achievement. He repeated the traditional notion that all wisdom and knowledge had begun in the East, in China, Ethiopia, Egypt, Chaldaea, Persia, Syria, and Judaea, from whence came the astronomy and astrology, magic, geometry, natural philosophy, and ancient history of the Greeks: of Orpheus, Lycurgus, Pythagoras, Plato, and the rest.[5] Pythagoras had been typical of the Greeks in traveling first to Egypt, where he spent some twenty-two years in study and conversation, and then to Babylonia for twelve years to learn from the Chaldaean magi, from where (so it was said) he went on to Ethiopia, Arabia, India, Crete and Delphi, and listened to all the famous oracles. What sort of learning he must have gained from this could best be illustrated, Temple thought, by the Indian Brachmans, who were dedicated to the service of the gods, to studies of wisdom and nature, and to the counsel of princes. They believed the earth was round and had had a beginning, that the author of it was a spirit or mind that pervaded the whole universe, and that souls lived on in transmigration after death. They had an estimable moral philosophy besides. In short, they sounded more than a little like deists! It seemed probable to Temple that Pythagoras had learned both his science and his morality from them and brought them back to Greece and Italy, just as those later Greek sages, Democritus and Lycurgus were to do. Thus the Eastern wise men were ancients to the Greeks, just as the Greeks are ancients to us.

Needless to say the moderns were offended. Temple's claims were sweeping and a lot of ground had to be covered. The philosophers of the Royal Society were particularly annoyed by Temple's disparagement of their achievement and they selected the precocious young scholar William Wotton to provide an "official" answer. The result was a large book that took up Temple's argument point by point and discipline by discipline. Oddly enough, Wotton pretty much conceded the humanities, allowing that the Greeks and Romans had set the standards there which the moderns were forced to imitate in order to succeed. On one point only did he proclaim a specifically modern victory. Philology, he argued (that is to say classical scholarship), appeared to him a glorious modern achievement through which it was possible for a modern to come to know an ancient author even better than they had known themselves! Textual and contextual criticism, along with archaeology (i.e. the study of classical antiquities), could lay bare the meaning of a classical text in a way that no one could do before modern times. In this matter Wotton was helped by his friend Richard Bentley, who showed how Temple and his friends had made a grievous error in elevating the letters of the ancient Greek tyrant, Phalaris, as a great literary classic, when in fact they were a late and inept forgery by an anonymous sophist. Not even the combined wit of Christ Church and the satire of Jonathan Swift, all hastily patched together to defend Temple, could quite obscure the serious claims of the new philology; the epistles of Phalaris died a lingering death while the battle over the uses and abuses of scholarship went merrily on.

Wotton was on stronger ground when he attacked the claims of ancient science and philosophy. In the preface to his *Reflections upon Ancient and Modern Learning* (1694), he argued that the oldest was not, indeed could not, always be the best, since most human achievement needed time to develop. It was clear to him that in many crucial parts of learning, "the Ancients were, comparatively speaking, grossly ignorant."[6] His book was an attempt to show this exactly by comparing the knowledge and achievement of the ancients and moderns in every field of human learning, using all the implements of modern scholarship to make his case. His assumption – and as A. O. Lovejoy once insisted, the guiding conviction of both the classicists and the deists – was that human nature had remained constant through all the ages; therefore, whatever advantage later times may have had must be in all those fields where the *accumulation* of knowledge mattered, in science and philosophy, for example, or in classical scholarship – and even in theology. Wotton was willing to exempt the humanities, which he thought needed less time to ripen and had had peculiarly favorable circumstances in ancient Greece and Rome, and which, he was willing to allow might have been perfected long ago. He was thus happy to divide the field, leaving literature and the arts and moral philosophy to the neoclassicists, but claiming all the rest for the moderns.

But what was a young Anglican clergyman doing writing about such a subject? In fact Wotton believed that his work could (among other things) serve a useful religious purpose. In this he seems to have taken his chief inspiration, and something of his argument, from Bentley's Boyle Lectures a year or two before.[7] Apparently there was an old notion still circulating then about the eternity of the world, or at least its very great duration, that Wotton believed was particularly unsettling to the Christian faith, since it tended to undermine the history in Genesis. The claims to a fabulous antiquity by Egyptians, Chaldaeans, and Chinese seemed only to threaten the authority of the Bible. Temple had argued that a succession of floods and barbarian invasions must have destroyed all the early records, leaving only the last five or six thousand Biblical years accessible – a notion, Wotton feared, only too convenient for anyone who wanted to believe that Christianity was a sham. The best answer to that, Wotton believed, was to show conclusively, "how the world had gone on from Age to Age, Improving; and consequently, that it is at present much more Knowing that it ever was since the earliest Times to which History can carry us." Such an improvement could only have occurred within a finite amount of time. In other words, Wotton was ready to propose a progressive version of history to replace the cyclical views of Howell and Temple in order to defend the truth and uniqueness of the Christian worldview. Paradoxically, it was Christian orthodoxy that seemed to require the idea of progress, while the radical deists, so apparently modern in other respects – for example, in their disparagement of all authority – seemed to prefer an essentially timeless past.[8]

Wotton's scholarship was up to date; he had the advantage of several generations of philologists who had set themselves the awkward task of sifting through all the evidence of classical antiquity. It was not only Phalaris who came under critical scrutiny, but in particular many of those very sources that had made claims for the ancient wisdom: the chroniclers of ancient Egypt and Chaldaea and Phoenicia whose lost works were quoted by Eusebius and others; the theosophical writings attributed to Hermes Trismegistus, Zoroaster and the sibylls; the Hebrew Cabala; even Homer, whose claims to a philosophical wisdom had long been asserted. Wotton says categorically that there were no histories older than Moses', none that did not, "by their Contradictions, betray their Falshood." In later chapters of the book he argues concretely against the pretended knowledge of Pythagoras, whose mathematics would have looked paltry indeed next to Barrow and Newton; of the Egyptians, whose claims to antiquity were inflated and whose natural philosophy was all magic and astrology; and to the pretensions of Chaldaeans and Arabians, Indians and Chinese.[9] There were no shortcuts to natural knowledge, which required time to make it good, as the examples of recent science and philosophy plainly demonstrated. Wotton argues that neither floods nor barbarian invasions could possibly have effaced all the useful inventions and achievements of earlier times. After all there had been but one universal flood, and neither Goths nor Vandals, Saracens nor Turks, not even the Tartars in China had scorned to borrow directly and eagerly from the cultures of their civilized victims. Wotton doubted that any useful invention had ever been lost, except to be replaced by a superior one. "Men are not such stupid Creatures, but if an Invention is at any time found out, which may do them . . . Service, they will learn it and make use of it." It was inconceivable to Wotton (men being the same in all ages), "that the History of Learning and the Arts should be of so confessedly late a Date, if the Things themselves had been many Ages older; much more if the World had been Eternal."

So the history of learning might be used to prove the truth of Christianity – or at least to disarm its critics. Wotton saw another possibility for religion in his enterprise. In an age when natural religion was denied by many and revealed religion by many more, he thought it might be useful to show how the knowledge of nature, which had so recently improved, might be used to disclose the wisdom and beneficence of God. Here again he followed Bentley, who had already pointed the way in his admirable discourses against atheism, showing how "an accurate search into Nature" might lead directly to its divine author, "so as to leave the unbelieving World without Excuse." Nor was it difficult for Wotton to show that theology had made great progress along with the rest of learning, not only in its new understanding of nature, but in its ability to recover the sources of Christian conviction more exactly and more capably than ever before. As a result modern controversialists, even heretics and Socinians, were superior to their ancient counterparts!

II

Wotton does not mention the deists directly, but Bentley had entitled the first of his Boyle lectures, "The Folly of Atheism and (what is now called) Deism," thereby conflating, and to some extent confusing, the two. Bentley's real target seems to have been Epicureanism both ancient and modern, that is to say materialistic atomism, and his chief weapon was Newtonian physics, which he first checked out with the master himself.[10] Bentley does not name the modern deists but insists that they were only concealing their atheism for fear of running foul of the magistrates, and giving lip service to a God they did not believe. He was certainly thinking of Thomas Hobbes[11] and possibly the Hobbist writer Charles Blount, who was then stirring the world with a series of provocative pamphlets that were meant to popularize the ideas of the first of the English deists, Lord Herbert of Cherbury. Blount was deliberately eclectic and never made a systematic statement. He seems rather to have tried to marshall every argument he could find, without worrying much about consistency, to harry the priesthood and proclaim the virtues of freedom of expression and religious toleration.

Lord Herbert, on the other hand, was no materialist. Already in 1624 he had set out something like a deist program, which he reiterated and defended for the rest of his life, but it was only after his death in 1648 that the full proportions of his heresy became gradually public.[12] *De Veritate* was Herbert's response to what he believed was the overriding problem of the age: the great religious quarrels that had divided and disturbed the world since the Reformation. His answer was to propose a true and indubitable common denominator for all religion to which everyone could give allegiance. And he found it in five simple propositions that recur in all his works and that were repeated with only small changes by Blount and many of his deist successors. They were, according to the formulation in Herbert's autobiography:, "(1) That there is one supreme God; (2) That he is to be worshipped; (3) That virtue and Piety joined with Faith in and love of God are the best ways to serve and worship him; (4) That wee ought to repent us of our Sinnes and seriously to return to God and the Right way; (5) That there is reward and Punishment both in this life and after it."[13] This natural religion, Lord Herbert believed, was imprinted on the minds of all men and was known by reason. Everything else that was claimed for religion was controversial, uncertain, and indifferent, although it was just those things about which men fought.

Lord Herbert tried to justify his views philosophically by attempting a neoplatonic epistemology and historically by employing the ancient wisdom. He wanted to establish that the five common notions both could be, and had actually been, known with certainty by wise men through all time. His rationalism (like that of the Cambridge Platonists or his correspondent, René Descartes) was thus an effort to meet the dogmatists on the one hand, who insisted on an exclusive revelation, and the skeptics on the other, who denied everything. This meant, for him, playing down all revealed truth in favor of a religious knowledge that was both certain and universal. Lord Herbert thought that he could demonstrate this by appealing to the two neutral grounds that could be put beyond interest and prejudice, that is to say reason and history, which he found nicely to agree. In the *De Veritate*, he attempted philosophy; in his posthumous works, the *De Religione Laici* and the *De Religione Gentilium*, he turned to history.

In looking backward, Herbert found two sources that pretended to religious knowledge: on the one hand a mixed bag of ancient writings about pagan beliefs; on the other, the miscellaneous Scriptures of Christians and Jews. He was eager to submit both to the test of reason. How else was one to determine the truth of the different and contradictory claims, of the strange and improbable stories that were set out there? Certainly, no tradition or authority could be accepted at face value; everyone knew now about the pious frauds that littered Christian history. Herbert was free, therefore, to pick and choose according to the dictates of his a priori reason. And so he found it not difficult to show that both pagans and Christians had shared an original wisdom, a belief in the common notions that was unavoidable to rational men. But he also found that the clergy from earliest times had deliberately fostered superstition out of self-interest, and this explained the great mass of pagan rites and ceremonies that filled his ancient sources. In the *De Religione Gentilium*, published in 1663 and translated in 1705 as *The Antient Religion of the Gentiles and Causes of their Errors Consider'd*, Herbert showed how pagan religion had begun in rational purity only to be corrupted by Egyptian priests who introduced rites and ceremonies, and pretended to prophecies to bolster their authority. Eventually they passed down their false religion to the Syrians, Greeks, and Romans, "for almost all Religion and Superstition came from the East."[14] With the help of continental erudition, particularly the work of G. J. Vossius, and the reports of modern travelers who had been to America, Herbert took his readers on a tour through the astral religion of the ancients, and the euhemeristic creation of many of their gods, comparing them with the pagan beliefs of modern Indians, to account for both the wisdom *and* the ancient superstition that he found everywhere, locked in a perpetual and timeless rivalry.[15] Lord Herbert taught the deists to believe in both the ancient wisdom *and* in the ancient superstition, caught up in a rivalry that had never changed.

The implications for Christianity were plain enough. In the *De Religione Laici* Herbert considered the claims of revelation.[16] There he insisted forthrightly that the only test of religious truth was reason. The Scriptures were fraught with difficulties of transmission and interpretation that left only reason competent to adjudicate the inevitable disputes. Antiquity and authority could hardly settle matters when it was clear that the canon was unsettled, the text full of interpolations and excisions, the original Hebrew ambiguous, and the narrative by different authors confused by obvious discrepancies. Nor was it clear what to do with the stories and miracles recounted there, since they were at odds with experience and common sense, and so were likely to be the invention of priests and politicians intent on establishing a new government or religion. It was not that Herbert wished to discard the Scriptures altogether; he preferred to submit them to reason and common consent and accept only those things that did not conflict with universal principles. On this point Christians could accept the teaching of the wisest pagans, who "did not think any Doctrines ought to be built on Faith only . . . for they easily discovered how they might be imposed on by that means."[17] In affirming natural religion Herbert was, of course, sharing the arguments of the many Anglican divines who were then opposing Puritan enthusiasm by endorsing reason; but in suggesting its self-sufficiency, he was stepping boldly into heresy.[18]

Much of this Charles Blount picked up and reiterated in a series of anonymous works that he began to print about 1679.[19] In one he dealt with ancient opinions about the soul; in another, about the origins of pagan idolatry, in particular about the gentile sacrifices. While he claimed to be defending Christianity, and specifically exempted it from the criticisms he applied liberally to ancient superstition, the implications were plain enough to rouse the ire of the censor, Sir Roger L'Estrange, and one offending pamphlet was burned. To a later writer it appeared that "his early dislike to superstition hurried him into dangerous mistakes, and induced him to believe all Religion priestcraft."[20] In the *Religio Laici* (1683) Blount directly resumed Lord Herbert's arguments for the five common notions. But generally Blount preferred to criticize rather than to construct, indirection rather than plain statement, perhaps because he had little choice, and his most interesting work may be the translation – published in 1680 – of *The Two First Books of Philostratus Concerning the Life of Apollonius of Tyaneus*, which he adorned with elaborate notes in his usual "Montaignizing" way. The choice of work was deliberately provocative, since Apollonius had long been proposed as a kind of pagan rival to Christ, a pure teacher and prophet who had also worked miracles. Blount knew that at least one heathen writer, Hierocles, had compared the two to the disadvantage of Christ, but he argued that Eusebius had long ago confuted Hierocles and that any comparison must work to the advantage of true religion. Blount protested his fidelity, too much it seems since everyone suspected his intentions anyway.[21]

It would not be easy to make a consistent treatise from his notes, and I shall not try. Blount alarmed his orthodox readers by quoting with approval from Hobbes, Lord Herbert, and even the notorious Vannini, asking only for charity and freedom of thought. Perhaps more disconcerting were his frequent comparisons between Christianity and paganism, and his constant reminders that all religions and religious sects condemned their rivals to perdition, so that none could easily proclaim authority. "If Preachers, Teachers and Pastors . . . disagree about Matters, which they preach up as necessary points of Faith, they deservedly lose all Credit and Authority." And again:

How vain it is for men to pretend every Opinion necessary in so high a degree, that if all said true, or indeed any two of them in 500 Sects . . . it is 500 to one that every man is damned. For 'tis naturall to all Zealots to call their own Enemy God Almighty's enemy, and we may as well hang all men that are not like us in feature as in opinion.[22]

Since self-love was the predominant passion in mankind, each religion naturally preferred its own vantage point. "This made *Hierocles* the *Heathen* so much extol *Apollonius* above *Christ*, and *Eusebius* the *Christian* prefer *Christ* to *Apollonius*."[23] It was only "narrowness of fancy" to assume our own opinions or customs to be infallibly the best.

Blount was plainly skeptical of the supernatural, of miracles, prophecies, and witchcraft, "for to believe any Stories that are not approved of by the publick Authority on our Church is superstition; whereas to believe them that are, is Religion." Nevertheless he agreed with Hobbes about the importance of religious ceremonies in preserving civic order. It was better, therefore, to rest religion on reason rather than general opinion or antiquity, "lest some *Jew* or *Pagan* come and supplant me."[24] Blount accepted the notion that all knowledge had been carried from East to West, and like Wotton later, that it had generally developed over time. But like Herbert, he believed that religion "was clearest at the beginning," and had been corrupted by priestly superstition; as a result, "All men ought to reverence Antiquity, but not conclude it infallible."[25] Besides how could we know that the ancients always wrote what they believed? As with us, "The Law and Religion of their Country, may often have obliged them to accomodate their Precepts to the Politicks of their Government."

Still, Blount continued to believe, as all the deists had to, in an original condition of simplicity, when the truths of natural religion were unsullied, "without any allay of Art or Custom."[26] Such notions as the immortality of the soul had, therefore, come down from the earliest times, from the Jews to the Egyptians (when Abraham lived in that country), to Pythagoras, who taught it to Socrates, and so on. In the end, however, Blount seems not to have been satisfied with either the ancient wisdom or the authority of the Bible; the immortality of the soul, he believed, had been proclaimed most effectively by legislators – not philosophers – who understood its practical value in prescribing morality. Whether it was true or not, it was undoubtedly useful, and that was what really mattered.[27] Religion was more important, more practical, because it was more influential than all the speculations of philosophy. And religion, for Blount, was always a matter of social convenience – or indeed inconvenience – too important to be left to the priests.

Blount died prematurely and it was left to his young disciple Charles Gildon to complete his work and reply to Bentley. In 1693 Gildon published the *Oracles of Reason*, a mixed collection of pieces, many by Blount, and a few in his own name. In one he pointed out that Bentley had expended great energy to develop arguments for a divinity when there was no one who actually doubted the matter! Deists were not atheists. Gildon doubted John Locke's antideist notion that there were in fact some peoples who had no notion of God and he reaffirmed the idea of Providence against Lucretius.[28] On the other hand he insisted that a strict chronology of six thousand years for the world's duration could not be maintained. Histories might have been lost, records might not have been kept, the Chinese, Brachman, and Egyptian claims could not be easily dismissed. He also found Bentley's arguments for a spirit independent of matter unconvincing and welcomed Thomas Burnet's recent work (partly translated by Blount) in which he had demonstrated that the Mosaic account of creation could not be taken literally, but was only a parable.[29] Of course if Genesis was nothing but a parable, who was to say that the Persians might not be just as right as the Jews? Among other things, Blount wondered whether the Pentateuch could actually have been written by Moses.[30]

III

Although deist writings had been few enough so far, the alarm rang furiously throughout the land. To the orthodox it seemed that subversive ideas were spreading everywhere, particularly in the coffeehouses and behind closed doors, beyond the reach of the law. Worst of all, deist ideas were turning up apparently right within the camp of the faithful, particularly among those rational Anglicans, the Cambridge neoplatonists and Latitudinarian divines, who were so intent on exalting reason and combatting enthusiasm that they seemed to anticipate, perhaps even to originate, much of the deist position.[31] It is not altogether surprising that some thought the Archbishop of Canterbury (Tillotson) and his cohorts to be deists in disguise – though, needless to say, they (like their Platonic friends) continued to cling to the necessity of revelation and even to some vestiges of clerical privilege. Since the deists insisted on maintaining, or pretending, that they too were honest Christians, the confusion was real and may account for some of the vitriol in the controversy. In any case, all sides continued to appeal to reason and to history as the arbiters.

It was Bentley's patron, Edward Stillingfleet, who first launched the Anglican attack on deism in 1677 with an appeal to history, after which historical scholarship remained the constant recourse of the orthodox clergy.[32] So for example William Nicholls, the learned rector of a little church near Chichester, used the same kind of philological criticism against Blount that Bentley was shortly to employ against Phalaris. He showed that the chief source which Blount had directed against Moses, the ancient Greek writer Occelus Lucanus, was certainly no contemporary of the Pentateuch, but had written many years later. No use relying on such testimony! And he repeated Wotton's argument that "the late Invention of the Arts, and the Shortness of the History of the World, are invincible Arguments against its Eternity."[33] But Nicholls was no modern; he managed still to cling to the notion of the world's decay, which together with a literal reading of Biblical history made him suspect any real idea of progress.[34]

Nevertheless it was just about this time that the idea began to dawn in the orthodox camp.[35] In 1696 the indefatigable John Edwards, a prominent divine with strong Calvinist convictions, launched the first of a torrent of tracts aimed at defending the literal meaning of Scripture with a work entitled *A Discourse Concerning the Authority Stile and Perfection of the Books of the Old and New Testaments*. The Bible was for him (as for Nicholls) the oldest and truest of historical writings; it furnished the only reliable account of the creation of the world and the early history of mankind, including the rise of nations, the origins of civil government, and the first invention of all the useful arts and sciences. Edwards followed his *Discourse* at once with *Some Thoughts Concerning the Several Causes and Occasions of Atheism*, a work he directed again at Burnet but also at John Locke, whose *Reasonableness of Christianity* suggested an affinity with deism that Locke tried staunchly but in some ways vainly to resist. It was the beginning of a long and frustrating exchange.[36]

It was while struggling to find an answer to the deists and their Christian allies that Edwards came upon Wotton's defense of modernity and put it immediately to work. He had seen that one of the great stumbling blocks to accepting Scripture was that the picture of ancient life represented there was so very different from the present. (This, of course, is just what the moderns were then discovering about ancient Greek life in the *Iliad*).[37] The Old Testament stories seemed now so strange, so unsuitable to the manners and customs of the present age, that modern readers were tempted to think that they had never happened. "These men do not well consider, nor distinguish between those times and these, which are exceedingly Different." He pointed out that to call the Biblical stories into question on these grounds would necessitate doing the same for much of ancient history, for the equally strange stories in Herodotus and Pliny, for example. But suppose, "the World is not now as it was then." Then the strangeness of the old stories could be explained by the distance of time, "the Posture of the World having much changed since these things happened."[38] It was just here that the scholarship of the moderns could be employed.

In 1699 Edwards attempted a definitive statement in two thick volumes entitled, *A Compleat History or Survey of all the Dispensations and Methods of Religion from the Beginning of the World.* He was conscious of entering uncharted territory; no one that he knew about had ever attempted as much on this theme before.[39] He meant to set out a universal history of mankind since creation, foretelling the future as well as describing the past. And he meant his history to show the progress of the human condition through a series of divine dispensations. He was, as R. S. Crane suggested long ago, the first in a long line of Anglican apologists to develop the idea of progress.[40] Edwards begins by disposing of Burnet once again and also the argument of Blount and the *pre-Adamites* that there were men before Adam. He then proceeds step by step to show how all the things in this world developed, "from things more imperfect to things that are perfecter," God revealing himself by degrees, "to discover his Will as it were by Parcels."[41] From Adam to Noah to Abraham to Moses, to the coming of Christ and the growth and spread of the Christian church, true religion is shown steadily to have advanced. Along the way Edwards disposes of the claims of Egypt over the ancient Jews, of Apollonius of Tyanaea, and other deist errors, as well as the notion that the early church was already perfect. When at last he comes to modern times he turns for particular help to William Wotton.

Edwards saw that he must find an answer to Temple and all those who had argued for a general decay. And so he enters now upon a long "digression" to demonstrate that many inventions had been discovered and all the arts and sciences improved in recent times. In this context, it was absurd to pretend that only theology and religion had declined. Edwards shows how modern theology had advanced over the fathers and the medieval schoolmen, until "all the more important Doctrines of Christianity are more plainly and clearly delivered than before."[42] And all this was but a prelude to what was still to come, for if we surpass all who went before, so the future was bound to bring further improvement in life and knowledge, even to perfection, just as the Bible and some early churchmen had predicted.

When, a few years later, a skeptical Thomas Baker joined the battle of the books and offered his own pessimistic canvas of ancient and modern learning, "wherein is shewn the Insufficiency thereof . . . in order to evince the Usefulness and Necessity of Revelation," Edwards renewed his argument that "Religion, even the Christian Religion, admitteth of some new Discoveries." "Truth," he believed, "was more surely purchas'd by Later Times . . . The further it moves, the more Strength and Force it gets."[43] Of course, true religion, Edwards had to admit in a telling qualification, was "ever the same, and as old as the Author. The Eternal Laws of Good and Evil do never alter."[44] But in the knowledge of particulars, "many things may be said to be new, and indeed are so, and there are Fresh Discoveries made in different Ages." Once again he attempted a broad canvas of modern learning to demonstrate its undeniable progress.[45]

IV

Edwards was a learned man who did his best to keep up with modern scholarship. But modern scholarship had won a kind of autonomy that was not always kind to Christian pretensions. This is particularly evident throughout the career of Richard Bentley. In his very first work, a commentary on the obscure Greek chronographer, Malelas, the young scholar took up a passage purporting to be by Sophocles, which declared an unambiguous monotheism. Although some of the Greek fathers had employed it in their apologetics, Bentley found it clearly spurious and made it plain that he felt the same way about those other pagan props of Christianity, the verses of Orpheus, the sibylline oracles, and the Jewish cabala. As Anthony Grafton has pointed out, Bentley "set out not only to discredit one bit of fake Sophocles but to destroy the whole armory of dubiously ancient texts with which Christian scholars had tried to show that the best of the Greeks agreed with them."[46] No wonder that his conservative friend Edward Bernard urged him to reconsider – with the only consequence that he inspired Bentley to a postscript in which he now ascribed the

Sophoclean fragment to some early Jews who hoped to show that the Greeks were monotheists like themselves. The ancient wisdom was thus being put in serious jeopardy by an Anglican clergyman and defender of the faith, though much to the discomfort of his fellows. When Bentley turned next to Phalaris, his critics saw at once how the same philosophical method applied to Scripture could bring the whole house down.

He would prove that Phalaris could not possibly be the Author of those Letters . . . Does he know Whose this sort of Proof is, and to what Ill Purpose it hath been employ'd? It is famous for being made use of by Spinoza to ruine the Authority of Moses's Writings . . . He cares not whether the Authority of the Sacred Writings sink with him.[47]

And when Bentley began to contemplate a new edition of the Greek Bible itself, which would confirm the critical labors of his old patron, John Mill, the panic grew. Mill, it was said, had found over thirty thousand variants in the old manuscripts!

It is not surprising, then, that Edwards began to have some second thoughts. Without retracting his earlier work, he set out in 1714 to say something deliberately on the other side in a book he called *Some New Discoveries of the Uncertainty, Deficiency, and Corruptions of Humane Knowledge and Learning*. He allowed that some knowledge was certainly useful in understanding ancient authors, but he seems to have been impressed by the arguments of the "ancients" in the battle of the books, whose suspicion of scholarship he now echoes. "It was but a poor and mean Employment to spend our Days in turning over Dictionaries, Vocabularies, Thesauruses, Etymologisms, Lexicons, Glossaries," and so on. In his attack on "pedantry", Edwards almost sounds like the Christ Church wits or Jonathan Swift against Richard Bentley. If Mill's findings were true, the Bible (like the *Epistles of Phalaris*) must be a "very uncertain Book."[48] What use could there be in pointing out omissions, faults and corruptions, except to give comfort to the deists? Suddenly Edwards wanted to restrain the scholarship he had once admired, not only for the sake of the Bible, but for other sensitive matters too, like the history of the Anglo-Saxon church, in which Humfrey Wanley and Elizabeth Elstob had lately resurrected some Catholic practices better forgotten. Nor was Edwards willing to allow any value to the reports of modern travelers to America or the Indies.[49] The theologian genuinely admired the new science and the new history as long as they favored his reading of

Scripture; but now he began to see with Temple and Baker that in many things modern knowledge remained uncertain and unhelpful. His opposition to the deists thus exposed some real limits to his modernity and qualified his optimism, even though it had helped him to frame an idea of progress that he never quite gave up. In the end he remained equivocal, unwilling to relinquish the fundamental modernist insight that the ancient past was unlike the present and so not repeatable.[50] And he even remembered to praise Bentley, in a postscript at the end of his work, for having used his formidable scholarship to defeat the latest of the deists, Anthony Collins.

It would require at least another chapter on this scale to describe how Bentley took on Collins, and Wotton the troublesome Toland, as deism provoked a host of orthodox moderns to train the weapons of their new scholarship on their rivals' stubborn recourse to history.[51] Suffice it to say that the issues remained much the same, with the deists' subversion of Scripture being met by a generally superior scholarship, a scholarship that, however, was not nearly enough to squelch either the a priori conviction that "Christianity was as old as creation," or the growing tide of skepticism. The deists kept their guns trained on "superstition" and the miraculous, and merely shifted their "ancient" sympathies from the Eastern sages to the classical Romans, especially Cicero.[52] The moderns kept their sights squarely on the spurious sources of the ancient wisdom which they continued to deride, but would just as little give up on the Greek and Latin classics.

And so both the deists *and* their Christian opponents eventually abandoned the wisdom of the East, although much less readily the wisdom and authority of their neoclassical schoolbooks. But it is the final paradox of our story that in the end it was the Christian moderns, perhaps even more than the radical deists, who contributed most to the ultimate decline of Christian conviction. By introducing an incipient idea of progress and a historicist reading of Biblical history, and by criticizing all the ancient sources – much as they were doing for classical literature – they gradually undid the universalist claims of both revealed religion and the pagan authors, and so left the way open to that historical relativism that is the characteristic mode of modern thinking about the past. Needless to say that did not happen all at once and was never their intention. In the meantime, they should probably be read first of all in their own setting, as staunchly, and for the time being successfully, holding up the dikes against the threatening flood.

NOTES

1 James Howell, *Instructions for Forreine Travel*, ed. Edwin Arber (London, 1868), p. 14; George Berkeley, "Verses on the Prospect of Planting Arts and Learning in America," first published in *A Miscellany* (Dublin, 1752).

2 I hope to deal with the English scene in a forthcoming book. For two episodes, see Joseph M. Levine, "Sir Walter Ralegh and the Ancient Wisdom," in Bonnelyn Kunze and Dwight Brautigam (eds.), *Court, Country, and Culture: Essays in Honor of Perez Zagorin* (Rochester, 1992), pp. 89–108; "Latitudinarians, Neoplatonists, and the Ancient Wisdom," in Richard Kroll, Richard Ashcraft, and Perez Zagorin (eds.), *Philosophy, Science, and Religion in England: 1640–1700* (Cambridge, 1992), pp. 85–108. In general, see Francis Yates, *Giordano Bruno and the Hermetic Tradition* (1964; rptd. New York, 1969) and D. P. Walker, *The Ancient Theology* (Ithaca, 1972).

3 In a way I shall be offering a kind of commentary on A. O. Lovejoy's famous article on "The Parallel Between Deism and Classicism" (1932), though from a rather different point of view; see his *Essays in the History of Ideas* (Baltimore, 1948), pp. 78–98.

4 For what follows, see Joseph M. Levine, *The Battle of the Books: History and Literature in the Augustan Age* (Ithaca, 1991).

5 William Temple, "An Essay upon the Ancient and Modern Learning," *Miscellanea*, part 2 (1690), in *The Works of Sir William Temple*, 4 vols. (London, 1814), III, pp. 449–58.

6 William Wotton, *Reflections upon Ancient and Modern Learning* (London, 1694), p. iv.

7 Richard Bentley's "Eight Boyle Lectures," were printed in *The Folly and Unreasonableness of Atheism* (London, 1692–93), and are reprinted in *The Works of Richard Bentley*, ed. Alexander Dyce, 3 vols. (London, 1838), III.

8 According to Bentley the reason of the deists, which is their only guide to religious knowledge, was given at the beginning and "does not lead the way further." Revelation, on the other hand, was for him progressive, and may yield "further discoveries and new prospects of things." In this it parallels the experience of science which (as Wotton showed and Bentley repeats in the third of his Boyle lectures) is also cumulative. See the sermon, "On Revelation and the Messias," July 5, 1696, in Bentley, *Works*, III, p. 223. And for the progress of science, sermon 3 (May 2, 1692), pp. 64–69.

9 The Brachman's teaching about the transmigration of souls, Wotton added later, "is a precarious idle Notion, which these besotted Indians do so blindly believe, that they are fearful of killing a Flea for a Louse, for fear of disturbing the Soul of one of their Ancestors" (Wotton, *Reflections*, 2nd edn [1697], p. 140).

10 For the exchange of letters (1692–93), see Isaac Newton, *Correspondence*, ed. H. W. Turnbull, 7 vols. (Cambridge, 1961), III, pp. 233–44.

11 See Bentley to Bernard, May 28, 1692, *The Correspondence of Richard*

Bentley, ed. Christopher Wordsworth, 2 vols. (London, 1842), I, pp. 38–41.

12 There is a translation of the 1645 edition with a useful introduction by Meyrick H. Carre, *De Veritate* (Bristol, n.d.). For Lord Herbert see the unsympathetic but wonderfully complete study by Mario M. Rossi, *La Vita, Le Opere, I Tempi di Edoardo Herbert di Chirbury*, 3 vols. (Florence, 1947); and more recently, R. D. Bedford, *In Defense of Truth: Lord Herbert of Cherbury and the Seventeenth Century* (Manchester, 1979), and Eugene D. Hill, *Edward, Lord Herbert of Cherbury* (Boston, 1987).

13 *The Life of Edward, First Lord Herbert of Cherbury*, ed. J. M. Shuttleworth (London, 1976), pp. 29–30.

14 Herbert of Cherbury, *The Antient Religion of the Gentiles and Causes of their Errors Consider'd*, trans. William Lewis (London, 1705), p. 13. The original version appeared first in Latin in Amsterdam, 1663.

15 Thus the heathen religion was neither "so absurd as is generally believ'd, being receiv'd for so many Ages by the most Learned Philosophers, the greatest and best magistrates and most Valiant Heroes," nor was it free from the grossest errors of wily priests; sacrifices, sacred mysteries, oracles, auguries, rites, and ceremonies, all deliberately contrived to conceal or stifle true religious principles. (*Antient Religion*, p. 270.)

16 *De Religone Laici*, edited and translated with a long useful introduction by Harold R. Hutcheson (New Haven, 1944).

17 Herbert of Cherbury, *Antient Religion*, p. 300.

18 The distinction between the two is made clear in Roger Emerson, "Latitudinarianism and the English Deists," in J. A. Leo Lemay (ed.), *Deism, Masonry, and the Enlightenment* (Newark, DE, 1987), pp. 19–48. See also, William M. Spellman, *The Latitudinarians and the Church of England 1660–1700* (Athens, GA, and London, 1993).

19 See J. A. Redwood, "Charles Blount (1654–93), Deism, and English Free Thought," *Journal of the History of Ideas*, 35 (1974), 490–98; Ugo Bonanati, *Libertinismo e deismo nel seicento inglese* (Florence, 1972). There is a lively sketch of Blount in T. B. Macaulay, *The History of England*, ed. Charles Firth, 6 vols. (London, 1913–15), V, pp. 2302–304.

20 *Biographia Britannica*, ed. Andrew Kippis, 5 vols. (London, 1780), II, p. 383.

21 Pierre Bayle, who could not read the English, was assured that the work was "full of poison," tending to destroy revealed religion and bring Christianity into contempt – not by a serious argument but by irony and jest; see his *Dictionary Historical and Critical*, trans. Pierre Des Maizeaux (London, 1734), II, p. 379, art. "Apollonius." For some other contemporary opinions, see G. R. S. Mead, *Apollonius of Tyanaea* (London, 1901), pp. 43–45.

22 Charles Blount, *Two first Books of Philostratus Concerning the Life of Apollonius Tyaneus* (London, 1680), pp. 4, 20.

23 Ibid., p. 5.

24 Ibid., pp. 82, 20.

25 Ibid., p. 20.

26 Ibid., p. 81. As he wrote in 1692, "Since the Notions of God and a good Conscience are written on our Souls at this day, so we cannot justly think, any of our Forefathers were deprived of them" (Blount to Major A, December 12, 1692, in *The Oracles of Reason* [London, 1693], p. 134).

27 Ibid., pp. 82, 230; cf. letter dated February 7, 1680, in *The Oracles of Reason*, pp. 123–26.

28 "Charles Gildon to Dr. R. B.," in *The Oracles of Reason*, pp. 178–94.

29 Ibid., pp. 191–95, 198; and Blount's letter to Gildon in defense of Burnet, March 23, 1693, pp. 1–19.

30 Ibid., p. 16. Skepticism of the Mosaic authorship had recently been voiced in a number of inflammatory works by Hobbes and Spinoza, Isaac La Peyrere, and Richard Simon, each of whom was well known to the deists and raised a storm of orthodox opposition. See for example, Josiah King, *Mr. Blount's Oracles of Reason Examined and Answered* (Exeter, 1698). Gildon seems to have returned to something like orthodoxy in his later work, *The Deists Manual: Or a Rational Inquiry into the Christian Religion* (London, 1705).

31 See Joseph M. Levine, "Latitudinarians, Neoplatonists, and the Ancient Wisdom," in Kroll et al., *Philosophy, Science and Religion*, pp. 85–108; and Emerson, "Latitudinarians and the English Deists," in Lemay, *Deism, Masonry and the Enlightenment*, pp. 19–48.

32 Edward Stillingfleet, *A Letter to a Deist* (London, 1677; 2nd edn 1697).

33 William Nicholls, *A Conference with a Theist* (London, 1696), pp. 21–23, 80. In 1697, Bentley too argued against Boyle that Occelus was a later author than was usually maintained – a Pythagorean writing in the Doric dialect – and even his opponent, the "examiner," had to agree that he wrote long after Moses. Nicholls seems to have considered the problem for himself; he believed that the offending work depended on Aristotle and was probably no older than Simplicius.

34 Nicholls's target is George Hakewill (see note 40). "For those Arts which are supposed to be invented in these late times, were in all probability only revived after a long time of disuse, or they might have been several times lost and as many times reinvented" (Nicholls, *Conference*, p. 84).

35 There is a forecast of it in the answer of Samuel Parker to the Platonist argument about the preexistence of souls.

> My Hypothesis is this, that it pleased Providence to place mankind here in an immature and imperfect state, that we might . . . by degrees be fitted for, and at length arrive at a better and more raised condition of life. As in nature all things commence their Beings in a rude and immature state, and make orderly progresses, to farther degrees of maturity, 'till they arrive at the utmost perfections their Beings are capable of; so is mankind Created and born into the World as it were in the Spring, in a Budding and Blossoming season, that so we may by proceeding forward in the differing Periods of our lives, grow up to higher and more excellent Capacities, 'till at length we ripen into a state of maturity and perfection. *An Account of the Nature and Extent of the Divine Dominion and Goodness* (Oxford, 1666), pp. 61–62.

36 For Edwards, see Joseph M. Levine, *Dr. Woodward's Shield: History, Science and Satire in Augustan England* (Berkeley, 1977), pp. 66–72; for Edwards and Locke, see Maurice Cranston, *John Locke: A Biography* (1957; rptd. London, 1968), pp. 390–92, 429–33; and H. O. Christophersen, *A Bibliographical Introduction to the Study of Locke* (1930; rptd. New York, 1968), pp. 57–66.

37 See Joseph M. Levine, "The Battle of the Books and the Shield of Achilles," *Eighteenth Century Life*, 9 (1984), pp. 33–61; Levine *Battle of the Books*, chapters 4–6.

38 John Edwards, *A Discourse Concerning the Authority Stile and Perfection of the Books of the Old and New Testaments* (London, 1696), p. 303.

39 Among Edwards's many sources, he cites a number of efforts at a universal history: Walter Ralegh's *History of the World* (pp. 28–31), George Hakewill, *An Apologie of the Power and Providence of God in the Government of the World* (pp. 618, 634), and Thomas Burnet's *Archaeologia* (pp. 26, 61). In addition, he was much absorbed in the quarrel among the geologists about the history of the world, even to making his own contribution: *A Demonstration of the Existence of God from the Contemplation of the Visible Structure of the Greater and Lesser World* (London, 1696). See *Dr. Woodward's Shield*, pp. 66–72. He also drew inspiration for the idea of progress from two ancients: Vincent of Lerins (p. 611) and Seneca (p. 615).

40 R. S. Crane, "Anglican Apologetics and the Idea of Progress, 1699–1745," *The Idea of the Humanities and Other Essays*, 2 vols. (Chicago, 1967), I, pp. 214–87.

41 John Edwards, A *Compleat History or Survey of all the Dispensations and Methods of Religion from the Beginning of the World* (London, 1699), pp. 396–97.

42 The digression on the progress of learning begins at p. 621; he gets to religion at p. 634.

43 John Edwards, *A Free Discourse Concerning Truth and Error Especially in Matters of Religion* (London, 1701), pp. 190, 634 ff. Baker's work, *Reflections on Learning* (London, 1699) quickly went through seven editions.

44 Ibid., p. 196.

45 The same argument is attempted a little later in a work dedicated to William Wotton, namely Roger Davies, *An Essay in the Socratic Way of Dialogue on the Existence of the Divine Being in Imitation of Tully's Tusculan Disputations* (London, 1724).

46 Anthony Grafton, *Defenders of the Text* (Cambridge, MA, 1991), pp. 14–17.

47 Charles Boyle, *Dr. Bentley's Dissertation on the Epistles of Phalaris Examin'd* (London, 1698), p. 121. For the quarrel generally and the authorship of "Boyle against Bentley," see Levine, *Battle of the Books*, chapters 2–3.

48 John Edwards, *Some New Discoveries of the Uncertainty, Deficiency, and Corruption of Human Knowledge and Learning* (London, 1714), pp. 11–12, 21.

49 Ibid., pp. 43–44, 56.

50 "There are no certain Rules in Policy now, for from what hath been, we cannot tell what shall be; because there are new Scenes, and Variety of

Changes continually starting up in all Parts of the World" (ibid., p. 63).

51 Collins's *Discourse of Free-Thinking* (London, 1713), was swiftly answered by Bentley (under the pseudonym Phileleutherus Lipsiensis) in his *Remarks upon a Late Discourse of Free-Thinking* (London, 1714). "You have shewn," according to a contemporary, "that their Misrepresentation of the Antients is . . . very gross." [Hare], *The Clergyman's Thanks to Phileleutherus for the Remarks on the Late Discourse of Free-Thinking* (London, 1713), p. 15. Leslie Stephen describes the mismatch between the "shabby and shrivelled little octavos" of the (generally anonymous) deists and the ponderous tomes of the orthodox, "very goliaths of books," by the most venerable names in English letters: Bentley, Locke, Berkeley, Clarke, Butler, Waterland, and Warburton. (Leslie Stephen, *History of English Thought in the Eighteenth Century*, 2 vols. (New York, 1949), I, p. 72.) Even Collins's biographer accepts the contemporary view that Bentley's victory was a genuine triumph of scholarship; see James O'Higgins, *Anthony Collins: The Man and his Works* (The Hague, 1970), p. 93. Toland's *Letters to Serena* (London, 1704) was quickly answered by William Wotton in his *Letter to Eusebia* (London, 1704). For Toland and the *philosophia perennis*, see Robert Sullivan, *John Toland and the Deist Controversy* (Cambridge, MA, 1982), chapter 6.

52 Thus Toland, who found the Battle of the Books very much alive in 1703, "all the perfections of the Moderns beyond the Schoolmen, have been revealed to them by the Ghosts of the Antients, that is, by following their rules, reading their works, imitating their method, and copying their stile, which last holds true in prose as in verse." "A Letter Concerning Roman Education," *A Collection of Several Pieces*, 2 vols. (London, 1726); Gunter Gawlich, "Cicero and the Enlightenment," *Studies on Voltaire and the Eighteenth Century*, 25 (1963), pp. 657–82; Stephen Daniel, *John Toland: His Methods, Manners and Mind* (Kingston and Montreal, 1984), p. 130.

CHAPTER 10

Henry Fielding and the problem of deism

Ronald Paulson

> It was deism that taught us to accept the pain of historicity. By granting God powers of initiation and then putting him to sleep forever, deism freed the mind from the puzzle of origins and cleared the way for historical consciousness. Without such a tacit premise, the novel could not have gotten very far, since it really has no room for a will superior to natural law.

These words are by Irving Howe in an essay called "History and the Novel."[1] Deism is not a phenomenon that is ordinarily related to the origins of the novel.[2] This is because it has usually been taken to mean ethical deism, one consequence of the view that God created the world and, having set it going, abandoned it. In Fielding's own words in *The Champion*, without an immanent God "then Mankind might be left to pursue their Desires, their Appetites, their Lusts, in a full Swing and without Control."[3] Owen Apshinken in *The Welsh [Grub-Street] Opera* (1731) is an ethical deist. His argument for seduction is that "Nature never prompts us to a real crime. It is the imposition of a priest, not nature's voice, which bars us from a pleasure allowed to every beast but man."[4] But in Fielding's works the emphasis more often falls on the priest, who masks nature with his doctrine.[5]

The association of Fielding with ethical deism is based on his supposed identification in *Joseph Andrews* with Mr. Wilson and his freethinking club.[6] The "young Men of great Abilities" in the club are Shaftesburian deists who profess a commitment to "the infallible Guide of Human Reason" and "the utmost Purity of Morals," denying "any Inducement to Virtue besides her intrinsic Beauty and Excellence." In practice, however, benevolence does not hold passion in check, and innate virtue is overbalanced by an equally innate but more powerful "unruly Passion," and one member of the club runs off with another's wife.

Samuel Richardson and his followers, hardly well-wishers, transmitted

Fielding to the nineteenth century as a debauched skeptic whose novels were low, immoral, and possibly blasphemous. But since James Work's corrective essay "Henry Fielding, Christian Censor" (1949), and Martin Battestin's book-length *Moral Basis of Fielding's Art* (1959), Fielding has been generally accepted as a Latitudinarian Anglican. Although in Fielding's day Latitudinarian meant to many no more than a safe deist, Battestin has emphasized his orthodoxy, and in an essay by Aubrey Williams he can be mistaken for an Anglican divine.[7] In their 1989 biography of Fielding Martin and Ruthe Battestin judge deism narrowly and censoriously from the Anglican perspective. They mention Benjamin Franklin's ethical deist tract *A Dissertation on Liberty and Necessity, Pleasure and Pain* (1725), "which, to his credit, he later repented of and tried to destroy"; and after referring to Franklin's failure to repay a debt to his (and Fielding's) deist friend James Ralph, the Battestins comment grumpily: "Such is the cement binding the friendships of deists." When they quote (another friend) Thomas Cooke's deist sentiment, "We should divest ourselves of all Prejudices . . . we should disjoin the monstrous Associations of Ideas of the tru [*sic*] God from the Idea of such a god as the Schools teach us to worship," the Battestins refer with heavy irony to "this noble enterprise" of Cooke ("an utter enemy to Christian doctrine").[8]

To see deism as simply a version of "God is dead and so everything is permitted," which Fielding repudiated and Ralph and Cooke played down in their writings, is to miss the real impact of deist thought on Fielding.[9] Irving Howe, in my epigraph, was referring to deism as a critical attitude, one with parallel sources in the Protestant Reformation and the English Enlightenment. As an extension of anti-Popery, deists questioned any priestcraft, and as an extension of empiricist reason, they questioned the authority of readings imposed on Scripture by the clergy, the evidence of the Scriptures themselves, and doctrines that flew in the face of reason.[10] The arch-heretic Bernard Mandeville distinguished deism from atheism: "He who believes, in the common acceptation, that there is a GOD, and that the world is rul'd by providence, but has no faith in any thing reveal'd to us, is a deist; and he, who believes neither the one nor the other, is an atheist."[11] While believing in God and his providential order, deists regarded the Bible and the church as purely human inventions; while subscribing to Christianity's moral principles, they could not believe they were mysteriously revealed in Scripture. Although critical deism was intertwined with ethical, it was the former that primarily affected Fielding and became instrumental in the "new Province of Writing" he founded, which he referred to as his own "great Creation."

HOGARTH

On the walls of the rooms in his "modern moral subjects" of the 1730s Fielding's friend William Hogarth represented old master paintings that include, but from which he has pointedly omitted, the figure of the deity. In the second plate of *A Harlot's Progress* (1732) he replaces the Old Testament God striking Uzzah dead with an Anglican bishop stabbing him in the back. In *Marriage A-la-mode*, plate 1 (1745) he reproduces a *Martyrdom of St. Agnes* but omits the upper level on which Christ and his angels wait to receive the soul of the saint. In *The Sleeping Congregation* (1736) he represents the inside of a church in which the "*Dieu*" of the royal motto is blocked out, leaving only "*et mon droit*," the civil authority, manifested by two clergymen.

Internal evidence for critical deism in *A Harlot's Progress* begins with the elision of God from the paintings and, as any sort of an effectual presence, from the scene itself: there is no divine intervention in the lives of his harlots and rakes in a world dominated by self-interested clergy and magistrates. The scenes are informed by parodic echoes of New Testament stories; for example, in plate 2 the angel of the Annunication is replaced by a London magistrate. Most often it is a clergyman: In plate 1 a parson turns his back on the girl to read the address of the Bishop of London, the source of clerical patronage (Bishop Edmund Gibson himself); in plate 2 a bishop stabs Uzzah; and in plate 6 a clergyman, who should be officiating at the Harlot's funeral, is making tipsy advances to the whore next to him. The most striking piece of external evidence is Hogarth's defecating on a church porch in Kent during the five-days "peregrination" that celebrated the successful publication of the *Harlot*.[12]

We can add Hogarth's belief, evident throughout his prints but emphasized in his writings on art culminating in *The Analysis of Beauty* (1753), that reason and not authority is the only basis for certitude. This is essentially the deist assumption, applied by John Toland and others to Christianity and by Hogarth to art, that ordinary human understanding is the only criterion of meaning and belief. The key word of Toland, author of *Christianity not Mysterious* (1696), was "priestcraft," the argument that a clergy maintained itself by focusing on the mysterious activity of God and arguing that they alone understood the mysteries of religion. Toland believed that laymen were the real measure of intelligibility, and he extended the concept, arguing that laymen were excluded equally from the mysteries of medicine, law, scholarship, and politics. Hogarth's attacks on the clergy also extended "priestcraft" to connoisseurs, picture dealers, and "men of taste."

Scriptural demystification is an aspect of Hogarth's revision of history painting – the highest painterly genre according to the art treatises, which he was attempting to recreate as a "new province" of painting in 1730s London. The first plate of the *Harlot* is constructed on two gestalts – the parson, harlot, and bawd; the harlot, bawd, and gentleman rapist lurking in a doorway. One parodies the model for history painting in Shaftesbury's *Tablature of the Judgment of Hercules* (1713) and the other evokes the satiric deflation of New Testament miracles by the deist Thomas Woolston in his *Six Discourses on the Miracles of Our Saviour* (1727–30). The Choice of Hercules can be inferred from the internal evidence of the three figures at the center of the plate; Woolston's portrait is on the wall in some versions of Plate 2.[13] The vigorously antideist Bishop Gibson, who persecuted Woolston, is alluded to in plates 1, 2, and 3.[14]

From these groupings, and from the visual–verbal references to the *Harlot* as a new art form in the subscription ticket, we can conclude that Hogarth's first "modern moral subject" (or, in Fielding's words in the preface to *Joseph Andrews*, "comic history-painting") is a response to Shaftesbury's dictum that history painters should model their histories on the classical Choice of Hercules (Heroic Virtue choosing Virtue over Pleasure). But Hogarth first substitutes for Shaftesbury's classical a Christian gestalt, and not the Life of Christ but the life of the Virgin (the parody of a visitation); he then replaces the New Testament figures of Mary, Elizabeth, and Zacharias with recognizable, living Londoners (Kate Hackabout, Elizabeth Needham, and Francis Charteris). For critical deists, once the classical myth was compromised by juxtaposition with the Christian, the Christian itself could be submitted to reason, which meant, in the terms of deist ridicule, revealing the historical reality beneath the myth. For Hogarth this meant carrying skepticism to the edge of blasphemy and probably explains why he removed the portrait of Woolston in the subscription edition of the *Harlot*.[15]

Cooke's contemporary *Letter to the Archbishop of Canterbury, concerning*

Persecution for Religion and Freedom of Debate (1732) was provoked by the case of Woolston, though he is not named. Cooke argues "that Freedom of debate about Religion is not only consistent with Christianity, but recommended in the *New Testament*, as previously necessary before we can arrive at a certainty of Truth"; he attacks "the Wickedness of persecuting for religion, and the Folly and Baseness of attempting to lay any Restraint on the Minds of Men," an attack which can be read as a defense of liberty in moral matters (Cooke places much emphasis on both charity and love). He reads the Gospels "in their original Purity," against the perversions and self-serving interpretations of the clergy.[16] Cooke's tract coincides with the publication of Hogarth's *Harlot* (its writing is dated February 1732); he cites Samuel Clarke (pp. 34–35) against persecution, which could explain the presence of Clarke's portrait alongside Woolston's in the *Harlot*, plate 2.[17] Cooke was also a friend of Hogarth, who etched a frontispiece for his translation of Hesiod (1727/28), and, in the context of his pamphlet and Hogarth's portraits of Woolston and Clarke, *A Harlot's Progress* can be interpreted as a plea for freedom from religious persecution.

For Hogarth deism was a contemporary form of Protestant iconoclasm, one which focused not only on the deity but primarily on the clergy that exploited the notions of revealed religion and an immanent deity for its own ends. For Fielding, however, deism was a much more complex and ambiguous phenomenon, including both critical and ethical aspects. In the 1750s both Cooke and Ralph attacked him for apostasy to his more liberal views of the 1730s – views that this chapter will attempt to recover.[18]

FIELDING'S FARCES AND *CHAMPION* ESSAYS

Demystification of the sort practiced in *A Harlot's Progress* also appears in Fielding's stage farces of the 1730s. The question, however, is where if anywhere among the overdetermined sources for these plays does Woolston's critique of Christ's miracles fit? Besides the dialogues of Lucian, the primary and most admired of his models, Fielding also drew upon Scriblerian satire, in particular *The Dunciad*, which represented Grub Street authors imitating Virgilian heroes, and even upon the Grub Street puppet shows and pantomimes that amused rather than satirized by "contrasting" (to use Fielding's own term) heroic, mythological, and high-literary actions with banal everyday doings.[19] But Lucian, who held up all religions and philosophies, including that of the early Christians, to a standard of reason and common sense, would have evoked the sort of impious skepticism associated with deism. He was particularly unpopular with the Anglican clergy. The Revd. Edward Young commented that "Some Satirical Wits, and Humorists, like their Father *Lucian*, laugh at every thing indiscriminately."[20]

Fielding's use of Lucian extended from the theatrical adaptations in *Tumble-Down Dick* (1736) and *Eurydice* (1737) to direct imitations such as "An Interlude between Jupiter, Juno, Apollo, and Mercury" and *A Journey from this World to the Next* gathered in his *Miscellanies* (1743). His persona of the 1730s derives from the Lucianic protagonist (a Menippus, Cyniscus, Damis, Diogenes, or Lucian himself) who asks questions, probing appearance, idealization, myth, and custom. This questioner begins on earth with pseudo-oracles and prophets, charlatans, and sophistical philosophers, then travels up to Olympus or down to Hades. He questions the gods themselves and throws them into confusion, revealing their shoddy pretensions to omniscience. They prove to be only humans who think most persistently about sacrifices, the sign of man's loyalty to them; but they have long since shirked their part of the agreement, and there is no causal relationship between prayers or deeds and rewards or punishments. The Lucianic questioner points to the disorder of experience, bringing this empirical reality to bear on the illogic of the myths of deity. He shows that Fate is on the one hand superior to the gods themselves, preventing them from answering prayers that were not foreordained anyway; on the other hand, superior to man, who therefore bears no responsibility for his misdeeds and has no reason to sacrifice to the gods or obey their laws. Consequently sacrifices have fallen off and man's duty to the gods is in abeyance.

The resemblance to deism, and in particular to the works of Woolston, would have been obvious to Fielding. Both Lucian and Woolston brought common sense (that is contemporary, domestic) reality to bear upon false prophets: for Lucian most notably in the story of Peregrine, for Woolston in the story of Christ.[21] But the most significant fact is that, unlike his friend the always bolder Hogarth (perhaps because of the potential for ambiguity in his visual medium), Fielding travesties only the safe classical myths of Lucian, neither Old nor New Testament stories.[22] Nevertheless he goes beyond mere travesty (in the manner of Scarron's *Virgile travestie* and its imitators) to analysis: his plays, like Woolston's *Discourses*, are really about the bad critics and exegetes, often associated with clergymen; their structure – in both staging and book publication – surrounds a text or action with comically divergent commentaries.[23]

The plays obsessively exploit the self-reflexive theatrical metaphor, which was a favorite explanatory model for providential design – life is a playhouse, we are the actors, and the manager who assigns roles is to an immanent God as the magistrates and clergymen were in *A Harlot's Progress*. Because of its pragmatic and provisional quality this was a metaphor appropriated by the deists.[24] When, as in *The Author's Farce* (1731), a play has a happy ending, and rewards and punishments are distributed, it is plainly the work of the playwright who is demonstrating the discrepancy between his and the real world. In the last, strongly political plays of 1736–37, a prime minister (Walpole) writes a (political) farce, manipulates his actors, and deceives his audience; and Fielding associates himself, the author of the play, with the minister as another surrogate (for the king in this case) and farceur.[25] He explores the discrepancy between what is shown and what is hidden behind the scenes, between actor and role, but also between the playwright's "providence" and the actual performance, marred by "chance" (that other crucial Fielding term): the bailiff who intercepts the actor before he can get to the theater, or even the audience that, for extraneous reasons, hisses the play.

With the Licensing Act of 1737 the plays came to an end, surrounded by accusations of scurrility, obscenity, and impiety that dogged Fielding into the 1750s.[26] In 1739–40 he specifically attacked deism in a series of *Champion* essays. The series began with two on January 22 and 24, 1739/40, continuing with four more (the essays "defending" the clergy) on March 29, and 5, 12, and 19, 1740. These essays express a more "official" view than the plays, for whose irreverence they may serve as an apology. Fielding criticizes deism in its three aspects: (1) the deletion of an immanent God (or, as he puts it, the desire to "believe the deity a lazy, unactive being" who will not intervene on our behalf); (2) the subsequent opening up of a libertine ethics; and (3) the denigration of the clergy (the climactic and most extended argument, clearly the most important for Fielding).

At the outset we notice that in these essays, while ostensibly condemning deism, Fielding utilizes the deist strategy of shifting attention from the question of revealed religion to the observable facts of human virtue and happiness in a social situation. The validity of religion for Fielding is based less on whether it is true or false than on whether it fulfills a social function. Moreover, though ostensibly statements of orthodoxy, these essays are Lucianic in their rhetoric.

The argument of the opening essay, against the deist assumption that God does not interfere in events, is couched in the subjunctive, as if hypothetical: "even *supposing* these Allegations were true, and Religion as false as they would have it imagined," and: "Was there no future state, it would be surely the *interest* of every virtuous Man to *wish* there was one" (emphasis added). Instead of a theological argument, Fielding offers a pragmatic one:

What a rapturous Consideration must it be to the Heart of Man to think the Goodness of the Great God of Nature concerned in his Happiness? How must it elevate him in his own opinion? How transported must he be with himself? What extatic Pleasure must he feel in his Mind. . . . If this be a dream, it is such a one as infinitely exceeds all the paultry Enjoyments this Life can afford. It is such a Delusion as he who undeceived you might be well said *Occidere & non servare*, to destroy, not preserve. How cruel woud it be in a Physician to wake his Patient from Dreams of purling Streams, and shady Groves, to a State of Pain and misery? How much more cruel then is this pretended Physician of the Mind [the deist], who destroys in you those delightful Hopes, which, however vain, would afford such a Spring of Pleasure during the whole Course of your Life.[27]

To begin with, the passage unmistakably recalls Swift, for example his satire in *The Mechanical Operation of the Spirit* (1704) on the notion, held primarily by enthusiasts and radicals who believed in unmediated inspiration, that God the Creator could be expected to intervene in human events: "Who, that sees a little paultry Mortal, droning, and dreaming, and drivelling to a Multitude, can think it agreeable to common good Sense, that either Heaven or Hell should be put to the trouble of Influence or Inspection upon what he is about?"[28] More precisely, Fielding echoes Swift's account in "The Digression on Madness" of "Happiness . . . convey'd in the Vehicle of Delusion" ("How shrunk is every Thing, as it appears in the Glass of Nature?"), which is the "sublime and refined Point of Felicity, called, *the Possession of being well deceived*; The Serene Peaceful State of being a Fool among Knaves."[29] However, he modulates Swift's savage irony with Addison's more sedate story in the *Spectator* issue 413 of the romantic knight errant wandering in a world of primary qualities:

our souls are at present delightfully lost and bewildered in a pleasing delusion, and we walk about like the enchanted hero of a romance, who sees beautiful castles, woods and meadows; and at the same time hears the warbling of birds, and the purling of streams [all of these, secondary qualities]; but upon the finishing of some secret spell, the fantastic scene breaks up, and the disconsolate knight finds himself on a barren heath, or in a solitary desert.

Addison's "purling of streams" and Fielding's "Dreams of purling Streams, and shady Groves" recall that "purling streams" and "shady groves," as a conventional image for romantic dreams of love, appeared, for example, in Eliza Heywood's dedication to *The Fatal Secret; or, the Lucky Disappointment: A Novel* (1724).

Most revealingly, Fielding's passage recalls the dialogue between Queen Ignorance and Queen Common Sense in his play *Pasquin* (1736), in which the former (whose adviser, and the chief villain of the piece, is significantly the cleric Firebrand) argues that "thinking makes men wretched; And happiness is still the lot of fools":

> While the poor goose in happiness and ease,
> Fearless grows fat within his narrow coop,
> And thinks the hand that feeds it is its friend.

This is Fielding in his satiric mode, anticipating the stripping away of sentimental illusion a few years later in his critique of Ricardson's *Pamela*. But in *The Champion* he speaks as a moralist, analogous to the Pope of the ethic epistles or *The Essay on Man* rather than *The Dunciad*.

SHAFTESBURY

Fielding's invocation of "happiness," and in particular the vocabulary of *rapture, ecstasy,* and *transportation*, probably owes more to Shaftesbury than to Swift or even Addison.[30] In his *Inquiry concerning Virtue and Merit* (1699, 1711) Shaftesbury denies Hobbes's view that virtuous behavior does not produce happiness, arguing that only the virtuous individual can experience true happiness, which consists in the ability to share the joy of benevolent acts. In the sequel he sums up a benevolent God and his providential design:

For 'tis impossible that such a divine order should be contemplated without ecstasy and rapture, since in the common subjects of science and the liberal arts, whatever is according to just harmony and proportion is so transporting to those who have any knowledge or practice in the kind.[31]

Rejecting Locke's *tabula rasa*, Shaftesbury posits a "moral sense" prior to education, prior to religious persuasion, but the Christian religion can supplement this moral sense as one agent (among others) of moral instruction. In the *Inquiry* his basic argument is that belief in a deity is of two kinds: it "must be either in the way of his power, as presupposing some disadvantage or benefit to accrue from him; or [as in the quotation above] in the way of his excellency and worth, as thinking it the perfection of nature to imitate and resemble him" (I, pp. 266–67). If, as in the first case,

> through hope merely of reward, or fear of punishment, the creature be incited to do the good he hates, or restrained from doing the ill to which he is not otherwise in the least degree averse, there is in this case . . . no virtue or goodness whatsoever. (I, p. 267)

In the second case the virtuous act is imitative, not prudential or pragmatic, and it supposes a deity as "an example" of beauty, virtue, and order that "must undoubtedly serve . . . *to raise and increase* the affection toward virtue, and *help* to submit and subdue all other affections to that alone" (I, p. 268):

> the admiration and love of order, harmony, and proportion, in whatever kind, is naturally *improving* to the temper, *advantageous* to social affection, and *highly assistant* to virtue, which is itself no other than the love of order and beauty in society. (I, p. 279, emphasis added)

Nevertheless Shaftesbury admits that "the fear of future punishment and hope of future reward, added to this belief," might contribute to the virtue of some people; though this "attention to self good and private interest . . . must insensibly diminish the affections towards public good or the interest of society, and introduce a certain narrowness of spirit, which (as some pretend) is peculiarly observable in the devout persons and zealots of almost every religious persuasion" (I, p. 269). Again, "the principle of fear of future punishment, and hope of future reward, how mercenary or servile soever it may be accounted, is yet in many circumstances a great advantage, security, and support to virtue." And:

> Thus in a civil state or public we see that a virtuous administration, and an equal and just distribution of rewards and punishments, is of the highest service, not only by restraining the vicious, and forcing them to act usefully to society, but by making virtue to be apparently the interest of every one, so as to remove all prejudices against it, create a fair reception for it, and lead men into that path which, afterwards they cannot easily quit. (I, p. 270–72)

Finally, he extends punishments in the afterlife to public executions in this life in which

we see generally that the infamy and odiousness of their crime, and the shame of it before mankind, contribute more to their misery than all besides; and that it is not the immediate pain of death itself which raises so much horror either in the sufferers or spectators, as that ignominious kind of death which is inflicted for public crimes and violations of justice and humanity. (I, p. 273)[32]

Here, in a nutshell, is the trajectory followed by Fielding's views of religion: from beautiful order (the world is a work of art), to pragmatic and provisional order based on fear and hope, to grim necessity in order to hold together a collapsing society.

Fielding could have been thinking of Shaftesbury when he declared repeatedly in *Tom Jones* that this work of art (like his hero, Tom) may appear to some observers flawed but is nevertheless a "great Creation." Shaftesbury describes a world that seems to the religious bigots, as well as atheists, fallen and flawed but to him a perfect, harmonious "system" made up of other systems, parts subordinated to a unified whole. Some men "find fault, and imagine a thousand inconsistencies and defects in this wider constitution," but others ("you, my friend, are master of a nobler mind") "are conscious of better order within, and can see workmanship and exactness in yourself and other innumerable parts of the creation" (II, p. 62).

Theocles (whose sermon on order this is in *The Moralists*) wonders that "there should be in Nature the idea of an order and perfection which Nature herself wants!" He admits that "Old Father Chaos (as the poets call him)" is ever threatening to extend "his realms of darkness. He presses hard upon our frontier, and one day, belike, shall by a furious inroad recover his lost right, conquer his rebel state, and reunite us to primitive discord and confusion" (p. 71). This leads to the implication that the philosopher-artist's substitute cosmos is called for precisely because the actual world, in the imaging of priestcraft, is marred with "a thousand inconsistencies and defects." Thus Theocles, in his ascending scale of forms, asserts "That the beautiful, the fair, the comely, were never in the matter, but in the *art and design*; never in *body itself*, but in *the form or forming power*" – that is of the artist, whether originally God or, in historical time, man (emphasis added).

There is a delicate irony in Shaftesbury's writing, which says that if religion in its Anglican forms proves conducive to happiness, he is willing to tolerate the orthodoxy necessary to preserve virtue and order, especially among the lower orders who need good examples. This is an aristocratic irony Fielding would have found elucidated in Shaftesbury's writings on enthusiasm and ridicule, which came to be known as deist irony: Shaftesbury's "defensive raillery," John Toland's "exoteric and esoteric distinctions," Anthony Collins's "irony" or, the blunter term, "theological lying." In Collins's words, the freethinker can "sacrifice the privilege of irony" only when there is freedom of expression, or in Toland's: "considering how dangerous it is made to tell the truth, 'tis difficult to know when any man declares his real opinion." Fielding's words in *The Champion* come very close to echoing Shaftesbury's "'Tis real Humanity and Kindness to hide strong Truths from tender eyes," by which he means both the ecclesiastical authorities and the lower orders. In *Tom Jones* he cites Shaftesbury's objection to "telling too much Truth," a reference to "defensive Raillery," which Shaftesbury explained as "when the Spirit of Curiosity wou'd force a Discovery of more Truth than can conveniently be told. For we can never do more Injury to Truth, than by discovering too much of it, on some occasions."[33]

If Toland and Woolston were Hogarth's models, the more genteel and polite Shaftesbury was Fielding's – not only his subtle pragmatism but his equation of beauty and virtue, the principle of internal balance and harmony, shared by the work of art and the virtuous individual. Fielding the artist, in his "comic epic in prose," gives art the primary didactic importance it carried for Shaftesbury. As a unique power to influence those who have not yet reached a state of virtuous equilibrium, this, more than any other formulation, sums up Fielding's sense of his audience, his persuasive function, and his "new Province of Writing." It proclaims that the representation of a perfectly well-ordered world will produce similar order in the minds of men; that, though a fiction, the representation of the world as a beautiful and harmonious construction is on the one hand the greatest work of art and on the other the most powerful agency for improving morals.[34] It is, of course, a formulation intended primarily for the elite, whom Fielding will designate in *Tom Jones* as his "sagacious Readers" (as opposed to those who require the hope and fear of rewards and punishments).

Most important, Fielding follows Shaftesbury in not presuming to assert (with Anglican clergymen) that this providential order corresponds to reality. I am distinguishing between the providential assumptions of the clergy, cited by Battestin and Williams (and attributed to Fielding), and the deists' view that providential design, however essential to our happiness and social stability, is a human fiction.[35] This is not so much to claim that Fielding is necessarily himself a deist as that he accepts the consequences of deism; he recognizes the providential order as having been rendered by the deists no longer valid except as a fiction – as "Dreams of purling Streams, and shady Groves" (in the *Champion*) or "poetic justice" and a happy ending (in *Joseph Andrews* and *Tom Jones*).

Considering the two forms of providential design, as his *Champion* essays make clear, Fielding the man – as opposed to the artist – keeps returning to the specifically Christian doctrine of rewards and punishments in the afterlife (especially a happy reunion with loved ones).[36] This is most strikingly evident in his proposal for dealing with the "Affliction for Loss of Friends" in his *Miscellanies* of 1743: after dismissing the "remedies" of philosophy, and focusing on his own bereavement and his wife Charlotte's existential response ("comforting herself with reflecting, that *her Child could never know what it was to feel such a Loss as she then lamented*"), he concludes, in the same language he used to defend religion against the deists, that

Religion goes much farther, and gives us a most *delightful* Assurance, that our Friend is not barely no Loser, but a Gainer by his Dissolution. . . . Lastly, It gives a Hope, the sweetest, most endearing, and *ravishing*, which can enter into a Mind capable of, and *inflamed* with, Friendship. The Hope of again meeting the beloved Person, of renewing and cementing the dear Union in *Bliss* everlasting. This is a *Rapture* which leaves the warmest Imagination at a Distance.

Among many other examples, we can recall Fielding's joyous meeting with his deceased daughter in *Journey from this World to the Next* and Allworthy's *consolatio* for the death of his wife in *Tom Jones*.[37] Perhaps because of the long series of bereavements he suffered (children, wife, sisters), this "hope" seems to have been Fielding's own entrée to the Christian religion. He uses this "proper matter of faith" in his personal essays but not, until the 1750s, as a guiding principle in his fiction.

ETHICAL DEISM

The second subject of the *Champion* essays attacking deism is virtue. Again Shaftesbury is the key figure, from whom Fielding takes an affective, response-oriented morality. He recalls Shaftesbury's figure of Virtue, projected by Theocles in *The Moralists* (Theocles' version of Prodicus and Cebes), leading a Roman triumph over "monsters of savage passions . . . ambition, lust, uproar, misrule, with all the fiends which rage in human breasts . . . securely chained" (2. 44). But to this the skeptical Philocles opposes "an authentic picture of another kind," in which Virtue is the captive and "by a proud conqueror triumphed over, degraded, spoiled of all her honours, and defaced, so as to retain hardly one single feature of real beauty" (2. 45). While Philocles' picture is characterized by his more pious companions as libertine and atheist, Theocles recognizes that the "proud conqueror" is not the atheist but "religion itself" – those who, pretending to expose "the falsehood of human virtue, think to extol religion," but "strike at moral virtue as a kind of step-dame, or rival to religion." These are the clerics who "would value virtue but for hereafter" – the advocates of rewards and punishments in the afterlife. Virtue, in short, even Theocles admits is better without religion of *this* sort.

But Fielding goes beyond Shaftesbury. As if recalling Hogarth's *Harlot*, plate 1, he summons up Shaftesbury's Choice of Hercules but rejects both Pleasure, a harlot, *and* Virtue, seen as "disagreeable," "rigid," with "intolerable penances," "thirst and hunger, whips and chains." To get at true Virtue he must strip both women. He begins with the mistranslation of Plato, which he will use again in the dedication to *Tom Jones*, "That could Mankind behold Virtue naked, they would all be in Love with her."[38] Under the "tawdry, painted Harlot," Pleasure will prove to be "within, all foul and impure," and under Virtue's clerical/puritanical demeanor she will prove not "of that morose and rigid Nature" but alluring. "Virtue forbids not the satisfying our Appetites," he writes, "Virtue forbids us only to glut and destroy them. The temperate Man tastes and relishes Pleasure in a Degree infinitely superior to that of the voluptuous." Fielding keeps her within Shaftesbury's ascending scale of aesthetics to ethics, body to mind, and his two women (though both stripped naked) prepare us for the figures of lust and love, Molly and Sophia, in *Tom Jones*. (The stripping of Sophia is done only in the imagination of the lecherous puppet master.)

Nevertheless orthodox Christian virtue as a humanized, sexually desirable young female is a surprisingly provocative metaphor for a warning against deist libertinism. The metaphor involves not only dressing and undressing Virtue but her "embraces," the "pursuit" and "possession" of her. As *Tom Jones* shows, while Fielding retains the Shaftesburian scale, he allows Tom his sensual "pleasure allowed to every beast but man" with other women; he distinguishes Tom's lust for Molly (and Jenny Waters and Lady Bellaston) from his love for Sophia, which however clearly includes the other.

Shaftesbury's central term (for his ethics as well as aesthetics) is "disinterestedness," which in the religious context is focused on the distinction between a disinterested love of God and an interested one based on "belief in a future reward and punishment": he concludes that "to serve God by compulsion, or for interest merely, is service and mercenary" (2: 55). Fielding's own moral program, however, is devoted to justifying the "interestedness" of virtue: Tom's benevolence is based on neither the religious principles of Thwackum nor the Shaftesburian "natural Beauty of Virtue" advocated by Square. It is based on a "love" of the *other* which, though extended to a general sympathy, is posited on a physical desire. This "love" can lead Tom to sacrifice his own feelings when he knows they will be harmful to her. What Fielding has produced out of the Shaftesburian principles of order and harmony, mind over body, and "disinterested" pleasure is an alternative aesthetics of pleasure centered on the body of a real woman, which anticipates in significant ways Hogarth's *Analysis of Beauty* (1753).[39]

There is a strong possibility that Fielding, as was certainly the case with Hogarth, draws on Mandeville for the "interested" aspect of his ethics. Mandeville revealed the interest beneath the vaunted disinterestedness of Shaftesbury's civic humanist (or man of taste) to be human desire. Although Fielding plainly disagrees with Mandeville's view of human nature as unredeemedly selfish, and when he refers to him by name he is "Mand-evil" (though this is many years later, when he is unmistakably speaking for orthodoxy), these disavowals divert attention from a fundamental indebtedness to Mandeville in the "new" mode of discourse he initiates in *Joseph Andrews* and *Tom Jones*.[40] Though the content differs, the method Mandeville employed in his critique of Shaftesbury is similar to Fielding's of Richardson. Mandeville's subject, in this sense, was the discrepancy between moral language and reality, and his strategy was to investigate words such as "virtue" (or "honor" or "reason") by testing them against empirical evidence, the "daily Experience" of human behavior.[41] He played off the abstractions of Shaftesbury, as Fielding does of Richardson's *Pamela*, against specific examples, in the process undermining the meaning of stock moral and ecclesiastical terminology.

Fielding follows him in suggesting the artificial nature of "virtue," as an imposition of the clergy, and specifically as self-denial and repression of the senses. "Virtue," as Mandeville said (in his own version of Shaftesbury's fictionality of religion), is the work of "Lawgivers and other wise Men, that have laboured for the Establishment of Society"; not "the pure Effect of Religion" but "the Contrivance of Politicians . . . the skilful Management of wary Politicians," a "contrivance" necessary for both social order and personal happiness.[42]

In his "Essay on the Characters of Men", Fielding redefines virtue as "Good Nature," which "disposes us to feel the Misfortunes and enjoy the Happiness of others; and consequently pushes us on to promote the latter, and prevent the former; and that" – he significantly adds – "without any abstract contemplation on the Beauty of Virtue, and without the Allurement or Terrors of Religion."[43] But in fact, as he explains in his *Champion* essay on Good Nature (March 27, 1740), Good Nature may need the support of one or both of these. In unusually tangled syntax, with ambiguous referents, he says that Christianity is necessary because it "hath taught us something beyond what the Religion of Nature and Philosophy [deism] could arrive at."[44] Once again Christianity is a useful addendum because it keeps people happy, but to that is added the particular necessity of Good Nature to go beyond harmless benevolism to the rigorous judgment of good and evil, based on a belief in rewards and punishments in the afterlife.

THE CLERGY AND TEXTUAL AUTHORITY

The climactic essays defending the clergy against deist attack make a strange defense, one that devotes most of its time to outlining the reasons for the contempt in which its individual members, as distinct from the "order," are held.[45] Fielding's censures are of the privileges bestowed on the clergy by the civil law, their honors, revenues, and immunities from the law – in sum (using a favorite term in his writings of the 1730s), their "greatness."[46] A preponderance of space is given to the lurid stories of Guinandus de Briland and other clergymen who murdered and raped and used the law to escape punishment. The third and the fourth essays, which are separated by an essay on vanity, define a "clergyman" simply as a good shepherd whose task it is to "feed his flock with meat, precept, and example," who is "entrusted with the care of our souls, over which he is to watch as a shepherd for his sheep . . . To live in daily communication with his flock, and chiefly with those who want him most (as the poor and distressed), nay, and after his blessed Master's example, to eat with publicans and sinners." When he asks, "Can such a man as this be the object of contempt?" he is anticipating Parson Adams (in particular at the hands of the roasting squire in book 3): "perhaps indeed boys and beaus, and madmen, and rakes, and fools, and villains, may laugh at this sacred person; may shake those ridiculous heads at him." The final essay then concludes with another vivid description of what the good clergyman is *not*, rendered in great and savage detail.[47]

Clergymen are twice distinguished from deists and atheists, and Fielding, the public spokesman and (by this time) respectable barrister, wants to dissociate himself from the name of deist. But he makes it quite clear that his sense of the clergy is not unlike the bugbear of the deists: the authoritarian interpreter of the law, Scripture, and doctrine. It is significant that in his plays and in *Shamela* he names as his examples of the clergy's "rotten members" Parsons Murdertext, Tickletext, and Puzzletext, names which emphasize the authority of the clergy over texts, and so focus attention on the interpretation of texts.

JOSEPH ANDREWS

Though it originated as literary parody, *Joseph Andrews* (1742) is essentially an attempt to resolve the religious tensions evident in the *Champion* essays. The issue of Richardson's *Pamela* (1740), greeted as it was by clerical praise, is closely linked to the clerical authority of texts, and Fielding brings in a bad Parson Tickletext to recommend and a good Parson Oliver to demystify the text as if he were Thomas Woolston. But *Pamela*'s claims to represent "Virtue Rewarded" also focus attention on the problem of ethics. Richardson's "virtue" was founded on principle, which meant Christian orthodoxy; Fielding sets out to advocate an alternative based on something other than revealed religion.

The locus for the distrust of textual authority in *Shamela* and *Joseph Andrews* is, of course, Pamela's own text, the letters by which the servant girl controls her betters and raises her social status.[48] Pamela's actions, like the miracles of Scripture, are in themselves nonsense (or as she, or her editor, Richardson or Tickletext interprets them); but tested against history and human psychology, they reveal Mandevillian desire.

Whereas in his farces Fielding travestied only classical myths, now in *Joseph Andrews*, in the context of Richardson's elevation of principle, he travesties the Old Testament stories of Joseph and Potiphar's wife and Abraham's sacrifice of Isaac. In 1740 in the third volume of his deist tract *The Moral Philosopher*, Thomas Morgan had treated Joseph and Abraham much as Woolston had Christ; and similarly Fielding corrects the implausibilities of the biblical stories, revealing the real contemporary Joseph and Abraham under the biblical paragons.[49] He is writing about "examples", both good and bad, the former based on love, the latter on principle masking antisocial passions. Joseph rejects Lady Booby (Potiphar's wife), ostensibly because he acts according to the examples of the Old Testament, Pamela's letters, and Parson Adams's sermons (Joseph as model of chastity), but in reality because he is in love with a buxom young maid, Fanny Goodwill.

At the same time, however, Fielding privileges a New Testament text, the parable of the Good Samaritan, which informs as a positive model the central sections of Joseph's trip back from London to Booby Hall. A coachload of "respectable" folk leave the wounded Joseph to die; one poor postilion gives him his coat; in the Tow-wouses' inn, the single exception is the "love" of Betty the chambermaid.[50] The lawyers, innkeepers, physicians, clergymen, and other respectable people who act from selfish motives are implicitly analogous to Pamela, but we do not forget that in the Good Samaritan parable they were priests. The parable, employed earlier by Hogarth (in his 1736 painting in St. Bartholomew's Hospital),[51] could be read in the Woolstonian way as in fact about the priests and the Letter (versus the Spirit) of the Law. It is certainly the parabolic embodiment of the Christian ethic *outside* doctrine and clerical structure.

Chapters 13 and 17 of book 1 focus on Parson Barnabas, whose name suggests what he *should* be (a "son of consolation," a companion of St. Paul's in Acts 4.36) first to Joseph and then to Parson Adams. In chapter 13 Joseph invokes a theology of love focused on his beloved Fanny; Barnabas of doctrine. Thinking he is dying, Joseph says his only sin is "the Regret of parting with a young Woman, whom he loved as tenderly as he did his Heartstrings," and Barnabas assures him "that any Repining at the Divine Will, was one of the greatest Sins he could commit; that he ought to forget all carnal Affections, and think of better things."[52] Barnabas, who has treated the wounded Joseph with anything but Samaritan charity, tells him he must "divest himself of all human passion, and fix his Heart above," which he can only do "by Grace," that is "By Prayer and Faith." Pamelian virtue, grace, clergy, and the church are being contrasted to an ethic founded on charity and sexual love.

In chapter 17 Barnabas is brought together with Parson Adams; the subject is sermons, and Adams's religion is defined in terms of the Methodist sermons of George Whitefield: "such Heterodox Stuff," as Barnabas says, "levelled at the clergy. He would reduce us to the example of the Primitive Ages forsooth! and would insinuate to the People, that a Clergyman ought to be always preaching and praying." Barnabas associates the Methodist Whitefield with "the Principles of *Toland, Woolston,* and all the Freethinkers," but Adams says that in fact he agrees with Whitefield in so far as his aim is to strip the church, or the clergy, of its political authority and to return to a primitive Christianity: "I am as great an Enemy to the Luxury and Splendour of the Clergy as he [Whitefield] can be. I do not, more than he, by the flourishing Estate of the Church, understand the Palaces, Equipages, Dress, Furniture, rich Dainties, and vast Fortunes of her Ministers." However he does object to Whitefield's doctrine of faith over works and the concomitant "Nonsense and Enthusiasm" – that is, the irrational belief in the direct intervention by God in man's affairs, the existence of ghosts and other superstitions, which were the object of the deist attack on the church.

Adams's criticism of the principle of faith over works leads him to assert the prototypical deist commonplace "that a virtuous and good *Turk*, or Heathen, are more acceptable in the sight of their Creator, than a vicious and wicked Christian, tho' his Faith was as perfectly Orthodox as St. *Paul's* himself."[53] When Barnabas and the bookseller cry him down, he responds by citing the authority of Bishop Hoadly's *A Plain Account of the Nature and End of the Sacrament of the Lord's-Supper* (1735), "a Book written (if I may venture on the Expression) with the Pen of an Angel" – a work (one of which was to be found in Shamela's library) that has survived the enmity and attacks of the clergy. Barnabas responds by calling Adams a Woolstonian deist, a Hobbesian materialist, a Muslim, and the Devil himself.

Just as Adams asks Barnabas whether he has ever actually read Hoadly's book, there is a great uproar: Mrs. Tow-wouse, who has discovered Mr. Tow-wouse in *flagrante delicto* with Betty, is calling her a bitch. Betty, of course, is the one person in the Tow-wouse household who has shown kindness to the poor, battered Joseph. She objects not to the empirical fact that she was in bed with Mr. Tow-wouse but to being called a bitch – which, in fact, given her history of charity, and the facts of Mr. Tow-wouse's seduction of her, is a matter of dispute. That Betty's natural act can be mislabeled by the angry Mrs. Tow-wouse raises the question of whether the religion of Adams and Hoadly is similarly misconstrued by the angry Barnabas.

In the episode of Mr. Wilson's freethinking club, Fielding shows that the deists, however cogent their critique of Christianity, failed to formulate a convincing positive alternative, a version of "natural religion" grounded in the unaided human reason. But if Shaftesbury is wrong, and "natural religion" does not work, the same applies to the externally imposed order of the clergy, which serves only as a hypocritical cloak for such as Barnabas and Parson Trulliber, who judges a clergyman's worth solely by the quality of his clothes.

By contrast with both, Parson Adams so little resembles a clergyman that he is seldom recognized until he brings his learning into play. Beneath his tattered and discolored cassock, he is a lusty man, the progenitor of six children, and able to outrun a coach. He exemplifies the Good Nature described in the *The Champion*, which combined "perfect simplicity" with strong fists and a crabstick (his equivalent of Hercules' club) used to chastise obvious knavery, especially as it threatens those he loves. The crabstick is the physical manifestation of the religion that is required to accompany Good Nature.

But Adams's natural good nature is at odds with his sermons, his superstitions, and – as seems clear – his whole order. He is inordinately vain of his teaching abilities and his sermons (especially the one on vanity). He preaches the word of the Bible, significantly the Old Testament, while he acts according to the New. Thus the model of Abraham (his namesake, and the sacrifice of his son Isaac) causes Adams to defend the father's sacrifice of his son, but he reacts with love and grief when he hears his own son has drowned. This was the paradigmatic Old Testament story, which Hogarth affixed to his harlot's wall; it summed up the patriarchal family, filial obedience, and arbitrary justice, while the New Testament story was Christ's attempt to bring man back to the undefiled source of religion in love, in opposition (as in the parable of the Good Samaritan) to a priesthood that exalted the law.

In practice, moreover, except for the influence he has had on

Joseph and Fanny, Adams's example (the "piety, meekness, humility, charity, patience, and all the other Christian virtues") has no effect on the Pamelas and Cibbers, Trullibers and Barnabases, roasting squires, dishonest justices, and greedy landlords he encounters. ("Bless us!" he exclaims, "how good-nature is used in this world!") If Lucian was the literary model behind the farces, then Cervantes is behind *Joseph Andrews* ("Written in Imitation of the Manner of Cervantes"), and that means that we are invited to read Adams as a Quixote fighting a losing battle with windmills – Joseph as his down-to-earth Sancho. Indeed if Adams is seldom recognized as a priest, Joseph himself, though no priest at all, becomes the reader's model, and this is because he comes closest to representing the beautiful harmony of virtue and passion posited by Shaftesbury and lacking in both the freethinking club and Adams. True, he is anything but "disinterested" in his feelings for Fanny. True also, he mediates his actions through the "religious" authority of Pamela's letters and the sermons of Adams (though obviously Fielding privileges one more than the other). Joseph implies that without such texts *even* his love of Fanny might not have kept him out of Booby's arms. He requires Adams to insist that he and Fanny declare the banns before they consummate their passion. All in all Joseph illustrates the ability of the good-natured man, assisted by the "divine example" offered by an Adams, to learn to control his passions and at crucial moments to instruct Adams himself.[54]

Joseph also requires the author, for in this eponymous novel the real world is the world of chance, little affected by either the false fictions of Pamela or the true ones of Adams. Mr. Wilson goes (as Fielding may have seen himself going) from the freethinking deists to gambling and a lottery by way of the playhouse and playwriting, finally narrating his early life in the formula of a "rake's progress."[55] But within the plot of the novel, the structure of authorial artifice and control, Wilson's lottery ticket, the symbol of chance, serves to reorder his life, now reformed, and reflects externally the internal order he has achieved and that his son Joseph will achieve as well.

In *Joseph Andrews*, and *Tom Jones*, Fielding follows Shaftesbury in preferring the analogy of beauty and virtue, aesthetics and morality, to theological indoctrination. Thus he reproduces providential design not as a reactionary metaphysical doctrine to be foisted on his readers (as he believed Richardson did) but as a principle of art.

In *Tom Jones* the demystification – now of Jacobite mythology – is carried out by the Abbé Banier's euhemerism, a safe version of Woolston's critical deism.[56] The alternatives of deism and Anglicanism of *Joseph Andrews* reappear in equally bad alternatives, those Allworthy surrogates, Thwackum and Square; but only Square the deist (a lusty man who shares Molly with Tom) is capable of reformation. He is converted on his deathbed to religion, specifically to belief in an afterlife. Battestin points to the influence on Fielding of Lord Lyttelton's *Observations on St. Paul*, published at about the time he was writing the concluding books of *Tom Jones*. Clearly Square's conversion is an analogue to Tom's success at controlling his potentially anarchic impulses; but, knowing he is dying, Square needs consolation, the belief in an afterlife which was the feature of Christian belief that most obsessed Fielding. It is Square the deist who is converted and confesses the truth he knows about Tom, while Thwackum the clergyman remains to the end cold-hearted, self-righteous, self-seeking, and hypocritical. This says, as Fielding has reiterated since the *The Champion* essays, that deist morality of the Shaftesbury sort can be corrected – as both control and consolation – by a pragmatic belief in Christian examples and eschatology; the Christian clergy, although there is an occasional Parson Adams, is hopeless. Parson Supple, the best the clergy can show in *Tom Jones*, is summed up in his name (he cannot control the violent impulses of Squire Western) and his ultimate marriage to Jenny Waters.

Like St. Paul, Square was a persecutor and is now converted. But he has no Pauline vision, no divine intervention (nor is the recovering of his sight a miracle), only the same pragmatic belief advocated by Fielding at the end of his essay on bereavement. This is a matter of some importance because Lyttelton's aim in his book is no less than to prove, on the strength of this Pauline text, that Paul's conversion and its aftermath "did all really happen, and therefore the Christian religion is a divine revelation."[57] I do not mean to suggest that Fielding is subverting his friend Lyttelton's pious tract. But *Tom Jones* is written in a generic form that, as defined by Fielding, cannot advocate both divine presence *and* belief in the divine: the one, as the deists taught him, is not historical; the other is necessary for human survival.

By book 7, however, with the news of the Pretender's invasion, Fielding no longer permits himself to be equivocal in his respect for the clergy and belief in Protestant Christianity. The cloth and patriotism are at this time and place in history of necessity equated.[58]

This event decidedly changed his attitude toward religion, albeit still in a pragmatic way. After *Tom Jones*, as Westminster Magistrate and official spokesman for the government he speaks for orthodoxy without irony or ambivalence. If earlier his reliance on rewards and punishments in the afterlife had seemed to satisfy a personal need, in his later years it satisfied a social one. In the 1750s he simply materialized doctrine in *Examples of the Interposition of Providence in the Detection and Punishment of Murder* (1752), though in an advertisement he explains that "No Family ought to be without this Book, and it is most particularly calculated for the Use of those Schools, in which Children are taught to read."[59]

Fielding's last novel, *Amelia* (1751), advocates the Christian religion, pious education, and the necessity of belief on the one hand, and a strong and honest judiciary and police force on the other. A final mention of rewards and punishments comes from Dr. Harrison, the grim successor to Parson Adams: he believes that religion is useful *because* it "applies immediately to the strongest of these Passions, Hope and Fear, chusing rather to rely on its Rewards and Punishments, than on that native Beauty of Virtue" advocated by the deists and Shaftesbury.[60]

Looking back from the 1750s, Fielding defined "Religion" in the "modern Glossary" of his *Covent-Garden Journal* as "A Word of no Meaning; but which serves as a Bugbear to frighten Children with" (issue 4, January 14, 1752). Issue 6, an imitation of Swift's "Dedication to Prince Posterity," takes up the uses to which forgotten books are put: too great a dissemination (e.g., through the use by pastry cooks) of deist tracts is dangerous because they were meant for "the Use and Inspection of the few" but "are by no means proper Food for the Mouths of Babes and Sucklings."[61]

But, as often is the case, Fielding's irony includes a hard Mandevillian truth: not only that the old deist tracts are impious and now unread, used to line trunks and pastry cases, but that there *was* in those days (when Fielding was young) a distinction between the thinking few, who were entitled to play around with these skeptical, freethinking ideas, and the public as a whole who must be guided and guarded by religion. In the *Enquiry into the late Increase in Robbers*, other legal tracts of 1751, and in the *Covent-Garden Journal* he shows that to keep order in a disintegrating society religion is as essential as the law; in *A Charge to the Grand Jury* he draws attention to the statutes against irreligious writings; and in *Amelia* he includes as his own surrogate, a deist, Billy

Booth, who believes in a world governed by chance and who, at the end, is converted to Christianity. The *Covent-Garden Journal* too draws our attention back to the way Fielding felt before he bore responsibility for public order, before he saw society as dangerously degenerate, and to the pragmatic function he assigned to religion in public life, as well as (in the matter of grieving) in his own private life. And the reference to children (which recalls Locke on the simplicity of children) exposes, at least to the "few" (those he referred to as his "sagacious readers" in *Tom Jones*), his realistic appraisal of the public, as his portrait of Booth exposes his realistic appraisal of himself in middle age.

While not ruling out the possibility of a "conversion" like Booth's (perhaps down to the specifics of reading Barrow), I see deism and orthodoxy as coexisting for Fielding on different levels of belief; but, for both personal and professional reasons, orthodoxy gained the final ascendancy. Even then one can imagine the old Fielding still joking while the official voice proclaimed whatever was necessary to maintain order.

NOTES

1 Irving Howe, "History and the Novel," *The New Republic*, 3 (September 1990), 29.
2 Michael McKeon does include a mention in *Origins of the Novel, 1600–1740* (Baltimore, 1987), pp. 81–82. He involves the deists in what he calls the "Question of Truth," where he mentions Woolston.
3 *The Champion*, January 22, 1739/40; my text is the collected *Champion* of 1740.
4 *The Welsh [Grub Street]* act II, scene 2. But this may be partly as a contrast and comparison with his mother (Prince Frederick with Queen Caroline), a supporter of religion who admired such controversial divines as Samuel Clarke.
5 In *The Letter-Writers* of the same year, Commons is having his final fling before taking orders. His friend Rakel asks him if he has "the Impudence to pretend to a Call." Commons: "Ay, Sir; the usual Call: I have the Promise of a good Living. Lookee, captain, my Call of Piety is much the same as yours of Honour – you will fight, and I shall pray for the same Reasons I assure you" (1731 edn, p. 7).
6 *Joseph Andrews*, II.3 (Martin C. Battestin [ed.] [Middletown, CT, 1967] edition). Aurélien Digeon presumed that Fielding was a deist until late in life and that his conversion explains the changes of perspective in *Amelia* (*Les romans de Fielding* [Paris, 1923], pp. 260–62); and Battestin believes that Fielding had a brush with deism in his youth but swiftly turned straight (Martin C. and Ruthe Battestin, *Henry Fielding: A Life* [London, 1989], pp. 154–55).

7 James A. Work, "Henry Fielding, Christian Censor," in *The Age of Johnson: Essays Presented to Chauncey Brewster Tinker* (New Haven, 1949), pp. 139–148; Battestin, *The Moral Basis of Fielding's Art: A Study of "Joseph Andrews"* (Middletown, CT, 1959); Aubrey Williams, "Interpositions of Providence and the Design of Fielding's Novels," *South Atlantic Quarterly*, 70 (1971), 265–86. On the association of deism and Latitudinarianism (a charge often leveled at Bishop Benjamin Hoadly, Fielding's favorite contemporary clergyman), see Roger L. Emerson, "Latitudinarianism and the English Deists," in J. A. Leo Lemay, (ed.), *Deism, Masonry, and the Enlightenment*, (Newark, DE, 1987); John Redwood, *Reason, Ridicule and Religion: The Age of Enlightenment in England, 1660–1750* (Cambridge, MA, 1976), p. 175; Robert E. Sullivan, *John Toland and the Deist Controversy* (Cambridge, MA, 1982), p. 35; Leslie Stephen, *History of English Thought in the Eighteenth Century* (1876; rptd. New York, 1962), II, p. 129; see also Henry Knight Miller, *Essays on Fielding's "Miscellanies"* (Princeton, 1961), pp. 76–83. For a more detailed analysis of Hoadly's influence on Fielding's religious positions, see Paulson, *Henry Fielding: A Critical Biography* (Oxford, forthcoming).

8 Thomas Cooke, *A Demonstration of the Will of God by the Light of Nature* (1733), introduction; cited in Martin and Ruthe Battestin, *Henry Fielding*, pp. 153, 156. This work, a collection of Cooke's periodical essays in *The Comedian*, is carefully couched in terms of Christianity, with none of Thomas Woolston's satiric thrust or obvious disrespect for the Christian Fathers or the New Testament itself. Cooke urges that instead of the institutional deity of the clergy and the biblical texts, man should "cast his Eye into the Book of *Nature*, which the bounteous Hand of *God* has opened to him" (p. xiii). *The Comedian*, issue 2, sets out "to prove that God, requires no more of us than *Nature* requires" (p. 5); issue 4 concerns observance of the Sabbath "and some Cases in which we ought to break it" (pp. 14–17), concluding that one ought "not to offend God hereafter by neglecting to gather in his Harvest on the sabbath day when he cannot on another Day" (p. 17); and subsequent papers are on the immortality of the soul and a future state (issue 5), on liberty, necessity, and the freedom of the will (issue 6), on the origin of evil (issue 7), and climactically on God, Providence, and Nature (issue 8).

9 For the history of deism, see John Orr, *English Deism: Its Roots and Fruits* (Grand Rapids, MI, 1934) and – for our purposes, the most useful source – Roland N. Stromberg, *Religious Liberalism in Eighteenth-Century England* (Oxford, 1954); but Leslie Stephen's chapters in his *History of English Thought* remain of interest. I have also benefited from the work on deism of my students, Andres Virkus and Peter Mortensen.

10 As the deist John Toland wrote, "Popery in reality is nothing else, but the Clergy's assuming a Right to think for the Laity" ("A Word to the Honest Priests," in *An Appeal to Honest People against Wicked Priests* [1713], p. 38; see Stephen H. Daniel, *John Toland: His Methods, Manners, and*

Mind [Kingston and Montreal, 1984], pp. 28–29).

11 Bernard Mandeville, *Fable of the Bees*, ed. F. B. Kaye (Oxford, 1924), p. 3. Later, in the chapter "Of Mysteries," Mandeville acknowledges that "I incur the censures of our zealous clergy, who will call this the advice of a latitudinarian, if not worse" (p. 82) – suggesting the narrow line that separated Latitudinarian and deist for many contemporaries.

12 See Paulson, *Hogarth*, 3 vols. (New Brunswick, 1991), I, pp. 322–23. For the prints see Paulson, *Hogarth's Graphic Works*, 3rd edn (London, 1989), nos. 120–26.

13 See John Nichols, *Biographical Anecdotes of William Hogarth* (1782), p. 90.

14 Gibson's three *Pastoral Letters* between 1728 and 1731 attacked deism and in particular Woolston; a parody appeared in the antiministerial *Craftsman*, November 16, 1728 (Gibson was Walpole's chief ecclesiastical adviser). A *Pastoral Letter* is used as a butter wrap in *Harlot*, 3, and again in Fielding's *Shamela*, where it is predicted that the next *Letter* will praise *Pamela*.

15 See Paulson, *Hogarth*, I, pp. 288–92.

16 Cooke, *Letter*, pp. 6, 5.

17 Cooke also cites Benjamin Hoadly (ibid., 35; see above, n. 7).

18 See Battestin, *Moral Basis of Fielding's Art* pp. 493 ff.

19 For "contrast," see *Tom Jones*, V.1; for an account of how an example, Settle's *Siege of Troy*, operated, see Paulson, *Hogarth*, I, pp. 139–40.

20 Preface to *Love of Fame* (2nd edn, 1728), sig. a verso. On Lucian, see Levi R. Lind, "Lucian and Fielding," *Classical Weekly*, 29 (1936), 84–86; Christopher Robinson, *Lucian and his Influence in Europe* (Chapel Hill, 1979), pp. 211–23; Miller, *Essays*, pp. 366–86; Paulson, *The Fictions of Satire* (Baltimore, 1967), pp. 31–42.

21 I am paraphrasing my remarks in *Fictions of Satire*, pp. 33–34. For Fielding's continuing utilization of the Lucianic persona, see Paulson, *Satire and the Novel* (New Haven, 1967), chapter 4, "The Lucianic Satirist." It is difficult to dissent from Miller's judgment that "Fielding did not share Lucian's thoroughgoing skepticism; and his love of the good showed itelf more clearly and more often" (*Essays*, p. 368).

22 Unless the lost *Deborah: or, A Wife for You All* was possibly a burlesque of the Old Testament story (or of Handel's *Deborah* of 1733).

23 See Paulson, *Satire and the Novel*, pp. 85–95.

24 For example, in *The Comedian*, (April 1732) Cooke opened his deist argument by introducing the metaphor: "I shall look on the whole World as the Scene of Action on which a continual tragic-comedy is represented" (p. 4). For the prominence of this metaphor, its origins, and its influence, see Paulson, "Life as Journey and as Theater: Two Eighteenth-Century Narrative Structures," *New Literary History*, 8 (1976), 43–58, reprinted in *Popular and Polite Art in the Age of Hogarth and Fielding* (Notre Dame, 1979), II.2.

25 This procedure is materialized again in *The Champion* of April 22, 1740.

Whenever the reference is political, the politician is accompanied by a clergyman, as Robin the butler was by Puzzletext the chaplain in *The Welsh [Grub-Street] Opera*.

26 The plays, fiercely attacked by writers in the *Grub-Street Journal* and elsewhere, had in effect been suppressed by the Licensing Act of 1737. See Paulson and Thomas F. Lockwood, *Fielding: The Critical Heritage* (London, 1969).

27 *The Champion* (1740 edn), pp. 208–209.

28 Jonathan Swift, *The Mechanical Operation of the Spirit*, in *A Tale of a Tub* (1704), ed. A. C. Guthkelch and D. Nichol Smith, 2nd edn, (Oxford, 1958), p. 276.

29 Swift, "Digression on Madness," in *A Tale of a Tub*, pp. 173–74. The passage also includes a sentence condemning "*Unmasking*, which I think, has never been allowed fair Usage, either in the *World* or the *Play-House*," which connects "Delusion" with the important strand of theatrical metaphor in Fielding's works.

30 Fielding's passage invites comparison with Cooke's nonsatiric *Demonstration*, where he wrote of "that *Power* to which Man owes his Desire of Happyness, and his Aversion to Misery, which Power is *God*." Cooke claims that obedience to "the rule of Right [v. Christianity] advances our Happyness here; and consequently every Deviation from it is a Deviation from the Road which leads to Happyness" (xiii). The discussion of providence (8–11) concludes that Nature is "that *Power* to which Man owes his Desire of Happyness, and his Aversion to Misery, which Power is *God*": in short, Nature, God, and Happiness are one.

31 *Inquiry*, 1.2.3, in *Characteristics*, ed. John M. Robertson (1900 rptd. Indianapolis, 1964), I, p. 279.

32 In *The Moralists* (1709, 1711) the most respectable of the deist tracts on the subject of morality (perhaps because it is presented as a dialogue, with Theocles balanced by Philocles), Shaftesbury presents the world as ordered and humans as naturally sociable and benevolent – a vision that is hindered by the belief, promulgated by clerics as well as atheists, that human nature is depraved and fallen. He obsessively returns to the danger of the Christian religion's carrot stick fiction of rewards and punishments in the afterlife. But, argues Shaftesbury (or rather, Theocles' freethinking friend), this sort of religion *can* serve as a way station toward a more disinterested love of God:

although this *service of fear* be allowed ever so low or base, yet religion still being a discipline and progress of the soul towards perfection, the *motive of reward and punishment* is *primary and of the highest moment* with us, *till*, being *capable of more sublime instruction*, we are *led from this service state* to the *generous service of affection and love*. (p. 55, emphasis added)

He first made the point about reward/punishment in his preface to *Select Sermons of Dr. [Benjamin] Whichcot* (1698): his point is that the Christian view of human sinfulness is no different from Hobbes's atheistic materialist view of man; that this was the result of priestcraft's need to emphasize rewards and punishments in the afterlife, thus replacing the love of goodness for its own sake – *dis*interested virtue (*Sermons*, sigs. a5v, a6r–6v, a7r). Hoadly also took this position aginst the idea of morality based on rewards/punishments in the afterlife. (See Klein, p. 32 and n. 15.) Treated most fully in the *Enquiry*, it is also treated in *Enthusiasm* (I, p. 15).

33 Toland, "Clidophorus; or of the Exoteric and Esoteric Philosphy," in *Tetradymus* (1720); Shaftesbury, "An Essay on the Freedom of Wit and Humour" (1709), in *Characteristics*, I, p. 45; *Tom Jones*, XIV.12. See David Berman, "Deism, Immortality, and the Art of Theological Lying," in J. A. Leo Lemay (ed.), *Deism, Masonry, and the Enlightenment* (Newark, DE, 1987), p. 63 (see pp. 61–78). And, as Stromberg notes, "Thinking that the priests and their preachings were fraudulent, [deists] felt justified . . . in using fraud to fight fraud" (*Religious Liberalism*, p. 58).

34 For Cooke, too, beauty "is that which arises to the Mind in exact Proportion, and which gives that Pleasure which the Mind enjoys from Propriety of Action" (*Demonstration*, p. xii).

35 Cf. Melvyn New, "'The Grease of God': The Form of 18th-Century English Fiction," *PMLA*, 91 (1976), 235–43.

36 Although Fielding's emotional attachment to the idea of immortality is more emphatic, his position, at least until the 1750s, is basically the pragmatic one of Shaftesbury and, stated more forcefully, Toland. Toland assumed that the flunctuation between hope and fear produces superstition, but he concluded that while irresolvable as a speculative issue, "'as a practical issue the denial of immortality, and consequently the denial of all future rewards, 'is an opinion I think inconsistent with society'" (*Second Part of the State Anatomy of Great Britain* [1717], p. vi, in Daniel's, *John Toland: His Methods, Manners, and Mind* [Kingston and Montreal, 1984], p. 97).

37 *Miscellanies*, vol. I, ed. H. K. Miller (Middletown, CT, 1972), p. 225 (emphasis added); *Tom Jones*, I.2. Cf. Battestin's note to the latter (p. 35), which simply makes it a devotional commonplace; but this was Fielding's own personal concern. Another example is in *Tom Jones*, II.1, pp. 116–17. On the other hand Bishop Butler, among others, argued that if we are uncertain it is safer to assume the reality of future rewards and punishments.

38 Fielding frequently uses and alludes to the passage in Plato's *Phaedrus* (250d); for example in the dedication to *Tom Jones*, just following his declaration that there will be nothing prejudicial to the Cause of Religion and Virtue," he connects "Example" and "Picture" with "Virtue . . . an object of Sight, and strikes us with an Idea of that loveliness, which *Plato* asserts there is in her naked Charms": But the passage in *Phaedrus* does not have anything like the "naked Charms" or erotic overtones of these passages (see also in "'The Essay on Conversation" and "on the Characters of Men"). In the context of both *Tom Jones* and

Hogarth's *Boys Peeping at Nature*, cf. the opening of Cleland's *Fanny Hill, or Memoirs of a Woman of Pleasure* (1749): "Truth! stark naked truth, is the word, and I will not so much as take the pains to bestow the strip of a gauze-wrapper on it . . ." (ed. Peter Wagner [Harmondsworth, 1985], p. 39).

39 He may have based this female figure on Hogarth's. Starting with the *Harlot*, Hogarth set off Vice-Harlot against another, valorized woman – Sarah Young, the Poet's wife, Miranda, and his young actress "playing" "Diana" in *Strolling Actresses Dressing in a Barn*. For a fuller discussion, see Paulson, *Hogarth*, III, chapter 3.

40 See *Covent-Garden Journal*, March 14, 1752; also *Amelia* III.5. Without being named, Mandeville is with Hobbes the villain of the attack in *The Champion* for January 22, 1730/40. Cf. also Battestin's view of Mandeville's lack of influence on Fielding in *The Providence of Wit: Aspects of form in Augustan Literature and the Arts* (Oxford, 1974), p. 160.

41 Mandeville, *Fable of the Bees*, I, p. 324.

42 Ibid., I, pp. 42, 50, 51.

43 Fielding, *Miscellanies*, I, p. 158.

44 He goes on: "and consequently, that it is *not as old as the Creation* [alluding to Tindal's deist tract, which argued that God made the basic tenets of religion available to all men through the use of their reason alone, with no need of assistance from the Bible], nor is Revelation useless with Regard to Morality, if it had taught us no more than this excellent Doctrine, which, if generally followed, would make mankind much happier, as well as better than they are."

45 These essays Battestin sees as simply a reflection of the low standing of the clergy at the time – "contempt of the clergy" being "a stock phrase of the time," words he quotes from an ecclesiastical history of 1885 (J. H. Overton, *Life in the English Church [1660–1714]*, 1885, p. 302; Martin and Ruthe Battestin, *Henry Fielding*, p. 130). But the key word of the deists was "priestcraft": John Toland, author of *Christianity not Mysterious*, argued that a clergy maintained itself by focusing on the mysterious activity of God and arguing that they alone understood the mysteries of religion. Like Fielding, Toland distinguished bad priests from good – "an Order of Men not only useful and necessary, but likewise reputable and venerable" (he started a work called "Priesthood without Priestcraft"). See Toland, "A Word to the Honest Priests," in *An Appeal to Honest People against Wicked Priests* (1713); cited, Daniel, *John Toland*, p. 26.

46 Fielding's sense of bad clergy in the clergy essays is implicitly related to the bad stewards (lawyers, ministers, Walpole) of Opposition satire (see *The Champion* for February 12, 1739/40; cf. Howard Erskine-Hill, *The Social Milieu of Alexander Pope* [New Haven, 1975], pp. 243–59).

47 Fielding's positive touchstones, based on the Gospels, are humility and charity, which allow him to emphasize the spirit versus the letter of the law. He quotes Luke 20.46, 47: "to beware of the Scribes which desire to

walk in long Robes, and love Greetings in the Markets, and the highest Seats in the Synagogues, and the chief Rooms at Feasts, which devour Widows' Houses, and for Show make long Prayers."

48 At Mr. B.'s advance Pamela faints but exposes her stratagem by the words of her text: "I sighed, and scream'd, and fainted away. And still he had his Arms about my Neck"; on which Mr. B. comments: "As for *Pamela*, she has a lucky Knack at falling into Fits, when she pleases." Fielding's analysis of *Pamela* seen from one direction is libertine (Mr. B.'s analysis of Pamela's fainting fits), from another rationalist and deist. (See *Pamela*, ed. T. C. Duncan Eaves and Ben D. Kimpel [Boston, 1971], pp. 67, 68.)

49 J. Paul Hunter's argument that Fielding is *refuting* Morgan is unconvincing; following Battestin, he sees the Joseph-Abraham analogies as normative (*Occasional Form: Henry Fielding and the Chains of Circumstance* [Baltimore, 1975], pp. 101–05; Battestin, *Moral Basis of Fielding's Art*, pp. 30–43).

50 This proves to be lust, distinguished from Joseph's love of Fanny by Betty's willingness to settle for the next man who happens along.

51 See Paulson, *Hogarth*, vol. 2, chapter 4.

52 *Joseph Andrews*, ed. Battestin, p. 47.

53 The topos that Christians were morally inferior to non-Christians was, of course, deployed by Latitudinarians as well as deists. (See Isabel Rivers, *Reason, Grace, and Sentiment: A Study of the Language of Religion and Ethics in England, 1660–1780* [Cambridge, 1991], pp. 8–12.)

54 For a persuasive account of Joseph's development (as opposed to Adams' stasis), see Dick Taylor, Jr., "Joseph as Hero in *Joseph Andrews*," *Tulane Studies in England*, 7 (1957), 91–109.

55 It should be recalled that Mr. Wilson's narrative closely parallels Hogarth's *Rake's Progress* (1735), representing the same oppressive world of corrupt government, church, law, and medicine that destroys both the Rake and the Harlot.

56 See Paulson, *Popular and Polite Art*, II, p. 6. Banier, of course, never mentions the Scriptures, but it is obvious that, as in the earlier model of Lucian, the euhemerist interpretation of the Greek gods can apply equally well to the life and miracles of Christ.

57 George Lyttelton, "Observations on the Conversion and Apostleship of St. Paul" (1748), in *The Works of George Lord Lyttelton* (1776), II, p. 3.

58 In *The True Patriot* (1745–56) Fielding had used Roman Catholicism to sum up all the worst in priestcraft, the determination "to extirpate Heresy by all Methods whatever" and "inevitably destroy [England's] Civil Liberties" – which he opposes to "the Temper of Protestants." And in the dangerous situation of the Forty-Five he also lumps "the most noble Party of Free-Thinkers, who has no Religion" with the Jacobites. E.g., *Tom Jones*, IX.6.516–17; see also p. 373; Henry Fielding, *True Patriot and Related Writings*, ed. W. B. Coley (Oxford and Middletown, CT, 1987), pp. 124–25, 137. But the same reference to one bad

clergyman as opposed to the order (in *The Champion*, February 23, 1740, I, p. 259) reappears in *True Patriot* 14 (28 January-4 February 1746), pp. 207–208, where it is extended from clergy to writers.

59 *Covent-Garden Journal*, 29 (April 11, 1752), ed. Bertrand Goldgar (Oxford and Middletown, CT, 1993), p. 423.

60 *Amelia*, ed. Martin C. Battestin, pp. 511–12. This was an orthodox view. Fielding could have found support in the sermons of Robert South, one of his favorite Latitudinarian divines, that "hope and fear are the two great handles, by which the will of man is to be taken hold of, when we would either draw it to duty or draw it off from sin" (*Sermons* [1834], 3.136).

61 *Covent-Garden Journal*, p. 49:

There are certain Arcana Naturae, in disclosing which the Moderns have made great Progress; now whatever Merit there may be in such denudations of Nature, if I may so express myself, and however exquisite a Relish they may afford to *very* adult Persons of both sexes in their Closets, they are surely too speculative and mysterious for the Contemplation of the Young and Tender, into whose Hands Tarts and Pies are most likely to fall (p. 50).

See also issue 9 (p. 68) as an ironic but truth-telling account; pp. 43, 49; and cf. *Enquiry*, p. 172, on parents and children.

Select bibliography

PRIMARY WORKS

An Account of the Trial of Thomas Woolston, B.D. (London, 1729).

An Address to the Freeholders of the County of Sussex (n.p., December 1741).

Allestree, Richard, "Of the Exercise of Conscience," *Forty Sermons*, 2 vols. (London, 1684).

"The Ladies Calling," in *The Works of the Author of The Whole Duty of Man* (Oxford, 1704).

Aquinas, Thomas, *Summa Theologica*, Christian Classics edition, 5 vols. (Westminster, MD, 1981).

Astell, Mary, *Bartlemy Fair; Or, An Enquiry After Wit* (1709).

Atterbury, Francis, "A Scorner Incapable of True Wisdom" (1694), *Sermons and Discourses*, 2 vols. (London, 1820).

[Bagshaw, Edward], *The Great Question concerning Things Indifferent in Religious Worship* (London, 1660).

Baker, Thomas, *Reflections on Learning* (London, 1699).

Barrow, Isaac, *The Theological Works of Isaac Barrow, D.D.*, ed. Alexander Napier, 9 vols. (Cambridge, 1859).

Baxter, Richard, *Narrative of His Life* (1696).

Bayle, Pierre, *Dictionary Historical and Critical*, trans. Pierre Des Maizeaux (London, 1734).

Behn, Aphra, *Oroonoko, or the Royal Slave*, rptd. in *Works of Aphra Behn*, ed. Montague Summers (London and Stratford-on-Avon, 1915).

Bentley, Richard, *The Correspondence of Richard Bentley*, ed. Christopher Wordsworth, 2 vols. (London, 1842).

The Folly and Unreasonableness of Atheism (London, 1692-93); rptd. in *The Works of Richard Bentley*, ed. Alexander Dyce, 3 vols. (London, 1838).

Remarks upon a Late Discourse of Free-Thinking (London, 1714).

Berkeley, George, "Verses on the Prospect of Planting Arts and Learning in America," first published in *A Miscellany* (Dublin, 1752).

Bibliotecha Furleiana (Rotterdam, 1714).

Biographia Britannica, ed. Andrew Kippis, 5 vols. (London, 1780).

Blackmore, Richard, *A Satyr Against Wit* (London, 1700).

Blake, William, *The Poetry and Prose of William Blake*, ed. David V. Erdman, commentary by Harold Bloom (New York, 1970).

Blount, Charles, *A Just Vindication of Learning and the Liberty of the Press* (1695), rptd. in *Miscellaneous Works* (London, 1695).
The Oracles of Reason (1693), rptd. in *Miscellaneous Works* (London, 1695).
The Two First Books of Philostratus Concerning the Life of Apollonius Tyaneus (London, 1680).
Boyle, Charles, *Dr. Bentley's Dissertation on the Epistles of Phalaris Examin'd* (London, 1698).
Boyle, Robert, "Some Considerations Touching the Style of the Holy Scriptures," in *The Works of the Honourable Robert Boyle*, ed. T. Birch, 6 vols. (1773).
British Journal (1722-31).
Brooke, Lord, (Robert Greville) *A Discourse opening the Nature of that Episcopacie which is exercised in England* (1642), rptd. in *Tracts on Liberty in the Puritan Revolution*, ed. William Haller, 3 vols. (New York, 1934).
Browne, Philip, *The Sovereign's Authority* (London, 1682).
Browne, Simon, *A Fit Rebuke to a Ludicrous Infidel: In some Remarks on Mr. Woolston's Fifth Discourse on the Miracles of Our Saviour* (London, 1732).
Burke, Edmund, *Speech on Conciliation with America* (London, 1775).
Reflections on the Revolution in France (1790), rptd. in *The Writings and Speeches of Edmund Burke*, vol. VIII, ed. L. G. Mitchell (Oxford, 1989).
Burnet, Gilbert, *Charitable Reproof. A Sermon Preached to the Societies for Reformation of Manners* (London, 1700).
"The Life and Death of . . . John Earl of Rochester," in *The Lives of Sir Matthew Hale, . . . Wilmot, Earl of Rochester; and Queen Mary* (1774).
Bury, Arthur, *The Naked Gospel* (1690).
Butler, Samuel, *Prose Observations*, ed. Hugh de Quehen, (Oxford, 1979).
Calamy, Edward, *A Sermon Preach'd to the Societies for Reformation of Manners* (London, 1699).
Carroll, William, *A Dissertation Upon the Tenth Chapter of the Fourth Book of Mr Locke's Essay Concerning Human Understanding*, (1706; rptd. Bristol, 1990).
Chandler, Edward, *A Sermon Preach'd to the Societies for Reformation of Manners* (London, 1724).
Clarendon, Earl of (Edward Hyde), *A Brief View and Survey of the Dangerous and Pernicious Errors to the Church and State in Mr. Hobbes's Book Entitled Leviathan* (1676).
Clarkson, Laurence, *A Single Eye* (n.p., 1650).
Cleland, John, *Fanny Hill, or Memoirs of a Woman of Pleasure* (London, 1749).
Cobden, Edward, *The Duty and Reward of Turning Others to Righteousness. A Sermon Preach'd to the Societies for Reformation of Manners* (London, 1736).
A Collection of Certain Statutes in force . . . for the better Caution of such as are inclinable to Delinquency (London, 1643).
Collier, Jeremy, *Miscellanies Upon Moral Subjects, The Second Part* (London, 1695).
Collins, Anthony, *A Discourse Concerning Ridicule and Irony in Writing* (1729), ed. Edward A. and Lillian D. Bloom (Los Angeles, 1970).
A Discourse of Free-Thinking (London, 1713).

A Discourse on the Grounds and Reasons of the Christian Religion (London, 1724).
The Scheme of Literal Prophecy Considered (London, 1726).
Colnett, William, *A Sermon Preach'd to the Societies for Reformation of Manners* (London, 1711).
A Complete Catalogue of the Library of Anthony Collins, Esq., ed. T. Ballard (1731).
Cooke, Thomas, *A Demonstration of the Will of God by the Light of Nature* (1733).
Letter to the Archbishop of Canterbury, concerning Persecution for Religion and Freedom of Debate (1732).
Coppe, Abiezer, *A Fiery Flying Roll* (1650), rptd. *Abiezer Coppe: Selected Writings*, ed. Andrew Hopton (London, 1987).
Coxe, Thomas, *A Sermon Preach'd at the Assizes held at Bedford* (Oxford, 1730).
The Craftsman (1726-47).
Cudworth, Ralph, *A Treatise Concerning Eternal and Immutable Morality* (1731).
The True Intellectual System of the Universe (1678).
True Intellectual System of the Universe, prefaced by Johan Lorenz von Mosheim (Leyden, 1768).
Curteis, Thomas, *Advice to a Son at the University, Design'd for Holy Orders. By a Clergyman* (London, 1725).
Christianity, in its Nature and Design, Offers no Violence to the Reason or Conscience of Men. A Sermon preach'd in the Chapel at Tunbridge-Wells, on Sunday, the 31st of August, 1735 (London, 1735).
A Dissertation on the Unreasonableness, Folly, and Danger of Infidelity; Occasion'd by a late Virulent book [by Anthony Collins], intitul'd A Discourse on the Grounds and Reasons of the Christian Religion. (London, 1725).
Essays Moral and Divine, . . . Design'd to illustrate the Necessity, Authority, and Amiableness of Revealed Religion, 2nd edn, (London, 1715).
Genethlia: A Poem on the Blessed Nativity. Design'd to excite an Awful Sense of Religion both in the Indolent and Unbelieving Part of Mankind (London, 1727).
The Harmony between Natural and Revealed Religion, Asserted. In a sermon preached before the Worshipful the Master, Wardens, and Company of Apothecaries, in London, on the 23rd of September, 1731 (London, 1731).
Reflexions on Natural and Reveal'd Religion: Design'd as a Preservative against the Growing Scepticism of the Present Age: and Particularly against the Subtil Insinuations in a late Book [by Matthew Tindal], intitul'd, Christianity as Old as the Creation. (London, 1733).
Religious Princes the Greatest Blessing and Safety to the Church and State. A Sermon Preach'd in the Parish Church of Wrotham in Kent, on Thursday the 7th of June, 1716. Being the day appointed for a Publick Thanksgiving to Almighty God, for the suppression of the Late Horrid and Unnatural Rebellion (London, 1716).
Thankfulness and Unanimity the Proper Returns of National Blessings. A Sermon Preach'd on the late Day of Thanksgiving for his Majesty's Safe and Peaceable Accession to the Crown (London, 1715).
Davies, Roger, *An Essay in the Socratic Way of Dialogue on the Existence of the Divine Being in Imitation of Tully's Tusculan Disputations* (London, 1724).

Defoe, Daniel, *An Essay on the Regulation of the Press* (1704), ed. John Robert Moore (Oxford, 1948).
An Essay upon Projects (London, 1697).
Les Soupirs de la Grande Britaigne: Or, the Groans of Great Britain (London, 1713).
Poor Man's Plea to all the Proclamations, Declarations, Acts of Parliament, etc . . . . for a Reformation of Manners (London, 1698).
A Digest of the Law Concerning Libels (London, 1765).
Disney, John, *A View of Antient Laws against Immorality and Profaneness* (Cambridge, 1729).
The Distinction of High-Church and Low-Church Distinctly Consider'd and Fairly Stated. With Some Reflections upon the Popular Plan of MODERATION (London, 1705).
Dowel, John, *The Leviathan Heretical* (London, 1683).
Dryden, John, "Religion Laici," (1682), *The Poems and Fables of John Dryden*, ed. James Kinsley (London, 1962).
Drew, Robert, *A Sermon Preach'd to the Societies for Reformation of Manners* (London, 1735).
Edwards, John, *A Compleat History or Survey of all the Dispensations and Methods of Religion from the Beginning of the World* (London, 1699).
A Demonstration of the Existence of God from the Contemplation of the Visible Structure of the Greater and Lesser World (London, 1696).
A Discourse Concerning the Authority Stile and Perfection of the Books of the Old and New Testaments (London, 1696).
A Free Discourse Concerning Truth and Error Especially in Matters of Religion (London, 1701).
Socinianism Unmasked (London, 1696).
Some New Discoveries of the Uncertainty, Deficiency, and Corruption of Human Knowledge and Learning (London, 1714).
Edwards, Thomas, *Gangraena*, 2 vols. (London, 1646).
Evans, John, *Moderation Stated* (London, 1682).
An Expostulary Letter to Mr. Woolston, on Account of His Late Writings, By a Clergyman in the Country (London, 1730).
Fielding, Henry, *Amelia*, ed. Martin Battestin (Oxford and Middleton, CT, 1983).
The Champion, collected edn (London, 1740).
A Charge Delivered to the Grand Jury (London, 1749).
Covent-Garden Journal, ed. Bertrand Goldgar (Oxford and Middletown, CT, 1993).
An Enquiry into the Late Increase in Robbers (London, 1751).
Examples of the Interposition of Providence in the Detection and Punishment of Murder (London, 1752).
The History of Tom Jones A Foundling, introduction and commentary by Martin C. Battestin, ed. Fredson Bowers, 2 vols. (Oxford and Middletown, CT, 1975).
Joseph Andrews, ed. Martin C. Battestin (Oxford and Middletown, CT, 1967).

The Letter-Writers: or, a New Way to Keep a Wife at Home (London, 1731).

Miscellanies, vol. I, ed. Henry Knight Miller (Oxford and Middletown, CT, 1972).

Miscellanies, 3 vols. (1743).

The True Patriot and Related Writings, ed. W. B. Coley (Oxford and Middletown, CT, 1987).

The Welsh [Grub Street] Opera (London, 1731).

Fisher, Samuel, *The Rusticks Alarm to the Rabbies* (London, 1660).

Fog's Weekly Journal (1716-1737).

For God or the Devil, Or, Just Chastisement No Persecution (London, 1729)

Fowler, Edward, *The Principles and Practices of Certain Moderate Divines of the Church of England (Greatly mis-understood) Truly Represented and Defended* (London, 1670).

A Vindication of a Late Undertaking of Certain Gentlemen, In Order to the Suppressing of Debauchery, and Profaneness (London, 1692).

Franklin, Benjamin, *A Dissertation on Liberty and Necessity, Pleasure and Pain* (London, 1725).

[Anon.] *Free Thoughts Upon the Discourse of Free-Thinking* (London, 1713).

Freeman, Samuel, *A Sermon Preach'd at the Assizes, held at Northampton* (London, 1690).

The Freeholder's Journal, 36 (September 1722).

Gastrell, Francis, *The Principles of Deism Truly Demonstrated and Set in a Clear Light, in Two Dialogues Between a Sceptick and a Deist* (London, 1708).

Gibson, Edmund, *The Bishop of London's Pastoral Letter to the People of his Diocese* (London, 1728).

Codex Juris Ecclesiastici Anglicani (London, 1713).

Gildon, Charles, *The Deists Manual: Or a Rational Inquiry into the Christian Religion* (London, 1705).

Glanvill, Joseph, *A Blow at Modern Sadducism in Some Philosophical Considerations About Witchcraft* (London, 1668).

"The Agreement of Reason and Religion," *Essays on Several Important Subjects in Philosophy and Religion* (London, 1676).

Goodwin, John, *Divine Authority of the Scriptures Asserted* (1648).

Grant, Francis (Lord Cullen), *A Brief Account of the Nature, Rise, and Progress of the Societies for Reformation of Manners* (Edinburgh, 1700).

[Grove, Robert], *A Perswasive to Communion with the Church of England* (London, 1683).

Hall, Joseph, *A Sober Reply to Mr. Higgs' Merry Arguments* (London, 1720).

[Hare, Francis], *The Clergyman's Thanks to Phileleutherus for the Remarks on the Late Discourse of Free-Thinking* (London, 1713).

The Difficulties and Discouragements which Attend the Study of Scriptures in the Way of Private Judgment (1714; rptd. London, 1716).

Harris, John, *The Atheistical Objection Against the Being of God and his Attributes Fairly Considered, and Fully Refuted*, 2 vols. (London, 1698).

Hayley, Thomas, *A Sermon Preach'd to the Societies for Reformation of Manners* (London, 1718).

Herbert of Cherbury, *The Antient Religion of the Gentiles*, trans. William Lewis (London, 1705).

De Religone Laici, ed. and trans. Harold R. Hutcheson (New Haven, 1944).

De Veritate, ed. Meyrick H. Carre (1645; rptd. Bristol, n.d.).

Heylyn, John, *A Sermon Preached to the Societies for Reformation of Manners* (London, 1721).

Heywood, Eliza, *The Fatal Secret; or, the Lucky Disappointment: A Novel* (London, 1724).

Heynes, M[atthew], *A Sermon for Reformation of Manners, Preach'd . . . at the Assizes* (London, 1701).

Hilliard, Samuel, *A Narrative of the Prosecution of Mr. Sare and His Servant, for Selling the Rights of the Christian Church* (London, 1709).

Hoadly, Benjamin, *A Plain Account of the Nature and End of the Sacrament of the Lord's-Supper* (London, 1735).

Hobbes, Thomas, *Leviathan*, ed. C. B. Macpherson (Harmondsworth, 1981).

Horneck, Anthony, *The Nature of True Christian Righteousness* (London, 1689).

Howell, James, *Instructions for Forreine Travel*, ed. Edwin Arber (London, 1868).

Ibbot, Benjamin, *The Nature and Extent of the Office of the Civil Magistrate* (London, 1720).

Jachin and Boaz: Or the Stedfast and Unwavering Christian (London, 1676).

Johnson, John, *The Case of Occasional Days and Prayers: containing a defence for not solemnizing the Accession-Day . . . and for not using occasional prayers* (London, 1721).

The Clergyman's Vade-Mecum: or, an Account of the Ancient and Present Church of England; the Duties and the Rights of the Clergy; and of their Privileges and Hardships (3rd edn, London, 1709).

The Unbloody Sacrifice, and Altar Unvail'd and Supported; in which the Nature of the Eucharist is explain'd according to the Sentiments of the Christian Church in the Four First Centuries (London, 1714).

King, Josiah, *Mr. Blount's Oracles of Reason Examined and Answered* (Exeter, 1698).

L. P. "Two Essays," in *Somers Tracts* (1748-51), XI.

Lafite, Daniel, *No Lawful Ministry without a Divine Mission* (London, 1713).

Lardner, Nathaniel, *A Vindication of Three of Our Blessed Saviour's Miracles* (London, 1729).

Le Clerc, Jean, *Defense des sentiments de quelques theologiens* (Amsterdam, 1686).

Leslie, Charles, *The Charge of Socinianism Against Dr. Tillotson Considered* (1694).

The Second Part of the Wolf Stript of his Shepherd's Cloathing (London, 1707).

A Supplement Upon Occasion of A History of Religion (1694), rptd. *The Theological Works of the Rev. Charles Leslie*, 7 vols. (Oxford, 1832).

L'Estrange, Roger, *Considerations and Proposals in Order to the Regulation of the Press* (London, 1663).

A Letter Concerning Libels, Warrants, the Seizing of Papers and Sureties of Behaviour, 3rd edn (London, 1765).

Lewis, Richard, *The Robin-Hood Society: a Satire by Peter Pounce* (London, 1756).
The Life of Edward, First Lord Herbert of Cherbury, ed. J. M. Shuttleworth (London, 1976).
Locke, John, *Conduct of the Understanding*, with an introduction and notes by Thomas Fowler. 3rd edn (Oxford, 1890).
  Correspondence, Clarendon Edition of the Works of John Locke, ed. E. S. de Beer, 9 vols. (Oxford, 1976-).
  Epistola de Tolerantia: A Letter on Toleration, ed. Raymond Klibansky, trans. J. W. Gough (Oxford, 1968).
  An Essay Concerning Human Understanding, Clarendon Edition of the Works of John Locke, ed. Peter H. Nidditch (Oxford, 1975).
  Essays on the Laws of Nature, ed. W. von Leyden (Oxford, 1954).
  A Paraphrase and Notes on the Epistles of St Paul, Clarendon Edition of the Works of John Locke, ed. Arthur W. Wainwright. 2 vols., (Oxford, 1987).
  Reasonableness of Christianity (1695).
  Two Tracts on Government, ed. Philip Abrams (Cambridge, 1967).
  Two Treatises of Government, ed. Peter Laslett, 2nd edn (Cambridge, 1967).
  The Works of John Locke, 2nd ed. 3 vols. (London, 1722).
  "A Letter Concerning Toleration" in *The Works of John Locke*, 12th edn, 9 vols. (London 1824).
Lyttelton, George, "Observations on the Conversion and Apostleship of St. Paul" (1748), *The Works of George Lord Lyttelton*, 3 vols. (London, 1776).
Mandeville, Bernard, *Fable of the Bees*, ed. F. B. Kaye 2 vols. (Oxford, 1924).
  A Modest Defence of Publick Stews (1724), ed. Richard I. Cook (Los Angeles, 1973).
Marvell, Andrew, *The Rehearsal Transpros'd* and *The Rehearsal Transpros'd, The Second Part* (1672 and 1673), ed. D. I. B. Smith (Oxford, 1971).
Melanchthon, Philip, *Selected Writings*, ed. E. E. Flack and Lowell Satre, trans. C. L. Hill (Minneapolis, MN, 1962).
Memoirs of the Life and Writings of Matthew Tindall, LL.D. (1723).
The Memorial of the Church of England (London, 1705).
Meriton, George, *Immorality, Debauchery and Profaneness Exposed to the Reproof of Scripture and the Censure of the Law* (London, 1698).
Milton, John, *Complete Prose Works* (New Haven and London, 1953-).
[Anon.] *Moral Essays and Discourses Upon Several Subjects chiefly Relating to the Present Times* (1690).
More, Henry, *A Collection of Several Philosophical Writings of Dr. Henry More*, 4th edn (London, 1712).
  A Modest Enquiry into the Mystery of Iniquity (London, 1664).
Morgan, Thomas, *The Moral Philosopher* (London, 1737).
Newman, Thomas, *Reformation, or Mockery . . . A Sermon Preach'd to the Societies for Reformation of Manners at Salter's Hall* (London, 1729).
Newton, Isaac, *Correspondence*, ed. H. W. Turnbull, 7 vols. (Cambridge, 1961).
Nichols, John, *Biographical Anecdotes of William Hogarth*, 2 vols. (1782).
Nicholls, William, *A Conference with a Theist* (London, 1696).

Ogilvie, John, *An Inquiry into the Causes of the Infidelity and Scepticism of the Times* (London, 1783).

Osborn, Francis, *"Advice to a Son,"* in *Miscellaneous Works*, 11th edn, 2 vols. (London, 1722).

[Owen, John], *Truth and Innocence Vindicated: in a Survey of a Discourse concerning Ecclesiastical Politie* (London, 1669).

The Works of John Owen, ed. W. H. Goold, 24 vols. (1850-53).

Parker, John, *The Government of the People of England Precedent and President the Same* (London, 1650).

Parker, Samuel, *An Account of the Nature and Extent of the Divine Dominion and Goodness* (1666; 2nd edn Oxford, 1667).

The Case of the Church of England, Briefly and Truly Stated (London, 1681).

A Demonstration of the Divine Authority of the Law of Nature, and of the Christian Religion (London, 1681).

A Discourse of Ecclesiastical Politie, 3rd edn (London, 1671).

A Free and Impartial Censure of the Platonick Philosophie (Oxford, 1666; 2nd edn, 1667).

Reasons for Abrogating the Test, Imposed on all Members of Parliament (London, 1688).

Religion and Loyalty: Or, A Demonstration of the Power of the Christian Church within It Self (London, 1684).

Religion and Loyalty: The Second Part (London, 1685).

A Reproof to the Rehearsal Transprosed, in a Discourse to Its Author (London, 1673).

Pearse, Edward, *The Conformists Plea for the Nonconformists . . .* (London, 1681).

[Polhill, Edward], *The Samaritan: Shewing that Many and Unnecessary Impositions Are Not the Oyl that must Heal the Church* (London, 1682).

Proposals for a National Reformation of Manners (London, 1695).

Rawson, Joseph, *Righteousness the Exaltation, and Sin the Reproach of a People. In a Sermon Preach'd at the Lent Assizes* (London, 1714).

Ray, Thomas, *A Vindication of Our Saviour's Miracles, in Answer to Mr. Woolston's Five Last Discourses* (London, 1730).

Representation of the Present State of Religion Among Us, with Regard to the Late Excessive Growth of Infidelity, Heresy, and Profaneness (London, 1711).

A Representation of the State of the Societies for Reformation of Manners, Humbly Offered to his Majesty, (London, 1715).

Reverendi amodum in Christo Patri, S. Parker . . . de rebus sui temporis commentariorum libri quatuor (London, 1726). Translated Thomas Newlin, *Bishop Parker's History of His Own Time* (London 1727 and 1728).

The Review, (1704-11), ed. A. W. Secord, 22 vols. (New York, 1938).

[Richardson, Samuel], *The Apprentice's Vade Mecum*, ed. Alan Dugald McKillop (1734; rptd. Los Angeles, 1975).

Richardson, Samuel, *Pamela*, ed. T. C. Duncan Eaves and Ben D. Kimpel (Boston, 1971).

Sacheverell, Henry, *The Character of a Low Churchman* (London, 1702).

The Communication of Sin. A Sermon Preach'd at the Assizes held at Derby (London, 1709).

The Perils of False Brethren, both in Church and State. (London, 1709).

Sanderson, Robert, *Logicae artis compendium* (1615).

De Obligatione Conscientiae, Praelectiones Decem (1660).

Shaftesbury, Third Earl of (Anthony Ashley Cooper), *Characteristics of Men, Manners, Opinions, Times* (1711), ed. John M. Robertson (1900; rptd. Indianapolis, 1964).

Inquiry concerning Virtue and Merit (London, 1699, 1711).

A Notion of the Historical Draught or Tablature of the Judgment of Hercules (London, 1713).

Simon, Richard, *Critical History of the Old Testament*, trans. Henry Dickinson (1682).

Skelton, Philip, *Ophiomaches: Or, Deism Revealed*, ed. David Berman, 2 vols. (1749; rptd. Bristol, 1990).

Smalbroke, Richard, *Reformation Necessary to prevent our Ruine. A Sermon Preach'd to the Societies for Reformation of Manners* (London, 1728).

A Vindication of the Miracles of Our Blessed Saviour, 2 vols. (vol. i, London, 1729; vol. ii, London, 1731).

Smith, John, *Select Discourses*, 2nd edn (Cambridge, 1673).

Smith, Samuel, *A Sermon Preach'd to the Societies for Reformation of Manners* (London, 1738).

Smyth, George, *A Sermon Preach'd at Salter's-Hall to the Societies for Reformation of Manners* (London, 1727).

South, Robert, *Sermons* (1834).

Sermons Preached upon Several Occasions (London, 1737).

Spademan, John, *A Sermon Preach'd November 14, 1698 and Now Publish'd at the Request of the Societies for Reformation of Manners* (London, 1699).

Stamford, Thomas, Earl of, *Speech at the General Quarter-Sessions held at Leicester* (London, 1691).

Stanhope, George, *The Duty of Juries. A Sermon Preach'd at the Lent-Assizes, holden at Maidstone, in Kent* (London, 1703).

State Law, or the Doctrine of Libels Discussed and Examined (London, 1729).

Stebbing, Henry, *A Defence of the Scripture History* (London, 1730).

Stillingfleet, Edward, *Irenicum. A Weapon-Salve for the Churches Wounds: or, The Divine Right of Particular Forms of Church-Government Discussed and Examined* (1661), 2nd edn (London, 1662).

A Letter to a Deist (London, 1677; 2nd edn 1697).

Stubbe, Henry, *A Further Justification of the Present War Against the United Netherlands* (London, 1673).

Swift, Jonathan, *The Poems of Jonathan Swift*, ed. Harold Williams, 2nd edn, 3 vols. (Oxford, 1958).

The Prose Works of Jonathan Swift, ed. Herbert Davis et al., 16 vols. (Oxford, 1939–74).

A Tale of a Tub to Which is Added the Battle of the Books and the Mechanical Operation of the Spirit, ed. A. C. Guthkelch and D. Nichol Smith, 2nd edn (Oxford, 1958).

Taylor, Jeremy, *The Liberty of Prophesying, Ductor Dubitantium* (1648).

Temple, William, "An Essay upon the Ancient and Modern Learning," *Miscellanea*, part 2 (1690), rptd. in *The Works of Sir William Temple*, 4 vols. (London, 1814).

Tindal, Matthew, *An Address to the Inhabitants of the Two Great Cities of London and Westminster in Relation to a Pastoral Letter Said to be Written by the Bishop of London* (London, 1729).

A Defence of the Rights of the Christian Church (London, 1707).

A Discourse for the Liberty of the Press in a Letter to a Member of Parliament (London, 1698), rptd. in *Four Discourses* (London, 1709).

An Essay Concerning the Power of the Magistrate and the Rights of Mankind in Matters of Religion (London, 1697).

The Rights of the Christian Church Asserted, 3rd ed. (London, 1707).

The Rights of the Christian Church Asserted (London, 1706).

The Power of the Magistrate, rptd. in *Four Discourses* (London 1709).

A Second Defence of the Rights of the Christian Church (London, 1708).

Toland, John, *An Appeal to Honest People against Wicked Priests* (London, 1713).

Christianity Not Mysterious (London, 1696).

Letters to Serena (London, 1704).

Pantheisticon, English translation (London, 1751).

Vindicius Liberius (1702).

"Clidophorus," Tetradymus (London, 1720).

"A Letter Concerning Roman Education," *A Collection of Several Pieces*, 2 vols. (London, 1726).

The Travels of Cosimo III, Grand Duke of Tuscany, though England (London, 1821).

Troughear, Thomas, *The Magistrate's Duty to Honour God, Set Forth in a Sermon Preach'd at Southampton* (Oxford, 1733).

Tucker, Josiah, *Letter to the Right Honourable Edmund Burke . . . in Answer to His Printed Speech* (Gloucester, 1775).

Turner, John, *A Vindication of the Rights and Privileges of the Christian Church* (London, 1707).

Veneer, John, *An Exposition on the Thirty Nine Articles of the Church of England*, 2 vols., 2nd edn (London, 1734).

[W. D.] *The Gentleman Instructed*, part 3 (London, 1712).

Warburton, William, "The Divine Legation of Moses," *The Works of the Right Reverend William Warburton*, 7 vols. (London, 1788).

Ward, Edward, *The History of the London Clubs* (London, 1709).

Waterland, Daniel, *Christianity Vindicated Against Infidelity: A Second Charge Deliver'd to the Clergy of the Archdeaconry of Middlesex* (London, 1732).

Watson, Richard, *Anecdotes of the Life of Richard Watson, Bishop of Llandaff; Written by Himself* (London, 1817).

Whichcote, Benjamin, *Moral and Religious Aphorisms*, ed. Samuel Salter (London, 1753).

Wilkins, John, *A Discourse Concerning a New World and Another Planet* (London, 1641).

Williams, Daniel, *A Sermon Preach'd at Salter's-Hall to the Societies for Reformation of Manners* (London, 1698).

Woolston, Thomas, *The Moderator between An Infidel and an Apostate* (London, 1725).

Six Discourses of the Miracles of Our Saviour, and Defences of His Discourses (1727-1730; rptd. New York and London, 1979).

Wotton, William, *Letter to Eusebia* (London, 1704).

Reflections upon Ancient and Modern Learning (London, 1694).

Writer, Clement, *Fides Divina*, (1657).

Young, Edward, *Love of Fame: The Universal Passion*, 2nd edn, (London, 1728).

SECONDARY WORKS

Addy, John, *Sin and Society in the Seventeenth Century* (London, 1989).

Aldridge, A. O., "Shaftesbury and the Test of Truth," *PMLA*, 60 (1945).

Arnauld, Antoine, *The Art of Thinking*, trans. James Dickoff and Patricia James (New York, 1964).

Ashcraft, Richard, *Locke's Two Treatises of Government* (London, 1987).

Revolutionary Politics and Locke's Two Treatises of Government (Princeton, NJ, 1986).

"Latitudinarianism and Toleration: Historical Myth Versus Political History," in Richard Kroll, Richard Ashcraft, and Perez Zagorin, (eds.), *Philosophy, Science and Religion in England 1640-1700* (Cambridge, 1992).

"Political Theory and Political Action in Karl Mannheim's Thought: Reflections upon *Ideology and Utopia* and its Critics," *Comparative Studies in Society and History*, 23:1 (January 1981).

Ashcraft, Richard, and Goldsmith, M. M., "Locke, Revolution Principles, and the Formation of Whig Ideology," *The Historical Journal* 26 (1983).

Atheism from the Reformation to the Enlightenment, ed. Michael Hunter and David Wootton (Oxford, 1992).

Bate, Frank, *The English Indulgence of 1672: A Study in the Rise of Organized Dissent* (London, 1908).

Battestin, Martin C., *The Moral Basis of Fielding's Art: A Study of "Joseph Andrews"* (Middletown, CT, 1959).

The Providence of Wit: Aspects of Form in Augustan Literature and the Arts (Oxford, 1974).

Battestin, Martin C. and Ruthe R., *Henry Fielding: A Life* (London, 1989).

Baumer, Franklin, L., *Religion and the Rise of Scepticism* (New York, 1960).

Bedford, R. D., *In Defense of Truth: Lord Herbert of Cherbury and the Seventeenth Century* (Manchester, 1979).

Berman, David, *A History of Atheism in Britain from Hobbes to Russell* (London, 1990).

"Deism, Immortality, and the Art of Theological Lying," in J. A. Leo Lemay, (ed.), *Deism, Masonry, and the Enlightenment* (Newark, DE., 1987).

Biddle, John C., "Locke's Critique of Innate Principles and Toland's Deism," *Journal of the History of Ideas*, 37 (1976).

Bolam, C. G., Goring, Jeremy, Short, H. L., and Thomas, Roger, *The English Presbyterians: From Elizabethan Puritanism to Modern Unitarianism* (London, 1968).

Bonanati, Ugo, *Libertinismo e deismo nel seicento inglese* (Florence, 1972).

Bonner, Hypatia, *Penalties Upon Opinion* (London, 1943).

Boyer, Richard E., *English Declarations of Indulgence, 1687 and 1688* (The Hague, 1968).

Bradlaugh, Charles, *The Laws Relating to Blasphemy and Heresy: An Address to Freethinkers* (London, 1878).

Browning, Reed, *Political and Constitutional ideas of the Court Whigs* (Baton Rouge, 1982).

Bunyan, John, *Grace Abounding* (Oxford, 1977).

Burrow, J. W., *A Liberal Descent: Victorian Historians and the English Past* (Cambridge, 1981).

Burtt, Shelley, *Virtue Transformed: Political Argument in England, 1688-1740* (Cambridge, 1992).

Chamberlain, Jeffrey S. "Portrait of a High-Church Clerical Dynasty in Georgian England: The Frewens and Their World," in John Walsh, Colin Haydon and Stephen Taylor eds., *The Church of England c. 1689-c.1833: From Toleration to Tractarianism* (Cambridge, 1993).

Champion, J. A. I., *The Pillars of Priestcraft Shaken: The Church of England and its Enemies, 1660-1730* (Cambridge, 1992).

Christophersen, H. O., *A Bibliographical Introduction to the Study of Locke* (1930; rptd. New York, 1968).

The Church of England c. 1689–c. 1833: From Toleration to Tractarianism, ed. John Walsh, Colin Haydon and Stephen Taylor (Cambridge, 1993).

Clark, J. C. D., *English Society, 1688-1832: Ideology, Social Structure and Political Practice During the Ancien Régime* (Cambridge, 1985).

Clifford, Alan, *Atonement and Justification: English Evangelical Theology 1640-1790* (Oxford, 1990).

Colley, Linda, *In Defiance of Oligarchy: The Tory Party, 1714-60* (Cambridge, 1982).

Collinson, Patrick, *The Elizabethan Puritan Movement* (London, 1967).

A Complete Collection of State Trials, ed. T. B. Howell, 33 vols. (London, 1812).

Crane, R. S., "Anglican Apologetics and the Idea of Progress, 1699-1745," *The Idea of the Humanities and Other Essays*, 2 vols. (Chicago, 1967).

Cranston, Maurice, *John Locke: A Biography* (1957, rpt. London, 1968).

Curtis, T. C., and W. A. Speck, "The Societies for the Reformation of Manners: A Case Study in the Theory and Practice of Moral Reform," *Literature and History*, 3 (1976).

Cust, Lionel and Colvin, Sidney, *History of the Society of Dilettanti* (London, 1914).

Daniel, Stephen H., *John Toland: His Methods, Manners, and Mind* (Kingston and Montreal, 1984).

Davies, Horton, *Worship and Theology in England*, 5 vols. (Princeton, 1961-70).
Davis, J. C., "The Levellers and Christianity," in Brian Manning (ed.), *Politics, Religion and the English Civil War* (London, 1973).
Davison, Lee, "Experiments in the Social Regulation of Industry: Gin Legislation, 1729-1751," in Davison et al. (eds.), *Stilling the Grumbling Hive: The Response to Social and Economic Problems in England, 1689-1750* (New York, 1992).
De Bruyn, Frans, "Latitudinarianism and its Importance as a Precursor of Sensibility," *Journal of English and Germanic Philology*, 80 (July 1981).
Deism, Masonry, and the Enlightenment, ed. J. A. Leo Lemay (Newark, DE, 1987).
Dickinson, H. T., *Liberty and Property: Political Ideology in Eighteenth-Century Britain* (New York, 1977).
Digeon, Aurélien, *Les romans de Fielding* (Paris, 1923).
Dow, F. D., *Radicalism in the English Revolution, 1640-1660* (Oxford, 1985).
Emerson, Roger L., "Latitudinarianism and the English Deists," in J. A. Leo Lemay (ed.), *Deism, Masonry, and the Enlightenment* (Newark, DE, 1987).
"Heresy, the Social Order, and English Deism," *Church History*, 37 (December 1968).
English Historical Documents, 1660-1714, ed. Andrew Browning (London, 1954).
Erskine-Hill, Howard, *The Social Milieu of Alexander Pope* (New Haven, 1975).
Ewald, William Bragg, *Rogues, Royalty and Reporters: The Age of Queen Anne Through Its Newspapers* (Westport, CT, 1978).
Fissell, Mary E., "Charity Universal? Institutions and Moral Reform in Eighteenth-Century Bristol," in Davison et al. (eds.), *Stilling the Grumbling Hive: The Response to Social and Economic Problems in England, 1689-1750*, (New York, 1992).
Fox Bourne, H. R., *The Life of John Locke*, 2 vols. (London, 1876; rptd. Bristol, 1991).
Gascoigne, John, *Cambridge in the Age of the Enlightenment* (Cambridge, 1991).
Gawlich, Gunter, "Cicero and the Enlightenment," *Studies on Voltaire and the Eighteenth Century*, 25 (1963).
George, Edward A., *Seventeenth-Century Men of Latitude* (London, 1908).
Gillett, Charles Ripley, *Burned Books: Neglected Chapters in British History and Literature*. 2 vols. (New York, 1932).
Goldie, Mark. "The Civil Religion of James Harrington," in Anthony Pagden (ed.), *The Languages of Political Theory in Early Modern Europe* (Cambridge, 1987).
"Ideology," in Terence Ball, James Farr, and Russell L. Hanson (eds.), *Political Innovation and Conceptual Change* (Cambridge, 1989).
"John Locke and Anglican Royalism," *Political Studies*, 31 (1983).
"The Theory of Religious Intolerance in Restoration England," in Ole Peter Grell, Jonathan I. Israel, and Nicholas Tyacke (eds.), *From Persecution to Toleration: The Glorious Revolution and Religion in England* (Oxford, 1991).

Grafton, Anthony, *Defenders of the Text* (Cambridge, MA, 1991).
Greaves, R. L., *Enemies Under His feet; Radicals and Nonconformists in Britain, 1664-1677* (Stanford, 1990).
Greene, Donald, *The Age of Exuberance* (New York, 1970).
"Augustinianism and Empiricism: A Note on Eighteenth-Century English Intellectual History, *Eighteenth-Century Studies*, 1 (1967).
"How 'Degraded' was Eighteenth-Century Anglicanism?" *Eighteenth-Century Studies*, 24:1 (fall 1990).
"The *Via Media* in an Age of Revolution: Anglicanism in the Eighteenth Century," in Peter Hughes and David Williams (eds.), *The Varied Pattern: Studies in the Eighteenth Century* (Toronto, 1971).
Griffin, Martin I. J., Jr., *Latitudinarianism in the Seventeenth-Century Church of England* (Leiden, 1992).
Hanson, Laurence, *Government and the Press 1695-1763* (Oxford, 1936).
Harris, Tim, *Politics Under the Later Stuarts: Party Conflict in a Divided Society* (London and New York, 1993).
"Party Turns? Or, Whigs and Tories Get off Scot Free," *Albion*, 25:4 (winter 1993).
Harvey, Richard, "The Problem of Social-Political Obligation for the Church of England in the Seventeenth Century," *Church History*, 40:2 (June 1971).
Hill, Bridget, *"The Republican Virago": The Life and Times of Catharine Macaulay, Historian* (Oxford and New York, 1992).
Hill, Christopher, *Change and Continuity in 17th-Century England*, rev. edn (New Haven and London, 1991).
Economic Problems of the Church (London: Panther, 1968).
The English Bible and the 17th-Century Revolution (Harmondsworth, 1993).
The Experience of Defeat: Milton and Some Contemporaries (New York, 1984).
Milton and the English Revolution (New York, 1978).
Religion and Politics in 17th-century England (Brighton, 1986).
A Turbulent, Seditious and Factious People: John Bunyan and his Church (Oxford, 1988).
The World Turned Upside Down (Harmondsworth, 1975).
Hill, Eugene D., *Edward, Lord Herbert of Cherbury* (Boston, 1987).
Hilton, R. H., *The English Peasantry in the Later Middle Ages* (Oxford, 1975).
Holdsworth, William, *A History of the English Law*, 12 vols. (London, 1938).
Holmes, Geoffrey, *Politics, Religion and Society in England, 1679-1742* (London and Ronceverte, 1986).
Hooker, E. N., "Dryden and the Atoms of Epicurus," in H. T. Swedenberg, Jr. (ed.), *Essential Articles for the Study of John Dryden* (Hamden CT, 1966).
Horst, J. B., *The Radical Brethren* (Nieuwkoop, 1972).
Howe, Irving, "History and the Novel," *The New Republic*, 3 (September 1990).
Hunter, J. Paul, *Occasional Form: Henry Fielding and the Chains of Circumstance* (Baltimore, 1975).

Hunter, Michael, "The Problem of 'Atheism' in Early Modern England," *Transactions of the Royal Historical Society* (1985).

Innes, J., "Jonathan Clark, Social History and England's 'Ancien Régime,'" *Past and Present*, 115 (1987).

Isaacs, Tina, "The Anglican Hierarchy and the Reformation of Manners, 1688-1738," *Journal of Ecclesiastical History*, 33 (1982).

Jacob, J. R., *Henry Stubbe, Radical Protestantism and the Early Enlightenment* (Cambridge, 1983).

Jacob, Margaret C., *Living the Enlightenment: Freemasonry and Politics in Eighteenth-Century Europe* (New York, 1991).

The Newtonians and the English Revolution, 1689-1720 (Ithaca, 1976).

The Radical Enlightenment: Pantheists, Freemasons and Republicans (London, 1981).

Jolley, Nicholas, *Leibniz and Locke: A Study of the "New Essays on Human Understanding"* (Oxford, 1984).

Jones, J. R., *Country and Court: England 1658-1714* (Cambridge, MA, 1978).

Kaufman, Franz-Xavier, "The Sociology of Knowledge and the Problem of Authority," in Piet F. Fransen, (ed.), *Authority in the Church* (Leuven, 1983).

Keeble, N. H., *The Literary Culture of Nonconformity in Late Seventeenth-Century England* (Leicester, 1987).

Kelly, P. J., "John Locke: Authority, Conscience and Religious Toleration," in John Horton and Susan Mendus (eds.), *John Locke, A Letter Concerning Toleration, in Focus* (London, 1991).

Kennedy, Rick, "The Alliance between Puritanism and Cartesian Logic at Harvard, 1687-1735," *Journal of the History of Ideas*, 51 (1990).

Kenyon, John, *The Popish Plot* (London, 1972).

Revolution Principles: The Philosophy of Party, 1689-1720 (Cambridge, 1977).

Kilcullen, John, *Sincerity and Truth: Essays on Arnauld, Bayle, and Toleration* (Oxford, 1988).

Klein, Lawrence, *Shaftesbury and the Culture of Politeness: Moral Discourse and Cultural Politics in Early Eighteenth-Century England* (Cambridge, 1994).

Knox, R. A., *Enthusiasm* (Oxford, 1950).

Kors, Alan C., *Atheism in France, 1650-1729, Vol. I: The Orthodox Sources of Disbelief* (Princeton, 1990).

Kramnick, Isaac, *Bolingbroke and His Circle: The Politics of Nostalgia in the Age of Walpole* (Cambridge, MA, 1968).

Republicanism and Bourgeois Radicalism: Political Ideology in Late Eighteenth-Century England and America (Ithaca, 1990).

Lamont, William, *Godly Rule: Politics and Religion, 1603-1660* (London, 1969).

Marginal Prynne, 1600-1669 (London, 1963).

Richard Baxter and the Millennium (London, 1979).

Lamprecht, Sterling P., *The Moral and Political Philosophy of John Locke*, (New York, 1918).

Laski, Harold J., *Political Thought in England: Locke to Bentham* (London, 1920).

Lathbury, Thomas, *History of the Convocation* (London, 1853).

Leng, John, *A Sermon Preach'd Before the King at Newmarket* (London, 1699).

Lettinga, Neil, "Covenant Theology Turned Upside Down: Henry Hammond and Caroline Anglican Moralism: 1643-1660," *Sixteenth-Century Journal*, 24 (Fall 1993).

Levine, Joseph M., *The Battle of the Books: History and Literature in the Augustan Age* (Ithaca, 1991).

Dr. *Woodward's Shield: History, Science and Satire in Augustan England* (Berkeley, 1977).

"The Battle of the Books and the Shield of Achilles," *Eighteenth-Century Life*, 9 (1984).

"Latitudinarians, Neoplatonists, and the Ancient Wisdom," in Richard Kroll, Richard Ashcraft and Perez Zagorin (eds.), *Philosophy, Science, and Religion in England: 1640-1700* (Cambridge, 1992).

"Sir Walter Ralegh and the Ancient Wisdom," in Bonnelyn Kunze and Dwight Brautigam (eds.), *Court, Country, and Culture: Essays in Honor of Perez Zagorin* (Rochester, 1992).

Levy, Leonard. *Treason Against God: A History of the Offense of Blasphemy* (New York, 1981).

The Life of Edward, First Lord Herbert of Cherbury, ed. J. M. Shuttleworth (London, 1976).

Lind, Levi R., "Lucian and Fielding," *Classical Weekly*, 29 (1936).

Lovejoy, A. O., *Essays in the History of Ideas* (Baltimore, 1948).

Lund, Roger D., "Strange Complicities: Atheism and Conspiracy in *A Tale of a Tub*," *Eighteenth-Century Life*, 13 (November 1989).

Macaulay, T. B., *The History of England*, ed. Charles Firth, 6 vols. (London, 1913-15).

Maclear, James Fulton, "Popular Anticlericalism in the Puritan Revolution," *Journal of the History of Ideas*, 17:4 (October 1956).

Macpherson, C. B., *The Political Theory of Possessive Individualism*, (London, 1962).

Mannheim, Karl, *Ideology and Utopia*, (New York, 1936).

Manning, Brian, "The Levellers and Religion," in J. F. McGregor and B. Reay (eds.), *Radical Religion in the English Revolution* (Oxford, 1984).

"Puritanism and Democracy, 1640-1642," in Donald Pennington and Keith Thomas (eds.), *Puritans and Revolutionaries: Essays in Seventeenth-Century History Presented to Christopher Hill* (Oxford, 1978).

Marshall, John, "The Ecclesiology of the Latitude-Men, 1660-1689; Stillingfleet, Tillotson, and 'Hobbism'," *Journal of Ecclesiastical History*, 36:3 (July 1985).

John Locke: Resistance, Religion and Responsibility (Cambridge, 1994).

"John Locke and Latitudinarianism," in Richard Kroll, Richard Ashcraft and Perez Zagorin (eds.), *Philosophy, Science and Religion in England, 1640-1700* (Cambridge, 1992).

Martin, J. W., "Toleration 1689: England's Recognition of Pluralism," in Gordon J. Schochet (ed.), *Restoration, Ideology, and Revolution*, Proceedings of the Folger Institute Center for the History of British Political Thought, 4 (Washington, DC, 1990).

McKeon, Michael, *Origins of the Novel, 1600-1740* (Baltimore, 1987).

McLachlan, H., *The Unitarian Movement in the Religious Life of England* (London, 1934).

Mead, G. R. S., *Apollonius of Tyanaea* (London, 1901).

Mendus, Susan, *Toleration and the Limits of Liberalism* (Atlantic Highlands, NJ, 1989).

Miller, Henry Knight, *Essays on Fielding's "Miscellanies"* (Princeton, 1961).

Milton, John, "Locke at Oxford," in G. A. J. Rogers (ed.), *Locke's Philosophy: Content and Context*, (Oxford, 1994).

Mintz, Samuel I., *The Hunting of Leviathan* (Cambridge, 1962).

Morrill, J. S., *The Nature of the English Revolution* (London, 1993).

"The Religious Context of the English Civil War," *Transactions of the Royal Historical Society*, 5th series, 34 (1984).

"Sir William Brereton and England's Wars of Religion," *Journal of British Studies*, 24:3 (1985).

Mulligan, Lotte, "The Religious Roots of William Walwyn's Radicalism," *Journal of Religious History*, 12:2 (December 1982).

The New Eighteenth Century: Theory, Politics, English Literature, ed. Felicity Nussbaum and Laura Brown (New York, 1987).

New, Melvyn, "'The Grease of God': The Form of 18th-century English Fiction," *PMLA*, 91 (1976).

Nokes, G. D., *A History of the Crime of Blasphemy* (London, 1928).

NOMOS XI: Voluntary Associations, ed. J. Roland Pennock and John W. Chapman (New York, 1969).

O'Higgins, James, S. J., *Anthony Collins: The Man and his Works* (The Hague, 1970).

Orr, John, *English Deism: Its Roots and Fruits* (Grand Rapids, MI, 1934).

Overton, J. H., *The English Church in the Eighteenth Century*, 2 vols. (1878).

Life in the English Church (1660-1714) (London, 1885).

Overton, J. H., and Relton, F., *The English Church from the Accession of George I to the End of the Eighteenth Century* (1896).

Paulson, Ronald, *The Fictions of Satire* (Baltimore, 1967).

Henry Fielding: A Critical Biography (Oxford, forthcoming).

Hogarth, 3 vols. (New Brunswick, 1991).

Hogarth's Graphic Works, 3rd edn (London, 1989).

Satire and the Novel (New Haven, 1967).

"Life as Journey and as Theater: Two Eighteenth-Century Narrative Structures," *New Literary History*, 8 (1976); rptd. in *Popular and Polite Art in the Age of Hogarth and Fielding* (Notre Dame, 1979).

Paulson, Ronald and Lockwood, Thomas F. *Fielding: The Critical Heritage* (London, 1969).

Philosophy, Science and Religion in England, 1640–1700, ed. Richard Kroll, Richard Ashcraft and Perez Zagorin (Cambridge, 1992).

Pocock, J. G. A., *The Machiavellian Moment: Florentine Political Thought and the Atlantic Republican Tradition* (Princeton, 1975).
Virtue, Commerce, and History: Essays on Political Thought and History, Chiefly in the Eighteenth Century (Cambridge, 1985).
"Early Modern Capitalism: the Augustan Perception," in Eugene Kamenka and R. S. Neale (eds.), *Feudalism, Capitalism and Beyond* (Canberra, 1975).
"Post-Puritan England and the Problem of the Enlightenment," in Perez Zagorin (ed.), *Culture and Politics: From Puritanism to the Enlightenment* (Berkeley, 1980).
"Religious Freedom and the Desacralization of Politics; From the English Civil War to the Virginia Statute," in Merrill D. Peterson and Robert C. Vaughan (eds.), *The Virginia Statute for Religious Freedom: its Evolution and Consequences in American History* (Cambridge, 1988).
"Thomas Hobbes Atheist or Enthusiast? His Place in A Restoration Debate," *History of Political Thought*, 11:4 (1990).
The Political Works of James Harrington (Cambridge, 1977).
Pope, Alexander, *The Dunciad*, ed. James Sutherland, 3rd edn (London and New Haven, 1963).
Pastoral Poetry and An Essay on Criticism, ed. E. Audra and Aubrey Williams (London and New Haven, 1961).
Popkin, R. H. "Spinoza and the Conversion of the Jews," in C. De Deugd (ed.), *Spinoza: Political and Theological Thought* (Amsterdam, 1984).
"Spinoza, the Quakers and the Millenium," *Manuscrito VI* (Brazil, 1982).
Redwood, J. A., *Reason, Ridicule and Religion: The Age of Enlightenment in England, 1660-1750* (Cambridge, MA, 1976).
"Charles Blount (1654-93), Deism, and English Free Thought," *Journal of the History of Ideas*, 35 (1974).
Rivers, Isabel, *Reason, Grace, and Sentiment: A Study of the Language of Religion and Ethics in England, 1660-1780*, Vol 1: *Whichcote to Wesley* (Cambridge, 1991).
Robinson, Christopher, *Lucian and his Influence in Europe* (Chapel Hill, 1979).
Rossi, Mario M., *La Vita, Le Opere, I Tempi di Edoardo Herbert di Chirbury*, 3 vols. (Florence, 1947).
Sabine, George H., *A History of Political Theory*, 3rd edn (New York, 1961).
Schochet, Gordon J., "The Act of Toleration and the Failure of Comprehension: Persecution, Non-Conformity, and Religious Indifference," in Dale Hoak and Mordechai Feingold (eds.), *The World of William and Mary* (Stanford, 1995).
"Between Lambeth and Leviathan: Samuel Parker on the Church of England and Political Order," in Nicholas Phillipson and Quentin Skinner (eds.), *Political Discourse in Early Modern Britain* (Cambridge, 1993).
"From Persecution to 'Toleration,'" in J. R. Jones (ed.), *Liberty Secured? Britain Before and After 1689* (Stanford, 1992).
"Intending (Political) Obligation: Hobbes and the Voluntary Basis of

Society," in Mary G. Dietz (ed.), *Thomas Hobbes and Political Theory* (Lawrence, KS, 1991).

"John Locke and Religious Toleration," in Lois G. Schwoerer (ed.), *The Revolution of 1688-89: Changing Perspectives* (Cambridge, 1992).

"Why Should History Matter? Political Theory and the History of Political Discourse," in J. G. A. Pocock, Gordon J. Schochet, and Lois Schwoerer (eds.), *The Varieties of British Political Thought, 1500-1800* (Cambridge, 1993).

"Toleration, Revolution, and Judgment in the Development of Locke's Political Thought," *Political Science*, 40 (1988).

Scholtz, Gregory, F. "Anglicanism in the Age of Johnson: the Doctrine of Conditional Salvation," *Eighteenth-Century Studies*, 22:2 (winter 1988/89).

Scott, Jonathan, *Algernon Sidney and the Restoration Crisis, 1677-1683* (Cambridge, 1991).

Shepherd, Simon, *Marlowe and the Politics of the Elizabethan Theatre* (Brighton, 1986).

Shklar, Judith N., "Facing up to Intellectual Pluralism," in David Spitz (ed.), *Political Theory and Social Change* (New York, 1967).

Shoemaker, Robert B., "Reforming the City: The Reformation of Manners Campaign in London, 1690-1738," in Lee Davison et al. (eds.), *Stilling the Grumbling Hive: The Response to Social and Economic Problems in England, 1689-1750* (New York, 1992).

Skinner, Quentin, *The Foundations of Modern Political Thought*, 2 vols. (Cambridge, 1978).

Smith, The Reverend M. G., *Pastoral Discipline and the Church Courts: The Hexham Court, 1680-1730* (York, 1982).

Smith, Nigel, "The Charge of Atheism and the Language of Radical Speculation, 1640-1660," in Hunter and Wootton (eds.), *Atheism from the Reformation to the Enlightenment* (Oxford, 1992).

Somerville, John C., *The Secularization of Early Modern England*, (Oxford, 1992).

Spellman, William. M., *The Latitudinarians and the Church of England, 1660-1700* (Athens, GA, and London, 1993).

Spurr, John, *The Restoration Church of England, 1646-1689* (New Haven, 1991).

"The Church of England, Comprehension, and the Toleration Act of 1689," *English Historical Review*, 104 (1989).

"'Latitudinarianism' and the Restoration Church," *Historical Journal*, 31 (1988).

Stephen, James Fitzjames, *A History of the Criminal Law in England*, 3 vols. (London, 1883).

Stephen, Leslie, *History of English Thought in the Eighteenth Century*, 2 vols. (1876; rptd. New York, 1949).

Stromberg, Roland N., *Religious Liberalism in Eighteenth-Century England* (Oxford, 1954).

Sullivan, Robert, *John Toland and the Deist Controversy* (Cambridge, MA, 1982).

Sutch, Victor D., *Gilbert Sheldon, Architect of Anglican Survival, 1640-1675* (The

Hague, 1975).

Sykes, Norman, *From Sheldon to Secker* (Cambridge, 1959).

Taylor, Dick, Jr., "Joseph as Hero in *Joseph Andrews*," *Tulane Studies in English*, 7 (1957).

Thomas, Donald, *A Long Time Burning: The History of Literary Censorship in England* (London, 1969).

Thomas, K. V., "Cases of Conscience in Seventeenth-Century Europe," in J. Morrill, P. Slack and D. Woold (eds.), *Public Duty and Private Conscience in Seventeenth-Century England: Essays Presented to G. E. Aylmer* (Oxford, 1993).

Thomas, Roger, "Comprehension and Indulgence," in G. F. Nuttall, and O. Chadwick (eds.), *From Uniformity to Unity, 1662-1962* (London, 1962).

Thompson, E. P., *Witness Against the Beast: William Blake and the Moral Law* (Cambridge, 1993).

Trapnell, William H., "What Thomas Woolston Wrote," *British Journal for Eighteenth-Century Studies*, 14 (spring 1991).

"Who Thomas Woolston Was," *British Journal for Eighteenth-Century Studies*, 11 (1988).

Trevor-Roper, H. R., *Catholics, Anglicans and Puritans: 17th-century Essays* (Chicago, 1988).

Religion, the Reformation and Social Change (London, 1967).

Troeltsch, Ernst, *The Social Teachings of the Christian Churches*, 2 vols. (New York, 1931).

Trollope, Anthony, *Phineas Redux*, World's Classics edition (Oxford, 1983).

Tulloch, John, *Rational Theology and Christian Philosophy in the Seventeenth Century* (Edinburgh, 1872).

Tully, James, "Governing Conduct," in Edmund Leites (ed.), *Conscience and Casuistry in Early Modern Europe* (Cambridge, 1988).

Tyacke, Nicholas, *Anti-Calvinists: The Rise of English Arminianism, c. 1590-1640* (Oxford, 1987).

Verkamp, Bernard J., *The Indifferent Mean: Adiaphorism and the English Reformation to 1554* (Athens, OH, 1977).

Voluntary Religion, Studies in Church History, 23, ed. W. J. Shields and Diana Wood (Oxford, 1986).

Wade, G., *Thomas Traherne* (Princeton, 1944).

Walker, D. P., *The Ancient Theology* (Ithaca, 1972).

Wallace, Dewey D., Jr., *Puritans and Predestination: Grace in English Protestant Theology, 1525-1695* (Chapel Hill, 1982).

Wallace, John M., *Destiny His Choice: The Loyalism of Andrew Marvell* (Cambridge, 1968).

Watts, Michael R., *The Dissenters: From the Reformation to the French Revolution* (Oxford, 1978).

Weber, Max, *The Protestant Ethic and the Spirit of Capitalism*, (New York, 1958).

"The Protestant Sects and the Spirit of Capitalism," in H. H. Gerth and C. Wright Mills (eds.), *From Max Weber: Essays in Sociology* (New York, 1958).

"'Churches' and 'Sects' in North America: An Ecclesiastical Socio-Political Sketch," translated and introduced by Colin Loader and Jeffrey Alexander, *Sociological Theory*, 3:1 (Spring 1985).

Williams, Aubrey, "Interpositions of Providence and the Design of Fielding's Novels," *South Atlantic Quarterly*, 70 (1971).

Willman, Robert, "The Origins of 'Whig' and 'Tory' in English Political Language," *Historical Journal* 12:2 (1974).

Wilson, John, *Pulpit in Parliament: Puritanism during the English Civil War; 1640–48* (Princeton, 1969).

Wootton, David, "John Locke: Socinian or Natural Law Theorist?" in James E. Crimminis, (ed.), *Religion, Secularization and Political Thought* (London, 1989).

"New Histories of Atheism," in Hunter and Wootton, (eds.), *Atheism from the Reformation to the Enlightenment* (Oxford, 1992).

Work, James A., "Henry Fielding, Christian Censor," in *The Age of Johnson: Essays Presented to Chauncey Brewster Tinker* (New Haven, 1949).

Yates, Frances, *Giordano Bruno and the Hermetic Tradition* (1964; rptd. New York, 1969).

Yates, Nigel, "A Kentish Clerical Dynasty: Curteis of Sevenoaks," *Archaeologia Cantiana*, 108 (1990).

Yolton, John W., *Locke and French Materialism* (Oxford, 1991).

Thinking Matter: Materialism in Eighteenth-Century Britain (Oxford, 1983).

MANUSCRIPTS

Bodleian Library, Oxford

Locke MS C34, fo. 43; fos. 75, 120.
Locke MS C34, fos. 48-49.
Locke MS C34, fo. 11.
Locke MS C34, fo. 122.
Locke MS C34, fo. 18; fos. 71, 127-28.
Locke MS C34, fo. 42.
Locke MS d.1, fo. 125.
Journal, 20 March 1678, MS fo. 3.
Journal, 5 April 1677, MS fo. 2;
Journal, 26 June 1681, MS fo. 5.
Journal, 29 July 1676, MS. fo. 1.

Lambeth Palace

MS 1741. Curteis to Gibson, April 12, 1729.

East Sussex Records Office

ESRO Fre 5368: William Curteis to Joseph Tucker, October 20, 1715.
ESRO Fre 736.

ESRO AMS 2276: Sermons of Richard Ireland.
ESRO Fre. 1301: Thomas Frewen to Thankful, December 5, 1741.

Christ Church, Oxford

Arch. W. Epist. 9, fo. 232: Curteis to Wake, November 29, 1722.
Arch. W. Epist. 10, fo. 92: Curteis to Wake, October 31, 1724.
Arch. W. Epist. 7, fo. 56: C. Norwich to Wake, 9 February 1716. Arch. W.
    Epist. 9, fo. 273: Curteis to Wake, September 21, 1723.
Arch. W. Epist. 7, fo. 53: Curteis to Wake, November 23, 1717.
Arch. W. Epist. 9, fo. 277: John Johnson to ?

British Library

Add. MS 33, 344 fos. 70-90: "An Appeal to the Reason and Consciences of
all True Englishmen, concerning their Unhappy Prejudices, and the
Fomenters of them: But more particularly with regard to the Next Election
of the Representatives in Parliament. By an Impartial Hand," 1733.
Add. MSS 32, 688 fos. 246, 336, 393; 32, 693, fo. 406; 32, 698 fo. 371; 32, 693
fo. 406: Letters to the Duke of Newcastle.

Kent Archives Office

U269/C148/2, 8, 10, 18: Sackville of Knole Papers.
U269/C148/18/1 and 3.

Unpublished Works

Ashcraft, Richard, "John Locke and the Problem of Toleration." Paper
    presented to the Conference on Discourses of Tolerance and Intolerance
    in the Enlightenment, at the William Andrews Clark Library, University
    of California at Los Angeles, May 20-22, 1994.
Caplan, Neil. "An Outline of the Origins and Development of Nonconformity
    in Sussex: 1603-1803." Unpublished typescript in the British Library,
    Dr. William's Library, and the library of the Sussex Archaeological
    Society, Lewes, 1965.
DesBrisay, Gordon, "Fornication, Illegitimacy and Godly Discipline in the
    Early Modern Scottish Town." Unpublished paper, 1991.

Index

293